# Discourse Markers in Early Koine Greek

Septuagint and Cognate Studies

Martin Rösel, General Editor



Number 77

# Discourse Markers in Early Koine Greek

## Cognitive-Functional Analysis and LXX Translation Technique

Christopher J. Fresch

Atlanta



Library of Congress Control Number: 2023940188

# Contents

# Acknowledgments

This book represents five years of effort over a decade. As such, there is a plethora of friends, scholars, and family members who could be recognized and thanked. However, in the interest of space, I will keep this brief.

My thinking about linguistics, Greek, Hebrew, and the Septuagint has been positively influenced and informed by many over the years. In particular, I am grateful for conversations with and the insights provided by Luke Wisley, Michael Aubrey, William Ross, Marieke Dhont, Kim Phillips, Peter Myers, Andrew Keenan, Travis Wright, John Lee, Trevor Evans, Katy Davis, James Prothro, Joshua Harper, Christopher Thomson, Elizabeth Robar, and Ed Glenny. Special mention must be made of Stephen Levinsohn, who offered much feedback and wisdom over the years and has always been a willing conversation partner.

Editing is a slow and disheartening process. I am thankful for the encouragement of friends, of mutuals on Twitter, and especially of Luke Wisley and David Shaw, as we spurred each other on in our projects in conversations, emails, and video chats. In addition, my colleagues at the Bible College of South Australia have been a constant source of support. Our principal, Tim Patrick, deserves special mention for supporting his faculty in their research and creating an environment wherein research is promoted and possible.

I am indebted to Christopher Macindoe, who read an earlier draft of this book and offered pages of excellent feedback, helpful suggestions, and needed corrections.

Steve Runge regularly gave me his time and shared his knowledge of linguistics, Greek, and Hebrew. Dirk Jongkind provided invaluable insights and feedback to the project. I am incredibly thankful to both Steve and Dirk for their pushback, insights, advice, and friendship over the years.

This book would not exist if not for Jim Aitken. As my PhD supervisor at the University of Cambridge, he played a pivotal role in my life and in my development as a scholar. During the PhD, Jim was a constant source of encouragement, ever pushing me forward in my writing and research. He challenged me to be a more rigorous and critical thinker and to ask better questions of ancient texts and of those who produced them. He supported me, saw value in my work, and instilled in me a passion for the study of the Septuagint, Hellenistic Judaism, and texts from antiquity more generally (passions that are foundational to this book). One could not ask for a better supervisor, but Jim's influence went well beyond that of a supervisor. In the years after the PhD, Jim continued to be a valued friend and mentor. He never ceased to push and challenge me in my thinking, and he was always ready to be a resource when I needed him, a quality that aided me greatly as I was finishing this book. In everything, Jim was the very model of an excellent scholar and friend. I would not be the scholar I am today if not for him, and I am indebted to him. It causes me immense sadness that he will not hold this book in his hands. Jim's untimely death on 7 April 2023 was a shocking and devastating loss. His influence can be felt throughout the pages of this book, and it is my hope that it serves to further his legacy.

Lastly, I am immensely thankful to my family. To my daughters, Zoe and Emma, thank you for your patience, for bearing with your Papa, and for being a source of joy and delight. Thank you most of all to my wife, Laura, to whom I owe so much and yet who would never ask any of it from me. She has continually given of herself and has been my most constant source of support and encouragement. Her graciousness and kindness know no limit. I could not ask for a better partner, and it is to her that I lovingly dedicate this book.

מה־יפו דדיך אחתי כלה
מה־טבו דדיך מיין
How beautiful is your love, my sister, my bride!
How much better is your love than wine!
(Song 4:10a–b)

# Abbreviations

## Papyrological Conventions

| | |
|---|---|
| ( ) | Modern expansion of an abbreviation |
| [ ] | Text lost, restored by the editor |
| [ ....... ] | Up to eight characters lost—cannot be restored |
| < > | Characters erroneously omitted by the scribe, added by modern editor |
| \ / | Text added above the line in antiquity |
| { } | Superfluous letters removed by editor |
| α̣β̣γ̣ | Underdotted by editor to indicate characters ambiguous outside of context, damaged, illegible, or otherwise uncertain |
| ⟦ ⟧ | Characters deleted in antiquity |

## Other Abbreviations

| | |
|---|---|
| AB | Anchor (Yale) Bible |
| acc. | accusative |
| ASCP | Amsterdam Studies in Classical Philology |
| Bd’A | La Bible d’Alexandrie |
| BDAG | Danker, Frederick W., Walter Bauer, William F. Arndt, and F. Wilbur Gingrich. *Greek-English Lexicon of the New Testament and Other Early Christian Literature*. 3rd ed. Chicago: University of Chicago Press, 2000. |
| BDB | Brown, Francis, S. R. Driver, and Charles A. Briggs. *A Hebrew and English Lexicon of the Old Testament*. Oxford: Clarendon, 1907. Repr., Peabody: Hendrickson, 2008. |
| BDF | Blass, Friedrich, Albert Debrunner, and Robert W. Funk. *A Greek Grammar of the New Testament and Other Early Christian Literature*. Chicago: University of Chicago Press, 1961. |
| BDS | La Bible du Semeur |

*BGU* *Aegyptische Urkunden aus den Königlichen* (later *Staatlichen*) *Museen zu Berlin, Griechische Urkunden.* Berlin, 1863–.
BHHB Baylor Handbook on the Hebrew Bible
*BHK* *Biblia Hebraica.* Edited by Rudolf Kittel.
BHL Blackwell Handbooks in Linguistics
*BHRG* Merwe, Christo H. J. van der, Jackie A. Naudé, and Jan H. Kroeze. *A Biblical Hebrew Reference Grammar.* Biblical Languages: Hebrew 3. London: Sheffield Academic, 1999.
*BHRG2* Merwe, Christo H. J. van der, Jackie A. Naudé, and Jan H. Kroeze. *A Biblical Hebrew Reference Grammar.* 2nd ed. London: Bloomsbury T&T Clark, 2017.
*BHS* *Biblia Hebraica Stuttgartensia*
*BIOSCS* *Bulletin of the International Organization for Septuagint and Cognate Studies*
BKAT Biblischer Kommentar Altes Testament
Brenton Brenton, Sir Lancelot C. L., trans. *The Septuagint Version: Greek and English.* London: Bagster, 1882.
BTS Biblical Tools and Studies
BZAW Beihefte zur Zeitschrift für die alttestamentliche Wissenschaft
CC Continental Commentaries
CEI Conferenza Episcopale Italiana
*CGCG* Emde Boas, Evert van, Albert Rijksbaron, Luuk Huitink, and Mathieu de Bakker. *The Cambridge Grammar of Classical Greek.* Cambridge: Cambridge University Press, 2019.
CLR Cognitive Linguistics Research
ConBOT Coniectanea Biblica Old Testament Series
CSL Cambridge Studies in Linguistics
CTL Cambridge Textbooks in Linguistics
*DCH* Clines, David J. A., ed. *Dictionary of Classical Hebrew.* 9 vols. Sheffield: Sheffield Phoenix Press, 1993–2016.
*DFNTG* Levinsohn, Stephen H. *Discourse Features of New Testament Greek: A Coursebook on the Information Structure of New Testament Greek.* 2nd ed. Dallas: SIL International, 2000.
*DGGNT* Runge, Steven E. *Discourse Grammar of the Greek New Testament: A Practical Introduction for Teaching and Exegesis.* Lexham Bible Reference Series. Peabody, MA: Hendrickson, 2010.
DJD Discoveries in the Judaean Desert

| | |
|---|---|
| DM | discourse marker |
| EALT | Empirical Approaches to Language Typology |
| ESV | English Standard Version |
| FGS | Functional Grammar Series |
| FRLANT | Forschungen zur Religion und Literatur des Alten und Neuen Testaments |
| gen. | genitive |
| *GELS* | Muraoka, Takamitsu. *A Greek-English Lexicon of the Septuagint*. Louvain: Peeters, 2009. |
| GKC | Gesenius, Wilhelm. *Gesenius' Hebrew Grammar*. Edited by Emil Kautzsch. Translated by Arthur E. Cowley. 2nd ed. Oxford: Clarendon, 1910. |
| *HALOT* | Koehler, Ludwig, Walter Baumgartner, and Johann J. Stamm. *The Hebrew and Aramaic Lexicon of the Old Testament*. Translated and edited under the supervision of Mervyn E. J. Richardson. 2 vols. Leiden: Brill, 2001. |
| HCSB | Holman Christian Standard Bible |
| *IBHS* | Waltke, Bruce K., and Michael P. O'Connor. *An Introduction to Biblical Hebrew Syntax*. Winona Lake, IN: Eisenbrauns, 1990. |
| *JAJ* | *Journal of Ancient Judaism* |
| *JBL* | *Journal of Biblical Literature* |
| Joüon | Joüon, Paul. *A Grammar of Biblical Hebrew*. Translated and revised by Takamitsu Muraoka. 2 vols. SubBi 27. Rome: Pontifical Biblical Institute, 1991. |
| *JSCS* | *Journal of Septuagint and Cognate Studies* |
| JSJSup | Supplements to the Journal for the Study of Judaism |
| JSNTSup | Journal for the Study of the New Testament Supplement Series |
| JSOTSup | Journal for the Study of the Old Testament Supplement Series |
| K-G 2.2 | Kühner, Raphael. *Ausführliche Grammatik Der Griechischen Sprache: Zweiter Teil: Satzlehre*. Edited by Bernhard Gerth. 3rd ed. Hannover: Hahn, 1904. |
| KJV | King James Version |
| L-N | Louw, Johannes P., and Eugene A. Nida. *Greek-English Lexicon of the New Testament Based on Semantic Domains*. 2 vols. New York: United Bible Societies, 1989. |
| LBLA | La Biblia de las Américas |

| | |
|---|---|
| LCL | Loeb Classical Library |
| LES | Brannan, Rick, Ken M. Penner, Israel Loken, Michael Aubrey, and Isaiah Hoogendyk, eds. *The Lexham English Septuagint*. Bellingham, WA: Lexham, 2020. |
| LHBOTS | Library of Hebrew Bible/Old Testament Studies |
| LSAWS | Linguistic Studies in Ancient West Semitic |
| LSG | Louis Segond |
| LSJ | Liddell, Henry George, Robert Scott, and Henry Stuart Jones. *A Greek-English Lexicon*. 9th ed. with revised supplement. Oxford: Clarendon, 1996. |
| LXX | Septuagint |
| LXX.D | Septuaginta Deutsch |
| LXX.D 1 | Karrer, Martin, and Wolfgang Kraus. *Septuaginta Deutsch: Erläuterungen und Kommentare zum griechischen Alten Testament*. Vol. 1: *Genesis bis Makkabäer*. Wuppertal: Deutsche Bibelgesellschaft, 2011. |
| LXX.D 2 | Karrer, Martin, and Wolfgang Kraus. *Septuaginta Deutsch: Erläuterungen und Kommentare zum griechischen Alten Testament*. Vol. 2: *Psalmen bis Daniel*. Wuppertal: Deutsche Bibelgesellschaft, 2011. |
| MGS | Montanari, Franco. *The Brill Dictionary of Ancient Greek*. Edited by Madeleine Goh and Chad Schroeder. Leiden: Brill, 2015. |
| MSU | Mitteilungen des Septuaginta-Unternehmens |
| MT | Masoretic Text |
| Mur 88 | Hebrew Minor Prophets scroll from Wadi Murabba'at |
| NBD | Nueva Biblia al Día |
| NBLH | Nueva Biblia Latinoamericana de Hoy |
| NEG | negative statement, negation |
| NET | New English Translation |
| NETS | Pietersma, Albert, and Benjamin G. Wright, eds. *New English Translation of the Septuagint*. Oxford: Oxford University Press, 2007. |
| NICOT | New International Commentary on the Old Testament |
| NIV | New International Version |
| *NovT* | *Novum Testamentum* |
| NR | Nuova Riveduta 2006 |
| NRSV | New Revised Standard Version |
| NS | New Series |

| | |
|---|---|
| NTL | New Testament Library |
| *NTS* | *New Testament Studies* |
| NTTS | New Testament Tools and Studies |
| NTV | Nueva Traducción Viviente |
| NVI | Nueva Versión Internacional |
| *Oec.* | Xenophon, *Oeconomicus* |
| OG | Old Greek |
| P.Adl.G. | Adler, Elkan N., John G. Tait, Fritz M. Heichelheim, eds. *The Adler Papyri, Greek Texts*. Oxford: Oxford University Press, 1939. |
| P.Athen. | Petropoulos, Georgios A., ed. *Papyri Societatis Archaeologicae Atheniensis*. Athens: Academia Scientiarum Atheniensis, 1939. |
| P.Bad. | Spiegelberg, Wilhelm, et al., eds. *Veröffentlichungen aus den badischen Papyrus-Sammlungen*. Heidelberg: Winter, 1923–1938. |
| P.Cair.Zen. | Edgar, Campbell Cowan. *Zenon Papyri, Catalogue général des antiquités égyptiennes du Musée du Caire*. Cairo: Institut français d'archéologie orientale, 1925–1940. |
| P.Col. | *Columbia Papyri*. 1929–1998. |
| P. Dryton | Vandorpe, Katelijn, ed. *The Bilingual Family Archive of Dryton, His Wife Apollonia and Their Daughter Senmouthis*. Collectanea hellenistica 4. Brussels: Comité Klassieke Studies, Subcomité Hellenisme, Koninklijke Vlaamse Acad. van België voor Wetenschappen en Kunsten, 2002. |
| P.Erasm. | Sijpesteijn, P. J., and Ph. A. Verdult, eds. *Papyri in the Collection of the Erasmus University (Rotterdam)*. Papyrologica Bruxellensia 21. Brussels: Fondation égyptologique reine Élisabeth, 1986. |
| P.Hamb. | Meyer, Paul M., et al., eds. *Griechische Papyrusurkunden der Hamburger Staats- und Universitätsbibliothek*. Leipzig: Teubner, 1911–1998. |
| P.Lond. | Kenyon, F. G., et al., eds. *Greek Papyri in the British Museum*. London: British Museum, 1893–1974. |
| P.Mich. | *Michigan Papyri*. 1931–1999. |
| P.Oxy. | Grenfall, B. P., et al., eds. *The Oxyrhynchus Papyri*. London: Egypt Exploration Society, 1898–. |
| P.Tebt. | Grenfall, B. P., et al., eds. *The Tebtunis Papyri*. London: Egypt Exploration Society, 1902–2005. |

| | |
|---|---|
| POS | positive statement |
| PSI | Vitelli, G., et al., eds. *Papiri greci e latini*. Florence: Società italiana per la ricerca dei papiri greci e latini in Egitto, 1912–2008. |
| R-H | Rahlfs, Alfred, and Robert Hanhart, eds. *Septuaginta id est Vetus Testamentum graece iuxta LXX interpretes, editio altera*. Stuttgart: Deutsche Bibelgesellschaft, 2019. |
| SAOC | Studies in Ancient Oriental Civilizations |
| SB | *Sammelbuch griechischer Urkunden aus Aegypten*. 1915–. |
| SBLMS | Society of Biblical Literature Monograph Series |
| Schlachter | Schlachter-Bibel 2000 |
| SCS | Septuagint and Cognate Studies |
| SHBC | Smith & Helwys Bible Commentary |
| Sib. Or. | Sibylline Oracles |
| SiP | Studies in Pragmatics |
| SLCS | Studies in Language Companion Series |
| Smyth | Smyth, Herbert Weir. *Greek Grammar*. Harvard: Harvard University Press, 1956. |
| SubBi | Subsidia Biblica |
| *TESOL* | *Teachers of English to Speakers of Other Languages* |
| *TFG 1* | Dik, Simon C. *The Theory of Functional Grammar: Part 1: The Structure of the Clause*. 2nd rev. ed. FGS 20. Berlin: de Gruyter, 1997. |
| *TFG 2* | Dik, Simon C. *The Theory of Functional Grammar: Part 2: Complex and Derived Constructions*. 2nd rev. ed. FGS 21. Berlin: de Gruyter, 1997. |
| TSL | Typological Studies in Language |
| UPZ | Wilcken, Ulrich, ed. *Urkunden der Ptolemäerzeit (ältere Funde)*. Leipzig, 1927. Berlin: de Gruyter, 1935–1957. |
| *VT* | *Vetus Testamentum* |
| VTSup | Supplements to *Vetus Testamentum* |
| WBC | Word Biblical Commentary |

1

# Introduction

Comprehension of discourse is a complex process. At the most basic level, in oversimplified terms, a reader must understand the semantics of lexemes and constructions, the syntactic relationships between phrases and clauses, and how these two components of language interact and thereby result in the expression of meaningful information. But even then, such units do not occur in isolation. They are a part of larger discourses. A reader must not only comprehend words, phrases, and clauses in their own right but also how they relate semantically to the surrounding context and are relevant in the unfolding discourse.[1] In addition, while processing and comprehending each new word, clause, sentence, or paragraph, the reader is also evaluating the information. The reader makes assumptions and inferences with regard to what is being communicated as they are processing it. Further, they relate what they process and their evaluation of it to their own knowledge of the world.[2] The complexity only intensifies as the reader moves to a new unit of information. The reader does not forget what they have read, but neither do they keep an exact replica of the discourse in their mind. Instead, some of the most salient elements and relations may be replicated mentally, but much of what was processed will be combined with the reader's own understanding, evaluations, and

1. Throughout this study, the word *context* and its derivatives, unless stated otherwise, refer to cotext, i.e., the linguistic context.

2. One's own knowledge of the world is particularly crucial in text comprehension. Ludo Verhoeven and Charles Perfetti state, "Major models of text comprehension … have shown that text comprehension cannot be done with only the information present in the text, but that individuals also use their prior knowledge to construct new knowledge that is relevant to their individual experiences and situations" ("Advances in Text Comprehension: Model, Process and Development," *Applied Cognitive Psychology* 22 [2008]: 95).

reflections and incorporated into a synergistic, ever-growing mental representation of the discourse. Walter Kintsch summarizes the process well when he writes:

> We comprehend a text, understand something, by building a mental model. To do so, we must form connections between things that were previously disparate: the ideas expressed in the text and relevant prior knowledge. Comprehension implies forming coherent wholes with Gestalt-like qualities out of elementary perceptual and conceptual features.[3]

Successful comprehension of discourse is reliant on a complex web of interrelated and interdependent issues. It is, as Kintsch goes on to reflect, "a marvelous and wondrous achievement."[4]

However, this is not to say that the reader is left without any help in the comprehension task. There is a plethora of linguistic devices available that serve to aid the reader in their processing of a text by indicating the structure of the discourse, specifying the relations between propositions, correcting the presumed assumptions of the reader, and even demonstrating the attitude of the author (to name a few). When we use such devices, we are seeking to facilitate successful comprehension because we want to ensure successful communication. This study is concerned with one category of these devices, discourse markers (henceforth, DM). Discourse markers will be discussed in detail below, but broadly and briefly, DMs indicate the structure of the discourse and instruct the reader on how to process new linguistic material in relation to the wider context. In English, words such as *but*, *therefore*, *however*, *okay*, *well*, and *anyway* and constructions such as *you know*, *I mean*, and *so to speak* function or can function as DMs. As DMs, they serve as explicit linguistic cues to the reader on how to understand and fit the following material into the developing discourse. Discourse markers assist and guide the reader in their processing, clarifying discourse relations and structure, thereby easing the comprehension task.

The focus of this study is on a selection of DMs in early Koine Greek (third through first centuries BCE), namely, δέ, εἰ/ἐὰν μή, ἀλλά, ἀλλ᾽ ἤ, and μέν. This, of course, is not an exhaustive list of DMs in Koine Greek, but these were chosen for their occurrences in the LXX and because their

3. Walter Kintsch, *Comprehension: A Paradigm for Cognition* (Cambridge: Cambridge University Press, 1998), 93.

4. Kintsch, *Comprehension*, 93.

functions in particular are often not fully understood.[5] My purpose in this study is twofold: first, to investigate the use of these DMs in documentary papyri and the LXX in order to provide cognitive-functional descriptions of them and, second, to investigate the contribution of such an understanding to the study of LXX translation technique in, though not limited to, the Book of the Twelve.

With regard to the first purpose, there are two reasons a linguistic investigation of these DMs in the papyri and LXX is needed. First, DMs in this period have largely been neglected. There is some excellent scholarship to be found on the use of DMs both in Classical Greek and in Early Roman Greek (primarily as witnessed in the New Testament), but the use of DMs in the intervening period has rarely been investigated.[6] Second, in most Greek grammars and lexica, DMs are not described functionally, that is, according to how they aid the reader in processing and structuring the discourse. Instead, multiple meanings are attributed to them that primarily reflect the semantics of the contexts in which they may be found or that equate them, without any qualification, with various translational glosses.[7] Such misrepresentations thus result in misunderstandings of what the DMs actually accomplish.[8]

---

5. Regarding the term LXX, see §1.4 below.

6. These studies will be discussed in relevant chapters.

7. This will be observed in chs. 2–6. For a consideration of how DMs are typically handled in lexica, see the discussion in Christopher J. Fresch, "Discourse Markers in Lexica and the Benefit of Functional Descriptions: A Case Study of δέ," in *Koine Greek and the Evidence of Documentary Sources*, ed. Trevor Evans and Genevieve Young-Evans (forthcoming). Stephanie L. Black illustrates the problem well with her hammer analogy: "A hammer can be used for a number of things besides hammering a nail: as a doorstop, as a paperweight, or as a gavel. Should we then speak of a 'door-opening hammer,' a 'paper-weighting hammer,' or a 'table-banging hammer' as distinct entities? And more importantly, do any of these provide an adequate description of what a hammer *is*? Securing doors, weighting paper, and banging on tables may be atypical functions of a hammer used to make a point, but the principle is valid: a single object would not normally be construed as several distinct entities according to its different uses, and describing its uses is not tantamount to describing the object" (*Sentence Conjunctions in the Gospel of Matthew: καί, δέ, τότε, γάρ, οὖν and Asyndeton in Narrative*, JSNTSup 216 [London: Sheffield Academic, 2002], 145). Of course, Black's analogy is overstated, as it does not provide space for polysemy or even extended uses from a prototypical core—all analogies break down at some point—but it is a helpful illustration nonetheless.

8. Despite there being good Greek scholarship that has investigated these DMs from linguistically informed perspectives, the impact of such studies has hardly been

Concerning my second purpose, DMs are often used in the LXX even when not lexically motivated by a translator's *Vorlage*. Even when the DM can be argued as representing a feature of the underlying Hebrew, it is often the case that it is but one of multiple viable options. This is significant. Such uses evince contextually motivated decisions on the part of the translators and provide insight into how they themselves conceived of the flow and structure of the discourse.[9] In other words, in the LXX, DMs are often motivated by reasons other than lexemic representation and thus witness to the translators' own conception of the discourse and their desire to explicitly represent that conception. Because of this, I find DMs to be crucial in the study of translation technique.

## 1.1. Discourse Markers Defined

The category discourse marker is a functional one. It does not describe a formal part of speech.[10] Instead, as Maj-Britt Mosegaard Hansen explains, the category of DM comprises any linguistic item that is used to provide "instructions to the hearer on how to integrate their host utterance into a developing mental model of the discourse in such a way as to make that

felt. Most Greek grammars and lexica, the controlling authorities in the field, either lag far behind or simply do not pay attention to these investigations and thus do not benefit from the insights they provide.

9. Karin Aijmer writes, "The speaker's cognitive processes are hidden to observation. However, pragmatic markers (and other devices) can emerge as overt indicators of (or windows on) ongoing metalinguistic activity in the speaker's mind" (*Understanding Pragmatic Markers: A Variational Pragmatic Approach* [Edinburgh: Edinburgh University Press, 2013], 4).

10. See Maj-Britt Mosegaard Hansen, "A Dynamic Polysemy Approach to the Lexical Semantics of Discourse Markers (with an Exemplary Analysis of French *toujours*)," in *Approaches to Discourse Particles*, ed. Kerstin Fischer, SiP 1 (Amsterdam: Elsevier, 2006), 27–28; Hansen, *The Function of Discourse Particles: A Study with Special Reference to Spoken Standard French*, Pragmatics and Beyond NS 53 (Amsterdam: Benjamins, 1998), 357–58; Salvador Pons Bordería, "A Functional Approach to the Study of Discourse Markers," in Fischer, *Approaches to Discourse Particles*, 80, 82; Laurel J. Brinton, "Discourse Markers," in *Historical Pragmatics*, ed. Andreas Jucker and Irma Taavitsainen, Handbooks of Pragmatics 8 (Berlin: de Gruyter, 2010), 286; Carla Bazzanella, "Discourse Markers in Italian: Towards a 'Compositional' Meaning," in Fischer, *Approaches to Discourse Particles*, 451; Richard Waltereit, "The Rise of Discourse Markers in Italian: A Specific Type of Language Change," in Fischer, *Approaches to Discourse Particles*, 64.

utterance appear optimally coherent."[11] Discourse markers can include everything from particles and conjunctions to idiomatic phrases and even prosodic contours.

Thus, DMs are primarily pragmatic devices. As Richard Waltereit states, "DMs are nonpropositional. Their function lies outside the ideational realm of language. They belong to both the textual and the interpersonal language function."[12] Diane Blakemore labels this "procedural encoding," as opposed to conceptual encoding, explaining that DMs "do not encode a constituent of a conceptual representation (or even indicate a concept), but guide the comprehension process so that the hearer ends up with a conceptual representation."[13] In other words, DMs instruct hearers and readers on how to process the unfolding discourse, how to fit it together, as they go about the task of comprehension. This is needed in communication because, as mentioned earlier, comprehension of discourse is a complex process with a plethora of inputs. Furthermore, a discourse is not simply a collection of discrete utterances. The utterances of a discourse connect together to form larger segments. They interact with their contexts. They also may interact with nontextual material. Thus, DMs are incredibly useful devices because they clarify how the discourse fits together, thereby easing the comprehension task for the hearer or reader. They may be thought of as linguistic road signs—they aid the reader in navigating the discourse, informing them of the structure of the text, alerting them to what is coming, and providing them with instructions on how to proceed.[14] A simple example may suffice for now. Consider the use of sentence-initial "anyway" in English, as demonstrated in this excerpt from Brandon Sanderson's novel *Dawnshard*:

> She held out her hand—which glowed suddenly with a fierce light. The ardent wore gemstones on it, connected with silver chains.

---

11. Hansen, "Dynamic Polysemy Approach," 25. See also Waltereit, "Rise of Discourse Markers," 64; Aijmer, *Understanding Pragmatic Markers*, 4–8. Aijmer describes DMs (or "pragmatic markers") as "indicators of metapragmatic awareness." So also Jef Verschueren, *Understanding Pragmatics*, Understanding Language (London: Arnold, 1999), 189.

12. Waltereit, "Rise of Discourse Markers," 64.

13. Diane Blakemore, *Relevance and Linguistic Meaning: The Semantics and Pragmatics of Discourse Markers*, CSL 99 (Cambridge: Cambridge University Press, 2002), 90–91.

14. For seeing them as road signs, see Hansen, *Function of Discourse Particles*, 199.

> "Storms!" he said, "A Soulcaster?"
> "Yes," she said. "Let me see if I can remember how to use one of these...."
> "You know *how*?"
> "Of course," she said. "The Soulcasting ardents use them all the time. I went through a phase when I was *very* keen on joining them, until I discovered how boring their work was. Anyway, plug your ears and hold your breath."
> "Why—"
> He cut off as smoke *filled* the stairwell, making his ears scream with sudden pressure, as if he'd dived deep beneath the ocean.[15]

Sentence-initial "anyway" is not strictly necessary. It does not add a new concept to the discourse. If it were taken away, the meaning would not change. However, it guides the listener/reader in the processing task. It is a DM that indicates a return to the main idea after a digression. It tells the listener/reader that the former digression is now being cut off, as it is beside the point of the current discourse, and that the discourse is returning to its main point. In the case above, the speaker digressed into a background narrative, explaining how she gained familiarity with the device. Ultimately, though, that is not the point of the dialogue or the situation the characters find themselves in, which the speaker recognizes when she says "anyway" and returns to the issue at hand.

Lastly, it is important to note that DMs may operate in one or more of three macrofunctional domains: Interactional, metatextual, and cognitive.[16]

---

15. Brandon Sanderson, *Dawnshard* (New York: Tor, 2021), 209, emphasis original. I have also copied the typography of the text, which itself is a DM. Line breaks at the switch of speaker are not necessary, but they are eminently helpful.

16. As Pons Bordería notes, a DM may perform several functions simultaneously at different discourse levels. Pons Bordería, "Functional Approach," 93. I am adopting Bazzanella's general taxonomy for DMs, which she developed in her study of Italian DMs. See Bazzanella, "Discourse Markers in Italian," 456–57. A similar taxonomy that posits two macrofunctions, interpersonal and textual, is proposed by Brinton, "Discourse Markers," 286; Waltereit, "Rise of Discourse Markers," 64; Karin Aijmer, Ad Foolen, and Anne-Marie Simon-Vandenbergen, "Pragmatic Markers in Translation: A Methodological Proposal," in Fischer, *Approaches to Discourse Particles*, 104; and Alexandra Georgakopoulou and Dionysis Goutsos, *Discourse Analysis: An Introduction* (Edinburgh: Edinburgh University Press, 1997), 94. Interpersonal corresponds to Bazzanella's interactional, and textual corresponds to both Bazzanella's metatextual and cognitive. Four macrofunctions—cognitive, expressive, social, and textual—are posited by Yael Maschler and Deborah Schiffrin, "Discourse Markers: Language, Meaning, and Context," in *The Handbook of Discourse Analysis*, ed. Deborah Tannen,

The interactional domain is concerned mostly with conversation management and the relation between speaker and addressee.[17] The metatextual domain includes structuring markers (introduction/frame device, transition, list, digression, ending), direct and indirect speech markers, focusing devices, and reformulation markers.[18] The cognitive domain includes procedural markers ("related to cognitive processes, e.g., inference"), epistemic markers, and modulation devices ("related to propositional content and illocutionary force").[19] Given that the data in this study occur in text rather than spoken discourse, the focus will be on the metatextual and cognitive domains. Thus, functioning within these domains, the Greek DMs investigated, generally speaking, may be used to signal the structure of the discourse (metatextual) and/or to guide the reader in their interpretation of it (cognitive).[20]

## 1.2. Linguistic Frameworks and Considerations

### 1.2.1. Functional Grammar, Cognitive Linguistics, and Discourse Grammar

Given the nature of DMs, they are best investigated from a perspective informed by multiple linguistic subdisciplines.[21] They are functional

Heidi E. Hamilton, and Deborah Schiffrin, 2nd ed., BHL (Chichester: Wiley Blackwell, 2015), 189. The expressive and social are comparable to Bazzanella's interactional. For a more detailed hierarchy of functions, see the proposal in Pons Bordería, "Functional Approach," 86. Despite the difference of the number of macrofunctions posited, there is agreement concerning what DMs accomplish. The difference simply lies in how the functions are grouped and categorized. I prefer Bazzanella's taxonomy because I find the distinction between the metatextual and cognitive macrofunctions (also reflected in Maschler and Schiffrin) to be a helpful one. Though they are both concerned with the textual domain (which is why they are often grouped together), they represent notably different types of interaction with the discourse.

17. Bazzanella, "Discourse Markers in Italian," 457.

18. Bazzanella, "Discourse Markers in Italian," 457.

19. Bazzanella, "Discourse Markers in Italian," 456.

20. Brinton, describing the textual macrofunction, which corresponds to the metatextual and cognitive macrofunctions (see n. 16), writes, "Discourse markers assist in structuring discourse as text, by, for example, initiating or closing discourse; marking topic shifts, episodic boundaries, or turns; constraining the relevance of adjoining clauses; or introducing repairs or reformulations" (Brinton, "Discourse Markers," 286).

21. See Hansen, "Dynamic Polysemy Approach," 21. See also her discussion of previous studies and concluding remarks in Hansen, *Function of Discourse Particles*, 9–36.

devices that primarily exist to facilitate successful communication, so the framework of functional grammar is adopted here. In addition, cognitive linguistics informs my presuppositions and analyses. Its focus on language use as the basis of language meaning dovetails well with the foundational claims of functional grammar. Moreover, its recognition of the perspectival, encyclopedic, and flexible natures of linguistic meaning make it well-suited to examining linguistic devices that reflect the author's conception of the discourse, interact with linguistic context and the assumed knowledge and experience of the recipient, and evince core and peripheral usages.[22] Lastly, the reach and effect of DMs often goes beyond the sentences in which they appear, influencing the way the discourse is built and subsequently processed. Given this, a discourse-grammatical approach is taken throughout this study.[23] While there are other subdisciplines that inform my thinking and analysis, these three provide the overall framework. A brief description of each will now be provided.

Functional grammar is concerned with how language users succeed in communicating with each other.[24] As Simon Dik explains, whereas traditional perspectives prioritize syntax in the conceptualization of grammar, functional grammar prioritizes pragmatics, the study of language in use by its users, "as the all-encompassing framework within which semantics and syntax must be studied."[25] In this way, functional grammar considers language first "as an instrument of social interaction among human beings, used with the intention of establishing communicative relationships."[26] In other words, functional grammar, while not ignoring syntax, is less interested in the formal roles linguistic items play and is more interested in asking how humans *use* language to successfully communicate.[27] There-

22. The notion of core and peripheral usages will be discussed in more detail below in §1.2.2.3. "Prototypical Categorization."

23. Granted, discourse grammar is essentially a cognitive-functional approach, but it still merits specific mention.

24. *TFG 1*, 1.

25. *TFG 1*, 8. On pragmatics, George Yule offers the concise definition, "Pragmatics is the study of the relationships between linguistic forms and the users of those forms" (*Pragmatics*, Oxford Introductions to Language Study [Oxford: Oxford University Press, 1996], 4).

26. *TFG 1*, 2–3.

27. It is clear, then, when the linguists cited above claim that the category of DM is not defined by part of speech or syntactic role but rather function, they are assessing those linguistic items from a perspective informed by functionalism.

fore, in functional grammar, it is not enough to simply describe the grammatical system of a language. It is important to investigate the system in terms of functional motivations, to describe grammatical phenomena with respect to how they are used to achieve successful communication.[28] Dik writes:

> Since a natural language is an instrument used for communicative purposes, there is little point in considering its properties in abstraction from the functional uses to which it is put. The system underlying the construction of linguistic expressions is a functional system. From the very start, it must be studied within the framework of the rules, principles, and strategies which govern its natural communicative use. In other words, the question of how a language is organized cannot be profitably studied in abstraction from the question of why it is organized the way it is, given the communicative functions which it fulfills.[29]

As Christopher Butler explains, "One of the fundamental tenets of functional linguistics is that languages are primarily means of human communication. We might expect, then, that one of the factors which has shaped the forms which languages take is the need for the efficient transfer, from speaker/writer to hearer/reader, of information of various kinds."[30] Thus, given the role of DMs to facilitate successful communication and their primarily pragmatic nature, functional grammar provides a necessary foundation for their analysis. In order to analyze them well, one must consider the communicative task and the expectations and assumptions between text-producer and text-recipient. These are key considerations of functional grammar.

Cognitive linguistics shares significant overlap with functional grammar but also has unique and different priorities and emphases.[31] Dirk

---

28. *TFG 1*, 4.

29. *TFG 1*, 6.

30. Christopher Butler, *Approaches to the Simplex Clause*, vol. 1 of *Structure and Function: A Guide to Three Major Structural-Functional Theories*, SLCS 63 (Amsterdam: Benjamins, 2003), 12.

31. I am not differentiating here between cognitive linguistics and cognitive grammar. Though the latter may have some unique features, it is a subdomain of cognitive linguistics. See Ronald W. Langacker, "Cognitive Grammar," in *The Oxford Handbook of Linguistic Analysis*, ed. Bernd Heine and Heiko Narrog (Oxford: Oxford University Press, 2010), 89–90; Butler, *Approaches to the Simplex Clause*, 54; Dirk Geeraerts,

Geeraerts summarizes the discipline with the foundational principle that "language is all about meaning," explaining that language is not only something we know *about* but, given that it packages and transfers information, is itself a form of knowledge.[32] He then provides four tenets that elucidate this basic principle:[33]

> 1. Linguistic meaning is perspectival: Meaning cannot be reduced to objective description and classification. The use of language is necessarily embodied and contextual. It is based on the experience and perspective of the user.
> 2. Linguistic meaning is dynamic and flexible: Meaning changes as the world around us changes. "For a theory of language, this means that we cannot just think of language as a more or less rigid and stable structure.... If meaning is the hallmark of linguistic structure, then we should think of those structures as flexible."
> 3. Linguistic meaning is encyclopedic and nonautonomous: Related to the first tenet, humans are embodied beings and therefore our knowledge and use of language is also embodied. Because of this, linguistic meaning is not separate from other forms of knowledge but rather interacts with and is informed by our knowledge, experience, and context.
> 4. Linguistic meaning is based on usage and experience: Meaning cannot be separated from use. In fact, linguistic meaning *is* the use of language. "Cognitive linguistics is a usage-based model of grammar: if we take the experiential nature of grammar seriously, we will have to take the actual experience of language seriously, and that is experience of actual language use."

Thus, while cognitive linguistics largely assumes a functional perspective of language like functional grammar, it also has distinct features that are relevant to the study of DMs. The focus on encyclopedic knowledge and on meaning as perspectival and flexible, in particular, provide helpful groundwork for the study of DMs. Further, in addition to the above, Butler notes some assumptions cognitive linguistics makes when considering "the task of finding appropriate linguistic expression for a conceptualisation."[34] These include, but are not limited to, "the wish to

---

"Introduction: A Rough Guide to Cognitive Linguistics," in *Cognitive Linguistics: Basic Readings*, ed. Dirk Geeraerts, CLR 34 (Berlin: de Gruyter, 2006), 7–8.

32. Geeraerts, "Introduction," 3.

33. The following is drawn from Geeraerts, "Introduction," 4–6.

34. Butler, *Approaches to the Simplex Clause*, 54.

emphasise particular aspects of the conceptualization … assessment of the addressee's state of knowledge about what is to be communicated, the relationship of what is to be communicated with what has already gone on in the discourse, the intended effect on the addressee."[35] These, as will be seen in this chapter and throughout this study, are critical considerations for the study of DMs.[36]

Lastly, discourse grammar focuses on how grammatical phenomena function in the context of a discourse to convey meaning that has discourse implications. As I have explained elsewhere, "Discourse considerations motivate grammatical choices.… It is these choices, made on account of their function within a discourse, and the meanings they convey that are the object of discourse-grammatical study."[37] Grammatical phenomena do not exist in a vacuum. They can and often do have an effect on the interpretation, comprehension, and communication of the discourse beyond their host utterances. Such is not an accidental effect of grammatical choices but a motivation behind them. As Ronald Langacker writes:

> There is no exaggeration in saying that all of grammar is shaped by discourse and only exists to make it possible. It is atypical for the structures examined in grammar—such as phrases, clauses, and even sentences—to be used in isolation. Normally they occur as integral parts of longer discourse sequences that provide the reason for their being assembled and assuming the form they do. Fundamental grammatical notions can be characterized in terms of their discourse function.[38]

Discourse and grammar inform and work off of one another.[39] There is a circular relationship between the two. Mira Ariel summarizes it well:

---

35. Butler, *Approaches to the Simplex Clause*, 54. The whole list is not reproduced above but only the more salient considerations given the present study.

36. There are other insights from cognitive linguistics that are particularly useful when considering DMs, notably prototype theory and mental space theory, but these will be discussed in more detail below in §1.2.2. "Additional Linguistic Considerations."

37. Christopher J. Fresch, "The Septuagint and Discourse Grammar," in *T&T Clark Handbook of Septuagint Research*, ed. William A. Ross and W. Edward Glenny (London: T&T Clark, 2021), 83.

38. Ronald Langacker, *Cognitive Grammar: A Basic Introduction* (Oxford: Oxford University Press, 2008), 492.

39. This is described well by Robert E. Longacre and Shin Ja J. Hwang, who write, "The discourse as a whole, and the parts, greater and smaller, of which it is composed

"Discourse cannot but reflect grammar ... discourse makes selective use of grammar, choosing just those grammatical forms which suit the specific discourse goals of the speaker. Grammar too reflects discourse.... It also makes a selective use of discourse, 'choosing' some but not other discourse patterns for grammaticization."[40] Discourse grammar, then, investigates the discourse considerations that motivate grammatical choices and also what grammatical choices reveal about discourse considerations.

A particularly important aspect to the study of discourse grammar is the notion of choice. With respect to the grammar of a phrase or clause, speakers and authors often have multiple options available to communicate the same idea. When the same basic content can be conveyed through a variety of grammatical phenomena, then the choices between those grammatical options concern meaning that operates on a different level than the semantics of the phrase or clause. Recall the example above from Sanderson's *Dawnshard*. The meaning of the sentence hosting "anyway" would not be affected if the DM were removed. The choice to use "anyway" where it is not semantically necessary is a choice to explicitly convey meaning about the structure of the discourse and how its parts relate. Choices such as this are critical objects of study for discourse grammar. Rebecca Hughes and Michael McCarthy explain, "A discourse grammar ... foregrounds the kinds of choices that speakers and writers routinely deal with in production—that is, how can one best formulate a message to make it clear, coherent, relevant, appropriately organized, and so on?"[41] This is why Steven Runge writes, "One of the key presuppositions of discourse grammar is that *choice implies meaning*."[42] Such choices are not arbitrary.

---

are in living interplay with each other. The thrust or outline of the whole, as the hearer/reader begins to grasp it, affects his understanding of the parts. But, just as surely, it is information gleaned from each successive part of the discourse that facilitates the understanding of the whole" (*Holistic Discourse Analysis*, 2nd ed. [Dallas: SIL International, 2012], 15–16).

40. Mira Ariel, "Discourse, Grammar, Discourse," *Discourse Studies* 11 (2009): 6. So also Michael Hoey, who writes, "Discourse decisions have grammatical implications, and of course conversely every grammatical decision has potential discourse implications.... Patterns of text organisation are grounded in the details of the text" (*Textual Interaction: An Introduction to Written Discourse Analysis* [London: Routledge, 2001], 61).

41. Rebecca Hughes and Michael McCarthy, "From Sentence to Discourse: Discourse Grammar and English Language Teaching," *TESOL Quarterly* 32 (1998): 271.

42. *DGGNT*, 5 (emphasis original).

They are produced by a speaker or author in and for a specific communicative context and with respect to their linguistic context. Discourse considerations motivate grammatical choices, and it is incumbent on us that we seek to understand what is conveyed by those choices.

### 1.2.2. Additional Linguistic Considerations

Further to the linguistic framework provided above, there are a few linguistic issues that are particularly pertinent to the study of DMs and merit discussion. The first, monosemy and polysemy, concerns a debate within linguistic scholarship as to whether DMs should be investigated and described from the assumption of monosemy or polysemy. The second issue, scope, deals with the nature of DMs as devices that evince scope assignments over the discourse ranging from phrasal units to large sections of discourses. A DM that can be used with different scope assignments often has distinct (albeit related) usages at those different scopes. This, then, must be considered whatever position one takes with regard to monosemy and polysemy. Third, prototypical categorization must also be considered when investigating and describing DMs. As will be discussed below, humans tend to categorize different members of a category (e.g., different usages of a DM) as related to a prototypical member to greater and lesser extents. Determining the prototype, then, is important to understanding the category. This, too, has repercussions for how one understands the "meaning" or "meanings" of DMs in both monosemous and polysemous frameworks.[43] The final issue concerns how humans build mental representations of discourse. This is critical for the study of DMs because DMs primarily interact with those mental representations.

#### 1.2.2.1. Monosemy and Polysemy

There is no denying that DMs are polyfunctional devices.[44] However, how one describes the polyfunctionality of a DM differs based on their

43. In this way, the second and third issues, scope and prototypical categorization, expand on and further nuance the first issue of monosemy and polysemy.

44. See, e.g., Kerstin Fischer, "Towards an Understanding of the Spectrum of Approaches to Discourse Particles: Introduction to the Volume," in Fischer, *Approaches to Discourse Particles*, 12–14.

methodological presuppositions. Within current linguistic scholarship, the two primary positions are the monosemy approach and the polysemy approach.[45] The monosemy approach posits that DMs have one core function that is observable in all instances of use. The various interpretations that may arise in certain instances are not attributed to the DM itself but rather to other factors such as pragmatic processes, context, and prosody.[46] In this approach, then, it is always the invariant core function of a DM that motivates its use. Any additional meanings or interpretations associated with the DM are the result of how it interacts with a given context. The polysemy approach, on the other hand, posits that DMs have multiple functions *that are related in some way* but that do not all necessarily share one and the same *core* meaning.[47] Instead, DMs have one or more core meanings "from which new functions can be created in the interaction [with context]."[48] Except in their most extreme forms, monosemy and polysemy are not completely opposed; there is a methodological spectrum that exists between them.[49] For example, one may take a monosemous approach but regard the multiple senses that arise as individually lexicalized and as containing both the core meaning and additional specifications.[50] On the other hand, one may take a polysemous approach yet attempt to maintain the assumption of a core meaning as far as it is possible.[51]

---

45. For an overview of the positions and more detailed descriptions of the spectra of models employed, see Fischer, "Towards an Understanding," 12–20.

46. See Fischer, "Towards an Understanding," 13–14. See also Ler Soon Lay Vivien, "A Relevance-Theoretic Approach to Discourse Particles in Singapore English," in Fischer, *Approaches to Discourse Particles*, 154, 158.

47. See Fischer, "Towards an Understanding," 13. This should not be confused with how DMs are described in Classical and Postclassical Greek lexica. The descriptions of DMs in these lexica tend to be based off of different translational glosses and, often, a confusion between the semantics of context and the pragmatics of a DM, resulting in lists of a plethora of senses for a given DM in the target language. At best, lexica tend toward extreme versions of polysemy in their descriptions of DMs that lacks the rigor and nuance of current scholarship on DMs. (Granted, this may, in part, be due to the inherent constraints of producing a lexicon!) For some examples and discussion of this (beyond the chapters of this book), see Fresch, "Discourse Markers in Lexica."

48. Aijmer, *Understanding Pragmatic Markers*, 12.

49. The overview of scholarship in Fischer, "Towards an Understanding," 12–20, is particularly illuminating on this point.

50. Fischer, "Towards an Understanding," 14.

51. So Hansen, *Function of Discourse Particles*, esp. 87–89.

Generally, I find the polysemy approach to be the most satisfying in the study of DMs, and I assume that all of the DMs investigated in the following chapters are polysemous. However, one difficulty in applying polysemy in this particular study is the fact that, given the textual nature of this study, the interactional domain—conversation management and the relation between speaker and recipient—cannot be observed.[52] Most modern investigations of DMs are based on both text and spoken conversations. This allows one to observe all three macrofunctional domains, which makes polysemy a more likely reality, as there tends to be more variation in how DMs are used in the interactional domain. Without the interactional domain, there is far less variation in use.[53]

However, the issue of monosemy versus polysemy is perhaps not as critical as it first appears given my utilization of prototype theory. Prototype theory is a usage- and cognitive-based theory that posits category membership is a matter of degree, not of necessary and sufficient conditions, relative to the prototypical category member, the member that best characterizes the category.[54] In other words, if a DM evinces various uses, they can be explained as extensions from the prototype, sharing some but not all of its features. In this way, prototype theory allows one to sidestep the issue of monosemy versus polysemy, at least to some extent. It is fully

52. The interactional domain, as well as the other two macrofunctional domains, was introduced in §1.1 above. While it is, in theory, possible that the interactional domain could be observed in direct speech within a text, consider how direct speech is recorded in modern texts. It often does not share the same features of actual speech (e.g., space-building "well," "umm," and "you know" in modern English rarely occur in text except occasionally in news articles that reproduce speech) because it is composed for its place in a written text. Thus, even though direct speech may be recorded in Koine Greek or a letter may directly address its recipient(s), it likely does not provide insight into a DM's interactional function(s). See also n. 53 below.

53. Regarding the difference between spoken and written language and the functions of DMs in both, Hansen explains, "The norms of written language are typically more conservative than those of speech. Innovative structures and expressions that are common in speech will take some time to make their way into formal writing … assuming that they are at all appropriate to the goals of this mode of communication. Linked to this is the fact that … a certain standardization is indispensable to the establishment of a written norm, and some of the variation found in speech will therefore be naturally absent from writing" (Hansen, *Function of Discourse Particles*, 100).

54. Prototype theory is the psychological and linguistic outworking of the human tendency for categorization. This, and how it informs my research, is discussed in more detail below in §1.2.2.3. "Prototypical Categorization."

compatible with either approach. The extensions from the prototype can be viewed as distinct senses (polysemy) or as sense extensions (monosemy), but given the prototypical analysis, the labels are largely immaterial.

Therefore, in this study, I attempt to provide descriptions that posit a core prototypical function while recognizing that there may be uses in certain contexts that share core features with the prototype and are extensions from it but may not overlap with it completely. This approach allows me to err on the side of minimalism while not being constrained by it. If a single core function can be discerned and other uses can be understood as extensions from the prototype, this provides a succinct but also sufficiently broad analysis that does not result in a plethora of seemingly disparate senses being posited. In this way, my method shares some similarities to that of Hansen's, who follows Ad Foolen's methodological minimalism. Hansen writes, "As Foolen says, this is really a variant of Occam's razor which tells us, as it were, not to 'multiply senses beyond necessity,' or in other words to try as far as possible to maintain the minimalist assumption of a common core meaning, while aiming for relative precision of description."[55] By starting with a minimalist assumption, one first attempts an analysis that determines a core function and any nonconventionalized "side effects" that arise from the interaction of the DM and its context.[56] If, however, that cannot be satisfactorily accomplished, one is then able to move to a more explicit polysemous approach.[57]

#### 1.2.2.2. Scope

One factor that plays a significant role in the understanding and interpretation of a DM is that of scope, which refers to the level of discourse at which the DM occurs. For the sake of convenience, one may think of the levels of discourse as comprising sections, paragraphs, sentences, dependent clauses, adpositional phrases, and nominal phrases. Discourse markers vary with regard to the scope(s) with which they occur. Some will only ever exhibit one scope. Others, however, may be used at various levels of the discourse. With

55. Hansen, *Function of Discourse Particles*, 88. So also Hansen, "Dynamic Polysemy Approach," 24.

56. Hansen, *Function of Discourse Particles*, 88; Hansen, "Dynamic Polysemy Approach," 24.

57. Thus, I do not regard polysemy and monosemy as presuppositions to which one must rigidly hold. One should attempt to describe DMs on a case-by-case basis.

regard to these, it is often the case that different scopes bring about slight differences in the interpretation of the DM. As Regina Blass states, "Different scope assignments yield different interpretations."[58] This is even the case if the DM has one core function.[59] Its core function is observable in each instance of use, but its interaction at different levels of the discourse results in various additional senses arising. Thus, recognizing a DM's scope is crucial to interpreting it and understanding how its core function, if it has one, motivates its use at different levels of discourse and interacts with those contexts.

There are two important points to note. First, levels such as paragraphs and sentences are modern notions. They are convenient labels that are imposed on the Greek texts investigated and will not always be the best descriptions of the structure of the discourse. Moreover, with regard to DMs in general, not only in Greek, scope is relative to the discourse rather than to the syntactic structure. As Waltereit states, "The scope of DMs makes reference to discourse, not to grammar.... Given that the scope of a DM is highly variable and subject to discourse considerations, the syntagmatic sequence that can be considered their host unit cannot be determined in grammatical terms."[60] Second, the levels of sections, paragraphs, and sentences are gradient. Each level blends into its neighbors. Thus, owing to these issues, while it is sometimes sufficient and even helpful to use terminology such as "sentence-level scope" or "word-level scope," it is not necessarily best practice. Thus, I will tend to use the descriptors broad scope (section–sentence), moderate scope (sentence–adpositional phrases), and narrow scope (adpositional phrases–nominal phrases).

#### 1.2.2.3. Prototypical Categorization

When humans categorize, they often structure their categories around conceptual prototypes.[61] That is to say, humans conceive of a prototypical

---

58. Regina Blass, *Relevance Relations in Discourse: A Study with Special Reference to Sissala*, CSL 55 (Cambridge: Cambridge University Press, 2006), 24. So also Pons Bordería, who splits Spanish connectives into three distinct subfunctions according to their scope. Pons Bordería, "Functional Approach," 90–93.

59. Blass, *Relevance Relations in Discourse*, 24.

60. Waltereit, "Rise of Discourse Markers," 65. See also the discussion in Hansen, *Function of Discourse Particles*, 113–28.

61. See John R. Taylor, *Linguistic Categorization*, 3rd ed., Oxford Textbooks in Linguistics (Oxford: Oxford University Press, 2003), 41–83; Taylor, *The Mental Corpus: How Language Is Represented in the Mind* (Oxford: Oxford University Press,

member that stands at the center of a category and that contains certain features and attributes that are central to the category.[62] The nonprototypical members are still a part of the category, but they differ in some way from the prototype. They share certain features with it, but it cannot be said that they exemplify the prototype. Some will be quite similar to the prototype, thus having a more central place, conceptually, within the category, and some will be less similar, therefore existing on the periphery of the category.[63]

Often, this is how DMs are conceived. A certain use of a DM exemplifies the prototype. Most likely, this use is regarded as the prototype owing to high frequency, high productivity, and the presence of a cluster of features that are considered representative of the category.[64] Other instances of the DM will resemble the prototype, sharing various features with it, but they will differ in various ways (e.g., a particular context of use, an unusual collocation, a use that is an extension of the prototype's function, or exhibiting some but not all features of the prototype). Whether the DM is regarded as polysemous or monosemous, it is often the case that all uses can be traced to a prototypical center.[65] Though this may seem antithetical to the assumptions of polysemy, Karin Aijmer, Ad Foolen, and Anne-Marie Simon-Vandenbergen, in their work on DMs and polysemy networks, state, "We simply want to stress that within the polysemy network, one of the nodes often has a prototypical or core

---

2012), 186–87; Barbara Lewandowska-Tomaszczyk, "Polysemy, Prototypes, and Radial Categories," in *The Oxford Handbook of Cognitive Linguistics*, ed. Dirk Geeraerts and Hubert Cuyckens (Oxford: Oxford University Press, 2007), 144–46, 149–51.

62. Taylor, *Linguistic Categorization*, 64. See also Taylor, "Prototype Effects in Grammar," in *Handbook of Cognitive Linguistics*, ed. Ewa Dąbrowska and Dagmar Divjak, Handbooks of Linguistics and Communication Science 39 (Berlin: de Gruyter, 2015), §3; Lewandowska-Tomaszczyk, "Polysemy, Prototypes, and Radial Categories," 145–46.

63. Taylor refers to this difference of similarity between category members as "degrees of representativity" (Taylor, "Prototype Effects in Grammar," 563–64, 569).

64. Productive in the sense that it is the least restricted in what kinds of syntactic and semantic contexts in which it may occur. See Taylor, *Mental Corpus*, 173–75.

65. Contra Hansen (*Function of Discourse Particles*, 87), who seems to suggest that prototypical categorization entails polysemy. It does not. A prototypical center actually lends itself more to a monosemous approach than a polysemous one given that the central features of the prototype are typically shared by the nonprototypical members. Taylor, in fact, hesitates to use prototype terminology when describing polysemous lexemes (Taylor, *Linguistic Categorization*, 119–22).

status, or, alternatively, that an abstraction over the different nodes is possible, resulting in a core meaning."[66]

Thus, when investigating a DM and attempting to describe its function(s), one should bear in mind this feature of human cognition.[67] If multiple distinct uses are observed, it may be the case that they are related and are extensions from a core prototype. In this case, it would be inaccurate to posit multiple unrelated functions. Rather, the prototypical use should be recognized and then it should be determined to what degree the other uses resemble the prototype and how and why they differ. This will then provide an accurate portrayal of the core features of the DM and demonstrate how less prototypical uses still maintain enough of a resemblance to the prototype to remain category members.

#### 1.2.2.4. Mental Representations and Discourse Markers

A reader encountering a text is not able to cognitively store every piece of information, linguistic or otherwise. Despite this, while processing the text, the reader is able to maintain an awareness of the flow and structure of the discourse as well as comprehend the arguments being made or the story being told and their meaning. This is possible due to the ability to construct a mental representation of the discourse. Mental representations are not direct copies of the discourse; rather, they are "cognitive represen-

---

66. Aijmer, Foolen, and Simon-Vandenbergen, "Pragmatic Markers in Translation," 105. See also François Nemo, "Discourse Particles as Morphemes and as Constructions," in Fischer, *Approaches to Discourse Particles*, 381; Foolen, "Polysemy Patterns in Contrast: The Case of Dutch *Toch* and German *Doch*," in *Pragmatic Markers in Contrast*, ed. Karin Aijmer and Anne-Marie Simon-Vandenbergen, SiP 2 (Amsterdam: Elsevier, 2006), 60.

67. I am working with the assumption that the language faculty is not autonomous but is rather a part of human cognition and experience like any other human faculty. Thus, if prototypical categorization is a normal part of cognition and how humans experience the world, it likely affects and interacts with how humans understand, use, and categorize language. This assumption is based in cognitive linguistics, which can be perceived as the methodological umbrella under which all of my linguistic inquiry resides. Regarding the language faculty as a nonautonomous part of human cognition, see William Croft and D. Alan Cruse, *Cognitive Linguistics*, CTL (Cambridge: Cambridge University Press, 2004), 2–3; Geeraerts, "Introduction," 4–5, 19.

tations that interpret the linguistic input."[68] Instead of directly encoding the linguistic form of the text (though elements of the formal structure may certainly be incorporated and stored), mental representations store packages of information representing relevant individuals, events, and relations from the discourse.[69] In other words, a mental representation is an efficient packaging of information that conveys the meaning and structure of the discourse according to the reader's understanding of it. Along with the information in the discourse, the reader brings to the representation of it their knowledge of the world, expectations of what the author means to say and what the text will say, and assumptions about the author's own state of mind.[70] Because of this, a mental representation contains more than the information processed from the text; it also contains the reader's assumptions, inferences, evaluations, and reflections. As Kintsch writes:

> The mental representation of a text a reader constructs includes the textbase (not necessarily complete or veridical) plus varying amounts of knowledge elaborations and knowledge-based interpretations of the text—the situation model.... The reader must add nodes and establish links between nodes from his or her own knowledge and experience to make the structure coherent, to complete it, to interpret it in terms of the reader's prior knowledge, and last but not least to integrate it with prior knowledge.[71]

Mental representations are not completely built in one instance, nor are they static. Rather, they are constructed incrementally as the reader relates

68. Arthur C. Graesser, Morton A. Gernsbacher, and Susan R. Goldman, "Cognition," in *Discourse as Structure and Process*, ed. Teun A. van Dijk, Discourse Studies 1 (London: Sage, 1997), 292. See also Teun A. van Dijk, "The Study of Discourse," in Van Dijk, *Discourse as Structure and Process*, 18.

69. P. N. Johnson-Laird, "Mental Models in Cognitive Science," *Cognitive Science* 4 (1980): 106.

70. See Robert A. Dooley and Stephen Levinsohn, *Analyzing Discourse: A Manual of Basic Concepts* (Dallas: SIL International, 2001), 21, 52; Johnson-Laird, "Mental Models in Cognitive Science," 106; Kintsch, *Comprehension*, 96, 103, 107; Hoey, *Textual Interaction*, 18–26, 52–54; Catherine Emmott, *Narrative Comprehension: A Discourse Perspective* (Oxford: Oxford University Press, 1999), v–vi, 26–35; Susanna Cumming and Ono Tsuyoshi, "Discourse and Grammar," in Van Dijk, *Discourse as Structure and Process*, 116; Van Dijk, "Study of Discourse," 18, 31.

71. Kintsch, *Comprehension*, 50, 103. See also Verhoeven and Perfetti, "Advances in Text Comprehension," 296–97; Emmott, *Narrative Comprehension*, 26–35; van Dijk, "Study of Discourse," 18.

what has already been constructed with what is currently being processed. Thus, as a reader processes a discourse, they are able to build upon the mental representation, integrating new information with the old.[72] Gilles Fauconnier, who developed mental spaces theory, a significant theory in cognitive linguistics from which the notion of mental representations of discourse is derived, writes concerning the construction of mental spaces:

> The linguistic form will constrain the dynamic construction of the spaces, but that construction itself is highly dependent on previous constructions already effected at that point in discourse: available cross-space mappings; available frames and cognitive models; local features of the social framing in which the construction takes places; and, of course, real properties of the surrounding world.[73]

In the processing of a discourse, then, there is a constant retrieving, updating, building, and comprehending of the mental representation taking place.[74] In all of this, the linguistic form of the text, as Fauconnier points out, is essential. It not only provides the text, but it constrains the mental construction. However, the extent to which it provides explicit boundaries and signals to the reader will differ between texts and authors depending on the devices employed.

This brings us back to DMs. Discourse markers play a crucial role in the construction of mental representations. They guide the reader in their processing of the text, instructing them how to build the mental representation of the discourse by signaling how the new textual material fits into and is relevant to it.[75] In this way, DMs facilitate the recipient's understanding and comprehension by easing the processing effort it takes to arrive at the intended interpretation.[76] Sometimes, the relation signaled by a DM could

---

72. See Kintsch, *Comprehension*, 101–2; Talmy Givón, "The Grammar of Referential Coherence as Mental Processing Instructions," *Linguistics* 30 (1992): 9.

73. Gilles Faucconnier, *Mental Spaces: Aspects of Meaning Construction in Natural Language* (Cambridge: MIT, 1985; repr., Cambridge: Cambridge University Press, 1994), xxxvii, xxxix.

74. See Kintsch, *Comprehension*, 101–3; van Dijk, "Study of Discourse," 18.

75. See Hansen, "Dynamic Polysemy Approach," 25; Hansen, *Function of Discourse Particles*, 358; Waltereit, "Rise of Discourse Markers," 64.

76. Vivien, "Relevance-Theoretic Approach," 151. See also Thanh Nyan, "From Procedural Meaning to Processing Requirement," in Fischer, *Approaches to Discourse Particles*, 176; Brinton, "Discourse Markers," 286.

be inferred by the reader even if it were absent, but by using a DM, the author ensures (insofar as it can be ensured) that the reader arrives at the correct interpretation. As Henk Zeevat states, "It is in the speaker's interest to mark these relations: without marking, he or she may well be misunderstood."[77] This is especially the case for contexts in which multiple interpretations would be possible and equally feasible if the DM were absent.

It is important to note the significance of the fact that DMs connect the material they introduce to the *mental representation*. Hansen writes, "Discourse markers actually never mark a direct connection between their host utterance and the linguistic cotext, but always a connection between the utterance and *the mental discourse model under construction*."[78] Granted, often the piece of information in the reader's mental representation to which the DM's host utterance relates will be drawn from and mirror the information explicitly conveyed in the utterance or discourse preceding the DM. However, since a mental representation also includes elements such as assumptions, inferences, and evaluations, DMs may relate the textual material to those as well. Consider Eddy Roulet's remarks concerning the relations signaled by DMs:

> It is not appropriate to restrict TR [Textual Relations] to relations between text segments.... We define a TR as a relation between a constituent of the hierarchical structure of text—act, move or exchange—and a piece of information stored in discourse memory (this information may have its origin in the preceding constituent, in the immediate cognitive environment, or in our world knowledge). Thus a TRM [Textual Relation Marker = DM] can be defined as a linguistic form (lexical or syntactic) which indicates an illocutionary or interactive relation between a text constituent and a piece of information stored in discourse memory and which gives instructions in order to facilitate the access to the relevant information.[79]

Similarly, Kerstin Fischer writes, "Discourse particles/markers connect discourse *contents* rather than *segments*, including contents not explicitly

---

77. Henk Zeevat, "A Dynamic Approach to Discourse Particles," in Fischer, *Approaches to Discourse Particles*, 140.

78. Hansen, "Dynamic Polysemy Approach," 26 (emphasis added). See also Waltereit, "Rise of Discourse Markers," 64.

79. Eddy Roulet, "The Description of Text Relation Markers in the Geneva Model of Discourse Organization," in Fischer, *Approaches to Discourse Particles*, 120. See also Pons Bordería, "Functional Approach," 89.

mentioned. That is, they could create or mark relationships between actual, virtual (attributed), or presupposed utterances, as well as aspects of discourse memory."[80] In order to indicate a relation between the text and the information stored in the reader's mental representation, an author must make assumptions concerning the reader's mental state.[81] Authors are able to do this based on their own knowledge of the world and their expectations of what the reader will and will not know or assume as they process the discourse. For example, the English conjunction "but," as Blakemore demonstrates, activates "an inference which results in the contradiction and elimination of an assumption," even if the author is only presuming the intended recipient holds that assumption.[82] Thus, in a sentence such as, "I enjoy books by Brandon Sanderson, but I am not a Mormon," the author presumes that the reader may assume, based on knowledge that Sanderson is a Mormon, that the author is also a Mormon. By using "but," the author alerts the reader to contradict and eliminate that assumption. If the reader does not know that Sanderson is a Mormon, "but" will likely alert them to this, thereby effectively creating the assumption. In such a case, it would not be odd for the reader to think (or the recipient in a conversation to respond), "Oh, is Sanderson a Mormon?"—thereby deducing the assumption that "but" instructs them to eliminate. Thus, when investigating the use and function of any given DM, it is crucial to consider not only the linguistic context but also what the author may be presuming about the reader's mental representation, as that is the site of interaction for the DM. Blakemore argues, "The object of study is not discourse, but the cognitive processes underlying successful linguistic communication, and the expressions which have been labelled as discourse markers must be analysed in terms of their input to those processes."[83] Granted, Blakemore claims too much, as discourse, cognition, and the interaction between the two all must be considered in order to discern the function of a DM and the motivation of its use in a given context, but her point stands. Discourse markers interact with and guide

80. Fischer, "Towards an Understanding," 6, emphasis original. See also Nyan, "From Procedural Meaning," 176; Gisela Redeker, "Discourse Markers as Attentional Cues at Discourse Transitions," in Fischer, *Approaches to Discourse Particles*, 341; Aijmer, *Understanding Pragmatic Markers*, 13.

81. Regarding a speaker's assumptions about their addressee's mental state (and vice versa), see *TFG 1*, 10–11; Cumming and Tsuyoshi, "Discourse and Grammar," 116–17.

82. Blakemore, *Relevance and Linguistic Meaning*, 100, but see Blakemore's entire discussion in pp. 89–115.

83. Blakemore, *Relevance and Linguistic Meaning*, 5.

readers' cognitive processes, relating the material they introduce to the readers' mental representations of the discourse. This, then, is key to the successful analysis of them.

## 1.3. LXX Translation Technique and Discourse Markers in LXX Research

### 1.3.1. Translation Technique

The study of LXX translation technique is a descriptive exercise that investigates the relationship between a translated text and its assumed *Vorlage*.[84] Despite the terminology, such a study is not aimed at discerning a methodology that preceded the work of translation. As Jennifer Dines argues:

> "Technique" suggests something consciously chosen and systematic. It is unlikely that the early translators worked like this; their method is likely to have been *ad hoc*, experimental, not always consistent (Aejmelaeus 1991), as they grappled with the challenges and difficulties of a task for which there were at first no models.[85]

Thus, as Anneli Aejmelaeus writes, "Study of translation technique aims at describing the end-product of a translator's work."[86] The study of LXX translation technique is simply an investigation into what a translator did: It seeks to describe how a translator engaged with their source text and rendered it into the target language.[87] In doing this, one is given a sense of the

84. Anneli Aejmelaeus, "What We Talk about When We Talk about Translation Technique," in *On the Trail of the Septuagint Translators: Collected Essays*, rev. ed. (Leuven: Peeters, 2007), 205.

85. Jennifer Dines, *The Septuagint*, Understanding the Bible and Its World (London: T&T Clark, 2004), 118. See also Anneli Aejmelaeus, "Translation Technique and the Intention of the Translator," in *On the Trail of the Septuagint Translators*, 60–62; Aejmelaeus, "What We Talk about," 206; Staffan Olofsson, *The LXX Version: A Guide to the Translation Technique of the Septuagint*, ConBOT 30 (Stockholm: Almqvist & Wiksell, 1990), 19; R. Timothy McLay, *The Use of the Septuagint in New Testament Research* (Grand Rapids: Eerdmans, 2003), 57; Joshua L. Harper, *Responding to a Puzzled Scribe: The Barberini Version of Habakkuk 3 Analysed in the Light of the Other Greek Versions*, LHBOTS 608 (London: Bloomsbury T&T Clark, 2015), 21.

86. Aejmelaeus, "Translation Technique," 63.

87. So also Olofsson, *LXX Version*, 65; and Harper, who defines translation technique as "a neutral description of how the translator has worked, used in order better to understand him and his work" (Harper, *Responding to a Puzzled Scribe*, 21).

translator's tendencies, abilities, and preferences as well as insight into how they read and understood the source text. By having an accurate and holistic understanding of a translator's translation technique, one is presented with a clearer picture of the translator and how they went about their work. One is also then able to explore and speak to issues such as the translator's theological motivations and the text-critical value of the translation.

Traditionally in LXX scholarship, a translator's free renderings (so called) have been viewed as especially significant for the study of translation technique. It is argued that LXX translators, on the whole, followed their *Vorlagen* rather closely and tended toward literal translation. Thus, when they demonstrate freedom in their translation, it is notable and provides rich evidence of how they read their source texts and went about the work of translation.[88] As Aejmelaeus writes, "Free renderings are like fingerprints that the translators have left behind them. By these fingerprints it is possible to get to know them and to describe their working habits, their actual relationship with the original, and their talent as translators."[89] The choice to use a free rendering is a conscious one, in that the translator made a decision to produce a text that exhibits a movement beyond the minimal requirements of the *Vorlage*. The translator forewent literal representation for a translation that, even if faithful to the source, was not necessarily required nor formally motivated by it.[90]

There are useful insights to gain from how LXX scholarship has traditionally approached issues of literal versus free translation. Indeed, such

---

88. With respect to the study of translation technique, Dines defines literal as "a close approximation to the (supposed) source-text, word for word, or phrase for phrase, and including grammatical and syntactical idioms and word order; this is called 'formal equivalence.'" She defines free as "a style which is more paraphrastic and idiomatic, and which apparently aims to give the translator's understanding of the original rather than to reproduce it quantitatively; this is called 'dynamic equivalence'" (Dines, *Septuagint*, 119–20).

89. Anneli Aejmelaeus, "The Significance of Clause Connectors in the Syntactical and Translation-Technical Study of the Septuagint," in *On the Trail of the Septuagint Translators*, 43–44.

90. I appreciate Aejmelaeus's remarks on literalness and faithfulness. She writes, "A distinction should be made between literalness and faithfulness. A good free rendering is a faithful rendering" (Aejmelaeus, "Significance of Clause Connectors," 56). Though this remark and the sentence to which this footnote is connected illuminate that these terms are not as helpful or descriptive as they may first appear.

insights inform parts of the present study. However, these categories can be reductionistic. The literal versus free dichotomy is a false one and, as such, it is not a helpful or even descriptive means of categorizing.[91] Translational decisions, and translations as a whole, do not exist on a binary spectrum. Languages and their users are too complex for such simplistic categorization. This becomes clear in the following survey of a few issues that defy categorization as literal or free.[92]

(1) When a translator uses a middle-voice verb for a Hebrew verb in the *qal* stem, such as λούσασθαι for רחץ as in Exod 2:5, is the translation literal because of the semantic overlap between the two or is it free because of the choice to use a (contextually appropriate) middle-voice form for an active-voice form? The labels do not helpfully describe what the translator has done or why they did it.

(2) When a translator uses a present-tense verb in narrative as a historic present for a *wayyiqtol*, where does that fall on the literal/free divide? A historic present would be "literal" with regard to lexical semantics (in most cases), "literal" with regard to verbal semantics (if one understands the historic present effectively as a past perfective), "free" with regard to verbal form, and "free" with regard to pragmatics!

(3) Discourse features, as I have argued elsewhere, defy literal versus free categorization altogether. For example, a given Hebrew narrative may indicate a new discourse unit with a break in a *wayyiqtol* chain (a distinctive Hebrew feature) and an explicit preposed topic switch. If a translator represents this with a similar preposed topic switch and the use of a DM such as δέ (a distinctive Greek device), trying to categorize according to literal versus free is a fruitless endeavor. As I have written elsewhere, "A Greek translation that represents a movement to a new scene [by utilizing a feature not available to Hebrew] cannot be satisfactorily described as literal or as free simply construed. It is 'free' in the sense that the translator did not feel restricted by his *Vorlage*. Yet it is 'literal' in the sense that the translator is attempting to represent formal features of his *Vorlage*, but

91. Though this is recognized by some (e.g., Dines, *Septuagint*, 120), the problematic language persists.

92. The first two examples are taken from the discussion of John A. L. Lee, *The Greek of the Pentateuch: Grinfield Lectures on the Septuagint 2011–2012* (Oxford: Oxford University Press, 2018) in Christopher J. Fresch, "Illuminating the Path Ahead for Septuagint Studies: A Consideration of John A. L. Lee's *The Greek of the Pentateuch*," *JSCS* 54 (2021): 25–42.

these features are pragmatic in nature, rather than semantic or syntactic."[93] The literal and free categories are tied to issues of syntax and semantics.[94] Any usefulness they may have in those linguistic domains is lost when applied to pragmatics.

Marieke Dhont also critiques the tendency to categorize according to a literal versus free dichotomy and argues, "The fact that translation is an intricate sociocultural activity implies that it cannot be described along a single binary axis, and that a translator's decisions during the translation process are governed by a multidimensional interplay of various factors that are determined by the translator's context."[95] Dhont is correct, and she rightly highlights the inherent complexity of the factors underlying translation. Thus, in this study, for this reason and those stated above, the work of translators is not described in reductionistic and misleading terms such as "literal" or "free." Nevertheless, the freedom of the translator *is* important for the study of translation technique. However, rather than appealing to a false dichotomy of literal or free translation, it is much more interesting and illuminating to focus on a translator's freedom of choice in any given instance. That is, when a translator has multiple viable options in the target language from which to choose, insights may be drawn by analyzing the source text, the translation, and what different options were available to the translator.[96] The question of the translator's freedom of choice is central to this study, as will be evinced in the following chapters.

Related to this discussion are the notions of quantitative and qualitative representation. Generally speaking, the LXX translators tended to render their source text both quantitatively (one word in Hebrew = one word in Greek) and qualitatively (the Greek gloss is lexically motivated by its counterpart in the Hebrew), for example, causal ὅτι for causal כי. However, sometimes, a translator may render quantitatively but not qualitatively, For example, ἀλλά for אך, or qualitatively but not quantitatively, for example, ἀλλά for כי־אם. Other times, there may be a plus in the

93. Fresch, "Septuagint and Discourse Grammar," 85.

94. On the privileged place of syntactic and semantic investigation in LXX scholarship, see the discussion in Fresch, "Septuagint and Discourse Grammar," 79–83. Syntax and semantics are critical, but LXX scholarship has tended to treat them as the only domains of linguistic investigation.

95. Marieke Dhont, "Septuagint Translation Technique and Jewish Hellenistic Exegesis," in Ross and Glenny, *T&T Clark Handbook of Septuagint Research*, 24.

96. Lee does this to great effect in *Greek of the Pentateuch*, ch. 6.

translation, for example, μέν without any corresponding lexeme in the Hebrew text, which defies these categories altogether. As this last example demonstrates, these categories are not sufficient in themselves to describe the work of a translator and the choices they made; they merely offer a helpful starting point. Given that translators generally tended toward both quantitative and qualitative representation, it is notable when they depart from this. It raises the question as to what motivated the translation beyond lexemic representation. It is often the case in these situations that a larger contextual awareness, a desire to render into Greek idiom, and/or discourse-level concerns were at least some of the motivating factors. Again, this concerns the translator's freedom of choice. In the above paragraph, it was the freedom of the translator to choose from multiple viable options in Greek to render the source text. Here, it is the freedom to make decisions in their rendering that are informed by more than lexemic representation and lexical consideration. Thus, in the present study, attention will be paid to issues of quantitative and qualitative representation, not as sufficient descriptors of the translator's work but as necessary points from which to begin. The goal of considering quantitative and qualitative representation is to investigate the choices made by the translator and the motivations behind them.[97]

97. To be sure, quantitative and, more so, qualitative representation can be unhelpful categories similar to "literal" and "free." Qualitative representation, in particular, can be an imprecise and subjective label. Furthermore, as LXX scholarship has tended to prioritize syntactic and semantic issues (see Fresch, "Septuagint and Discourse Grammar," 79–83), the pragmatic domain of language is typically not considered when making claims pertaining to qualitative aspects of translation. This is an unfortunate lacuna. Moreover, in some LXX scholarship, categorizing a translator's work according to quantitative and qualitative aspects (on these aspects, see Anneli Aejmelaeus, "Characterizing Criteria for the Characterization of the Septuagint Translators: Experimenting on the Greek Psalter," in *The Old Greek Psalter: Studies in Honour of Albert Pietersma*, ed. Robert J. V. Hiebert, Claude E. Cox, and Peter J. Gentry, JSOTSup 332 [Sheffield: Sheffield Academic, 2001], 58) is done precisely in order to inform discussions of literalness and freedom. Hans Ausloos writes, "Several criteria have been developed which can be helpful in determining different types of literalness or freedom. They can thus contribute to the characterization of the translation techniques of the different Septuagint translators. In general, these criteria can be divided into two main categories. The first three criteria below are mainly quantitative, which means that they can be expressed statistically, whereas the other criteria are more qualitative, taking into consideration mainly the manner in which the translator deals with the content of the *Vorlage*" ("Translation

In the end, the study of translation technique has traditionally been an endeavor that narrows its focus to issues of grammatical, semantic, and/or syntactic relationships between a linguistic phenomenon in a translation and its counterpart in the *Vorlage*. While there is value to be found there, there is much more that needs to be investigated with respect to a translator and their translation. Moreover, the study of LXX translation technique frames its discussions by assuming an end goal of describing the product in terms of literalness or freedom, thereby guiding those discussions down certain avenues and unhelpfully closing off others. Translators and translations are complex. Though there have been exciting developments in LXX research in recent years that recognize this and have moved beyond the traditional paradigm, there is more work to be done.[98] One of the goals of this study is to contribute to this by demonstrating how translation technique research stands to benefit from a broader and more defined linguistic framework that leads us to consider more of the complexities of language, comprehension, and discourse, and how such factors and considerations motivate the choices of translators.

Discourse markers, in particular, demonstrate the significance of a translator's freedom of choice and the complexities at play in translation. No DM in one language is completely coextensive in function with a DM in another language. One need look no further, for example, than כי and ὅτι. The two DMs share extensive overlap but also exhibit distinct differences. The same could be said even of ו and καί. They share more similarities but there is not a complete overlap in function. Moreover, what one language accomplishes with a DM, another may accomplish by other means. For instance, as will be observed in chapter 2, δέ with a broad scope achieves what Hebrew can accomplish with marked word order in certain contexts. Because of this, using DMs in a translation is rarely a simple case of lexically representing the source text. A DM may be used to represent nonlexical features of the source text, or a DM may be used owing to linguistic requirements of the target language. Even when

Technique," in *The Oxford Handbook of the Septuagint*, ed. Alison G. Salvesen and Timothy Michael Law [Oxford: Oxford University Press, 2021], 168). Such is not my purpose here. Translation technique is too interesting a topic to begin all linguistic analyses with an a priori commitment that they will help define a translation in terms of literalness and freedom.

98. See, e.g., Marieke Dhont, *Style and Context of Old Greek Job*, JSJSup 183 (Leiden: Brill, 2018); and Lee, *Greek of the Pentateuch*.

a DM is used to render one in the source text, there may have been two or more viable options in the target language from which the translator had to choose. This is all the more pronounced in the LXX. Koine Greek had a rich repository of DMs. This stands in stark contrast to the handful of DMs in Biblical Hebrew. It is often the case that Greek DMs are used even when not lexically motivated by the translator's *Vorlage* or when the DM chosen is one of multiple viable options given the underlying Hebrew. Thus, frequently when DMs are used in the LXX, they indicate some level of choice on the part of the translator that evinces a consideration of factors beyond lexemic representation and that also reveals a translator who was keen to render their source text into idiomatic Greek.

The question, then, is what motivates the choice to use a DM in any instance given the many factors at play and complexities to consider. Discourse markers are intrinsically tied to context, the flow and structure of the discourse, and crucially, the mental representation under construction.[99] Thus, in order to use a DM, a translator must necessarily make a decision based on contextual factors, their understanding of how the text was structured and ought to be put together, and how to facilitate successful communication, that is, how to aid the reader in their building of their mental representation of the text. Therefore, these are the considerations that are most salient for us in order to answer the question of what motivates the use of a DM. As such, they are foundational to this study.

Because DMs rarely have one-to-one correspondences across languages and since they are functional, context-based devices that interact with the mental representation, they offer unique insights into a translator and their work. Traditional categories of literal and free are not relevant descriptors, and assessing them in terms of quantitative and qualitative representation is only helpful insofar as it leads us to ask further questions of the text, the translator, and their motivations. By the end of this study, it will be clear that DMs are a crucial part of the study of translation technique that provide more complex and nuanced pictures of translators and their work.

### 1.3.2. Discourse Markers in LXX Research

Discourse Markers have not been investigated in LXX research as such. However, there has been a good deal of interest in conjunctions, a type of

---

99. See §1.2, "Linguistic Frameworks and Considerations" above.

DM, though not as DMs. There is a justified sense that attention to conjunctions will provide insights into translation technique and, perhaps, even the translator. At the same time, these studies do not typically incorporate broader linguistic research into conjunctions/DMs, and they are not interested in providing a linguistic analysis of the Greek DMs under investigation. As a result, their insights only go so far before, not having the necessary linguistic resources to go further, veering prematurely into descriptions of translation technique or issues of textual criticism, and/or settling on statistical data that merely reports certain aspects but does not offer explanations. Nevertheless, the interest in at least a subset of DMs is encouraging, and there have been fruitful insights and findings as a result.

Philippe Le Moigne investigated the use of particles in Greek Isaiah in his dissertation "Le livre d'Ésaïe dans la Septante: ecdotique, stylistique, linguistique."[100] Of the particles considered, δέ, ἀλλά, and μέν are particularly relevant as they feature in this study as well. Le Moigne rightly sees significance in the use of particles for providing insight into a translator, particularly given the lack of direct correspondences for many Greek particles.[101] The overall investigation is insightful. However, Le Moigne does not establish functions for the particles investigated but rather relies on lexica, good but outdated studies, and translational glosses. As a result, there is a plethora of uses attributed to the particles that could be consolidated and better explained. His work is interacted with in relevant chapters of this study, but because of the lack of a functional framework and of an understanding of scope, prototypical categorization, and mental representations, it is often the case that our approaches are simply incongruous. Moreover, he often uses his investigations as jumping off points into text-critical discussions, which is beyond the interest or purview of this study.

Frank Polak has provided helpful insights into connections between clauses that is informed by discourse analysis. In his article "Context Sensitive Translation and Parataxis in Biblical Narrative," he argues that

---

100. Philippe Le Moigne, "Le livre d'Ésaïe dans la Septante: Ecdotique, stylistique, linguistique" (PhD diss., L'École pratique des hautes études, 2001).

101. Le Moigne, "Le livre d'Ésaïe dans la Septante," part 2: "L'emploi des particules dans Ésaïe-LXX." See also his concluding remarks in "Conclusion de la deuxième partie." Unfortunately, the dissertation has not been published, and the version I received from Le Moigne lacks page numbers. So, when making specific references, I have done my best to indicate where they may be found. Usually, this is done by reference to chapter and section headings, e.g., "ch. 4 §A."

connections between clauses need to be considered within the framework of discourse.[102] After a study into clausal connections in LXX Genesis and Exodus, he concludes with the claim, "Discourse structure conditions the way in which the LXX uses καί, δέ and the various participle constructions in order to render the clauses which in the MT are opened by *wāw*, or which are asyndetically connected to the previous clause."[103] This is similar to claims that I made in §1.2.1 above. Polak's study, though brief, evinces the necessity of an interdisciplinary approach that utilizes linguistic theory as well as the need to investigate and describe discourse-related phenomena with reference to their function within the discourse.

In his article "Tying It All Together: The Use of Particles in Old Greek Job," Claude Cox considers the significance of conjunctions as function words that affect the structure of the text.[104] However, Cox's purpose is not to provide functional analyses of the particles in question but to describe the nature of the text of OG Job according to whether the translator shortened the text or added to it. While this may sound promising for the present study, the result is a collection of lists and statistics stating what the translator did, with little consideration as to why they did it. Ambiguous reference is made to "style," and though reference is made to particles that connect the text together, there is no consideration of what the choices of the translator reveal about the translator, how they read and understood their text, or what may have motivated such choices.[105] The data are helpful, but there is much more to be considered from a linguistic perspective and as it pertains to translation technique.

James Aitken provides a unique perspective on particles in "The Characterisation of Speech in the Septuagint Pentateuch."[106] He considers particle usage in direct speech in light of register and as evidence for the

102. Frank Polak, "Context Sensitive Translation and Parataxis in Biblical Narrative," in *Emanuel: Studies in Hebrew Bible, Septuagint and Dead Sea Scrolls in Honor of Emanuel Tov*, ed. Shalom M. Paul, VTSup 94 (Leiden: Brill, 2003), 526.

103. Polak, "Context Sensitive Translation and Parataxis," 539.

104. Claude Cox, "Tying It All Together: The Use of Particles in Old Greek Job," *BIOSCS* 38 (2005): 41–54.

105. For style, see Cox, "Tying It All Together," 50, 54; for references to particles, 46–47, 53–54.

106. James Aitken, "Characterisation of Speech in the Septuagint Pentateuch," in *The Reception of the Hebrew Bible in the Septuagint and the New Testament: Essays in Memory of Aileen Guilding*, ed. David J. A. Clines and J. Cheryl Exum (Sheffield: Sheffield Phoenix, 2013), 9–31.

idiomatic Greek of the LXX translators. Given the focus on register, Aitken's claims are outside the purview of the present study (though they are interacted with at points). Nevertheless, Aitken helpfully points us to yet other factors that add to the complex nature of translators and their work.

In his book *The Greek of the Pentateuch*, John Lee devotes a section to particles in his chapter on educated language.[107] I have questioned Lee's association of particle usage with education elsewhere.[108] Apart from this point of disagreement, Lee offers clear and insightful investigations that consider koine idiom, the use of the particles in context, and what may have motivated the translators to utilize them beyond lexemic equivalence. In addition, though not the topic of the chapter in which they appear, Lee frequently demonstrates the translators' freedom of choice and draws insights from it. As Lee's interest is not in determining linguistic function or in the application of his claims to the study of translation technique, the present study stands to complement the kind of work Lee has produced.

I have investigated the use of DMs in the LXX in my article "The Peculiar Occurrences of οὖν" and briefly in my paper "The Septuagint and Discourse Grammar."[109] In the former, I demonstrate how a discourse-grammatical framework has explanatory power for analyzing the use of οὖν in LXX Genesis and Exodus and how such provides a more nuanced picture of the translators' translation technique. I also draw from Aitken's work on particles, register, and the use of particles in speech to offer further considerations that may have motivated the decisions of the translators. In the latter paper, I illustrate the usefulness of discourse grammar to the study of the Greek of the LXX and of translation technique, as it can complement traditional approaches by speaking to issues of pragmatics and discourse, linguistic domains typically not considered in the study of translation technique. To that end, DMs are discussed and illustrated as grammatical phenomena with discourse implications that thus require discourse explanations.

---

107. Lee, *Greek of the Pentateuch*, 92–110.

108. Christopher J. Fresch, "Illuminating the Path Ahead," 38–40.

109. Christopher J. Fresch, "The Peculiar Occurrences of οὖν in the Septuagint of Genesis and Exodus," in *XV Congress of the International Organization for Septuagint and Cognate Studies, Munich, 2013*, ed. Wolfgang Kraus, Michaël van der Meer, and Martin Meiser, SCS 64 (Atlanta: SBL Press, 2016); Fresch, "Septuagint and Discourse Grammar."

The most significant contributions to the study of conjunctions in the LXX and their relevance to the study of translation technique have been produced by Aejmelaeus, particularly her 1982 monograph *Parataxis in the Septuagint*, but also in a number of articles published in the years since.[110] In *Parataxis in the Septuagint*, Aejmelaeus investigates how the translators of the Greek Pentateuch rendered Hebrew clauses coordinated by ו. She successfully demonstrates the importance of connectives in translation-technical work and how the translators of the Pentateuch each exercised various degrees of freedom and creativity in how they rendered the Hebrew conjunction. While recognizing the importance of her work and following her in many respects, my study differs from Aejmelaeus's in four ways.[111] First, whereas Aejmelaeus begins with ו and investigates how it was translated into Greek, I start with a selection of Greek DMs and investigate how they are used and how they relate to their *Vorlagen*. Second, because of her focus on how ו is translated, Aejmelaeus is mostly concerned with providing an overall analysis, including statistical frequencies and comparisons. I, however, investigate the effects of the DMs used, that is, resultant meaning and discourse structure of the translation versus the meaning and discourse structure of the *Vorlage*, and what may have motivated the use of the DM on the part of the translator. Third, my study is interdisciplinary, in that I draw from and use insights from linguistics, particularly functional grammar, cognitive linguistics, discourse grammar, and research on DMs cross-linguistically and typologically.[112] This also is, at least in part, a result of my focus on the functions of DMs rather than on how a single lexeme in Hebrew is translated throughout a selection of books. Last, Aejmelaeus focused on the translators of the Pentateuch, in order to provide constructive insight into the descriptions

---

110. Anneli Aejmelaeus, *Parataxis in the Septuagint: A Study of the Renderings of the Hebrew Coordinate Clauses in the Greek Pentateuch*, Dissertationes Humanarum Litterarum 31 (Helsinki: Suomalainen Tiedeakatemia, 1982). For follow-up articles see, e.g., Aejmelaeus, "The Function and Interpretation of כי in Biblical Hebrew," *JBL* 105 (1986): 193–209; Aejmelaeus, "Significance of Clause Connectors." Particles are a topic of discussion in many of her other articles as well.

111. My purpose here is not to critique Aejmelaeus but rather to note how and why our studies differ. Both methodologies are beneficial and contribute to the study of translation technique.

112. It should be noted that many of the linguistic advances and research from which I benefit did not exist or were in their infancy stages when Aejmelaeus wrote *Parataxis in the Septuagint*.

of their translation techniques. I focus on the Book of the Twelve (henceforth the Twelve) for similar purposes; however, whereas Aejmelaeus's study was a translation-technical one, mine is not. My aim is not to posit a translation technique for any one translator of the LXX, save for some reference to the translator of the Twelve. Rather, my study is concerned, in addition to providing descriptions of a selection of DMs in early Koine Greek within a linguistic framework, with how a proper linguistic understanding of DMs may contribute to a study of translation technique. In this way, my investigation represents one piece of the linguistic inquiry that informs such a study.

However, in her work after *Parataxis*, Aejmelaeus claims that the Septuagint translators did not pay attention to even the most immediate context while translating. She states:

> The translator ... had to concentrate on the few words he was translating. It has been discovered that the translators were often blind *even to the most immediate context*, so that they could leave in it structural inconsequences, which they did not later return to correct, either.... The range of vision of the translator at work was very limited.[113]

This position should be challenged as the default assumption. To claim that the translators were blind to even the most immediate context is to disregard the necessity of contextual awareness to the translation process. Likewise, James Barr writes:

> Generally speaking, it is not possible in any text, in any language, to make even basic identifications of words without some attention to their context, which is the sole resource available to select between the multiple possible values of the signs.... The [LXX] translator was commonly not able to make his basic diagnosis word for word. Even the literalist had to work by the context, as the freer translator did. But—and this is the difference—having made his judgements, with the context taken into account at least to some degree, he then proceeded to express the results

113. Anneli Aejmelaeus, "What Can We Know about the Hebrew Vorlage?," in *On the Trail of the Septuagint Translators*, 84, emphasis added. So also Ilmari Soisalon-Soininen, "Beobachtungen zur Arbeitsweise: Der Septuaginta-Übersetzer," in *Isac Leo Seeligmann Volume: Essays on the Bible and the Ancient World*, ed. Alexander Rofé and Yair Zakovitch (Jerusalem: Rubinstein, 1983), 320; McLay, *Use of the Septuagint*, 46 n. 18.

> in a manner that as far as possible gave representation to each word or element as a separate unit of meaning for the purpose of translation.[114]

With respect to the object of the present study, the use of nonlexically motivated DMs necessarily demonstrates an awareness on the part of the translators of the immediate context *at the very least*. Often, it evinces an even broader awareness. In order to choose a DM, particularly when there is no corresponding lexeme in the Hebrew or when not qualitatively representing something in the source text, the translator had to have some conception of what was coming and how it fit within the structure and flow of the discourse. Interestingly, this is noted by Aejmelaeus as well, at least with regard to conjunctions. She writes:

> The choice between καί and these alternative free renderings [δέ, οὖν, ἀλλά, γάρ, ἵνα, εἰ, ὅτι, the relative pronoun, and others] is not indifferent. These free renderings demonstrate the translator's ability to handle larger units of text and his inclination to relieve excessive parataxis by use of more natural Greek expressions.[115]

In addition, she notes that context is a necessary consideration when translating a multipurpose conjunction (such as כי).[116] Thus, I am not certain how to reconcile the two positions that Aejmelaeus takes. If one can observe contextual awareness on the part of a translator by their use of DMs, then claiming that the LXX translators were "often blind to even the most immediate context" is inconsistent. By looking to the wider context as they use a DM, they are reminded of what they have translated and become aware of what follows (if not already aware). It may be that Aejmelaeus considers "larger units of text" to be equivalent to one or two clauses, as that is what she elsewhere claims the translator may have checked when encountering a conjunction.[117] Again, this counters her more generalized statement concerning the translators' awareness of context. However, even granting one or two clauses is often not enough for a translator to use some DMs, and this is to say nothing about how DMs

114. James Barr, *The Typology of Literalism in Ancient Biblical Translations*, MSU 15 (Göttingen: Vandenhoeck & Ruprecht, 1979), 22–23.

115. Aejmelaeus, "Significance of Clause Connectors," 50. See also her discussion on p. 46.

116. Aejmelaeus, "Significance of Clause Connectors," 52.

117. Aejmelaeus, "Characterizing Criteria," 58.

connect with mental representations and thus may interact with assumptions, inferences, evaluations, and considerations of discourse structure. Discourse marker usage requires comprehension and a complex awareness. Moreover, even if the free renderings mentioned by Aejmelaeus were in the minority, they demonstrate a contextual awareness that one may reasonably postulate was perpetually, or at least frequently, maintained. In addition, the literal representation of Hebrew DMs does not necessarily indicate a lack of contextual awareness. Rather, it could be the case that a literal translation was judged to be the best translation and the translator made that decision by maintaining an awareness of the wider context. This is, arguably, often the case with καί. It is the stereotypical equivalent to ו for good reason. In addition, even when a different Greek connective would have been more idiomatic, καί is, in many cases, still acceptable and has the advantage of representing the underlying Hebrew given its stereotyped status.[118] The end product may not evince a contextual awareness but neither does it witness against it. If the translator demonstrates throughout their work that they are cognizant of the wider context—an awareness which, according to Barr, is necessary in the task of translation—then the better default position is to assume at least some level of contextual awareness.

Throughout this study, I will argue that the use of DMs in the LXX evinces contextually motivated decisions on the part of the translators and provides insight into how they themselves understood the flow and structure of the discourse.[119] In other words, DMs are often motivated by more than simple qualitative or quantitative representation and witness to the translators' own awareness of the context, mental representation of the discourse and its structure, and their desire to explicitly represent that conception. A necessary part of this is to provide an analysis of DMs that is informed by a linguistic framework. An interdisciplinary investigation that combines LXX scholarship with modern linguistic theory is a rarity and, as the above survey demonstrates, has been practically nonexistent on the specific topic of DMs. This study aims to change that.

---

118. Such instances of καί are the result of "easy technique" (Aejmelaeus, "Translation Technique," 69).

119. Aijmer writes, "The speaker's cognitive processes are hidden to observation. However, pragmatic markers (and other devices) can emerge as overt indicators of (or windows on) ongoing metalinguistic activity in the speaker's mind" (Aijmer, *Understanding Pragmatic Markers*, 4).

## 1.4. The Corpora

The corpora investigated in this study are documentary papyri dated between the third and first centuries BCE and the translated books of the LXX, particularly the Twelve.[120]

The documentary papyri were chosen on account of their witness to natural Greek idiom of the period and owing to the fact that they have not featured prominently in Greek linguistic studies (particularly in biblical scholarship). Regarding their witness to natural Koine Greek, the papyri comprise a wealth of ample linguistic data. They provide insight into the features of the Greek language, evincing how proficient Greek speakers used the language on a day-to-day basis. On this, Geoffrey Horrocks writes:

> Ancient papyri from Egypt provide us with a wide cross-section of text-types reflecting both formal and informal styles of composition by both Greeks/Macedonians and native Egyptians. While some are clearly the work of barely literate authors of non-Greek origin, the majority of the informal documents composed by and for Egyptians in Greek … in fact display a surprisingly competent knowledge of the language.… Thus even those who have difficulties with the orthography … almost always control morphology, syntax and lexicon with some facility, and the differences between official and more informal private documents do not generally stem from imperfect knowledge, but simply reflect differences of stylistic level that are paralleled in other areas, and so provide us with valuable insights into the evolution of popular forms of Greek in the period.[121]

Similarly, Patrick James states, "The non-literary papyri differ significantly in character from the other evidence available for the late 4th century BCE to the 8th century CE and are invaluable for the study of the history of the phonology, morphology, syntax, personal names, and lexicon of Greek."[122] Thus, by investigating the papyri, one stands to gain a greater understanding and appreciation of Koine Greek idiom. With regard to the second

120. I used papyri.info and trismegistos.org to access the papyri consulted for this study. All translations that appear in this study are my own unless stated otherwise.

121. Geoffrey Horrocks, *Greek: A History of the Language and Its Speakers*, 2nd ed. (Chichester: Wiley-Blackwell, 2010), 89.

122. Patrick James, "Papyri, Language of," in *Encyclopedia of Ancient Greek Language and Linguistics*, ed. Georgios K. Giannakis, 3 vols. (Leiden: Brill, 2014), 3:11.

point, that the papyri have not featured prominently in Greek linguistic studies, most grammars and lexica are based on literary texts. In addition, linguistic studies of the papyri themselves are few in number. What Trevor Evans wrote in 2010 is still true years later:

> The linguistic significance of the Greek non-literary papyri has been recognized since the late nineteenth century. Nevertheless, although valuable work has been done over the last hundred years, it has to be acknowledged that language specialists have still barely begun to exploit the richness of the resource.[123]

This wealth of data has not been mined near its full potential, and there is still much light it can shed on Greek idiom, particularly in, for the purposes of this study, the early koine period.

The papyri examples provided in this study are a representative sample of what I observed in the papyri of the third to first centuries BCE more generally. They are selected based on how well they represent the data, their chronology (I attempt to provide examples from all three centuries in each chapter), and their preservation (well-preserved papyri with fewer lacunae and indistinguishable letters are preferred).

By the terminology *LXX* and *Septuagint*, I am referring to the Old Greek (that is, the earliest stage of a book that can be reconstructed) translations, produced between the third century BCE and first century CE, of the canonical Hebrew Bible and deuterocanon.[124] While it is common practice to refer also to the original Greek compositions of the deuterocanon, I have not included them in my investigation and therefore do not

---

123. Trevor Evans, "Standard Koine Greek in Third Century BC Papyri," in *Proceedings of the Twenty-Fifth International Congress of Papyrology Ann Arbor, July 29–August 4, 2007*, ed. Traianos Gagos (Ann Arbor: Scholarly Publishing Office, 2010), 197. See also T. V. Evans and Dirk D. Obbink, "Introduction," in *The Language of the Papyri*, ed. T. V. Evans and Dirk D. Obbink (Oxford: Oxford University Press, 2010), 2.

124. See Dines, *Septuagint*, 3; McLay, *Use of the Septuagint*, 6; James K. Aitken, "Introduction," in *The T&T Clark Companion to the Septuagint*, ed. James K. Aitken (London: Bloomsbury T&T Clark, 2015), 1–4. *LXX* and *Septuagint* are potentially misleading terms, as they denote one book. However, it should be recognized that the terms are widely used for the sake of convenience and that there is no monolithic Septuagint. Rather, on the whole, each book was translated independently and later collected in manuscripts and codices.

refer to them when using the above terms.[125] The LXX examples provided in the following chapters are taken from the Göttingen Septuagint or, for those books not available in the Göttingen collection at the time of this study, from Rahlfs-Hanhart.

Like the documentary papyri, the LXX is an important witness to koine idiom of the day. Horrocks writes:

> [The Septuagint] constitutes one of our most important examples of surviving "vernacular" literature of the period.... Given the nature of the material, the translation in general reflects neither the Greek literary tradition nor the preoccupations of the rhetoricians, and to that extent is a valuable source of information about the ordinary written Greek of the period.[126]

Though it is a translation and certainly evinces interference from the Hebrew of its sources, it is still genuine Koine Greek of the period. That this is the case is made clear by investigation of and comparison with contemporaneous papyri. As Horrocks goes on to state:

> While it is undeniable that, as a close translation of a sacred text, it embodies Hebraisms (especially where the obscurity or formulaic language of the original led to literalness), the analysis of the ordinary language of contemporary private papyrus documents from Egypt has now demonstrated conclusively that the Septuagint's general grammatical and lexical make-up is that of the ordinary, everyday written Greek of the times, and that it therefore constitutes an important source of information for the development of the language in the Hellenistic period.[127]

Thus, the LXX is investigated here not only for the purposes of translation-technical study but also for its inherent linguistic value as a Greek text. However, lest any doubt remain regarding the idiomatic use of the DMs in the LXX, the papyri serve as a control group against which the LXX is compared.

I survey portions of the LXX apart from the Twelve in every chapter except for chapter 2. The reason for this is the nature of the data. Chapter 2 covers the use δέ in the papyri and the Twelve. Given the sufficiency of the

125. See Aitken, "Introduction," 1.

126. Horrocks, *Greek*, 106.

127. Horrocks, *Greek*, 106.

data in the two corpora, there was no need to investigate further. Chapters 4 and 5 include data from the Pentateuch, in addition to the papyri and the Twelve, since the Twelve does not provide enough evidence on its own. Chapters 3 and 6 incorporate data from the entirety of the LXX, given the sparsity of the DMs investigated. The LXX examples provided throughout this study are representative of what I observed across the corpora referenced here.

When comparing the LXX examples to the underlying Hebrew, I compare against the MT as represented in *BHS*. This should not be taken as any indication of my presuppositions regarding the *Vorlage* underlying any LXX book. Rather, this is done for the sake of convenience. However, even if the text to which *BHS* witnesses does not match the *Vorlage* of every occurrence of each DM under investigation, those instances are statistically immaterial.[128]

Throughout this study, special reference is made to the Twelve. This is done in order to provide a consistent discussion of the contribution of DMs to the study of translation technique. The Twelve, though comprising twelve separate books, is regarded as a collection, since the earliest manuscript evidence indicates that they were always grouped together and, crucial to this study, since the consensus in LXX scholarship is that all twelve books were translated by one translator or collaboratively by a group of translators.[129] Either way, throughout the Twelve, one may hear one translatorial voice.[130] Because of this, I will refer to the "translator" of the Twelve.

---

128. I am referring here not only to the representative examples provided in this study but also all of the other instances investigated from which I selected the representative examples.

129. For the grouping together of the Twelve, see Jennifer M. Dines, "The Minor Prophets," in Aitken, *T&T Clark Companion to the Septuagint*, 439. For the current consensus, see Cécile Dogniez, "The Twelve Minor Prophets," in Salveson and Law, *Oxford Handbook of the Septuagint*, 310; Dines, "Minor Prophets," 439; Myrto Theocharous, *Lexical Dependence and Intertextual Allusion in the Septuagint of the Twelve Prophets: Studies in Hosea, Amos and Micah*, LHBOTS 570 (New York: Bloomsbury, 2012), 8–9; Takamitsu Muraoka, "In Defence of the Unity of the Septuagint Minor Prophets," *Annual of the Japanese Biblical Institute* 15 (1989): passim; W. Edward Glenny, *Finding Meaning in the Text: Translation Technique and Theology in the Septuagint of Amos*, VTSup 126 (Leiden: Brill, 2009), 261–62; Harper, *Responding to a Puzzled Scribe*, 11.

130. Credit for the phrase "one translatorial voice" is due to Jennifer Dines, who used it in a personal conversation with me in July 2012.

Based on internal evidence, it is usually assumed that the *Vorlage* of the Twelve was very similar to the MT.[131] Scholarly consensus has dated its translation to the middle of the second century BCE and placed the provenance of the translation in Egypt.[132] The Twelve is generally described as a faithful translation that typically demonstrates a literal translation technique.[133] Thus, the Twelve offer a unique opportunity for the study of DMs. While the translator does attempt to render his *Vorlage* closely, they are concerned with creating a faithful representation of the meaning of the original and are willing to move beyond quantitative and qualitative representation to achieve this goal. By this characterization, the translator's use of DMs should not always lexically match the underlying Hebrew but should, nevertheless, be used to render the text, or at least the translator's conception of it, faithfully.

## 1.5. The Layout of This Study

Each of the chapters investigating DMs are, on the whole, structured in the same manner. I first present the evidence from the documentary papyri. The examples are organized in chronological order, except in circumstances wherein examining a later text first is judged to be helpful to the reader. Sometimes, when relevant or helpful, the whole text of a papyrus is provided. Other times, if there is no need to reproduce the entire text, only the relevant portion is given. In the papyrus examples, the line breaks of the original text are not followed, as this would often result in unwieldy examples that take up more than one page lengthwise. In order to accommodate the reader who wants to look at the original layout of the text, I provide approximate line numbers in parentheses for each example. After investigating the representative sample from the papyri, there is a summative discussion. I then present the

131. Theocharous, *Lexical Dependence*, 9–11; Glenny, *Finding Meaning*, 14; Harper, *Responding to a Puzzled Scribe*, 11.

132. For the dating, see Dines, "Minor Prophets," 441; Dines, "The Septuagint of Amos: A Study in Interpretation" (PhD diss., University of London, 1992), 311–13; Theocharous, *Lexical Dependence*, 18; Harper, *Responding to a Puzzled Scribe*, 10; Glenny, *Finding Meaning*, 262–63. For the location, see Dines, "Minor Prophets," 441; Dines, "Septuagint of Amos," 313; Theocharous, *Lexical Dependence*, 18; Glenny, *Finding Meaning*, 264; Harper, *Responding to a Puzzled Scribe*, 11.

133. Dines, "Minor Prophets," 440; Glenny, *Finding Meaning*, 14; Harper, *Responding to a Puzzled Scribe*, 11–12.

representative sample from the LXX. Except for chapter 2, which only investigates the Twelve, this sample will contain examples representative of the Pentateuch (chs. 4 and 5) or of the entire LXX (chs. 3 and 6), which are typically given in order of their sequence in Rahlfs-Hanhart, unless, as with the papyri, a reordering is judged to be helpful to the reader. The LXX examples are then followed by a summative discussion that compares what was observed in the LXX with what was observed in the papyri, that provides a cognitive-functional description of the DM, and that engages other relevant linguistic studies. This is then followed by a discussion of the significance of the DM under investigation to the study of LXX translation technique. In every chapter except for chapter 2, I proceed to investigate examples from the Twelve and then discuss the developing translation-technical picture of the translator. I then end the chapter with a few concluding remarks. The chapters are laid out as follows:

Chapter 2 investigates δέ. This connective is typically overlooked, being regarded as a lesser equivalent, with respect to καί, of ו. However, δέ is not an equivalent to ו, and as my findings demonstrate, it is used in the LXX for the same pragmatic purposes as in the papyri.

Chapters 3 and 4 both deal with corrective DMs, and so are placed one after the other. Chapter 3 is concerned with the collocations εἰ μή and ἐὰν μή, and chapter 4 investigates ἀλλά. Given that these Greek DMs share some overlap when it comes to the Hebrew DMs they typically render, chapters 3 and 4 provide insight into the contextual choices that translators had to make when translating their *Vorlagen*.

Chapter 5 follows closely from chapter 4, in that its object of study is the collocation ἀλλ᾽ ἤ. It is separated from chapter 4, though, in order to facilitate a discussion of ἀλλ᾽ ἤ as a DM in its own right. The collocation has received little attention, despite the fact that it occurs relatively frequently in the LXX and the papyri. My investigation posits a discourse function for the collocation that has not, to my knowledge, been advanced before but that finds support throughout the corpora investigated.

Chapter 6 investigates μέν, which is unique compared to the other chapters in that there is no linguistic element in Biblical Hebrew that corresponds even in the least to it. This chapter, perhaps more than the others owing to the unique status of μέν, demonstrates an awareness of the surrounding discourse on the part of the translators.

Chapter 7 concludes the study. I summarize my findings and provide abbreviated summaries of the cognitive-functional descriptions of the

DMs investigated. I also revisit, with the findings of the study in mind, the significance of DMs to the study of translation technique.

# 2

# δέ

Generally, δέ has been regarded as an adversative particle that signals weak contrast. For example, Robert Funk writes, "δέ is a mildly adversative connector: it indicates the general contrast of a clause or sentence with one preceding."[1] Similarly, Maximilian Zerwick states, "The particle δέ nearly always implies some sort of contrast."[2] Samuel Green likewise comments that δέ is "most properly adversative."[3] Overall, this is the framework applied for understanding the uses of δέ.[4] Despite this consensus, however, the description of δέ as an adversative particle is insufficient, as there is a plethora of instances in which there is no adversative element or contrast that arises when processing the material δέ introduces. For instance, consider Jonah 3:3:

1. Robert Funk, *A Beginning-Intermediate Grammar of Hellenistic Greek*, 3rd ed. (Salem, OR: Polebridge, 2013), §632.

2. Maximilian Zerwick, *Biblical Greek: Illustrated by Examples*, trans. Joseph Smith (Rome: Pontifical Institute Press, 1963), §467.

3. Samuel Green, *Handbook to the Grammar of the Greek Testament*, rev. and improved ed. (London: Religious Tract Society, 1886), 344.

4. See also H. E. Dana and Julius R. Mantey, *A Manual Grammar of the Greek New Testament* (Upper Saddle River, NJ: Prentice Hall, 1957), §214(1); Stanley E. Porter, *Idioms of the Greek New Testament*, 2nd ed., Biblical Languages: Greek 2 (London: Continuum, 2005), 208; J. H. Moulton and Nigel Turner, *A Grammar of New Testament Greek, Vol. 3: Syntax* (London: T&T Clark, 1963), 331; BDF §447; William Douglas Chamberlain, *An Exegetical Grammar of the Greek New Testament* (New York: Macmillan, 1941), 151; G. B. Winer, *A Treatise on the Grammar of New Testament Greek*, trans. W. F. Moulton, 9th ed. (Edinburgh: T&T Clark, 1882), 551; Richard A Young, *Intermediate New Testament Greek: A Linguistic and Exegetical Approach* (Nashville: Broadman & Holman, 1994), 183; K-G 2.2:261–62; Félix Marie Abel, *Grammaire du Grec Biblique suivie d'un choix de papyrus*, 2nd ed. (Paris: Gabalda et Fils, 1927), 345.

καὶ ἀνέστη Ιωνας καὶ ἐπορεύθη εἰς Νινευη, καθὼς ἐλάλησε κύριος· ἡ δὲ Νινευη ἦν πόλις μεγάλη τῷ θεῷ ὡσεὶ πορείας ὁδοῦ ἡμερῶν τριῶν.
And Jonah stood up and went to Nineveh, just as the Lord had said. Nineveh *de* was a great city to God about a journey of three days by road.[5]

This occurrence of δέ cannot be regarded as indicating contrast. There is nothing to contrast between the preceding sentence and the DM's host utterance.[6] The grammars and lexica are aware of instances such as this, and it becomes evident that there is a struggle to offer a concise explanation for how the particle is used. Multiple functions for the particle are posited, attempting to account for various nonadversative uses. Some grammarians, for example, will posit an additional copulative function in addition to the adversative one.[7] Zerwick, positing more functions, writes, "The particle δέ nearly always implies some sort of contrast, but is sometimes also used with 'progressive' or 'explanatory' force, meaning 'and moreover,' 'and at that' (where the contrast is still there, namely with an existing or possible false estimate)."[8] This tension to account for the various uses of δέ may be most clearly seen in Daniel Wallace's grammar, wherein δέ is described as having six different functions: ascensive, connective, contrastive, correlative, explanatory, and transitional.[9] Similarly, BDAG contains three entries that correspond closely with Wallace's categories of connective, transitional, and contrastive, and two additional entries that can be classified as additive and emphatic.[10] It is more likely that this multiplicity of unrelated functions for δέ, including the frequent appeal to a contrastive

5. This instance of δέ will be revisited below in §2.2.1.

6. Even if one were to regard δέ as similar to "however" here, this would indicate a correction to a presumed assumption, not contrast.

7. See Chamberlain, *Grammar of the Greek New Testament*, 150; Smyth, §2836; Edwin Mayser, *Grammatik der Griechischen Papyri aus der Ptolemäerzeit, 2.3: Synthetischer Teil* (Leipzig: Teubner, 1934), §164.6.3. Robertson does as well (A. T. Robertson, *A Grammar of the Greek New Testament in the Light of Historical Research* [Nashville: Broadman, 1934], 1183–85, 1186), though he does note that δέ is not truly contrastive. This is discussed below.

8. Zerwick, *Biblical Greek*, §467. See also J. D. Denniston, *The Greek Particles*, 2nd ed. (Oxford: Clarendon, 1959), 162, 169–84; Abel, *Grammaire du Grec Biblique*, 345–46; BDF, §447.

9. Wallace, *Greek Grammar beyond the Basics* (Grand Rapids: Zondervan, 1996), 670–74. This tension can be observed in other Greek grammars as well, e.g., Dana and Mantey, *Manual Grammar*, §214; Porter, *Idioms*, 208.

10. BDAG, s.v. "δέ." See also LSJ, s.v. "δέ"; L-N, §§89.87, 89.94, 89.124, 89.136.

force that is frequently not observed, is better explained as deriving from the context in which the particle appears, rather than from δέ itself.

Given that DMs will either have a core function that may be observed in every instance of use or multiple functions that are related in some way, it is reasonable to expect the same to be true for δέ.[11] In what follows, I investigate the use of δέ in a representative sample from the documentary papyri of the third to first centuries BCE in order to determine how it functions in early Koine Greek. The determined function(s) will then be compared to the particle's use in the Twelve.

## 2.1. The Use of δέ in the Papyri

### 2.1.1. *BGU* 14.2417 (258/257 BCE)

In this letter, Philotas writes to Epistrotos. Most of the letter is concerned with well wishes and requests to be remembered by Epistrotos. The real request comes at the end of the letter, pertaining to Philotas's son.

> Φιλώτας Ἐπιστράτωι χαίρειν· καλῶς ποιεῖς, εἰ ἔρρωσαι· ἐρρώμεθα δὲ καὶ ἡμεῖς· ὑγιαίνει δὲ καὶ Πλείσταρχος, καὶ ἡδέως προσεδέξατο αὐτὸν ὁ βασιλεύς· χαρίζοιο δ᾽ ἂν ἡμῖν ἐπιμελόμενος σαυτοῦ, ὅπως ἂν ὑγιαίνῃς· καὶ μνημόνευε δὲ ἡμῶν ὥσπερ καὶ ἡμεῖς σοῦ ἐν παντὶ καιρῶι, καὶ ταῦτα πολὺ χαριεῖ ἡμῖν· καὶ περὶ τοῦ ἡμῶν υἱοῦ, ἐὰν τις τῶν παρ᾽ ἡμῶν καταπλεῖ, ἐπίστειλον ἡμῖν· ἔρρωσο.
> Philotas to Epistrotos. Greetings. You are well, if you are in good health. We *de* are in good health also. Pleistarchos *de* is also healthy, and the king pleasantly received him. You *de* would do us a favor by taking care of yourself, so that you are in good health. Also, remember *de* us just as we also remember you at every opportunity, and these things will be a great kindness to us. And concerning our son, if anyone of our people sails back, send a message to us. Farewell.

None of these instances of δέ can be regarded as adversative. The first occurrence is preceded by a wish for Epistrotos's good health and is then followed by a switch of reference to the letter writer, Philotas, and those with him, confirming that they too are enjoying good health. A contrastive relation here would result in incoherence. The second use is similar. It introduces a referent switch to a certain Pleistarchos, who is also doing

11. See §1.2.2.

well. The third instance differs in some respects. There is still no element of contrast between that which precedes and follows δέ, and the DM does occur with a referent switch (now Epistrotos is addressed directly). The difference is that the DM's host utterance does not continue the greetings and well-wishes. Instead, Philotas advances his letter to make a request of his recipient, requesting that he take care of himself in order to stay healthy. Directly following this is the final use of δέ. In this instance, the material following the DM makes another request of Epistrotos, namely that he remember Philotas and those with him as they remember Epistrotos. This then leads to the final request (and presumably the point of sending the letter): if anyone of Philotas's people who were with his son sails back, he requests a message be sent. In every case, note that δέ occurs at seams within the discourse, where there is some element of discontinuity, whether it be referent switches (first, second, and third occurrences) or new topics (third and fourth occurrences) and where the author is moving the letter forward to a new point. Given this, it would seem that the final part of the letter (the request concerning Philotas's son) would be ripe for δέ as well. At the very least, one can observe that the final portion differs from the rest in that it is headed by a clear point of departure marking the shift in topic (καὶ περὶ τοῦ ἡμῶν υἱοῦ), whereas the other seams of the discourse have no such clear thematic discontinuities. Perhaps it is due to this that δέ was not used in the last instance.

### 2.1.2. P.Cair.Zen. 1.59036 (257 BCE)

Apollodotos writes to Xanthippos concerning a sum of money that he sent to the latter for a ship. It seems there was an agreement that Xanthippos would refund this sum to Apollodotos but he had yet to do so. So, Apollodotos writes to remind Xanthippos of this need.[12]

> (10) Ἀπολλόδοτος Ξανθίππωι χαίρειν. εἰ τῶι τε σώματι ἔρρωσαι καὶ τὰ ἄλλα σοι κατὰ γνώμη[ν] ἐστίν, εἴη ἂν ὡς ἡμεῖς θέλομεν· ἐρρώμεθα <u>δὲ</u> καὶ αὐτοί. ἐγράψαμέν σοι πρότερον διότι δεδώκαμεν διὰ Περιγένους εἰς τὴν ναῦν ἣν τριηραρχεῖς Ἀντιπάτρωι τῶι ἐπιπλέοντι ἐπὶ τῆς νεὼς (δραχμὰς) Β. ὅπως οὖν τοῦτό τε καὶ τὸ δοθὲν Ἑκατωνύμωι εἰς τὴν (ἐννήρη) (δραχμὰς) υξε (διώβολον) χ(αλκοῦς) β, ἐάν τε φαίνηταί σοι, διαγράψῃς Μηδείωι εἰς τὰ ἰατρικά, ἐάν τε

12. For more context to this papyrus, see Roger S. Bagnall and Peter Derow, *The Hellenistic Period: Historical Sources in Translation* (Malden, MA: Blackwell, 2004), 199–200.

βούλῃ[ι], γράψῃις Ἱκεσίωι διορθώσασθαι ἡμῖν ἀπὸ τῶν ἐνηροσίων, οὐθὲν δὲ σοῦ ἐπεσταλκότ[ος] βέλτιον (15) ὑπελάβομεν εἶναι πάλιν γράψαι σοι περὶ τούτων. καλῶς ἂν οὖν ποιήσαις ἐπιστείλας ἡμῖν ὡς \βούλει/ ⟦δεῖ⟧ γενέσθαι, ἵνα καὶ ἡμεῖς οὕτω καταχωρίσωμεν. ἐὰν δὲ φαίνηταί σοι Χαρμίδει τῶι παρ' ἡμῶν τῶι τὴν ἐπιστολήν σοι ἀποδεδωκότι διαγράψαι, διάγραψον. ἔρρωσο.
(10) Apollodotos to Xanthippos. Greetings. If you are well in body and other things are in accordance with your will, it would be as we wish. We *de* ourselves are also well. We wrote to you before that we have given, through Perigenes, for the ship that you command, 2000 drachmae to Antipatros, who is sailing the ship. In any way whatever, if it pleases you, you may pay this sum and what was given to Hekatonymos for the nine-oar ship (465 drachmae, 2 obol, and 2 copper coins) to Medeios for the medical tax. If you wish, you may write to Hikesios to pay us out of the (15) ship's equipment account.[13] (As *de* you have sent no word, we supposed it to be better to write to you again concerning these things.) So, please send us what you wish to happen, in order that we also may record it accordingly. If *de* it pleases you to pay Charmides, who has delivered the letter from us to you, do so. Farewell.

The first instance of δέ occurs at the end of the letter's greeting. After wishing for Xanthippos's health, there is a topic switch from Xanthippos to "we," and this occurs alongside δέ: "If you are well in body and other things are in accordance with your will, it would be as we wish. We *de* ourselves are also well." From there, Apollodotos moves straight into the body of the letter ("We wrote to you before that we have given"). This first δέ certainly cannot be regarded as adversative. There is no contrast between the sentences but rather a movement from one topic to the next.

The second use of δέ also cannot be regarded as adversative. In the material prior to this sentence, Apollodotos reminds Xanthippos of the content of his previous letter (that the money was sent for the ship) and asks that he repay what is owed. The material following δέ does not continue this but rather explains why this current letter has been sent: Since Xanthippos has not sent word yet, Apolloditos thought it wise to write again. This is not contrastive material (there is nothing with which it can stand in contrast), but rather a new part of the letter that is distinct from what preceded. In fact, the material introduced by δέ is background information, hence the parentheses in the translation above. The purpose

13. "Ship's equipment account" is the translation provided for the enigmatic ἐνηροσίων by A. S. Hunt and C. C. Edgar, *Select Papyri, Vol. 2: Non-Literary Papryi; Public Documents*, LCL (Cambridge: Harvard University Press, 1934), 555.

of the letter is to procure repayment from Xanthippos. The foreground of such a discourse that aims to effect a certain behavior in its recipient will typically and primarily be comprised of requests and imperatives, such as what can be observed in the previous sentences ("you may pay this sum" and "you may write to Hikesios to pay us") and in the following sentences ("Please send us what you wish to happen" and "If it pleases you to pay Charmides, do so").[14] The sentence with δέ does not make a request or include an imperative. Moreover, the sentence topic is not Xanthippos but has switched to Apollodotos ("we"). As such, it is parenthetical; it does not move the discourse forward but is a distinct information unit that provides background content about the current letter.

The final instance of δέ, introducing the request to pay Charmides, is also clearly not adversative. There is no contrast being made. At the same time, it is more difficult to observe a shift in the discourse like what was seen with the previous two uses of the DM. This last sentence and the previous both address Xanthippos and make requests of him. However, the request to pay Charmides may still represent a shift in the discourse in two ways. First, it is the final request of the letter, and, in fact, the final sentence, of the letter. Such may have something to do with the appearance of δέ here. Second, the request that Xanthippos pay Charmides is a distinct event from the immediately preceding "send us what you wish to happen."[15] In the end, whatever the case, we can observe uses of δέ similar to those in example 1 above. The DM, rather than signaling adversative relations, seems instead to segment sections of the discourse.

### 2.1.3. P.Cair.Zen. 2.59148 (256 BCE)

The author of this letter, Hierokles, writes to Zenon to inform him of a servant named Onesimos who is coming to Herakleopolis selling garments.

14. On foreground, discourse types, and verb forms, see Longacre and Hwang, *Holistic Discourse Analysis*, 35–36, 169–72. Note that the sentence immediately following "Please send us what you wish to happen" is introduced by οὖν. This DM often occurs after background information and signals a return to the foreground. See *DGGNT*, 44–46. I observed this as well in LXX Genesis and Exodus. See Fresch, "Peculiar Occurrences of οὖν," 463, 467.

15. As is made clear earlier in the letter (not reproduced here), Apollodotos is here suggesting that Xanthippos pay the money to Charmides who can then take it to Medeios (mentioned in the excerpt above).

Apparently, these garments are well-priced, and so Heirokles asks Zenon to purchase two and send them back.

> Ἱεροκλῆς Ζήνωνι χαίρειν. εἰ ἔρρωσαι καὶ ἐν τοῖς λοιποῖς ἀπαλλάσσεις κατὰ νοῦν, εὖ ἂν ἔχοι· ὑγιαίνω δὲ καὶ αὐτὸς καὶ Ἐφάρμοστος. ἀπέσταλκεν Καλλικῶν παῖδα εἰς Ἡρακλέους πόλιν ὥστε καταγαγεῖν τι αὐτῶι, ὧι ὄνομα Ὀνήσιμος. ἠξίωσεν οὖν καὶ Πτολεμαῖος παρελθεῖν αὐτὸν πρὸς \σ/έ. σὺ οὖν καλῶς ἂν ποιήσαις πριάμενος ἱμάτιον καὶ \ἄλλο θερινὸν/ ⟦χιτῶνα⟧ Πτολεμαῖωι καὶ δοὺς τῶι παιδὶ ὅπως ἂν καταγάγηι, (5) ἐπειδὴ σὺ μακρότερ\ο/ν ποιεῖς, Πτολεμαίωι δὲ τυγχάνει χρέα οὖσα· ἀκούων γὰρ ἄνῳ εὔωνα εἶναι οὐκ ἠγόρακεν ἐνθένδε. ἔρρωσο.
> Hierokles to Zenon. Greetings. If you are healthy and you are getting along in the rest according to your wishes, it would be good. I *de* myself am healthy also and so is Epharmostos. Kallikon has sent a servant, whose name is Onesimos, to Herakleopolis to bring something down to him. So, Ptolemaios also requested that he go to you. So, please buy an outer garment and another one for summer for Ptolemaois and then give them to the servant so that he may bring them down, since you take too long. (5) Ptolemaios *de* happens to be in need, for hearing earlier there is a fair price, he has not bought here. Farewell.

Similar to both examples 1 and 2, the first instance of δέ is found at the end of the greeting where the author switches from wishing the recipient well to stating that he and those with him are well. Furthermore, like example 2, the author then moves straight into the body of the letter. There is no notion of an adversative relation here. The sentence topic has switched from Zenon to Hierokles and the contents of the sentences do not give rise to a contrastive reading. Note that the next two developments in this letter are signaled by οὖν.[16] In both cases, the discourse moves forward to distinct, new information units while maintaining an explicit continuative connection with what preceded. The second instance of δέ occurs in the last sentence, following the unit introduced by the second οὖν. Whereas the preceding content concerns Hierokles's request to Zenon to purchase garments for Ptolemaios and give them to Onesimos, the DM's host utterance conveys a new idea that does not continue prior material. Rather, it is a description of Ptolemaios's need that explains the basis for the request. In addition, it serves to close the body of the letter. Like the

16. Regarding the function of οὖν, see *DGGNT*, 43–48; Fresch, "Peculiar Occurrences of οὖν."

second instance of δέ in example 2, the informational value of the host utterance could be regarded as parenthetical. While it is a distinct shift within the discourse, it is, in some respects, independent offline material, a sidenote from the author to his recipient.[17] Thus in both cases in this letter, δέ occurs with distinct units of discourse, though the kind of information introduced is different. In neither instance does the particle occur with contrastive material.

### 2.1.4. P.Athen. 60 (323 BCE–30 BCE)

In this letter, Apollonia and Eupous write to their sisters, Rasis and Demarion. They demonstrate a concern that their siblings behave well, attending to their responsibilities, and also inform them of their mother's health.

> Ἀπολλωνία καὶ Εὔπους Ῥασίῳ καὶ Δημαρίῳ ταῖς ἀδελφαῖς χαίρειν. εἰ ἔρρωσθε ε[ὖ· ἐρ-]ρώμεθα δὲ καὶ αὐτα̣ί̣. κα[λῶς] δὲ ποιήσεις τοῖς ἱεροῖς λύχνον ἅπτουσα καὶ ἐκτινάσσουσα τὰ προσκεφάλαια. φιλομάθει δὲ καὶ μὴ λυποῦ περὶ τῆς μητρός· ἤδη γὰρ κομψῶς ἔχει. προσδέχεσθε δὲ ἡμᾶς. ἔρρωσθε. καὶ μὴ παῖζε ἐν τῇ αὐλῇ, ἀλλὰ ἔσω εὐτάκτει· ἐπιμέλου δὲ Τιτόας καὶ Σφαίρου.
>
> Apollonia and Eupous to Rasis and Demarion, their sisters. Greetings. If you are well, good. We *de* ourselves are also well. You *de* should light a lamp and shake out the pillows in the sanctuaries. Be *de* devoted to learning and do not be distressed about mother. For already she is well. Wait *de* for us. Farewell. P.S. Do not play games in the courtyard, but behave well inside. Take *de* care of Titoa and Sphairos.

As with the previous examples, δέ is not adversative in any of its five occurrences in this letter. The first instance is similar to what was observed in examples 2 and 3—it occurs within the second half of a formulaic greeting where the reference is switched to the authors and they state that they are well. The second use of δέ directly follows the first and is found not only at a topic switch (from "we" to "you") but also at the shift from the

17. In addition to this example and that of the previous papyrus, consider also the second occurrence of δέ (interestingly, in fifth position!) in this excerpt from P.Bad. 2.15: διασάφησον δέ μοι καὶ ἢ μεμίσθωκας τῷ Θεοδότῳ καθάπερ ἐγεγραφήκην σοι καὶ περὶ τοῦ Ξενεινέτου δὲ κλήρου, ἢ μεμίσθωκας ὁμοίως. "Now, also make clear to me whether you have hired Theodotos as I had written to you (also concerning Xeneinetos's *de* allotment) or whether you have hired someone similar."

introduction of the letter to its body. The third instance of the DM occurs in the next sentence, which is a movement within the behavioral discourse to the next exhortation to Rasis and Demarion. After instructing them to attend to their duties in the sanctuaries, Apollonia and Eupous encourage them to be devoted to learning and not to be concerned about their mother.[18] After a brief background clause explaining that the sisters' mother is in good health, a fourth δέ is used, appearing in the next and final exhortation of the letter's body: "Wait δέ for us." The last δέ is found in the postscript. The postscript begins with the imperative "Do not play games in the courtyard, but behave well inside." It then moves to a separate command to take care of Titoa and Sphairos (presumably younger children in the family), and this is where the final δέ is used, introducing this distinct utterance.[19]

In each instance, similar to the previous examples, δέ occurs where a block of new, distinct information is given, where a natural seam can be (but does not have to be) observed in the discourse. It also often occurs where there is some element of thematic discontinuity, that is, changes of time, place, kind of action, or participants.[20] This is important to note, as seams in a discourse that are explicitly signaled as such (e.g., a paragraph break) occur most naturally where there is thematic discontinuity.[21] Given this, δέ seems to be explicitly segmenting portions of the discourse, informing the reader explicitly of the seams, of where to create distinct sections within their mental representation. The presence of the DM not only seems to represent how the authors conceived of the discourse struc-

18. The care of household shrines was a responsibility given to children in Greco-Roman Egypt. See Youssri Abdelwahed, "The Illumination of Lamps (Lychnokaia) for Neith in Sais/Esna in Greco-Roman Egypt," *Abgadiyat* 10 (2015): 35. Interestingly, the next exhortation (μὴ λυποῦ) is connected to this one by καί, not δέ. This indicates a close connection between the first command "be devoted to learning" and the second "do not be distressed about mother." It would seem Apollonia and Eupous were concerned that their sisters' worry about their mother's health would have a negative impact on their studies.

19. For Titoa and Sphairos, see Roger S. Bagnall and Raffaella Cribiore, *Women's Letters from Ancient Egypt, 300 BC–AD 800* (Ann Arbor: University of Michigan Press, 2006), §B9.1.

20. On thematic continuity and discontinuity, see Dooley and Levinsohn, *Analyzing Discourse*, 37.

21. Dooley and Levinsohn, *Analyzing Discourse*, 36–41.

turally but also appears to indicate a desire to guide their recipients in correctly structuring the discourse and in how to process it.

### 2.1.5. P.Tebt. 1.19 (114 BCE)

Menches, Polemon's brother, had sent him letters concerning various matters of business. In this letter, Polemon responds and provides advice on issues pertaining to farmers, the need to make haste in their work, reports, and the collection of taxes.

> Πολέμων Μεγχεῖ τῶι ἀδελφῶι χαίρειν. ἐκομισάμεθα τὰ παρὰ σοῦ ἡμῖν γραφέντα καὶ ὑπὲρ ὧν ἐσήμαινες πέμψαι γεωργῶν ἀπροσδέητοί ἐσμεν. τοῦ δὲ Ἀσκληπιάδου ἐπιτετακότος τὰ πράγματα καὶ προσαγειοχότος ἐκτὸς τῶν ὑποκε[ιμ]ένων ἄλλας (πυροῦ) (ἀρτάβας) Α. χωρὶς ἀργυρίου βεβουλήμεθα σπεῦσαι. ὑπὲρ δὲ ὧν σημαίνεις κωμογραμματέων μόλις ἕως τῆς κε χωρισθήσονται. σὺ δὲ ὀρθῶς ποιήσεις τὸ προσάγγελμα μὴ ἐλαττώσας παρὰ τὸ πρῶτον ὅπως εὐπροσωπῶμεν, καὶ ἐν τοῖς δὲ ἄλλοις χαριῆι καταταχήσας τὰ τῆς εἰσαγωγῆς. ἐπιμελόμενος δὲ καὶ σαυτοῦ [ἵν' ὑ]γιαίνῃς, ἔρρωσο.
>
> Polemon to Menches his brother. Greetings. We received the letters you wrote to us, and concerning those farmers whom you were suggesting you would send, we are not in need of them. As *de* Asklepiades has commanded the matters and added another one thousand artaba of grain beyond what was established, beside money, we have wanted to make haste. Concerning *de* the village clerks whom you mention, they will hardly depart until the twenty-fifth. You *de* will do rightly by not reducing the report in comparison with the first, in order that we may make a good show. Also in the *de* other things, you would oblige me by speeding up the tax collection. Take *de* care of yourself also so that you may be healthy, farewell.

Unlike the other letters observed thus far, this one does not contain a full formulaic introduction. Instead, after greeting his brother, Polemon begins the body of the letter by recalling previous letters from Menches and responding to an issue in them. Polemon then advances to the next item of business—a certain Asklepiades has pressured Polemon to provide more grain and he is wanting to make quick progress. At the start of this section, which is fronted by a genitive absolute that signals a shift in circumstance and frames the main clause, the first δέ occurs. The second δέ follows in the next sentence, which begins with a prepositional phrase—ὑπὲρ δὲ ὧν σημαίνεις κωμογραμματέων—that introduces the new topic of the village clerks. The DM fits well here, given its tendency to occur with semantic discontinuities (i.e., changes of time, setting, topic, or event). Like the occurrence of δέ before, it appears to be segmenting out a new section in the discourse, even if it is only a sentence. The third instance of δέ is found in the sentence that follows. Not only does this sentence move on to yet the next item of business—an exhortation to Menches not to diminish the report—but it also contains a preposed topic switch: σὺ δὲ ὀρθῶς ποιήσεις. The sentence topic has been placed in a position marked for thematic prominence, which results in drawing attention to the switch being made.[22] The DM is found a fourth time in the sentence that follows. Here again, one may observe a preposed prepositional phrase (ἐν τοῖς … ἄλλοις) that serves as the point of departure for what follows, changing to a new discussion topic (speeding up the tax collection). The final use of δέ occurs in the closing of the letter. Polemon exhorts Menches to take care of himself and then bids him farewell. Not only can this be understood as another new, distinct movement within the discourse, but structurally, this sentence serves to formally end the letter.

As discussed in the previous example, thematic discontinuities such as shifts in time, place, action, and/or participants are typical features of communication. Thematic discontinuities naturally occur as a discourse progresses. For example, the situation time of a text may change, a narrative may move its characters to a new location, a hortatory text may shift from exhortations to narrative background, new participants may be added or addressed, or old characters may be left behind. When a communicator desires to explicitly segment a discourse or create a seam between what they feel are distinct units of a discourse, the most natural place to do this will be in contexts of moderate to high discontinuity, since moving on to a new point or changing topic necessarily involves some amount of felt discontinuity.[23] Note that such segmentation is usually not necessary

22. On preposed topics and thematic prominence, see *DFNTG*, 7–13, 22–28; *DGGNT*, §§9.2.5, 9.2.7, 10.1.

23. See Dooley and Levinsohn, *Analyzing Discourse*, 36–41. Consider the typographic features of paragraphing and chapter division in English. Paragraphs are often used when there is a moderate amount of discontinuity, such as a new topic/subtopic, a new argument, a new scene, a new participant, a new event (and usually a combination of two or more of these), but where there is still enough continuity between paragraphs to regard them as a part of the same chapter. Chapter divisions are used when the discontinuities are felt to be even greater (though, note that there is still enough continuity for the chapter to have a place in a book with other related chapters).

for understanding the basic content of the discourse. The words, phrases, clauses, and sentences convey the same meanings regardless.[24] However, by explicitly creating seams between units of discourse where there is discontinuity, a break is made that is regarded as natural and is therefore helpful when building the mental representation of the discourse. It allows one to mentally consolidate information and treat distinct units of the discourse separately, thereby easing the processing task. It provides a structural order and hierarchy to the mental representation. In this way, the presence of δέ in these contexts would seem to be pragmatically motivated, indicating segmentation within the discourse. Each occurrence of δέ in this letter stands at a potential seam, often where there is at least some element of thematic discontinuity. In every case, the particle divides the discourse into smaller meaningful parts, as the author conceived of it.

### 2.1.6. P.Tebt. 3.1.804 (112? BCE)

This fragmentary letter tells the harrowing tale of a home invasion. The author is the man whose home was broken into.[25] He writes to Poseidonios, the governor of Tebtynis, and informs him of the events that transpired.

> Ποσε[ιδωνίωι επισ-]τάτηι Ṭ[εβτύνεως(?)] παρὰ Πά[..]..[.....] τοῦ Πάσιτος γεω[ργοῦ] τῶν ἐκ τῆς α[ὐτῆς] κώμης. [τῆι νυκτὶ] τῆι φερο[ύση]ι εἰ̣ς̣ τ̣[ὴν] ε τοῦ Φαμενὼθ τοῦ ε (ἔτους) ἐ̣β̣ι̣ά̣σ̣α̣ν̣τ̣ό̣ τινες εἰ̣[ς τὴν] ὑπάρχουσάν μοι οἰκίαν καὶ ὑπορύξαντες τὸ σταθμὸν̣ ε̣ἰ̣σ̣ῆλθον εἰς τὴν προστάδα. ἐμοῦ δὲ διεγερθέντος καὶ βοήσαντος ἀνθρώπους [.]ν̣α̣λ̣α̣
> To Poseidonios, governor of Tebtynis. From Pa[ ... ], son of Pasis, farmer of the same village. In the night leading to the fifth of Phamenoth of the fifth year, some men forced their way into my house, and after they undermined the doorpost, they entered into the antechamber. When *de* I woke up and shouted out for men.

After introducing himself, the author recounts the story of how his home was invaded. He begins by setting the scene and then telling of the first event—men broke into his house and entered the antechamber. Most of the rest of the letter is lost, but one ought to observe how the author starts his next sentence. It begins with a genitive absolute, providing a frame of

24. Of course, their interaction with the surrounding context, including structural features, can affect their interpretation within the discourse.

25. The author's name is mostly lost.

reference for the following content. There is no doubt that this next sentence tells the next event in the story, taking place after the events of the prior sentence. This is an advancement of the story. The first sentence of the letter sets the scene and narrates the first event. The second sentence begins with a new setting that conveys moderate thematic discontinuity (change in participants, progression of time, change in location) and would certainly relate the next event to take place. It is at this seam, where one could naturally segment the discourse into smaller meaningful parts, that one finds δέ.

### 2.1.7. *BGU* 4.1147 (13 BCE)

This is a contract drawn up between a certain Dionysios and Eirene. Eirene has received a loan of six hundred silver drachmae from Dionysios, and the contract details the agreement made with regard to repayment, interest, and what will happen should Eirene not pay back what is owed.

> Πρωτάρχωι τῶι ἐπὶ τοῦ κριτηρίου παρὰ Διονυσίου τοῦ Διονυσίου καὶ παρὰ Εἰρήνης τῆς Πατρόκλου Περσίνης μετὰ κυρίου τοῦ ἀδελφοῦ τοῦ Πατρόκλου τοῦ Ἀμμωνίου. περὶ τῶν διεσταμένων συνχωρεῖ ἡ Εἰρήνη ἔχειν παρὰ τοῦ Διονυσίου δάνειον διὰ χειρὸς ἐξ οἴκου ἀργυρ[ίου] Πτολεμαικοῦ δραχμὰς ἑξακοσίας τόκων ἐνεωβόλων [τῆς] μ̣ν̣ᾶ̣ς̣ ἑ̣κ̣ά̣σ̣τ̣η̣ς̣ τοῦ μ̣η̣ν̣ὸ̣ς̣ ἑ̣κ̣ά̣σ̣τ̣ο̣υ̣, ὃ καὶ ἀποδώσειν ἐν μησὶν ἓ̣ξ̣ ἀπὸ Μεχεὶρ τοῦ ἐνεστῶτος ἑπτακαιδ[ε-][κ] άτου ἔτους Καίσαρος διδοῦσα τὸν μὲν τόκον κατὰ μῆνα εὐτάκτως τὸ δὲ κε[φά]λαιον ἐν τῶι ἐσχάτωι μηνὶ ἄνευ [π]ά[ση]ς ὑπερθέσε[ω]ς, ἢ εἶναι [αὐτὴν] [παραχ]ρῆμα ἀγωγίμην καὶ συνέχεσ[θα]ι μέχρι τοῦ ἐκτεῖσαι τὸ μὲν δάνειον σὺν ἡμιολίᾳ̣, τοὺς δὲ τόκους ἁπλοῦς, τοῦ δὲ ὑπερπεσόντος χρόνου τοὺς κατὰ τὸ διάγραμμα τόκους διδράχμους, [τῆς πράξ]εως γινομένης τῶι Διονυσίωι [ἔκ τε αὐτῆς] Εἰρήνης καὶ ἐκ τῶν ὑπαρχόν[των αὐτῇ πά]ντων καθάπερ ἐκ δίκη(ς), [ἔτι] δ̣ὲ̣ καὶ ἐκ τῆς ὑπαρχούσης τῇ Ἰρήνῃ δούλης Ἐ̣ρ̣ω̣τ̣ί̣ο̣υ̣, καθ' ἥσπερ κ̣α̣ὶ̣ ἀναδέδωκεν α̣ὐ̣τῶι Δ[ιο] νυσίωι ἐν ὑπαλλάγματι
> To Protarchos, who is over the court of judgment, from Dionysios, son of Dionysios, and from Eirene, daughter of Patroklos the Persian, with the brother of Patroklos, son of Ammonios, as guardian.[26] Concerning

26. For a similar use of κύριου, see Hunt and Edgar, *Select Papyri*, §299. Though the letter translated by Hunt and Edgar is dated to 186/187 CE, it reflects the same legal requirement as there was in 13 BCE in Greco-Roman Egypt for a woman to have a male guardian to engage in certain legal matters. See Uri Yiftach-Firanko, "Law in Graeco-Roman Egypt: Hellenization, Fusion, Romanization," in *The Oxford*

> the various issues, Eirene agrees to receive a loan of six hundred silver Ptolemaic drachmae from Dionysios by the hand of the bank, with an interest rate of nine obols per mina[27] each month, which she is to pay in six months from Mecheir of the present seventeenth year of Caesar, by giving the interest every month regularly the *de* sum in the last month without any delay, or she will be immediately liable to seizure and detainment until she pays the loan in full with half as much again, the *de* simple interest, the *de* two-drachmae interest for the time exceeded, according to regulation, the right of exaction belonging to Dionysious from both Eirene herself and all her possessions just as is right, further *de* also from Eirene's possession, the slave girl Erotion, concerning whom she has also delivered to Dionysios himself in exchange.

The DM is first used in a *μέν* … *δέ* construction (~line 10). The preceding content, in which *μέν* occurs, states that Eirene is to pay the interest regularly each month. Immediately following this is the utterance in which *δέ* is found, anticipated by the *μέν*. The particle's host utterance informs the reader of a different payment that must be paid, namely, the total sum in the last month. The DM has a narrower scope here than has been observed in the letters above. It occurs at the phrasal level, marking a relationship between its host utterance and the preceding *μέν* clause. Given that there are elements of discontinuity between the preceding information and the information conveyed in the *δέ* clause (interest payment monthly; sum payment in the final month) and given the anticipatory *μέν*, it would seem that *δέ* segments the discourse at a localized level, providing the "other side of the coin" to the *μέν* clause.[28] The DM's host utterance provides the second of two points to be made within the larger *μέν* … *δέ* structure. While the connective *καί* could have been used, the effect of segmenting into smaller units by *δέ* seems to be to unambiguously treat its host utterance as a distinct point within the larger thematic *μέν* … *δέ* unit. There is a cognitive purpose in this. By marking both points within the *μέν* … *δέ* construction as distinct segments, it draws equal attention to them both. In the reader's mental representation, they are closely connected (owing to *μέν*) but separate information units. The issue under discussion is remu-

---

*Handbook of Papyrology*, ed. Roger S. Bagnall (Oxford: Oxford University Press, 2009), 555; Bernhard Palme, "The Range of Documentary Texts: Types and Categories," in Bagnall, *Oxford Handbook of Papyrology*, 366.

27. That is, nine obols per one hundred drachmae.

28. See the discussion on *μέν* in ch. 6.

neration, so it is understandable that the author would want to be as clear as possible about what needed to be paid when.

The second and third instances of δέ are similar to the first. They are contained in the second and third parts of a μέν … δέ … δέ construction (between lines 15 and 20). Should Eirene not honor the agreement, she is liable to seizure and detainment until she pays the loan with half as much again, plus (δέ) the simple interest, plus (δέ) the two-drachmae interest for the time exceeded. Again, each distinct part of the remuneration is separated out by the use of δέ.

The fourth use of δέ occurs in the following participial clause. Dionysios has the right of exaction from Eirene and her possessions. This is then followed by an additional possession of Eirene's to which Dionysios has the right of exaction, the slave girl Erotion. Granted, this could have been joined to the rest of the list by means of καί, as happens between the first two members. However, the rest of what is extant from this letter continues to be about Erotion. She ought not have any debt, and should she run away or die, Eirene must still fulfill her part of the agreement. Given that there is some significance to Erotion as collateral, it would seem the author used δέ to indicate a certain level of distinction (which, given the context of a list where καί was used previously, may thereby make this final member stand out as more prominent). Note too the use of ἔτι "further" before δέ as a means of marking out this final list member as distinct from the previous two.

In sum, though these instances of δέ are narrower in scope than what has previously been examined, they work well in the context of the contract. They have the effect of marking each new item they introduce as a distinct information unit. In the last instance, this may even result in drawing special attention to its host utterance. All of this together would seem to have the purpose of creating a clear, well-ordered contract.

### 2.1.8. The Function of δέ as Evinced in the Papyri

Consistently, δέ appears to be used for structural purposes, explicitly marking out distinct segments within the discourse. As is natural, this typically occurs in contexts of semantic discontinuity, that is, changes of time, setting, topic, event, and so on. By using δέ in these contexts, rather than καί or asyndeton, the reader is explicitly instructed to "chunk" the discourse, understanding δέ, along with its interaction with any present discontinuities, to be signaling a distinct information unit. In the reader's mental representation, then, δέ functions to close off or begin new sections (relative to its scope), encouraging the reader to process smaller, more manageable pieces of the discourse at a time.

The DM is used at different levels of the discourse. In some cases, such as those observed in examples 1–4, δέ contributes to the overall structure of the letter. In each of these cases, unlike the other examples, one may observe a formulaic introduction (e.g., in example 2: εἰ τῶι τε σώματι ἔρρωσαι καὶ τὰ ἄλλα σοι κατὰ γνώμη[ν] ἐστίν, εἴη ἂν ὡς ἡμεῖς θέλομεν· ἐρρώμεθα δὲ καὶ αὐτοί). Formulaic introductions such as these always end with a topic switch to the author(s) + δέ + the conveying of the information "I am also well." The use of δέ is a part of the formula. This is understandable. Given its function to segment discourse, the use of the DM in this context simultaneously accomplishes two structuring effects. The first, as a result of interacting with the information in the surrounding context, is that δέ segments two portions of the introduction at the point where discontinuity is most strongly felt (at the topic switch). By using δέ, these related pieces are portrayed as two distinct parts of the introduction, which has the effect of focusing the reader's attention on each of them as discrete entities. The second effect, as a result of interacting with the letter's metastructure, is that δέ signals the end of the letter's introduction and, by extension, that the body of the letter will follow. The DM is thus used to provide an overall structure to the document. Sometimes, though, an additional δέ will be used at the start of the body, such as in examples 1 and 4. While there is certainly nothing wrong with this use of δέ, it is irregular.[29] Evans writes, "It becomes clear that it is regular to have no particle linking the body of the text to the greeting formula. And this is precisely what we should expect. Greeting and letter-body are discrete elements of the text."[30] Where I disagree with Evans is that, typically, because greeting and letter-body are discrete elements of the text, one *would* expect δέ. However, since the δέ signaling the close of the greeting would sufficiently

---

29. Examples such as 1 and 4 seem to be the rare exceptions to what is otherwise a consistent phenomenon. When a letter begins with a formulaic introduction, it is expected that one will find δέ at the end of the pleasantries and that the body of the letter will then begin (usually asyndetically). The DM rarely ever also occurs at the beginning of the body. Perhaps such occurrences are due to a rhetorical motivation to make the letter sound more official or educated.

30. Evans, "Standard Koine Greek," 201.

signal the separate sections to the reader, a δέ between the two sections is unnecessary, as it would overencode the discourse.[31]

In one case, the final δέ in example 1, the DM occurs with a broad scope within the letter body, signaling a segmentation between two larger discourse structures. The effect of δέ with this scope interacting with its context appears to be to signal a movement to a distinct unit of discourse in the development of the communication, similar to a new paragraph in English typography. The DM also has a moderate scope, typically corresponding to the sentential level. The effect of δέ segmenting at this level of discourse is to signal a movement to the next step or a new distinct point. In many respects, δέ occurring with this scope does not differ in function from its use above the sentence. Presumably, had the author desired it, the smaller (typically sentence-level) segments could have been more explicitly set apart, extended, and discussed in more depth. The high frequency of δέ with a sentence-level scope would seem to be due mostly to the nature of the documentary letter. These letters are not long and tend to move forward on a point-by-point basis. They spend little time on extended details unless further information is necessary. Each new point can understandably and naturally be regarded as the next step in the development of the letter.

On two occasions, once in example 2 and once in example 3, the particle segments what appears to be parenthetical material. While not the most frequent context of use for δέ, it is an understandable phenomenon. If δέ is a text-structuring device, used to segment discourse into smaller distinct parts, it is a clear choice for parenthetical material. Such information is naturally distinct from the surrounding context, and δέ would effectively signal to the reader to regard it as a discrete information unit.[32] This is not to say that δέ signals parenthetical information, but rather simply segments the material. It would then be up to the reader to understand how the information unit relates to its surrounding context.

In sum, based on the evidence in the papyri, δέ operates within the metatextual domain and functions to segment the discourse into

31. In the examples Evans investigates, however, there are none of the typical pleasantries. After χαίρειν, the body of the letter begins, as seen in example 5 above. In this case, one would *typically* still expect δέ, but χαίρειν is a clear enough signal of the closing of the greeting when pleasantries do not directly follow.

32. Another option would be to use γάρ, but this is only acceptable if the parenthetical information has a supportive relation to preceding material.

smaller, discrete information units. This is a more satisfying description of the particle than "adversative," especially given that none of the examples above are adversative, and it is a more useful functional description than "correlative."[33] The scope of the DM and the kind of information it introduces will result in different contextual effects. It can segment above the sentence level to signal the structure of a letter proper or to segment thematic units that contribute to the development of the overall communication. With a moderate scope, it can segment to indicate shifts to distinct parts of a larger structure, typically the next step or a new point in the discourse. Lastly, it can segment out parenthetical material. It is important to note that in none of these cases is δέ strictly required (except, perhaps, in the formulaic material). As a metatextual device, δέ is used according to the author's own conception of the flow of the discourse and where, in his mind and according to his communicative purposes, he feels a segmentation needs or ought to occur. In written Postclassical Greek, this would be a very helpful device. Greek at this time was written in capital letters and without spaces between words. Consider this image (see the next page) of the portion of P.Cair. Zen. 1.59036 discussed above in example 2.[34] This throws the usefulness and need for a segmenting device into even sharper relief. Not only are such devices useful for successful communication and the building of mental representations, but they also provide clear and practically necessary structuring cues in written text.[35]

---

33. This is not to say that δέ does not occur in adversative contexts within the papyri. It does. Some examples may be found in P.Cair.Zen. 1.59001 ("Isidorus should repay the loan.... If δέ he does not repay"), P.Cair.Zen. 2.59155 ("When you reap the grain, immediately water the land by hand. If δέ it is not possible"), and P.Grenf. 2.29 and SB.5.7532 (similar to P.Cair.Zen. 1.59001). However, given the many examples that are not adversative, an "adversative" label is unhelpful, especially given the fact that the so-called adversative uses of δέ can be better described as marking distinct segments. Moreover, as will be discussed in §2.2.2. "Cognitive Chunking and Metatextual Discourse Markers," below, contrastive and adversative relations arise from the semantics of the surrounding context, not from the choice of particle.

34. Images of this papyrus can be found at https://tinyurl.com/2568y9kt.

35. See the discussion below in §2.2.2. "Cognitive Chunking and Metatextual Discourse Markers." Typographic features work similarly in English. Consider how much more difficult and burdensome this book would be to read without paragraph and section breaks!

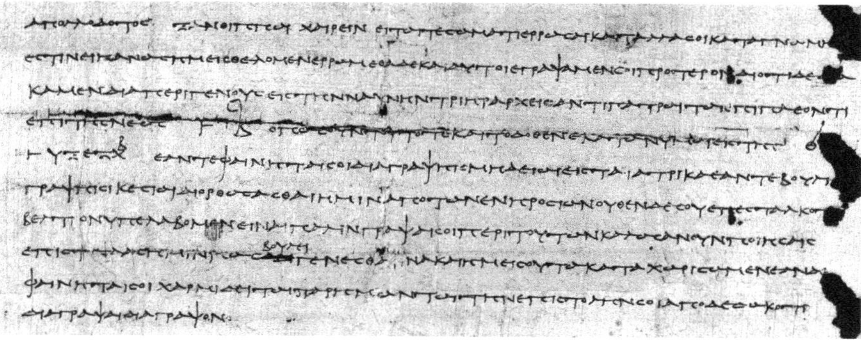

Fig. 2.1. P.Cair.Zen. 1.59036. Photograph by Adam Bülow-Jacobsen. I am grateful to the Centre for the Study of Ancient Documents in Oxford for granting me permission to use this photograph. The papyrus is held in the Cairo Museum, and the photograph of it has been made available by the Cairo Photographic Archive, which was sponsored by the Association Internationale de Papyrologues.

### 2.2. The Use of δέ in the Twelve

There are fifty-eight occurrences of δέ in the Twelve. In what follows, a representative sample is discussed.

#### 2.2.1. Examples from the Twelve

The first use of δέ in the Twelve is found in Hos 1:7. In verses 6–7, the Lord instructs Hosea to name his daughter "Not Pitied" and then explains the meaning of the name.

> (1:6) And Gomer became pregnant again and bore a daughter. And the Lord said to Hosea, "Name her 'Not Pitied,' for I will not again show mercy to the house of Israel, but rather I will align myself, an opposer, against them.
>
> (1:7) τοὺς δὲ υἱοὺς Ιουδα ἐλεήσω καὶ σώσω αὐτοὺς ἐν κυρίῳ θεῷ αὐτῶν καὶ οὐ σώσω αὐτοὺς ἐν τόξῳ οὐδὲ ἐν ῥομφαίᾳ οὐδὲ ἐν πολέμῳ οὐδὲ ἐν ἅρμασιν οὐδὲ ἐν ἵπποις οὐδὲ ἐν ἱππεῦσι.
> I *de* will show mercy on the sons of Judah and I will save them by the Lord their God. But I will not save them by bow nor by sword nor by battle nor by chariots nor by horses nor by horsemen."

ואת־בית יהודה ארחם והושעתים ביהוה אלהיהם ולא אושיעם בקשת ובחרב ובמלחמה בסוסים ובפרשים

> But, I will have compassion on the house of Judah, and I will deliver them by YHWH their God. But I will not deliver them by bow nor by sword nor by war nor by horses nor by horsemen.

A shift can be observed as the Lord's discourse moves from the topic of Israel to the topic of Judah. In 1:6, the Lord commands Hosea to name his daughter "Not Pitied" because he will not show mercy to Israel. In the move to verse 7, a preposed topic switch occurs, switching from τὸν οἶκον Ισραηλ in verse 6 to τοὺς υἱοὺς Ιουδα in verse 7.[36] Such a switch, and the resulting discontinuity, makes segmentation natural here. Though one may certainly feel a contrastive relation between verses 6–7, it does not arise because of δέ.[37] Contrast arises here owing to the semantics of the context, that is, because of the oppositely polarized predicates "will not show mercy" versus "will show mercy" and the contrastive topics Israel versus Judah. This contrast would be present without δέ. The translator could have employed καί or asyndeton and an adversative relation between the sentences would still arise. This can be observed in the latter half of the verse as well where the translator uses καί, translating *vav*, to link the contrasting sentences. Contrast arises owing not to a contrastive use of καί but to the semantics of the context. Thus, assigning an adversative function to δέ (or καί, for that matter) does not accurately nor sufficiently describe how the DM instructs the reader to fit the discourse together and build a mental representation of the text. Granted, it may be the case that by virtue of creating two distinct units here, at this switch, there is more of a heightened focus on the contrast. Further, the pragmatics of δέ naturally lend it to be used in adversative contexts. But the contrast is not created by nor reliant upon δέ. Similar to what was observed in the papyri, δέ segments the discourse into smaller chunks. Its scope and interaction with the surrounding information results in portraying what follows as advancing to the next point or subtopic in the Lord's speech, moving from the Lord and his merciless disposition toward Israel to his merciful disposition toward Judah.

---

36. Topics do not have to be grammatical subjects, and it is possible for a sentence to have two topics, in this case the Lord "I" and the sons of Judah. See Knud Lambrecht, *Information Structure and Sentence Form: Topic, Focus, and the Mental Representations of Discourse Referents*, CSL 71 (Cambridge: Cambridge University Press, 1998), 137–50.

37. Contra Martin Karrer and Wolfgang Kraus, LXX.D 2:291.

The fact that the translator chooses δέ rather than καί to render the conjunctive *vav* at the beginning of verse 7 should cause one to pause and consider why such a decision was made. The particle καί would be the natural lexical choice and is the stereotypical equivalent to conjunctive *vav* in the Twelve and across the Greek Old Testament. Qualitatively, the translator had every reason to use καί but instead employed δέ. There must be a reason why δέ was preferred here rather than the more lexically equivalent and much more typical καί. The motivation for δέ would seem to be the translator's judgment that the content of 1:7 constituted the next point in the Lord's speech and that it merited being marked as a distinct segment. In order to use δέ here, then, in order to justify its use over the lexically preferred καί, the translator necessarily had to have an awareness of the surrounding context and the ability to make an assessment of it that influenced the choice of connective.

In Jonah 3 the prophet returns to dry land and is commanded by the Lord again to go to Nineveh. In verse 3, the narrator describes Jonah setting off on his journey.

> (3:1–2) And the word of the Lord came to Jonah a second time, saying, "Stand up, go to the great city of Nineveh and proclaim in it according to the previous proclamation that I spoke to you."
>
> (3:3) καὶ ἀνέστη Ιωνας καὶ ἐπορεύθη εἰς Νινευη, καθὼς ἐλάλησε κύριος· ἡ <u>δὲ</u> Νινευη ἦν πόλις μεγάλη τῷ θεῷ ὡσεὶ πορείας ὁδοῦ ἡμερῶν τριῶν.
> And Jonah stood up and went to Nineveh, just as the Lord had said. Nineveh *de* was a great city to God about a journey of three days by road.
>
> (3:4) And Jonah began to enter into the city about one day's journey, and he proclaimed and said, "Three more days and Nineveh will be destroyed."
>
> ויקם יונה וילך אל־נינוה כדבר יהוה ונינוה היתה עיר־גדולה לאלהים מהלך שלשת ימים
> And Jonah arose and went to Nineveh, according to the word of YHWH. Now, Nineveh was a great city to God, a journey of three days.

With Jonah finally obeying the Lord and setting out for Nineveh, 3:3a effectively ends a scene of the story. The second half of verse 3 introduces a new setting with a preposed topic switch to Nineveh, thereby indicating and drawing the reader's attention to a scene change.[38] The story locale has changed to Nineveh, and Jonah, in verse 4, begins proclaiming the Lord's judgment. The change in setting creates a thematic break in the middle of verse 3, making a development in the theme-line natural. Thus, it should be no surprise that one finds δέ at this transition. It is not used to signal an adversative relation, but rather to structure the text, creating a break between two parts of the story—the narrative is moving forward to the next scene where the Lord's command from the previous scene will be carried out. The use of δέ instructs the reader to process the following content as a new segment. This encourages the reader to slow down and breathe, so to speak, in that it breaks the story down into manageable comprehension units. This then allows the reader to build their mental representation of the discourse at a macrostructural level, thus regarding the content of verse 3a and the few verses prior as a separate scene from the content of verse 3b and following.[39]

The advancement to a new scene is reflected in the Hebrew as well by the author interrupting the consecutive verb forms with a nonconsecutive *qatal* preceded by a nominal constituent.[40] Instead of continuing the chain of consecutives, the author marks the shift in the discourse by beginning the sentence with ונינוה, thereby switching the topic and motivating a scene change.[41] It is at least possible that the LXX translator was motivated to use

38. In stories, new scenes will frequently begin with background scene-setting material, in order to provide a framework for and introduction to what follows. See also Hoey, *Textual Interaction*, 59.

39. This example illustrates well Levinsohn's insight that δέ, when introducing background material, will typically be in topic-comment articulation and begin with a point of departure. See *DFNTG*, 90.

40. See Christo H. J. van der Merwe, "Discourse Linguistics and Biblical Hebrew Grammar," in *Biblical Hebrew and Discourse Linguistics*, ed. Robert D. Bergen, (Dallas: Summer Institute of Linguistics, 1994), 29–34, 40; Geoffrey Khan, *Studies in Semitic Syntax*, London Oriental Series 38 (Oxford: Oxford University Press, 1988), 86; *BHRG2*, 507.

41. Uriel Simon notes, "The opening of a narrative unit with the circumstantial *vav* is not unusual.... Even though here it comes in the middle of a verse, there is no doubt that the circumstantial clause is anticipatory, since it serves as an exposition that is essential for understanding the statement in the next verse about how far Jonah penetrates into the city" (*Jonah: The Traditional Hebrew Text with the New JPS Translation*, trans. Lenn J. Schramm, JPS Bible Commentary [Philadelphia: Jewish Publication Society, 1999], 27). See also Douglas Stuart, *Hosea–Jonah*, WBC 31 (Waco, TX: Word, 1987), 484; Hans Walter Wolff, *Obadiah and Jonah: A Commentary*, trans. Margaret Kohl, CC (Minneapolis: Augsburg, 1986), 145, 147; W. Dennis Tucker Jr., *Jonah: A*

δέ not only due to awareness of the transition and thematic break within the story, which would be a natural place to mark a new segment, but also because the translator took note of the break in verb forms in the Hebrew and the preposed change of setting.

The particle next occurs in Jonah 4:11. Here, the Lord is reprimanding his prophet for caring more for a plant than for an entire people.

> (4:10) And the Lord said, "You showed sympathy for the plant, for which you did not suffer regarding it, and you did not nurture it, which came into being overnight and perished overnight.
>
> (4:11) ἐγὼ <u>δὲ</u> οὐ φείσομαι ὑπὲρ Νινευη τῆς πόλεως τῆς μεγάλης, ἐν ᾗ κατοικοῦσι πλείους ἢ δώδεκα μυριάδες ἀνθρώπων, οἵτινες οὐκ ἔγνωσαν δεξιὰν αὐτῶν ἢ ἀριστερὰν αὐτῶν, καὶ κτήνη πολλά;

---

*Handbook on the Hebrew Text*, BHHB (Waco, TX: Baylor University Press, 2006), 67. Jack M. Sasson also recognizes the material of MT 3:3b as background information, but he regards it as background embedded within a narrative, not as background material that begins a new scene (*Jonah: A New Translation with Introduction and Commentary*, AB 24B [New York: Doubleday, 1990], 227–28). While there is certainly a level of subjectivity to discerning the relation of background information to the larger narrative structure, I am firmly in agreement with Simon, Stuart, and Wolff that 3:3b begins a new scene. Sasson seemingly views 3:1–4 as a self-contained unit. The break he observes between 2:11 and 3:1 is reasonable; as he notes, there is an empty space in Mur 88 and a petuhah in other manuscripts between the two verses (225). Moreover, 3:1 begins with ויהי, which can signal a new scene when followed by a state of affairs (*BHRG*, 332–33). Because of this and because of the parallel between 3:1–3a and 1:1–3 (see Simon, *Jonah*, 25), I do think Sasson is correct in his critique of Wolff, who runs 2:11 and 3:1 together (Sasson, *Jonah*, 225). However, the scene does not last long. Not only does 3:3b begin with a preposed topic switch to Nineveh that interrupts the *wayyiqtol* chain and provides scene-setting information for what follows, but 3:3a sums up the content of 3:2 and ends by recalling the beginning of the scene. Compare 3:1a with the end of 3:3a: ויהי דבר־יהוה and כדבר יהוה. Jonah 3:3a ends by bookending the small scene; 3:3b begins by providing a new setting for the next scene. This is similar to the envelope figure used in Hebrew poetry, which Wilfred G. E. Watson describes as "the repetition of the same phrase or sentence at the beginning and end of a stanza or poem" (*Classical Hebrew Poetry: A Guide to Its Techniques*, JSOTSup 26 [Sheffield: JSOT Press, 1986], 282–83). Watson notes that envelope figures may repeat only a word or words of a common root and that they are often used to delimit a poem (284). Granted, Jonah 3:1–3a is not a poem, but that does not preclude the use of such a device for structural purposes within a narrative. See also Simon, who writes that the scene (3:1–3a) "ends, as it began, with 'the word of the LORD' (3:3a), which exactly repeats the language of the beginning, 'The word of the LORD'" (Simon, *Jonah*, 25).

Shall *de* I not have sympathy for Nineveh, the great city, in which dwell more than one hundred twenty thousand men, who did not know their right hand or their left, and many animals?

ואני לא אחוס על־נינוה העיר הגדולה אשר יש־בה הרבה משתים־עשרה רבו אדם אשר לא־ידע בין־ימינו לשמאלו ובהמה רבה
Now, should I not show pity on the great city Nineveh, in which there are more than one hundred twenty thousand men who do not know the difference between their right from their left, and many animals?

Unlike Jonah 3:3, wherein δέ separates a new narrative-level information unit, the DM is used in Jonah 4:11 to segment an advancement within an argument, similar to what was frequently observed within the bodies of the papyri above (in terms of scope). There is a clear rhetorical move in the Lord's argument, moving from Jonah's regard for the plant to the Lord's potential regard for Nineveh. The Lord builds on what he has just said, that Jonah had sympathy toward something for which he did not care and that did not last long, then turns the argument around and finalizes it, defending his decision to relent from wrath against a group that holds much greater significance than Jonah's plant. It is at this advancement of the argument in verse 11 that δέ is used, co-occurring with a preposed topic switch. The use of δέ segments the Lord's speech into argument and conclusion, thus signaling the next (and final) step in the Lord's argument against Jonah. This aids the reader in the processing of the text, providing an explicit structure that facilitates comprehension and the building of the mental representation. While a slight adversative relation may be felt, this is not due to the presence of δέ but to the explicitly stated contrasts, that is, the contrastive topic switch ("you" versus "I") and the contrasting objects of the verb φείδομαι ("the plant" versus "Nineveh"). This contrast would be present without δέ, since it arises from the semantics of an adversative context and the explicit juxtaposition of contrastive members.

As with the previous examples, a conjunctive *vav* is attested in the MT. The fact that δέ was used rather than καί suggests a translator who considered more than just quantitative representation as they translated, one who also had an awareness and understanding of the flow of the discourse. Moreover, the fact that δέ is used evinces a desire on the part of the translator to clearly indicate the structure of the discourse.

In Hab 3, Habakkuk offers a prayer that imagines the Lord as the sovereign creator and divine warrior who fights for his people. The particle δέ occurs near the end of the prayer.

> (3:17) For a fig tree will not bear fruit,
> and there will not be produce on the vines;
> the work of the olive tree will deceive,
> and the plains will not produce food;
> sheep ran out of food,
> and the cattle are not at the stalls.
>
> (3:18) ἐγὼ <u>δὲ</u> ἐν τῷ κυρίῳ ἀγαλλιάσομαι,
> χαρήσομαι ἐπὶ τῷ θεῷ τῷ σωτῆρί μου.
> I *de* will exult in the Lord,
> I will rejoice in God my savior.
>
> ואני ביהוה אעלוזה
> אגילה באלהי ישעי
>
> But I will rejoice because of YHWH
> I will rejoice because of the God of my salvation.

In verse 18, the entire tone of the prayer shifts. Habakkuk has little reason to rejoice in light of the desolation he sees in the prior verse, yet despite this, he expresses his praise to God.[42] By marking a new segment with δέ at the start of the verse, the following material, while certainly connected to the preceding verses and following closely from them, is portrayed as a discrete information unit. The DM's host utterance is a potential seam, exhibiting slight thematic discontinuities such as a preposed topic switch consisting of the redundant pronoun ἐγώ and a shift in tone. The interaction of these thematic discontinuities with the DM results in the explicit realization of a seam and thereby alerts us to a movement forward in the development of the discourse. Such boundary marking also has the effect of heightening the sharpness of the transition between the two verses. This makes sense given that the content of verse 18 represents the next and final portion of the prayer, Habakkuk's response. Thus, the reader processes the text by segmenting at the seam of verses 17–18, understanding a distinct movement to be taking place on the theme-line.

---

42. In this way, the beginning of 3:18 may be best rendered in English by "nevertheless."

This is reflected in the Hebrew as well with the pronominal constituent ואני beginning the verbal clause, thus creating a stark thematic break between the preceding כי-clause in verse 17 and Habakkuk's response, which in turn makes an advancement to the next distinct point all the more natural for the reader to perceive. It is possible that it was an awareness of the flow of the Hebrew discourse that motivated the translator's use of δέ here. Had the translator not been aware of the surrounding context, both preceding and following, and paid attention only to the conjunctive *vav*, καί would have been used instead of δέ—indeed, there would have been no reason to use anything other than καί.

Zephaniah 3:1–4 describes the city, presumably Jerusalem, that did not listen to correction and whose leaders sinned against the Lord.[43] In verse 5, where the author shifts the primary topic from the city to the Lord, δέ occurs.

> (3:4) Her prophets are moved by spirits, despising men; her prophets profane the holy things and sin against the law.
>
> (3:5) ὁ <u>δὲ</u> κύριος δίκαιος ἐν μέσῳ αὐτῆς καὶ οὐ μὴ ποιήσῃ ἄδικον· πρωὶ πρωὶ δώσει κρίμα αὐτοῦ καὶ οὐκ εἰς νῖκος ἀδικίαν.
> The *de* Lord is just in her midst, and he will never do injustice; morning after morning, he will give his judgment and no injustice for victory.
>
> יהוה צדיק בקרבה לא יעשה עולה בבקר בבקר משפטו יתן לאור לא נעדר ולא־יודע עול בשת
> YHWH is righteous in her midst. He does no injustice. Every morning, he gives from his justice. At dawn, he is not missing. But the unjust do not know shame.

There is a clear transition from the first four verses to 3:5, which shifts the entire discourse to the Lord and how he is just and punishes the wicked. This topic switch creates a small thematic break that correlates well with a shift in the discourse to the next, albeit related, issue to be discussed. The verses that follow are concerned with the Lord, his righteousness, and his actions. Thus, the use of δέ at this seam fits nicely. It structures the text, segmenting the discourse into logical pieces for the reader to process.

43. For the city being Jerusalem, see Ralph L. Smith, *Micah–Malachi*, WBC 32 (Waco, TX: Word, 1984), 137–38.

The relation of this instance of δέ to its source text is different from those examined above. Assuming the MT represents the same reading as the translator's *Vorlage*, then the translator used a δέ even though there was no conjunction in the Hebrew. This would thus be clear evidence for a translator who considered the flow of the discourse as they translated and who sought to represent that understanding. There is no qualitative nor quantitative motivation for using δέ. Rather, its use necessarily arises from the translator's assessment of the discourse. Indeed, given the absence of a *vav* at the beginning of verse 5 and the explicit switch to YHWH, one may observe explicit discontinuities in the Hebrew text that naturally correlate with an advancement to something new. Similarly, Sweeney writes:

> Zephaniah 3:5–13 constitutes the second subunit of the prophet's exhortative speech in 3:1–20 in which he presents a scenario by which YHWH will restore Jerusalem as the holy center of the nations.... There are a number of reasons for the demarcation of this passage. First, v. 5 lacks an introductory syntactical connector that would join it to vv. 1–4. Second, the reference to YHWH as subject in v. 5 shifts the focus of attention from Jerusalem, which is the subject of vv. 1–4.[44]

Thus the translation provided by the LXX translator is fitting. Though δέ does not qualitatively nor quantitatively represent any lexeme in the *Vorlage*, it provides a structure to the text in conventional Greek idiom that mirrors, at least to some extent, the structure of the Hebrew.

The final example comes from Mal 1:3. The oracle begins in verse 2.

> (1:2) "'I loved you,' says the Lord, and you said, 'In what way did you love us?' 'Was Esau not Jacob's brother?' says the Lord; and I loved Jacob,

> (1:3) τὸν <u>δὲ</u> Ησαυ ἐμίσησα καὶ ἔταξα τὰ ὄρη αὐτοῦ εἰς ἀφανισμὸν καὶ τὴν κληρονομίαν αὐτοῦ εἰς δόματα ἐρήμου.
> Esau *de* I hated, and I made his mountain a destruction and his inheritance gifts of the wilderness."

---

44. Marvin A. Sweeney, *Zephaniah: A Commentary*, Hermeneia (Minneapolis: Fortress, 2003), 169. See also Marvin A. Sweeney, *The Twelve Prophets*, vol. 2: *Micah, Nahum, Habakkuk, Zephaniah, Haggai, Zechariah, Malachi*, Berit Olam (Collegeville, MN: Liturgical Press, 2000), 520–21.

> (1:4) Since Idoumaia will say, 'It is destroyed, and we will return and rebuild the desolate places.' The Lord Almighty says these things: 'They will build, and I will destroy; and they will be called borders of lawlessness and a people against whom the Lord is set forever.'"

> ואת־עשו שנאתי ואשים את־הריו שממה ואת־נחלתו לתנות מדבר
> but Esau I hated. I set his mountains as a desolation and gave his inheritance to the jackals of the wilderness.

One one level, this is a simple occurrence of δέ. Esau is old information that was already introduced in verse 2. As such, it is a topical constituent that is placed before the verb here for thematic prominence. This is a typical contrastive topic switch. Discourse markers such as καί, δέ, ἀλλά, or asyndeton would be acceptable here. However, given the thematic discontinuity that arises from switching to Esau and from the switch of the Lord's disposition, there is a fittingness to δέ. It creates a small seam in the argument being built.

However, given the flow of the discourse in verses 2–4, it may be that something more is going on. As the discourse shifts from Jacob to Esau, there is a clear transition that is more significant than just a narrow contrastive topic switch. It is not simply the case that a contrastive topic switch happens at the beginning of verse 3. Rather, this switch is the beginning of the next part of the argument. In verse 2, the Lord declares his love for Jacob. In verses 3–4, he advances the discourse to a new subtopic, the next point in the theme-line of the argument: His hatred toward Esau demonstrates his love for Jacob. By using δέ in verse 3, the translator, seemingly aware of that which follows in the text, marks verse 3 as the beginning of a new segment in the Lord's speech, wherein his love for Jacob is demonstrably observed in his judgment against Esau. By segmenting here and interacting with its context, the effect of the DM is to signal explicitly the next step in the argument that the Lord is building. Moreover, not only does the shift in verse 3a provide the topic for what continues in verse 4, but as Nogalski demonstrates, it is also the center of a series of ABBA parallelisms:[45]

---

45. James D. Nogalski, *The Book of the Twelve: Micah–Malachi*, SHBC 18b (Macon, GA: Smyth & Helwys, 2011), 1011. So also Arndt Meinhold, *Maleachi*, BKAT 14.8 (Neukirchen-Vluyn: Neukirchener Verlag, 2006), 30–32; Terry W. Eddinger, *Malachi: A Handbook on the Hebrew Text*, BHHB (Waco, TX: Baylor University Press, 2012), 9–10.

(A) “I loved you”
(B) says the Lord
(B) You said
(A) “In what way did you love us?”
“Was Esau not Jacob’s brother?” says the Lord
(A) “I loved
(B) Jacob
**(B) Esau (δέ)**
(A) I hated[46]
“I made his mountain a destruction and his inheritance gifts of the wilderness. Since Idoumaia will say,
(A) ‘It is destroyed,
(B) we will return and rebuild the desolate places.’
The Lord Almighty says these things:
(B) ‘They will build
(A) I will destroy’”

I cannot claim whether the LXX translator was aware of this structure since it automatically arises simply from following the underlying Hebrew. However, δέ is fitting. Not only does it stand at a thematic break and signal a distinct information unit that serves as the next step in the argument but it also segments and structures the parallelism into its two thematic halves.

As is typical, δέ quantitatively but not qualitatively renders the underlying Hebrew. The conjunctive *vav* does not find a lexical equivalent in δέ, but δέ nonetheless is a faithful translation of the Hebrew overall, albeit providing a more explicit discourse structure for the reader than the Hebrew *Vorlage*.

### 2.2.2. Cognitive Chunking and Metatextual Discourse Markers

When humans tell stories or form arguments, we structure the discourse not only linearly but also hierarchically.[47] That is, while we do move from one unit of information to the next, the discourse is not simply presented as a single block of linearly structured information units. Rather,

46. It may be simpler here to regard 1:2c–3a as an A//A′ contrastive parallelism rather than an ABBA parallelism (see also Eddinger, *Malachi*, 10). Either way, δέ is found in the middle of the overall structure where the crucial shift occurs.

47. Hoey, *Textual Interaction*, 55–56; Talmy Givón, *Syntax: An Introduction*, vol. 2, rev. ed. (Amsterdam: Benjamins, 2001), 329.

we group units together that share strong thematic ties. We treat these larger groupings as related but discrete information units that represent the overall structure of the discourse, and we seek to convey that structure (in English) by using words and phrases such as *now*, *so*, *then*, *alright*, *okay*, and *anyway*; by utilizing paragraphs, line breaks, section headings, and chapter breaks; and by engaging in audible cues such as vocal inflections and pauses.[48] This happens naturally and often subconsciously, and it is done because it facilitates the mental processing of the discourse as a whole. First, though grouping smaller units together creates larger pieces of information to process, their thematic coherence makes such grouping possible, comprehensible, and even desirable, as it aids us in understanding how the smaller bits of information relate to the whole. Second, and moreover, by conceiving of the discourse as groups of related but discrete groupings of information units, we are segmenting the discourse, something that is too large to process effectively, into smaller meaningful units that allow for efficient and productive processing. On this, Robert Dooley and Stephen Levinsohn write:

> Humans typically process large amounts of information in chunks, somewhat like we eat a meal in bites. This helps us deal with complexity.... In a longer discourse there will indeed be many items of information; the speaker chunks material into parts which can be dealt with separately. What thematic groupings of sentences reflect, then, is conceptual chunking.[49]

We mentally chunk texts because it makes something complex less complex, and we signal such discrete groupings for our listeners and readers because it reflects our hierarchical conception of the discourse and so that we may aid their processing, thereby facilitating successful communication.

However, segmenting a discourse into hierarchically organized information units is not a strictly objective practice. It is up to the text-producer when to segment a text. It is important to ask, then, What motivates grouping and segmenting? As mentioned in the paragraph above, the grouping

48. Consider what it would be like attempting to comprehend a discourse, oral or written, without any of these features. It is not impossible, but neither would it be an easy process. It would be exhausting and would likely lead to some information being lost as well as to some misunderstanding.

49. Dooley and Levinsohn, *Analyzing Discourse*, 36.

of smaller information units into larger ones is done on the basis of thematic ties. Dooley and Levinsohn state:

> If chunking in texts were no more than this, it would not matter where the chunks were made, as long as the pieces were "bite-size." However, it turns out that chunking is responsive to content as well as to size.... Even though the mental representation for a coherent text is (by definition) a connected structure overall, its component parts have even tighter internal connections.[50]

Thus, there is an overall coherent and connected structure, but the component parts, those sections representing thematic groupings that have been chunked, share tighter internal thematic ties.[51] It follows, then, that while the different segments are a part of the same mental representation, certain thematic discontinuities will tend to occur between them.[52] It is at these places of thematic discontinuity where a text-producer is most likely to take advantage of the natural seam and segment the text. This was realized by Wallace Chafe in his research on how information is packaged in discourse. At the level of the paragraph in oral discourse, he noticed verbal cues indicating breaks between units that coincided with "a significant change in scene, time, character configuration, event structure, and the like."[53] Such contexts of discontinuity provide a clear place for segmentation. Granted, they do not *require* segmentation—such depends on the text-producer and whether they feel it is necessary according to their purposes within the discourse—but they are where segmentation, which needs to happen, will most naturally occur.[54] As Dooley and Levinsohn conclude, "Chunking, then, is necessary so that people can handle large

---

50.Dooley and Levinsohn, *Analyzing Discourse*, 36.

51. Dooley and Levinsohn list ties such as time, place, action, and participants (Dooley and Levinsohn, *Analyzing Discourse*, 37). Givón lists seven "well-marked" elements of discourse coherence: "referents ('participants'), location, temporality, aspectuality, modality, perspective ('narrative voice'), and action/events" (Givón, *Syntax*, 329).

52. Dooley and Levinsohn, *Analyzing Discourse*, 36.

53. Wallace Chafe, "Cognitive Constraints on Information Flow," in *Coherence and Grounding in Discourse: Outcome of a Symposium, Eugene, Oregon, June 1984*, ed. Russell S. Tomlin, TSL 11 (Amsterdam: Benjamins, 1987), 42.

54. See also Hoey's comments on the hierarchical organization of texts and the natural chunking of narrative episodes in contexts of discontinuity (Hoey, *Textual Interaction*, 55). This was observed in both the papyri and the LXX. There was a fairly consistent pattern whereby δέ would cooccur with contexts of thematic discontinu-

amounts of information, but discontinuities in content provide well-motivated occasions for it."[55]

Segmenting discourse, then, is a subjective decision on the part of the text-producer that is also responsive to the nature of the information being communicated. Whether owing to size and/or to certain elements of discontinuity that make chunking natural and useful within the story or argument, they may choose to signal a new, distinct segment. But it is also a necessary feature for cognition and for successful communication. At some point, segmentation needs to happen in order to aid the recipient in their processing of information and in their building of their mental representation of the discourse. They need to be able to group information units together as a means of consolidating the information and in order to understand how the various parts of a discourse relate. If this is not done for the reader, then they will likely either give up the task or they will create their own segments of the discourse, risking potential misunderstanding of the structure of the discourse.

Languages have various and different means of structuring discourse and marking distinct segments. Discourse markers functioning within the metatextual domain are one type of device often used. Regarding this, Aijmer writes:

> Pragmatic markers function as indicators of metapragmatic awareness.... This property accounts, for example, for the ability of pragmatic markers to reflect on and organise the discourse, for example to make it more coherent on the local and global level.... Their ability to project a new stage in the discourse (a new activity, speech act, or text) is an important aspect of metalinguistic indicators. They therefore have a crucial role in controlling and changing the progress of the discourse.[56]

---

ity, from a slight single discontinuity (switches of sentence topic) to more significant clusters of discontinuities (movements to new scenes).

55. Dooley and Levinsohn, *Analyzing Discourse*, 37. See also the related discussion of verbal paragraphing and changes in peripheral consciousness in Chafe, "Cognitive Constraints," 42–45; Chafe, "The Deployment of Consciousness in the Production of Narrative," in *The Pear Stories: Cognitive, Cultural, and Linguistic Aspects of Narrative Production*, ed. Wallace L. Chafe, Advances in Discourse Processes 3 (Norwood, NJ: Ablex, 1980), 40–47.

56. Aijmer, *Understanding Pragmatic Markers*, 5. See also Aijmer, Foolen, and

Similarly, Salvador Pons Bordería notes that one function involved in the treatment of DMs is a "metadiscoursive" function that has a structuring dimension.[57] He describes this dimension as "organizing the linguistic constituents of the message" and further states, "Structuring makes reference to the hierarchical, organizational aspects of connection, in other words, to the way a speaker builds and structures a message."[58] One example provided by Pons Bordería is the suprasentential use of *y* in Spanish to add a second sequence to a story.[59] Another example from Spanish is provided by Catherine Travis—a reorientation use of *bueno*. She describes this use as marking a reorientation in topic, which "includes introducing a new topic, closing a topic, prefacing a digression from the main topic, returning to a prior topic following a digression, and moving on to the key point of a topic."[60] Anna-Brita Stenström examines the various uses of *pues* and writes, "On [the discursive level], the connector *pues* serves to structure what the speaker says and maintains the discourse coherence.... When used as a discourse organizer, *pues* has a demarcating effect by chunking units of information, as well as a unifying effect by linking what is currently being said to what preceded."[61] She also demonstrates its use as a topic transition marker.[62] In English, Gisela Redeker notes the use of *so* to transition into a new segment and the use of *well* to signal a transition back to the mainline after parenthetical material.[63] Similarly, Aijmer describes a turn-taking use of *well*, which draws attention to something

---

Simon-Vandenbergen, "Pragmatic Markers in Translation," 105–6; Verschueren, *Understanding Pragmatics*, 189.

57. Pons Bordería, "Functional Approach," 86.

58. Pons Bordería, "Functional Approach," 89–90. See also Kerstin Fischer, "Frames, Constructions, and Invariant Meanings: The Functional Polysemy of Discourse Particles," in Fischer, *Approaches to Discourse Particles*, 430; Diana M. Lewis, "Discourse Markers in English: A Discourse-Pragmatic View," in Fischer, *Approaches to Discourse Particles*, 57; Bazzanella, "Discourse Markers in Italian," 457.

59. Pons Bordería, "Functional Approach," 90–91.

60. Travis, "The Natural Semantic Metalanguage Approach to Discourse Markers," in Fischer, *Approaches to Discourse Particles*, 234.

61. Stenström, "The Spanish Discourse Markers *O Sea* and *Pues* and Their English Correspondences," in Aijmer and Simon-Vandenbergen, *Pragmatic Markers in Contrast*, 164.

62. Anna-Brita Stenström, "Spanish Discourse Markers," 165.

63. Redeker, "Discourse Markers," 342–43.

new in the discourse, "whether a new turn, topic, an elaborate answer or clarification, etc."[64] She further notes the transitional use of the particle to signal "a change of topic or speech act according to an agenda or an 'interpretative frame'" or to signal a transition to a new stage of discourse.[65] Fischer demonstrates that, when used at a thematic break, *okay* may be used to mark a transition to a new phase in an interaction.[66] She also shows that it may be used to signal the conclusion of a conversation.[67] Diana Lewis examines the function of *of course* and, among other uses, argues for a background in narrative function, a topic shift function, and an end of list function.[68] Barbara Johnstone has argued that the DM *so* can be used to mark boundaries in discourse.[69] Concerning continuatives, M. A. K. Halliday writes, "A continuative is one of a small set of discourse signalers, *yes*, *no*, *well*, *oh*, *now*, which signal that a new move is beginning: a response, in dialogue, or a move to the next point if the same speaker is continuing."[70] Nontemporal *now*, in addition to the Norwegian *nå*, is also discussed by Hilde Hasselgård. She states that both may be used as continuatives, marking a new move or point.[71] In French, Hansen describes a reperspectivization or reorientation function for *alors*. She claims, "*Alors* is not infrequently used to mark shifts to new topics, particularly subtopics or digressions."[72] She also states that it may signal a return to a topic, a shift of frame, and frame-breaks.[73] In an investigation of two pragmatic markers in Sùpyìré, Robert Carlson concludes that the DM *kà* simultaneously

---

64. Aijmer, *Understanding Pragmatic Markers*, 34.

65. Aijmer, *Understanding Pragmatic Markers*, 35, 58–60.

66. Fischer, "Frames, Constructions, and Invariant Meanings," 434.

67. Fischer, "Frames, Constructions, and Invariant Meanings," 434. See also her discussion on p. 440, wherein she discusses what "okay" signals at its core (jointly agreed upon topic) and how that contributes to its "topic function."

68. Lewis, "Discourse Markers," 54.

69. Johnstone, *Discourse Analysis*, 2nd ed., Introducing Linguistics 3 (Malden, MA: Blackwell, 2008), 240–42.

70. Halliday and Christian Matthiessen, *An Introduction to Functional Grammar*, 2nd ed. (London: Arnold, 1994), 53.

71. Hasselgård, "'Not *Now*': On Non-correspondence between the Cognate Adverbs *now* and *nå*," in Aijmer and Simon-Vandenbergen, *Pragmatic Markers in Contrast*, 95, 103–4, 109.

72. Hansen, *Function of Discourse Particles*, 335.

73. Hansen, *Function of Discourse Particles*, 338–42.

fills continuity/development- and discontinuity-marking functions. It begins a new section within the larger theme (continuity/development) and also marks discontinuity, at a local level, with what precedes.[74] Lastly, Dooley and Levinsohn mention the particle *na* in Suruwahá and the particle *ka* in Inga, both of which signal a movement to the next point in the discourse.[75]

Thus, the use of certain DMs to structure and segment discourse is a phenomenon that occurs cross-linguistically. Much of what may be observed in modern languages corresponds to the function of δέ in Koine Greek.[76]

### 2.2.3. A Cognitive-Functional Description of δέ

The use of δέ in the Twelve further confirms what was seen in the papyri. Based, then, on what has been observed in those corpora and based on the cross-linguistic evidence, the following description may be offered.

- The DM δέ functions within the metatextual domain and is used to organize and structure the discourse. At its core, it signals a break between segments, introducing a new, distinct information unit. By using δέ to segment, the communicator both clearly indicates the structure of the discourse and divides it into smaller meaningful units. This aids the reader in the building of their mental representation of the text, explicitly informing them of where to chunk information

74. Robert Carlson, "Narrative Connectives in Sùpyìre," in Tomlin, *Coherence and Grounding in Discourse*, 15, passim.

75. Dooley and Levinsohn, *Analyzing Discourse*, 93–94.

76. Since many of the linguistic studies referenced here use recorded speech as a part of their data set, many of the different uses of DMs may be differentiated prosodically. Unfortunately, there are no native Koine speakers to whom we can listen. It may be the case that some of the slight variations of function one may observe with δέ were differentiated prosodically as well. The limits of our investigation, due to the nature of the data set, are something we must accept. This makes attentive study of texts from the koine period all the more crucial in our understanding of how the language functioned. In addition, this requires an even greater awareness of linguistic research and cross-linguistic studies on the part of biblical scholars. By gaining deeper understandings of how language functions and what typological trends there are across languages, we place our analyses of features within the biblical languages on firmer ground.

units. The advantage of this is that it makes the processing of the discourse easier for the recipient. By indicating a new, distinct segment, δέ naturally directs the recipient's current mental attention to this new information unit and thus allows the recipient to reduce at least some of their mental effort on actively holding onto prior information. Naturally, δέ will tend to co-occur with thematic discontinuities, that is, where it would be natural to create a seam in the discourse.

- The interaction of the DM with different levels of discourse in various contexts results in a few typical uses. First, with a broad scope and high or stark discontinuity, the segment marked by δέ typically corresponds with a new development within the discourse, such as a new scene or a new topic to be discussed. Second, with a moderate scope, typically occurring at the sentence-level, and moderate discontinuity, the segmenting corresponds with a new subtopic within a larger unit or the next part of an argument being built. Third, similar to the previous but typically occurring with offline information, δέ can separate off parenthetical information. Lastly, δέ may occur with a narrow scope segmenting out small steps in a discourse that the writer considered merited being separated out as distinct units.[77]
- It would seem that, given their frequency and productivity, the first two uses best exemplify the prototypical center of δέ, that is, segmenting at seams within the discourse and providing explicit organization

77. This last use may be observed in Hos 7:9 and twice in Obad 18. Hosea 7:9: *κατέφαγον ἀλλότριοι τὴν ἰσχὺν αὐτοῦ, αὐτὸς <u>δὲ</u> οὐκ ἔγνω· καὶ πολιαὶ ἐξήνθησαν αὐτῷ, καὶ αὐτὸς οὐκ ἔγνω.* "Foreigners devoured his strength; he *de* did not know. And gray hair burst forth on him, and he did not know." This instance of δέ segments at a very localized level. It seems odd that the same construction is not used in the parallel statement following. It would appear that the effect (and perhaps purpose?) of chunking the first *αὐτὸς οὐκ ἔγνω* would be to heighten the already present contrast between it and the preceding statement, particularly given the switch from "foreigners" (something external) to "he." By indicating a small distinct unit here, the reader's attention would inevitably be drawn to the sharp distinction being made. Obadiah 18: *καὶ ἔσται ὁ οἶκος Ιακωβ πῦρ, ὁ <u>δὲ</u> οἶκος Ιωσηφ φλόξ, ὁ <u>δὲ</u> οἶκος Ησαυ εἰς καλάμην, καὶ ἐκκαυθήσονται εἰς αὐτοὺς καὶ καταφάγονται αὐτούς, καὶ οὐκ ἔσται πυρφόρος τῷ οἴκῳ Ησαυ, διότι κύριος ἐλάλησε.* "'And the house of Jacob will be a fire; the *de* house of Joseph will be a flame; the *de* house of Esau will become plant stubble, and they will be kindled against them and they will devour them. And there will be no fire-bearer in the house of Esau,' for the Lord has spoken." Similar to these uses are occurrences of δέ such as those in Jesus's genealogy in Matt 1:2–16 or the listing of virtues Christians are to add to their faith in 2 Pet 1:5–7.

to its hierarchical structure. The other uses are less prototypical but nonetheless retain the DM's core segmenting function.

- Given its function and its typical co-occurrence with thematic discontinuities, it is not surprising that δέ is often found in adversative contexts. Adversative relations arise owing to the juxtaposition of contrastive options, which often correlates with some level of thematic discontinuity. Thus, understanding the pragmatic function of δέ provides us with a satisfying explanation for so-called adversative δέ.[78] The DM is well-suited to such contexts.

This description of δέ is not all that different from other recent linguistic investigations. Within recent Classical and Postclassical Greek scholarship, similar suggestions have been made.[79] Consider C. M. J. Sicking's comments on δέ:

> The difference between δέ and καί at the beginning of independent sentences as it is found in Lysias I and XII can be accounted for as a difference between (καί) *including* a further item within the context of that which precedes, and (δέ) *opening* a new section of the text. The use of δέ therefore results in a certain *discontinuity*, unlike that of καί, which establishes a *connection* between what precedes and what follows: an instance of δέ placed after a constituent indicates the beginning of a new section, and an instance of καί placed before a constituent is a mark of continuity.… Δέ marks the beginning of a portion of text which the speaker wishes to subjoin to what precedes as a new unit. In the sequence "*a*. *b* δέ …" there is a *discontinuity* between *a* and *b* to the extent that the speaker does not suggest that *b* forms part of the same context in a narrow sense as *a*, as well as a *continuity* to the extent that both *a* and *b*, other things being the same, form part of a larger argumentative or narrative whole which is coherent at its own level.[80]

---

78. Whereas starting with "adversative δέ," as is often done, does not adequately describe the pragmatics of the DM, does not address the present cognitive issues of mental processing and discourse segmentation, and does not provide a satisfying explanation for how the DM is used elsewhere (i.e., how other uses relate to or are derived from a supposedly more central adversative use).

79. As noted before, grammars and lexica still have not caught up with or paid attention to such studies. See n. 8 in ch. 1.

80. Sicking, "Devices for Text Articulation in Lysias I and XII," in *Two Studies in Attic Particle Usage: Lysias & Plato*, Mnemosyne Supplements 129 (Leiden: Brill, 1993), 11–12, 47, emphasis original. When Sicking uses the term "discontinuity," he is using

This is essentially how I have described δέ. What Sicking observes in Lysias 1 and 12 mirrors what was observed in the papyri and the Twelve. The DM is used to segment the discourse, indicating the beginning of a new unit.

Similarly, Egbert Bakker argues that δέ is a boundary marker. Regarding Homeric material, he claims that δέ separates (and simultaneously links) clausal intonation units, marking a new step in the progression of the narrative.[81] In Classical Greek, Bakker argues that δέ functions as a boundary marker that has a range of uses depending on its scope: Topic-switch/referential tracking (e.g., ὁ δέ …), marking a new thematic segment, marking a change of perspective, presenting pieces of information as small-scale discourse units, and marking the movement from an item to be identified to its identification in a new discourse unit.[82] For Bakker, each of these uses fall within the DM's function as a boundary marker. The slight differences between them are due to the scope of the particle in a given instance and the nature of the information being communicated.[83] However, I do prefer describing δέ in terms of segmentation or chunking rather than as a boundary marker, since "segmentation" and "chunking" more clearly present how the DM is functioning at every level of discourse and how it instructs the reader to chunk information units within their mental representation.[84]

Other classicists have made similar claims. Rutger Allan comments on the function of δέ and claims, "The particle δέ is typically used to indicate a slight boundary in the discourse.... In many cases, a new discourse topic is introduced.... In other words, by means of the particle δέ, the narrator divides the text into thematic units. These thematic units tend to

---

it differently than it has been used in this chapter. As is clear from his discussion, he uses discontinuity to refer to the effect of δέ creating a structural break in the discourse.

81. Egbert J. Bakker, "Boundaries, Topics, and the Structure of Discourse: An Investigation of the Ancient Greek Particle δέ," *Studies in Language* 17 (1993): 280.

82. For topic switch/referential tracking, see Bakker, "Boundaries, Topics, and the Structure of Discourse," 282–84. Without employing prototype terminology, Bakker helpfully notes the peripheral nature of the use of ὁ δέ as a disambiguating device. He writes, "Referential disambiguation is not so much a phenomenon in itself as the one extreme of a continuum of discourse boundaries ranging from local to global" (284). For marking a new thematic segment, see pp. 284–90; for a change in perspective, 290–92; for small-scale discourse units, 295–96; and for marking movement, 296–98.

83. Similar to the description of δέ provided at the beginning of this section.

84. "Boundary marker" is fitting when δέ occurs with a broad scope but is a less helpful descriptor when the DM occurs with a moderate or narrow scope.

have an internal temporal, causal and referential unity."[85] Gerry Wakker notes that, prototypically, the basic value of δέ is to signal the next new item within a discourse.[86] Frank Scheppers states, "δέ typically marks the transition to a 'new step' in a sequence … whether a Plot sequence … or e.g. a Topic-Chain."[87] Annamieke Drummen claims, "[δέ] marks a new step in the discourse … it signals a transition to something new."[88] With respect to an example of δέ in a contrastive context, she argues, "The particle itself does not signal this contrast, but merely marks the new step in the discourse."[89] In his work on Homeric Greek, Mark de Kreij regards δέ as a boundary marker that helps the audience compartmentalize discrete acts in a scene step by step.[90] Anna Bonifazi remarks that the functions of δέ "must exceed matters of contrast and continuation, as well as matters of coordination and subordination."[91] She goes on to state, "The only consistent meaning of δέ is pragmatic, and it consists in marking separate or new discourse acts."[92] Lastly, *CGCG* posits that the basic function of δέ is to indicate "a shift to a new, distinct, text segment, often with a change of topic."[93] Thus, what classicists have recognized as the function of δέ,

85. Rutger Allan, "Sense and Sentence Complexity: Sentence Structure, Sentence Connection, and Tense-aspect as Indicators of Narrative Mode in Thucydides' *Histories*," in *The Language of Literature: Linguistic Approaches to Classical Texts,* ed. Rutger J. Allan and Michel Buijs, ASCP 13 (Leiden: Brill, 2007), 105.

86. Gerry Wakker, "'Well I Will Now Present My Arguments': Discourse Cohesion Marked by οὖν and τοίνυν in Lysias," in *Discourse Cohesion in Ancient Greek*, ed. Stéphanie Bakker and Gerry Wakker, ASCP 16 (Leiden: Brill, 2009), 81.

87. Frank Scheppers, *The Colon Hypothesis: Word Order, Discourse Segmentation and Discourse Coherence in Ancient Greek* (Brussels: VUBPress, 2011), 413.

88. Annamieke Drummen, "A Construction-Grammar Analysis of Ancient Greek Particles," in *Toward a Cognitive Classical Linguistics: The Embodied Basis of Constructions in Greek and Latin*, ed. Egle Mocciaro and William Michael Short (Berlin: de Gruyter, 2019), 58–59. Drummen makes similar claims in Anna Bonifazi, Annemieke Drummen, and Mark de Kreij, *Particles in Ancient Greek Discourse: Exploring Particle Use across Genres*, Hellenic Studies 79 (Washington, DC: Center for Hellenic Studies, 2016), 854–58.

89. Drummen, "Construction-Grammar Analysis," 59.

90. Bonifazi, Drummen, and de Kreij, *Particles in Ancient Greek Discourse*, 464–65.

91. Bonifazi, Drummen, and de Kreij, *Particles in Ancient Greek Discourse*, 1248.

92. Bonifazi, Drummen, and de Kreij, *Particles in Ancient Greek Discourse*, 1249. Bonifazi, drawing from Bakker, uses the term "discretizing force" to describe the element that underlies all uses of δέ (1254).

93. *CGCG*, 671.

that it signals a new segment within the discourse, further confirms the conclusions reached above based on the use of the DM in the papyri and the Twelve.

In LXX scholarship, while there has been some interest in the usage of δέ, it is usually in the context of studies of translation technique, where its function(s) is assumed based on traditional scholarship. Thus, though δέ has received some attention in LXX studies, its function is rarely critically considered.[94] However, one study bears brief mention. Polak investigates the use of δέ in LXX Genesis and Exodus. Like what has been discussed above, Polak concludes that the particle is a marker of distinct units, typically introducing new stages of narrative.[95]

In New Testament Greek studies, similar descriptions may be found. Levinsohn writes, "The basic function of δέ is the same in narrative and nonnarrative text. In both it is used to mark new developments, in the sense that the information it introduces builds on what has gone before and makes a distinct contribution to the argument."[96] In the same way, Steven Runge observes:

---

94. E.g., Le Moigne discusses δέ in his study of LXX Isaiah (Le Moigne, "Le livre d'Ésaïe dans la Septante," ch. 6). However, he is simply interested in cataloguing the occurrences of the particle and offers no argument with respect to its function. He posits three primary uses—succession (whether chronological or logical), adversative, and the hinge between synonymous lines—and makes frequent reference to Denniston's *The Greek Particles*. Le Moigne's categories are sufficiently descriptive of the contexts in which δέ is used in LXX Isaiah, but they do not provide a satisfactory description of the pragmatics of the particle and why it is suitable to these contexts or why it is chosen rather than other connectives.

95. Polak, "Context Sensitive Translation and Parataxis," 528–39.

96. *DFNTG*, 112. Levinsohn claims too much in some of his descriptions of the DM, in that he ties its use to story and argument development (72). While this works for prototypical usage, it does not quite explain peripheral instances. Though the units that δέ segments will frequently correlate with developments in stories and arguments, such developments arise from the interaction of the DM's segmenting function within a given context. Related to this is how Levinsohn almost seems to conflate the particle's pragmatic function with literary analysis. For example, he writes, "Matthew's Gospel has a number of passages in which only the *conclusion* is introduced with δέ. This suggests that the author's primary intent in relating the episode is to lead up to that conclusion" (74, emphasis original). This claim, which he supports with Matt. 9:1–8, goes too far in extrapolating the significance of δέ to the purpose of the text. The DM, in that instance, is simply segmenting a distinct unit within the scene as the scene shifts from the event itself to the crowd's reaction to it. Moreover, DMs operat-

> Δέ is a coordinating conjunction like καί, but it includes the added constraint of signaling a new development.... The use of δέ represents the writer's choice to explicitly signal that what follows is a new, distinct development in the story or argument, based on how the writer conceived of it.[97]

I am hesitant to use the term "development marker," as it could easily be conflated with literary development. So long as development is simply regarded as new, distinct information, the terminology is fine, though I prefer the more neutral and more aptly descriptive "segmentation device" or "chunking device."

Kathleen Callow posits multiple functions of δέ that all share a common basic meaning. Crucially, she first mentions the importance of identifying the particle's scope. She states:

> Even a superficial reading of Corinthians reveals that δέ occurs at a variety of different discourse levels. It may occur with high-level significance, initiating a new topic which will form a major discourse-block.... It may occur with low-level significance, being relevant only to the clause or sentence in which it is located.... It therefore appears that the span or domain of a δέ in any instance is a considerable clue to its function.[98]

She then describes three uses: long-span, short-span, and intermediate-span. The long-span use may either signal a switch to a new discourse topic that will be discussed for some time or signal the termination of a discussion.[99] The short-span use signals either contrast or an aside.[100] With respect to contrast, Callow does note the presence of obvious contrastive lexical signals. Given this, one should question whether δέ is used to signal the contrast itself. The examples she provides can simply be considered segmentation at a very local level where there is a movement in the dis-

---

ing within the metatextual domain can often be used both to open a new segment *or to close a current segment* (on this, see the cross-linguistic studies cited above), which δέ was observed as accomplishing in some papyri, signaling the end of the letter's introduction. This appears to be a motivation behind the use of δέ at least in Matt 9:8.

97. *DGGNT*, 31.

98. Callow, "The Disappearing Δέ in 1 Corinthians," in *Linguistics and New Testament Interpretation: Essays on Discourse Analysis*, ed. David Alan Black, Katharine G. L. Barnwell, and Stephen H. Levinsohn (Nashville: Broadman, 1992), 184–85.

99. Callow, "Disappearing Δέ in 1 Corinthians," 185.

100. Callow, "Disappearing Δέ in 1 Corinthians," 185–86.

course to the next distinct point. Positing that the short-span use signals contrast ignores how δέ as a segmentation device works with a narrow scope and interacts with its context. Regarding δέ as a marker of an aside, Callow helpfully discusses how this use of δέ is accompanied by a certain package of signals. She writes, "Some lexical item already mentioned is taken up again in the δέ clause, and something new is added, which is not then further referred to."[101] The intermediate-span use is similar to the long-span use. However, rather than introducing a new discourse topic, it often introduces "a new aspect of an existing topic, and this new subtopic does not terminate with the δέ clause."[102] Callow also notes that after a topic or subtopic is introduced, major successive points tend to be marked with δέ.[103] In her conclusion, Callow provides the following description of the particle:

> We may say, therefore, that δέ characteristically occurs where there is linear development of thought, and that it marks new development in the progression of the message.... The speaker uses δέ as a signal, saying, "This is the next step." It may be a little step or a big one, it may be a step forwards, or sideways, or even backward-looking, but it is always the next step, and with it the speaker or writer is progressing one thought at a time along a purposeful line of development.... We can say that δέ knits thoughts together into a chain, very reasonably and rationally, one thought at a time.[104]

A similar description is given by Jakob Heckert. Based on his examination of δέ in the Pastoral Epistles, he concludes:

> Δέ has a single function, neither contrastive nor copulative, nor, for that matter, introducing only change, but marking development. If δέ functions as a copula, it marks a proposition as a development of a previous one. If it introduces a contrast, the proposition introduced by δέ builds

101. Callow, "Disappearing Δέ in 1 Corinthians," 185–86. In addition, she states, "Asides frequently have an introductory formula signaling their removal from the mainline" (187). She also mentions the short-span use of δέ in listing (186).

102. Callow, "Disappearing Δέ in 1 Corinthians," 186.

103. Callow, "Disappearing Δέ in 1 Corinthians," 186.

104. Callow, "Disappearing Δέ in 1 Corinthians," 192, 193. So also Young, *New Testament Greek*, 183.

> on the preceding conjunct as a foil. Even when δέ occurs in some set construction, it does not lose its basic developmental function.[105]

Thus, despite the differences in terminology, New Testament Greek scholarship also confirms the findings of the present study. Moreover, given that similar metatextual descriptions of δέ are posited both for Classical Greek and for the Greek exhibited in the New Testament, one would expect that δέ would function in the same way during the intervening period.[106]

---

105. Heckert, *Discourse Function of Conjoiners in the Pastoral Epistles* (Dallas: Summer Institute of Linguistics, 1996), 57.

106. One other New Testament study bears mentioning. Based on her analysis of conjunctions in Matthew, Black regards δέ as a marker of discontinuity. She observes that it frequently collocates with other signals of discontinuity, such as changes in referent, time, and place, and concludes that they all, including δέ, serve as mutually redundant cues for discourse processing (see Black, *Sentence Conjunctions*, 153, 173–74, 333–34). It seems to me that she is confusing the DM's function with the contextual features with which it naturally occurs. Discontinuity is a property of discourse that would be present with or without δέ (and often is present even when δέ is absent). As segmentation will tend to occur at seams within discourse (since this is the most natural and cognitively simplest place to chunk discourse), the issue is whether to take advantage of a given context of discontinuity and signal a new segment. This is a decision that will be dependent on the size of the current information unit, the topic under discussion, the author's purposes locally and globally, and the nature of the forthcoming material.

In addition, in contradistinction to καί, Black regards δέ as a marked choice and thus as a marker of potential prominence (66, 70, 334). Thus, when she states that the choice to use δέ "can be an attempt to guide the audience to turn their attention … to a particular participant or action in the discourse" (334), this is not a claim that attention is turned in such a way as to move to a new segment in the active building and structuring of the mental representation (as I claim). Rather, it is a prominence claim, i.e., that attention may be drawn to material that is highlighted because it is introduced by the marked connective. However, καί and δέ are not two binary options. They are used to structure discourse in two different ways. They are chosen not based on markedness but based on how the author wants to structure the discourse and instruct his recipient in the construction of their mental representation. Lastly, and perhaps most important, Black insists on a description of δέ that is applicable in every single case. Critiquing Levinsohn, she writes, "Unless 'development' can be shown unequivocally to be present in all uses of δέ in the Synoptic Gospels and Acts, Levinsohn's claim that 'development' is what δέ itself adds to discourse cannot be sustained." (147) While I do not agree entirely with Levinsohn's claims (see n. 96 above), it is Black's line of reasoning here that cannot be sustained. Many studies on DMs find that they are polysemous (see §1.2.2.1). Thus, by that alone, the argument that development must be present in

Some of the traditional Greek grammarians did recognize the use of δέ as a segmentation device, though not in such terms. The traditional grammarians had intimate knowledge of Greek and often provided satisfying and insightful descriptions of elements of the language, even though they did not have the linguistic terminology or framework. Consider what A. T. Robertson writes concerning the particle:

> However we take it, there is in the word no essential notion of antithesis or contrast. What is true is that the addition is something new and not so closely associated in thought as is true of τέ and καί. I prefer therefore to begin with the narrative and transitional (copulative) use of δέ.[107]

Similarly, although he does list an adversative function for the particle, G. B. Winer claims that δέ introduces something new to the discourse. He writes, "Δέ is often used when the writer merely subjoins something new, different and distinct from what precedes, but on that account not sharply opposed to it.... Sometimes δέ introduces a climax ... or marks the steps in a regular progression of clauses."[108] In like manner, William Chamberlain writes, "The earliest usage seems to have been a 'continuative' use in narrative with the meaning 'in the next place.'"[109] Thus, there is a sense among these grammarians that δέ signals a transition to something new or introduces the next step in the discourse. As observed and argued above, this is prototypically how δέ, as a segmentation device, is used in context. The observations of the grammarians were insightful and laid the ground-

all uses is not necessarily valid. Even if δέ is monosemous, DMs tend to interact differently with certain contexts (though still motivated by their core function). Moreover, regardless of whether δέ is polysemous or monosemous, it is likely that δέ is conceived of prototypically (see §1.2.2.3). This is not to say that Black is necessarily incorrect in her assessment of δέ, but rather that her presuppositions are contrary to linguistic scholarship on DMs and that her stated reasons for disagreeing with Levinsohn, on the whole, are not valid.

107. Robertson, *Grammar*, 1184. Smyth, though not as clear as Robertson and also committed to the notion that δέ is adversative to some extent, offered a similar insight into the connective: "δέ serves to mark that something is different from what precedes, but only to offset it, not to exclude or contradict it; it denotes only a slight contrast ... δέ is adversative and copulative; but the two uses are not always clearly to be distinguished" (Smyth, §2834).

108. Winer, *New Testament Greek*, 552–53.

109. Chamberlain, *Grammar of the Greek New Testament*, 150. See also Green, *Grammar of the Greek Testament*, 344.

work for what would be discerned with regard to the particle's function in years to come.

It was demonstrated above that, in many cases, δέ cannot be regarded as a marker of adversative relations, as there is simply no contrast present. Moreover, even when there was contrast, it was noted that it would be present regardless of the connective used. Levinsohn discusses this as well. He demonstrates that "true contrast" arises out of two opposed pairs of lexical items, regardless of whether or not δέ is present. Thus, he concludes, "In the context of 'true' contrast, δέ is either redundant or *conveys something other than contrast*, viz., development."[110] Levinsohn's insight illustrates well the fact that it is not conjunctions nor particles that create a coherent text but rather it is the realization of the underlying semantic relations between propositions.[111] Contrast is one such semantic relation. By their nature, contrastive semantic relations contribute to discontinuity. As noted throughout this chapter, discontinuity correlates well with δέ, since discontinuous contexts provide natural seams for discourse segmentation. Thus, the suitability of δέ to contrastive contexts is understandable and expected, but frequent co-occurrence and correlation should not be conflated with the function of the particle, what it explicitly signals to the recipient in their processing of the text.[112]

### 2.2.4. Switches between ἐγὼ δέ and καὶ ἐγώ in LXX Hosea as Stylistic Patterning

One of the advances in noting structural features in a translation has been the recognition of rhetorical techniques (e.g., Dines). Insight into how a certain translator utilizes these techniques often offers a clearer picture of the translator and their own style. However, it is important to keep in mind that rhetorical techniques do not supersede linguistic function. Style and rhetoric exist on a plane dependent upon and secondary to a language's

110. *DFNTG*, 113 (emphasis original). See also *DGGNT*, 28; Blakemore, *Relevance and Linguistic Meaning*, §4.2.1.

111. See M. A. K. Halliday and Ruqaiya Hasan, *Cohesion in English*, English Language Series 9 (Harlow: Longman, 1976); Gillian Brown and George Yule, *Discourse Analysis*, CSL (Cambridge: Cambridge University Press, 1983), 190–98; Dooley and Levinsohn, *Analyzing Discourse*, 31–32, 91–94.

112. See also Heckert, *Discourse Function*, 47–49; Black, *Sentence Conjunctions*, 174–77.

syntax, semantics, and pragmatics. In other words, style and rhetoric can only be determined after linguistic analysis. Because of this, I am unconvinced by Dines's argument that the translator of the Twelve alternated between ἐγὼ δέ and καὶ ἐγώ as translations for both ואני and ואנכי in Hos 5:2–13:4 for stylistic patterning purposes and, therefore, that the translations themselves did not have anything to do with their appropriateness to the context.[113] There are several issues with this claim. First, one must consider the function of δέ. If δέ is a text-structuring device that partitions the discourse and the translator alternated between ἐγὼ δέ and καὶ ἐγώ for the purpose of style, then they were purposefully ignoring the function of δέ in Koine. The readers could not have known this and would assume that the translator is using δέ conventionally. Thus, the translator would be allowing for the possibility that their translation would be misunderstood by the readers and hearers. It seems unlikely that a translator would allow for something like this. Second, one must ask why the translator limited the alternating chain only to 5:2–13:4. There are two other occurrences of ואנכי in 1:9 and 2:4, but the translator renders both with καὶ ἐγώ. Is there really an unbroken chain present in 5:2–13:4, as Dines claims, with these two nonalternated instances in Hosea 1 and 2?[114] Third, the supposed pattern consists of nine alternations spread across more than seven chapters. Would any reader or hearer of the text have noticed this pattern? It does not seem likely. Finally, one must also consider that there are other instances of καὶ ἐγώ in Hosea that do not translate either of the Hebrew pronouns (2:2; 3:3; 5:14; 11:3; and 14:9). Given these other occurrences of the collocation, there is no alternating pattern that arises in the Greek text. In the end, there are eleven occurrences of καὶ ἐγώ and five occurrences of ἐγὼ δέ, not in an alternating pattern and not all translating the Hebrew pronouns. From the reader's or listener's perspective, particularly, a pattern would not have been discernible nor would there have been any way to know which occurrences were and were not translating ואני and ואנכי.

Dines's argument proceeds by observing two examples of καὶ ἐγώ and ἐγὼ δέ from Hos 5:12 and 13:4, respectively, and positing that the opposite phrase would have been more contextually appropriate. This

113. Jennifer M. Dines, "Stylistic Invention and Rhetorical Purpose in the Book of the Twelve," in *Et sapienter et eloquenter: Studies on Rhetorical and Stylistic Features of the Septuagint*, ed. Eberhard Bons and Thomas J. Kraus, FRLANT 241 (Göttingen: Vandenhoeck & Ruprecht, 2011), 40; Dines, "Minor Prophets," 444.

114. Dines offers no explanation as to why she ignores these two instances of καὶ ἐγώ.

is thus regarded as evidence that the translator's choice was not based on context but rather on style.[115] Concerning Hos 5:12, she states, "ואני would have been more appropriately rendered by the adversative ἐγὼ δέ." As I have argued throughout this chapter, however, there is no adversative function inherent to δέ. The only reason that δέ will occur in an adversative context is because the material it introduces is conceived of as a distinct segment. Thus, when one reads Hos 5 and arrives at verse 12, since it begins with καί, it is processed as connected to and continuing Hos 5:11, not as a new information unit.[116] The context concerns the sinfulness of Ephraim and Judah and the Lord pouring his wrath on them. Hosea 5:12 states, "And I [καὶ ἐγώ] am like a cause of upheaval for Ephraim and like a spiked stick for the house of Judah." Verse 13 then continues the discussion of Ephraim and Judah. Understandably, the translator did not regard 5:12 and what followed as a new segment, and therefore did not use δέ. Regarding Hos 13:4, Dines states that the verse would have made more sense with καὶ ἐγώ, since there is no contrast present.[117] First, δέ is frequently used in noncontrastive contexts, as demonstrated above in the papyri and the Twelve. Thus, the lack of contrast does not in itself make καί more suitable to this context. Second, there is a discernible progression in the Lord's argument at the seam of verses 3–4. Hosea 13:1–3 speaks of Ephraim and his sin and what he will become. Hosea 13:4 switches the topic to the Lord, expressing who he is and what he has done: "Now, I [ἐγὼ δέ] am the Lord your God who establishes heaven and creates earth, whose hands created all the host of heaven, and I did not reveal them to you so that you would go after them. And I led you up out of Egypt and you will not know a god but me, and there is no one who saves besides me." The theme of the discourse does not shift again until 14:2. Thus, there is clear reason to use δέ at 13:4. It segments the discourse at a seam where the Lord advances his argument to its next major point. Chunking the discourse here is eminently reasonable and provides a clear discourse structure.

The stylistic patterning claim does not hold up. It cannot account for the other occurrences of the Hebrew pronouns in Hosea nor the other instances of καὶ ἐγώ. Furthermore, no Greek reader would have been able to comprehend the pattern or its underlying Hebrew. Lastly, and most

115. Dines, "Stylistic Invention and Rhetorical Purpose," 40.

116. I take καί as a simple marker of thematic continuity. See *DGGNT*, §2.2.

117. Dines, "Stylistic Invention and Rhetorical Purpose," 40.

importantly, the discourse function of δέ is not taken into account, which, once considered, reveals that the choice of δέ by the translator was due to appropriateness to the context.[118]

### 2.2.5. δέ and Translation Technique in the Twelve

The DM δέ does not have a lexical equivalent in Hebrew.[119] When it is used, the translator of the Twelve is making a decision that goes beyond qualitative lexemic representation. In the cases where it quantitatively represents conjunctive *vav*, the first question to ask is why the translator chose δέ over the more qualitatively equivalent and stereotypical καί. By choosing δέ, the translator is explicitly segmenting the discourse, instructing his reader to create a distinct component in their mental representation of the text. In order to make this decision, the translator, at the very least, must have been aware of the surrounding context and willing to encode their conception of the discourse structure in the translation.[120] The translator does this *even though* it did not lexically match the Hebrew *Vorlage* and also often changed the word order, given that δέ is a postpositive.[121] Without this awareness of context and conception of the flow of the discourse, there

118. Though an argument from silence, one could also ask why such a pattern does not occur anywhere else in the books of the Twelve (or across the books). Granted, Hosea has more occurrences of ואני and ואנכי than any of the other books, but Jonah and Zechariah each contain three occurrences of ואני.

119. Just because it frequently appears where there is a *vav* in the *Vorlage* does not therefore indicate that a translator regarded δέ as equivalent to *vav*, as Aejmelaeus seems to suggest (Aejmelaeus, *Parataxis in the Septuagint*, 42). The "relationship" is one of necessity and statistical probability. If a translator were motivated to use δέ to signal a new segment, it will be the conjunction within its host utterance. As *vav* appears with incredible frequency in Biblical Hebrew, usually regardless of whether or not the discourse is being chunked, it is to be expected that the two will almost always coincide.

120. Likewise, in his study of LXX Genesis and Exodus, Polak concludes that the discourse structure conditioned the way the translators used δέ (Polak, "Context Sensitive Translation and Parataxis," 538–39).

121. John A. L. Lee writes, "δέ is used with great frequency in some of these books [of the LXX], despite the availability of the more literal equivalent καί. I conclude that the translators were not necessarily constrained by the original in their use of particles, just as in general they show readiness, especially in the Pentateuch, to employ idiomatic Greek where appropriate" ("Some Features of the Speech of Jesus in Mark's Gospel," *NovT* 27 [1985]: 2–3).

is no other justification for the use of the DM in the Twelve. In addition, the use of δέ may evince the translator's awareness of discourse features in the underlying Hebrew, such as breaks in verb-forms with preposed topic switches or asyndetic topic switches that correlate with advancement of the discourse.[122] It is not necessary to posit that the translator was always conscious of these features in his Hebrew *Vorlage* or even of a decision-making process regarding how various words, clauses, and paragraphs were related to one another. Segmentation in discourse is a natural and cognitively necessary feature of language. I think it likely that, intuitively, the translator well-versed in Hebrew would translate accordingly—thus using δέ rather than καί or inserting δέ when they, based on their understanding and knowledge of the movement and structure of the discourse, sensed the need to partition a distinct information unit in the text.

When δέ is present, it indicates, at least to some extent, that the translator was concerned with more than literally translating the words in front of them, but also with rendering the flow of the text and portraying how the discourse fit together based on their consideration of the wider context. In other words, the use of δέ evinces a desire on the part of the translator not just to render the syntactic and semantic components of their *Vorlage*, but also to faithfully represent it and to create a structured text in genuine Greek idiom (and perhaps even render certain structural features of the Hebrew) that reflects their own conception of the discourse.[123] In addition, because δέ cannot be said to be lexically motivated and cannot be used without a certain level of contextual awareness, especially when it has a broader scope, its use challenges the assumption that the Septuagint translators did not pay attention even to the immediate context when translating. If this were a generally true statement, δέ would never be used. Lastly, it should be noted that the explicit segmentation δέ signals will often instruct the reader to create a mental representation of the text that does not necessarily mirror the representation one would build of the Hebrew text.

The presence of δέ in the Twelve demonstrates that translation is a complex and nuanced practice. It is a small word, but the implications of its use are rather large. It signals the structure of the discourse, which is thus often a more explicitly portrayed structure than what may be observed in

122. E.g., Jonah 3:3; Hab 3:18; and Zeph 3:5 in §2.2.1 above.

123. See also Polak, "Context Sensitive Translation and Parataxis," 538–39.

the Hebrew, and it cannot be reduced to a simple correspondence with its source text. Of course, this is only one very small piece of a translator's work, but it is an important one nonetheless that deserves more attention than it has received in translation-technical studies.

## 2.3. Conclusion

Based on its use in the documentary papyri and the Twelve, it has been demonstrated that δέ is a metatextual DM. It structures the text by signaling segmentation within the discourse, partitioning distinct information units. Its use at different levels of the discourse and in different contexts will result in various particular conventions, but prototypical usage is exemplified by occurrences of δέ signaling a new segment that is the next development in the discourse, whether the next part of a story, the next topic, or next step in an argument. This discourse-pragmatic description finds support in classical scholarship, linguistic investigations into the Greek of the New Testament, and even in the work of some of the traditional Greek grammarians.

In the Twelve, it was observed that the translator used δέ despite the lack of a lexical equivalent in the Hebrew *Vorlage*. Their use of δέ evinces an awareness of the wider discourse as they went about their work as well as an intention to represent their conception of the structure and flow of the text. The translator's end product demonstrates that their translation was concerned with more than simply qualitative lexemic representation, but also with producing a cohesive, structured text in koine idiom. Much of the time, by using δέ, the translator creates a text with a different structure or at least a more explicit structure than the Hebrew text. Sometimes, however, the Greek text's structure mirrors the Hebrew's, such as in cases like Jonah 3:3; Hab 3:18; and Zeph 3:5. In the end, the translator displays an intuitive sense for discourse segmentation with δέ, using it where appropriate for the purposes of their translation.

With regard to the study of translation technique, understanding the function of δέ is a crucial component to understanding how the translator went about their work. It provides insight into a translator's conception of the flow and structure of the discourse. Its very use indicates a willingness to use a particle that is not lexically motivated and also evinces a motivation either to mirror the structure of the *Vorlage* or to partition the translation for its own sake. The use of δέ is also relevant when considering a translator's awareness of context as well as issues of interlinearity.

Regarding the former, the presence of δέ necessarily evinces a translator who was considering the wider discourse as they translated. Regarding the latter, the use of δέ cannot be argued for in terms of linguistic dependence and subservience. Despite it frequently standing in for *vav*, it is not a transparent translation. It changes the word order of the text and, crucially, it often explicitly structures the discourse in a way not mirrored in the Hebrew. Moreover, in most cases, its use is dependent not upon the Hebrew text but rather upon the needs and structure of the Greek text.

# 3
# εἰ μή and ἐὰν μή

The function of the set phrase εἰ/ἐὰν μή as a marker of exception is not disputed.[1] However, a more precise pragmatic description of the collocation than is typically provided is necessary, as this facilitates a better understanding of the nature of exceptive relations and how they direct the hearer/reader to process the discourse. Moreover, such an understanding is needed in order to differentiate εἰ/ἐὰν μή from other DMs that signal similar relations. In what follows, then, examples of εἰ/ἐὰν μή in the papyri and LXX will be investigated, in order to determine how the DM functions in early Koine Greek. I will focus here primarily on occurrences of the collocation that follow the clause they modify. This has the benefit

---

In this chapter, I am not distinguishing between εἰ μή and ἐὰν μή, since, pragmatically, they accomplish the same function. In Greek conditional clauses, as noted by Tjen, the choice of conditional particle is related to the grammatical requirements of the mood of the dependent verb, i.e., εἰ for the indicative and optative and ἐάν for the subjunctive. Anwar Tjen, *On Conditionals in the Greek Pentateuch: A Study of Translation Syntax*, LHBOTS 515 (New York: T&T Clark, 2012), 35–36. My research in the papyri and the translated books of the LXX confirms that this is the case (with the possible exceptions of [1] Sib. Or. 3.6011: εἰ μή + κ[αταβῃ] is a postulated editorial restoration of the text and [2] Ps 18:14: the manuscript tradition attests both to ἐὰν μή + indicative, which is preferred by Göttingen, and to ἐὰν μή + subjunctive).

1. See BDF, §376; K-G 2.2:487; Dana and Mantey, *Manual Grammar*, §§216–17; Antonius N. Jannaris, *An Historical Greek Grammar: Chiefly of the Attic Dialect* (New York: Macmillan, 1897; repr., Hildesheim: Olms, 1968), 407–8; Porter, *Idioms*, 209; Smyth, §2346; Winer, *New Testament Greek*, 599–600; Zerwick, *Biblical Greek*, §468; Gerry Wakker, *Conditions and Conditionals: An Investigation of Ancient Greek*, ASCP 3 (Amsterdam: Gieben, 1994), 283–84; Frederick William Danker, *The Concise Greek-English Lexicon of the New Testament* (Chicago: University Of Chicago Press, 2009), s.v. "ἐάν, εἰ"; BDAG, s.v. "ἐάν, εἰ"; LSJ, s.v. "εἰ," VII.3.a; L-N, s.v. "ἐάν, εἰ μή"; *GELS*, s.v. "εἰ."

of narrowing the discussion and of providing an implicit comparison to ἀλλά, which is the topic of the next chapter.

## 3.1. Exceptives and Negated Conditionals

Before investigating the use of εἰ/ἐὰν μή in early Koine, one should observe what appears to be the collocation's spectrum of use. The discourse-marking exceptive function of the collocation is a natural extension of the interaction between the semantics of its constituent parts, εἰ/ἐάν and μή, and certain contexts.[2] What may be observed in third to first centuries BCE Greek is a continuum that has negated conditional (non-DM) εἰ/ἐὰν μή at one end and exceptive (DM) εἰ/ἐὰν μή, which is not concerned with communicating a negated conditional, on the other end. Between these

2. Negated conditionals typically implicate exceptions to the statements they modify. In English, e.g., in the sentence "You will not get dessert *if* you do *not* eat your vegetables," the negated conditional implicitly informs the recipient of the exception to the otherwise set-in-stone "You will not get dessert." The terms "implicate" and "implicitly" are important. The communicative effect of a negated conditional differs from that of an exceptive. In the example just given, the negated conditional confirms the preceding claim; it does not counter it. The negated conditional provides the condition that makes what precedes a true claim. Its content can be regarded as an exception, but it is not communicated as such. An exceptive, on the other hand, *explicitly counters* the preceding claim and offers the exception, e.g., "You will not get dessert *unless* you eat your vegetables." The exceptive explicitly counters the truth claim of the preceding. The focus is now on the condition that reverses the polarity of the preceding. A similar example is given by Barbara Dancygier and Eve Sweetser, "I'll be happy if you don't fail" versus "I'll be happy unless you fail" (*Mental Spaces in Grammar: Conditional Constructions*, CSL 108 [Cambridge: Cambridge University Press, 2005], 188). They also note that, in English, "unless" and "if not," though sharing certain features, are not interchangeable. It may sometimes be small, but there is a difference of communicative intent and what is implicated and explicated between negated conditional clauses and exceptive clauses. Consider the following: "Marking an essay is tedious if it is not well-formatted" versus "Marking an essay is tedious unless it is well-formatted." Here, the negated conditional and the exceptive effect rather different meanings. The example with the negated conditional is true enough—it is tedious to mark a poorly formatted essay. It may be tedious for other reasons as well, but such is not precluded by the negated conditional. The exceptive, on the other hand, does preclude any other possible worlds. To claim that marking an essay is tedious *unless* it is well-formatted is to say that marking a well-formatted essay is *not* tedious (a claim that would be disputed by lecturers everywhere). This is an altogether different claim from that of the nearly identical example with the negated conditional. For more on this, see the discussion on Deut 11:28 below.

two ends of the spectrum is where most occurrences of εἰ/ἐὰν μή reside, that is, in a position that allows for the collocation to be interpreted as either a negated conditional that carries an exceptive implication or an exceptive that is concerned with communicating a condition.

1. Negated Conditional: Deuteronomy 11:28
   (11:27) τὴν εὐλογίαν, ἐὰν ἀκούσητε τὰς ἐντολὰς κυρίου τοῦ θεοῦ ὑμῶν, ὅσας ἐγὼ ἐντέλλομαι ὑμῖν σήμερον, (28) καὶ τὴν κατάραν, ἐὰν μὴ ἀκούσητε τὰς ἐντολὰς κυρίου τοῦ θεοῦ ὑμῶν
   (11:27) The blessing, if you hear the commandments of the Lord your God, as many as I command you today. (28) And the curse, *if* you do *not* hear the commandments of the Lord your God.

2. Negated Conditional/Exceptive: P.Lond. 7.2007
   οὐ μὴ βόσκω τὰς ὗς ἐὰν μή μοι τὸν μισθὸν ἀποδῶις τετραμήνου.
   I will not tend to the animals *unless* you pay/*if* you do *not* pay me four months' worth of wages!

3. Exceptive: Daniel 2:11
   καὶ οὐδείς ἐστιν, ὅς δηλώσει ταῦτα, εἰ μή τις ἄγγελος
   And there is no one who will make these things clear *except* some angel.

This spectrum of use should not be taken as evidence for three separate yet related uses of the collocation of εἰ/ἐάν and μή. Rather, it represents the two related functions of εἰ/ἐὰν μή at the two ends of the spectrum—negated conditional and exceptive DM—and a shared space comprising contexts of use that are suitable to either. The shared space typically contains occurrences of εἰ/ἐὰν μή that occur with a scope over a clause or adverbial phrase rather than a noun phrase.[3] This is due to the overlap between a negated conditional clause, which can implicate an exceptive, and a clausal exceptive, which assumes a condition.[4] Therefore, the contexts in which εἰ/ἐὰν μή introduces a clause-level exception are absolutely exceptive, but one can clearly perceive by them the overlap and relationship between the DM εἰ/ἐὰν μή and the simple negated conditional.[5] It

3. The distinction to be made here is between free and connected exceptives. See the discussion in §3.4.2 below.

4. See the discussion and examples in n. 2 above.

5. This is why Tjen, in his work on conditionals in the LXX Pentateuch (*On Conditionals*, 86–87, 98), always refers to postposed εἰ/ἐὰν μή as a conditional with an

should be noted that the position of the negative particle will sometimes help in differentiating the two, as it will tend to stand before that which it is negating when not a part of the DM.[6] Thus, the ἐὰν μή in P.Lond. 7.2007 is likely an occurrence of the DM, as one would otherwise expect the negator to occur directly before the verb. The positioning of ἐὰν μή in Deut 11:28 is ambiguous, however, and context must be the deciding factor.

Despite the close relationship between negated conditionals and exceptive markers, they do present their content differently. Consider Deut 11:28 in context:

> (11:26) Ἰδοὺ ἐγὼ δίδωμι ἐνώπιον ὑμῶν σήμερον εὐλογίαν καὶ κατάραν, (27) τὴν εὐλογίαν, ἐὰν ἀκούσητε τὰς ἐντολὰς κυρίου τοῦ θεοῦ ὑμῶν, ὅσας ἐγὼ ἐντέλλομαι ὑμῖν σήμερον, (28) καὶ τὴν κατάραν, <u>ἐὰν μὴ</u> ἀκούσητε τὰς ἐντολὰς κυρίου τοῦ θεοῦ ὑμῶν, ὅσας ἐγὼ ἐντέλλομαι ὑμῖν σήμερον, καὶ πλανηθῆτε ἀπὸ τῆς ὁδοῦ, ἧς ἐνετειλάμην ὑμῖν, πορευθέντες λατρεύειν θεοῖς ἑτέροις, οἷς οὐκ οἴδατε.
> (11:26) Pay attention! I am giving before you today a blessing and a curse! (27) The blessing, if you hear the commandments of the Lord your God, as many as I command you today. (28) And the curse, *ean me* you hear the commandments of the Lord your God, as many as I command you today, and you are led astray from the way, which I commanded you, going to serve other gods, which you do not know.

While one could translate 11:28 as "And the curse, *unless* you hear the commandments of the Lord your God," it is more probable given the context that it is meant to be read not as an exceptive but rather as a negated conditional statement without an exceptive nuance. The purpose of the statement is not to communicate the exception to the curse but to detail what actions will bring about the curse. This is made clear by the parallel in verse 27, which details the actions that will bring about the blessing: "The blessing, if you hear the commandments of the Lord your God." Thus, verse 28 should be understood in the same way, explaining how the curse may be brought about: "And the curse, *if* you do *not* hear the commandments of the Lord your God." The effect of the negative operator μή (the only new element in 11:28a) is a much more salient relation, given the

---

exceptive nuance; he is simply viewing the collocation from the other side of the spectrum. However, as I discuss in n. 2 above and also below, it is important to note the functional differences between its use as a DM and as a negated conditional.

6. BDF, §433.

context, than an exception. Because the reader's attention is drawn to the polarity inversion in verse 28 (contrasting with v. 27), ἐὰν μή is disallowed its usual discourse-marking function. It is not signaling an exception; instead, it is signaling the condition for receiving the curse.

Moreover, if ἐὰν μή were regarded as an exceptive DM in Deut 11:28, the communicative intent of the statement would change. It would no longer focus on the actions that will bring about the curse but rather on detailing the exception, that is, actions that will allow Israel to avoid the curse. The negated conditional and the exceptive DM result in two different mental representations of the discourse, as they present the information and its relation to the preceding in slightly different ways. Negated conditionals do not explicitly counter the truth-propositional content of the preceding, rather they provide the condition that brings about the preceding proposition. Exceptives, on the other hand, as will be observed in this chapter, explicitly signal a counter to the truth-propositional content of the preceding and focus on the potential inversion of the situation.[7]

Therefore, it is important to distinguish between the two functions of εἰ/ἐὰν μή. While they are certainly related and do exist on the same spectrum, sharing a space of suitable contexts of use, they have distinct purposes and guide the reader down two different mental processing routes.[8]

## 3.2. Oath Formulas and Affirmations

The use of εἰ/ἐὰν μή in oath formulas and affirmations merits a brief mention. A few occurrences of the collocation are used not to mark exception nor to indicate a negated conditional but rather to make an oath. This is a Hebraism, imitating the Hebrew oath formula אם־לא, which by extension, is also found in nonoath affirmations.[9] Examples may be found in 3 Kgdms 21:23; 4 Kgdms 5:20; Ezek 17:16, 19; and Jer 15:11. Whether a Greek reader would have understood what was being communicated is difficult to know for certain, though Zerwick argues the formula was intelligible Greek based on the use of εἰ to signal an emphatic negation in the

7. See, e.g., the examples given in n. 2 above.

8. It is expected that they are related. DMs often arise in a language from non-DMs repeatedly being used idiomatically in certain contexts. See Lewis, "Discourse markers," 52; Waltereit, "Rise of Discourse Markers," 66.

9. *BHRG*, 296, 310; Joüon, §165*c*, *e*, *g*–*h*, *j*; GKC, §149.

form of an oath in 3 Kgdms 1:52 despite the lack of אם in the MT.[10] Even more difficult to ascertain is whether the translators were consciously using εἰ/ἐὰν μή in this way or whether they simply did not understand this function of אם־לא and thus resorted to a literal representation of it.

### 3.3. The Use of εἰ μή and ἐὰν μή in the Papyri

In what follows, I investigate a representative sample of postposed εἰ/ἐὰν μή and also two examples of preposed εἰ/ἐὰν μή. My purpose in examining the latter is to demonstrate that the core function of εἰ/ἐὰν μή is consistent regardless of position but also that positioning does pragmatically affect the communicative act.

#### 3.3.1. P.Lond. 7.2007 (248 BCE [postulated])

Horos writes to Pemenas, an associate of Zenon's, about a salary dispute with a swineherd. Horos describes the situation and then asks Pemenas to appeal to Zenon to send the demanded funds.

> (1) ῟Ωρος Πεμενῆτι χαίρειν. Ἑριενοῦφις \ὁ ὑοφορβὸς/ ἀπεχώρησεν ἐπὶ τὸν βωμὸν τοῦ βασιλέως, λέγων ὅ̣τι οὐ μὴ βόσκω τὰς ὗς ἐὰν μή μοι τὸν μισθὸν ἀποδῶις τετραμήνου, λέγων ὅτι ναύτης εἰμί, οὐθείς με μὴ δύνηται ἅψα̣σ̣θαι οὐδὲ ἀναγκάσαι βόσκειν τὰς ὑμετέρας ὗς. καλῶς ἂν οὖν ποιήσαις ἐντυχὼν Ζήνωνι καὶ εἴπας αὐτῶι περὶ τοῦ ὀψωνίου ὅπως ἂν ἡμῖν ἀπο[σ]τ̣είληι ἵνα ἄνθρωπος μὴ ἀπέλθηι ἀλλὰ βόσκηι̣.
> (1) Horos to Pemenas. Greetings. Herianouphis, the swineherd, withdrew to the altar of the king saying "I will never tend to the sows *ean mē* you pay me four months' worth of wages," and "I am a sailor! No one would be able to lay hands on me or force me to tend to your sows!" So, please appeal to Zenon and talk to him about the salary so that he may send it to us in order that the man would not leave but would tend.

Herianouphis, the swineherd whose demands were the impetus of this letter, is rather clear on what he wants and the lengths he is willing to go to get it. By stating "I will never tend to the swine," Herianouphis makes

10. Zerwick, *Biblical Greek*, §400. On the Hebraism, also see Winer, *New Testament Greek*, 627; F. C. Conybeare and St. George Stock, *A Grammar of Septuagint Greek* (New York: Ginn, 1905; repr., Grand Rapids: Zondervan, 1980), §§101–2; *GELS*, s.v. "ἐάν."

an absolute claim—there is no possible future in which he will care for the animals. It is interesting, then, that an exceptive clause follows, completely negating the claim: if he is paid four months' worth of wages, then he *will* do his job. By communicating the absolute statement first and then following it with the exceptive, Herianouphis counters the truth-propositional content of the preceding. The claim that he will not tend to the animals turns out to be not necessarily true; there is an exception that, if realized, reverses the polarity of the claim. This exceptive relation requires the recipient of the communication to fix their mental representation of the discourse, since it significantly changes the nature of the information being communicated. There is nothing ambiguous about "I will never tend to the swine." Without explicit instructions to do so, the recipient will not process the claim with an exceptive framework already in mind. Because of this, the resulting mental representation of the discourse would not leave any room for the possibility that Herianouphis will do his job. Therefore, when the reader processes the exceptive clause following the claim, it is not as simple as building on top of and relating the new information of the exceptive clause to the already constructed mental representation. This new information counters and thereby necessarily alters the recipient's understanding of the communication; it changes the nature of the established mental representation. The recipient must process the exceptive clause as a *correction* to what was previously processed and stored. This results in a "fix" to the mental representation. The original processing of the claim as absolute is countered, and the prior information is now, in a sense, modalized—the reader recognizes that the original claim is contingent on whether or not the action communicated by the ἐὰν μή clause is realized. If it is, then the polarity of the preceding claim is reversed (i.e., "I *will* tend to the swine"). In other words, the exceptive relation informs the recipient that, in fact, Herianouphis *may* or *may not* tend to the animals, despite the wording of the claim prior to the exceptive clause.

By requiring the hearer or reader to go back and "fix" their mental representation of the discourse, the exceptive relation slows down the building of it. This cognitive processing route naturally highlights the exception itself, both its content and its bearing on the communicative act, as it is the very cause of the delay. This would therefore appear to be the pragmatic purpose in presenting the information in this way and is certainly the case here. Herianouphis is most concerned with being paid. He thus uses an ἐὰν μή clause and places it after the statement it modifies, drawing attention to and highlighting its content and the correction it bears on the discourse.

Herianouphis could have presented the same propositional content by other means. He could have framed the statement "I will never tend to the swine" with the *ἐὰν μή* clause: "*ἐὰν μή* you pay me four months' wages, I will never tend to the swine." Or he could have foregone the exception altogether: "I will tend to the swine if you pay me." However, presenting the information in these ways does not achieve the same pragmatic effect of drawing the attention to the content of the *ἐὰν μή* clause or the rhetorical effect of starting with the absolute claim. Framing the claim with the exceptive clause presents the exceptive relation as background information that provides a frame of reference for what follows and thus does not force a correction to the hearer's/reader's mental representation. This also has the effect of lessening the force of the following claim. Foregoing the exceptive altogether results in a straightforward communication that does not require any significant amount of extra processing effort. It also lacks the force that starting with the absolute claim "I will never tend to the swine" brings to the communication. The claim is evocative and counterexpectational. As such, it is intended to achieve a reaction in the hearer/reader. Thus, Herianouphis's choice to use a postposed exceptive clause is a rhetorically and pragmatically motivated one. It allows him first to use a strong, evocative absolute claim, which communicates the seriousness of the situation, and then draws the recipient's attention to that which counters and (in hindsight) mitigates the claim and to what Herianouphis conceived of as the most salient information: being paid his wages.

### 3.3.2. P.Cair.Zen. 3.59509 (Mid-Third Century BCE)

The author, Somoelis, is a guard in Philadelphia. He writes to Zenon about a couple of business matters as well as some pressing issues for which he needs Zenon's assistance. The penultimate issue Somoelis raises is the need for another granary, as the year's crop is too much for the current granary, which Somoelis guards. This, then, leads into the final issue, which is, presumably, the most pressing to Somoelis: his lack of resources for feeding his family.

> καὶ εἰ δυνατ[όν ἐστι]ν, προσκατασκεύασον θησαυρόν·[ὁ γὰρ ὑ]πάρχων οὐχ ἱκαν[ός ἐστι] χωρεῖν τὸν σῖτον τὸν ἐνιαυτὸν [τοῦ]τον. φυλάσσω δὲ καὶ τ[ὸν] τηνεῖ θησαυρὸν λαμβάνων οὐθέν, [οἱ δ]ὲ ἐκ Φιλαδελφείας δίδ[ουσ]ίν μοι πυ(ροῦ) ἀρτ(άβας) α ∠. οὐχ ἱκανὸν οὖν [ἐστ]ιν οὐδὲ τὰ παιδάρια [διαβό]σ̣κειν, <u>εἰ μὴ</u> αὐτός τι προσεργάζο[μαι]. εὐτύχει.

(10) And if it is possible, provide a granary. For, the present one is not sufficient to hold this year's grain. Now, I am also guarding the granary there,[11] taking nothing, but those from Philadelphia give me one and a half artabs of grain. So, it is not enough, not even to feed the children, *ei mē* I earn (15) something in addition. Farewell.

Somoelis reports that he receives one and a half artabs of grain for guarding the granary. This, however, is not sufficient for his needs. Thus, at the end of his letter, he writes that it is not enough, *not even to feed the children*! This is an evocative statement that is sure to get Zenon's attention (and hopefully his pity). However, Somoelis does not end the letter there. Instead, he counters his claim: "εἰ μή I earn something in addition." While Someolis's current earnings truly are not enough to provide for his family, the exceptive clause forces the reader to modalize the absolute claim: It *could* be enough, *if* the right circumstances come about—in this case, if Somoelis earns something in addition. Thus, even though the claim that he is not making enough money is a true one, the modalizing effect of the exceptive relation counters the truth-propositional content by communicating a situation that, *if realized*, reverses the polarity of the original claim (i.e., "It is not enough" becomes "It is enough"). Moreover, this is where Somoelis wants to direct Zenon's attention. He needs to earn something more in order to feed his children, and Zenon is able to provide a means for him to do that. The sentence could have been written with the εἰ μή clause at the beginning ("εἰ μή I earn something in addition, it is not enough, not even to feed the children."), which would communicate the same propositional content. However, by placing the εἰ μή clause after the claim it modifies, Somoelis is able to use an unmitigated evocative claim, presumably with the hope of effecting a reaction in his reader. The εἰ μή clause is then naturally highlighted. By altering or "fixing" the reader's mental representation and providing the one exception—the answer—to the problem just stated, the reader's attention is drawn to it as especially salient information.

### 3.3.3. P.Cair.Zen. 3.59393 (Mid-Third Century BCE)

A potential buyer has approached Apollonios about purchasing Zenon's horse. Apollonios, however, does not know how much Zenon wants for

11. Presumably, this refers to a granary in Philadelphia, despite the distal adverb. See the final comment in LSJ, s.v. "τηνεῖ."

the horse. So, he writes to Zenon, informing him of the buyer and asking that he respond and inform Apollonios of the price.

> (1) Ἀπολλώνιος Ζήνωνι χαίρειν. προσῆλθέν μοι ὠνητὴς περὶ τοῦ ἵππου τοῦ μεγάλου τοῦ (5) παρὰ σοῦ, ἐγὼ δὲ οὐ δύναμαι περιεργάσασθαι περὶ τῆς τιμῆς, ἐὰν μὴ παρὰ σοῦ ἀκούσω. σὺ οὖν γράψον μοι πόσου σοι πρατέος ἐστί. σὺ οὖν γράψον μοι, εἰμὶ γὰρ ἐν (10) Κερκῆι, ὅπως ἂν εἰδῶ. ἔρρωσο.
> (1) Apollonios to Zenon. Greetings. A buyer came to me concerning the big (5) horse of yours. Now, I am not able to bargain concerning the price, *ean mē* I hear from you. So, write to me how much it is to be sold for you. So, write (10) to me, for I am in Kerke, in order that I may know. Farewell.

Zenon's response is crucial for Apollonios to move forward, and thus Apollonios wants to draw his intended reader's attention to that fact. He does this by using an ἐὰν μή clause that counters the truth-propositional content of the statement that precedes. Apollonios is, in fact, able to bargain; he only needs information from Zenon to do so. Thus, the importance of Zenon responding, in relation to Apollonios's ability to bargain, is highlighted. Further evidence that Zenon's response is the most important issue at hand is corroborated by the content immediately following the exceptive clause. Apollonios moves to the next step in the argument, which is explicitly linked to the preceding (signaled by οὖν). He picks up on the preceding salient information and addresses Zenon with an imperative: "So, write to me how much it is to be sold for you!" Not only does Apollonios highlight the need of a response by using a postposed exceptive clause but he also exploits where his reader's attention has been drawn by immediately continuing the idea that was introduced in the exceptive clause.

### 3.3.4. SB 18.13171 (101 BCE)

The author, Philammon, writes to two military commanders, Pates and Pachrates, with regard to the upcoming joining together of soldier companies. He provides instructions to them to be ready to travel.

> (5) ἐπεὶ γέγραφεν ὁ πατὴρ συνμίσγειν ἄγων τοὺς Κροκοδιλοπολίτας καὶ ὑμᾶς ἅμα, ὀρθῶς ποιήσετε καὶ κεχαρισμένως ἑτοίμους γενέσθαι ὡς ἅμα ἡμῖν συνεξορμήσητε, ἐὰν (10) δὲ μὴ ἔχητε πλοῖον, συνεμβήσητε ἅμα ἡμῖν εἰς τὴν ῥῶμσιν.
> (5) Since the father has written to join forces by leading those from Krokodilopolis and you all together, please also be ready so that you may set

> out together with us. Now, *ean mē* you have a boat, you should embark (10) together with us in the reed boat.

This instance of ἐὰν μή differs from the previous examples in that the ἐὰν μή clause is positioned before the content it modifies. As mentioned earlier, this chapter is concerned with postposed εἰ/ἐὰν μή rather than preposed. However, in order to fully appreciate the use and effect of exceptives, it is beneficial to consider briefly their preposed occurrences.

By using ἐὰν μή, the author signals to his readers that what follows provides a counter to the main clause: The letter recipients should embark together with the author and those with him in the reed boat; however, if the conditions of the ἐὰν μή clause are satisfied, if the readers do, in fact, have a boat, then the assertion of the main clause is canceled—they will *not* embark together. This is in line with the basic function of the DM observed thus far. Pragmatically, however, the information is processed differently. By preposing the exceptive clause, the readers are led down a straightforward mental processing route. When they first read the ἐὰν μή clause, they understand it as a frame of reference into which the following material will be integrated. Though the DM signals a counter to the main clause, because it precedes that content, the readers necessarily process it with the exception already in mind. Thus, they are never required to "fix" their mental representation of the discourse. This, then, does not result in any special attention being drawn to the exceptive clause; it is simply regarded as offline material that provides a frame of reference for what follows. Also, it is worth noting that, unlike most of the above examples, the primary assertion can in no way be considered evocative or counterexpectational. "You should embark together with us in the reed boat" does not grab the readers' attention in the way that "I will not tend to the animals" or "It is not enough, not even to feed the children" do. This nonevocative proposition correlates well with the use of the preposed exceptive; by virtue of first framing the assertion with the exceptive, any claim made is already necessarily mitigated. Because of this, the rhetorical force that can be felt in the above examples is not felt here.[12]

---

12. Regarding the difference here between how εἰ/ἐὰν μή interacts with *irrealis* versus *realis*, see the discussion in n. 58 below. Given the discussion there and the content of this letter, it may be the case that this is not an example of the exceptive DM but rather simply a negated conditional with an exceptive implication. It is, admittedly, hard to tell (and likely depends on whether one takes συνεμβήσητε as a mitigated

### 3.3.5. P.Erasm. 1.16 (4 BCE)

In this letter, the author writes to a certain Athenodoros.[13] The first matter that needs to be brought to Athenodoros's attention is how the author will transport some wheat to Koma in order to sell it. All boats have been commandeered by the army, so the author is in a bind.

> (5) [γίγνωσκε ὅτι τὰ] πλοῖα ἅπαντα ἐγγεγάρευται ὑπὸ τῆς λεγεῶνος καὶ οὐχ εὑρίσκω πως νῦν [τὸν πυρὸν] μεταγάγω εἰς Κόμα· εἰ οὖν ἐ[θέλεις] πέμψον μοι πλοῖον ἕ̣τερον ὅπως π̣[ορεύωμαι] εἰς τὴν̣ Κόμα· ἐὰν γὰρ μὴ μεταχθῆ[ι ὁ πυρὸς] ἄ̣πρατος ἔσται·
> (5) Know that all the boats have been taken into service by the legion, and now, I cannot find by what means I could take the wheat to Koma. So, if you are willing, send another boat to me so that I may go to Koma. For, *ean mē* the wheat is taken, it will be impossible to sell.

Similar to example 4, ἐὰν μή is positioned before the proposition it modifies. The DM signals to the reader that its host utterance provides a counter to the following assertion. If the wheat is transported to Koma, then the polarity of the claim "it will be impossible to sell" is reversed. Pragmatically, by preposing the ἐὰν μή clause, a frame of reference is given that provides background information to the more salient assertion "it will be impossible to sell." The reader is able to process this without having to correct the mental representation of the discourse.

Had the ἐὰν μή clause been postposed ("It will be impossible to sell, ἐὰν μή the wheat is taken"), then the reader would have been led down a different mental processing route. The reader would have taken the statement at face value, without any exceptions being made. However, upon encountering the ἐὰν μή clause, the construction of the mental representation would be slowed down, as the new information necessarily alters the reader's impression of what they already processed, forcing the reader to understand the preceding claim as contingent rather than absolute. In addition, the postposed ἐὰν μή clause would not be background information but highlighted foreground material. More of the focus would be on the information communicated in the exceptive clause and the effect it has

---

exhortation ["you should"] or a potential situation ["you may"]). If it is not the DM, the above discussion is not without purpose. It still demonstrates, by contrast, the unique effect of the postposed DM.

13. The name of the author is unknown.

on the previously asserted information. This, then, may be the reason the exceptive is preposed here.

This example would seem, at first glance, to be a good candidate for postposed εἰ/ἐὰν μή. Owing to its additional pragmatic and rhetorical effects, it appears to be better suited to contexts in which the primary assertion is evocative or counterexpectational, whereas preposed εἰ/ἐὰν μή may be better suited for the more mundane assertions, so to speak. A postposed exceptive could have made good sense here. However, the request for a boat had already been made, making the exceptive clause weaker rhetorically (as it does not lead into the imperative but follows it). Rather, the most salient information in the sentence in question is the assertion itself—it alerts Athenodoros to the seriousness of the situation—though it is not particularly evocative, given the context of a letter concerning business matters. The salience of the primary assertion may be further confirmed by what follows in the letter, though it is fragmentary. The next two sentences are γάρ clauses, referencing a farmer from Nea Agora (a village in the region where the letter was written), the army, and the price (of something).[14] It seems plausible that the author is elaborating on why it is impossible to sell in the region, thus building upon the primary assertion from the sentence under investigation.

### 3.3.6. The Function of εἰ/ἐὰν μή as Evinced in the Papyri

In examples 1–3 above, εἰ/ἐὰν μή signals that the information communicated by its host utterance is an exception to the preceding assertion. This, in itself, is not surprising. What is significant, though, is how the exceptive marker can achieve different pragmatic effects depending on its position relative to the content it modifies. When an exceptive is preposed, as in examples 4 and 5, it provides a frame of reference for what follows (e.g., "Unless you eat your vegetables, you will not get dessert"). The reader first processes the exception and then processes what follows with that exception already in mind. This allows for a fairly straightforward construction of the mental representation of the discourse. The reader first processes the exceptive clause, which then prepares them to properly process the following content by providing a framework into which the following

14. Lines 9–11 read: ἕκαστος γὰρ . . .[ -ca.?- ] [.]ου γεωργὸς ἀπὸ Νέας Ἀγορᾶ<ς>· οἱ γὰρ ἑλόντες τὴν νέαν ἤδη οἱ πλείονες πεδ̣ . .τα[ι] τὴν τιμὴν τῆι λεγεῶνι̣·

information may be integrated. Because the exception is processed first, it does not counter previously processed information but instead informs the reader to regard what follows as a contingent claim. This, then, allows them to build the mental representation of the discourse without encountering any processing hindrances. The preposed exceptive clause serves as background information that provides a frame of reference for the more salient part of the communication.

On the other hand, postposed exceptives affect the mental representation differently. Since these exceptive clauses occur after the utterances they modify, they cannot provide a frame of reference into which the preceding assertion may be integrated. Thus, the effect of a postposed exceptive is to signal to the reader that its host utterance counters the truth-propositional content of what preceded. This was observed in each of the above examples. The reader first processes the assertion (e.g., example 1: "I will not tend to the sows") and takes its truth-propositional content at face value. In constructing the mental representation of the discourse, the reader naturally assumes the information they are incorporating is an absolute claim. When the reader then encounters the exceptive clause ("*unless* you pay me four months' worth of wages"), the constructed mental representation is revealed to be inadequate, as there is new information that requires a reassessment of the preceding claim and its truth-propositional content. Thus, when the exceptions signaled by εἰ/ἐὰν μή are integrated into the mental representation, it results in the modalization of the preceding absolute claim. The prior information is recognized as being necessarily contingent on whether the action communicated by the exceptive clause is realized. If the conditions of the exceptive clause are met, then the polarity of the preceding claim is inverted (thus, "I *will* tend to the sows"). Therefore, when the reader processes the exceptive clause, the mental representation of the original claim ("I will not tend to the sows") is reevaluated and restructured. The claim's truth-propositional content has been countered, and the claim is viewed not as absolute but as contingent. In other words, since the mental representation of the discourse had previously understood the claim to be absolute, the reader must now correct and reconstruct the mental representation to incorporate the exception's effect on the communication as a whole.

Because of this, the building of the mental representation of the discourse is slowed down. The reader cannot simply add the new information to the old but must process how the new information affects and *changes* what was already processed. The natural effect of forcing the reader through this mental processing route is to draw extra attention to the excepted content, to that which required the reassessment and restructuring of the mental representation, and its effect on the communication as a whole. Thus, whereas the pragmatic purpose of *pre*posing an exceptive clause is to provide a frame of reference for foreground content, the pragmatic purpose of *post*posing an exceptive clause is to highlight it because it contains what the communicator conceives of as the most salient information, both in terms of content and in terms of how it affects the communication as a whole.[15]

Lastly, it is worth noting what appear to be the typical contexts in which postposed εἰ/ἐὰν μή occur. It seems there is a correlation between evocative or counterexpectational utterances and postposed εἰ/ἐὰν μή. As was observed in examples 1 and 2 there is a certain rhetorical force that is achieved by first allowing the reader to process an evocative or counterexpectational proposition and then countering that claim with εἰ/ἐὰν μή. The communicator is able to produce statements likely to elicit a reaction in their recipient and that will convey the gravity of the situation; they are then able to counter the statement, highlighting the desired conditions that will produce the inverse reality than that which was priorly communicated. This is not a necessary contextual condition for postposed εἰ/ἐὰν μή, as example 3 evinces, but it is understandable why it may be typical, as strong, evocative claims naturally, and often necessarily, lend themselves to being corrected.[16]

---

15. Thus, by "most salient information," I am not only referring to the propositional content of the exceptive utterance but also to the communicative value and effect of the whole (i.e., the intended resultant effect on the reader's mental representation of the interaction between the propositional content, the exceptive relation, and the preceding context).

16. It is possible that the claim is counterexpectational. However, it is impossible to know without more knowledge of the situation and what, if any, expectations Zenon had regarding the horse, its sale, and Apollonios's involvement. Preposed εἰ/ἐὰν μή, as mentioned above in the discussions of examples 4 and 5, does not benefit from this rhetorical synergy, since it lessens the rhetorical force of whatever follows it by framing the utterance for the reader up front.

## 3.4. The Use of εἰ μή and ἐὰν μή in the LXX

There are eighteen occurrences of postposed DM εἰ μή and twenty-one of postposed DM ἐὰν μή in the LXX.[17] A representative sample of this corpus is investigated here.

### 3.4.1. Examples from the LXX

The first example comes from Gen 32:26 (27 MT). Jacob has been wrestling with a man through the night, and the man is trying to get away.

> *καὶ εἶπεν αὐτῷ Ἀπόστειλόν με· ἀνέβη γὰρ ὁ ὄρθρος. ὁ δὲ εἶπεν Οὐ μή σε ἀποστείλω, ἐὰν μή με εὐλογήσῃς.*
> And he said to him, "Send me away, for the dawn rose." But he (Jacob) said, "I will never send you away *ean mē* you bless me."

> ויאמר שלחי כי עלה השחר ויאמר לא אשלחך כי אם־ברכתני
> And he said, "Let me go, for the dawn has risen." But he (Jacob) said, "I will not let you go unless you bless me."

The point of Jacob's statement is to force a blessing out of the man with whom he is wrestling. That is where the focus lies; that is what Jacob desires and without which he will not leave. The man, the recipient of the communication, first hears and processes the absolute statement that Jacob will not send him away. This is an evocative assertion, especially considering the emphatic negation construction. Jacob then follows this with ἐὰν μή, signaling to the recipient that what follows will counter the truth-propositional content of the preceding. This, in turn, will require the recipient to reassess his understanding of the previously processed proposition. Jacob's claim, as it turns out, is not true, as Jacob will indeed send the man away if a certain condition, giving a blessing, is met. Thus, the mental representation of the discourse is restructured to account for the modalizing effect of the ἐὰν μή clause on the communication. This mental process, requiring more cogni-

---

17. εἰ μή: Gen 3:11; Deut 32:27, 30; Judg 11:10; 2 Kgdms 19:14; 3 Kgdms 17:1; 21:23; Neh 2:2, 12; Esth 6:6; Ps 105:23; Eccl 3:12, 22; 8:15; Job 22:20; Sir 16:2; Jer 15:11; Dan 2:11. ἐὰν μή: Gen 32:26; 42:15, 37; 43:3, 5; Exod 3:19; Lev 22:6; 25:20; Josh 7:12; 1 Kgdms 27:1; 2 Kgdms 3:13; 2 Chr 23:6; Esth 2:14; 1 Macc 3:53; Ps 136:6 (twice); Prov 4:16; Amos 3:3, 4, 7; Mic 3:8. Thus, in this count, I have not included occurrences where the two particles are acting independently.

tive effort than simply constructing one's mental representation, results in drawing attention to the exception that required this mental route be taken. There are simpler ways to communicate the same propositional content, but by using ἐὰν μή and positioning it after the statement it modifies, Jacob is able to first make an evocative claim and then draw his hearer's attention to the condition that can reverse the claim if fulfilled, namely, receiving the blessing, which is what Jacob wants to ensure takes place.

The Hebrew requires the reader go through the same mental route. The collocation כי אם frequently communicates an exceptive relation between pieces of information.[18] Thus, in this instance, one can observe the LXX translator representing the Hebrew in a fitting manner.[19] The Greek DM both quantitatively represents the Hebrew and guides the reader on a similar mental processing route as כי אם. However, in order to represent the Hebrew in this way, the translator did have to make a decision. Depending on what is being communicated in context, כי אם can be appropriately rendered by collocations such as ἐὰν μή, ἀλλά, ἀλλ᾽ ἤ, or ὅτι εἰ/ἐάν—each with its own particular constraint and nuance. In order to know how to translate the Hebrew DM in this instance, the translator had to consider its function within its context.

Another example may be found in Exod 3:19. Here, the Lord is instructing Moses as to what he will say to the elders of Israel in order to convince them to leave Egypt with him.

> ἐγὼ δὲ οἶδα ὅτι οὐ προήσεταί ὑμᾶς Φαραὼ βασιλεὺς Αἰγύπτου πορευθῆναι, <u>ἐὰν μὴ</u> μετὰ χειρὸς κραταιᾶς.

---

18. Barry Louis Bandstra, "The Syntax of Particle 'KY' in Biblical Hebrew and Ugaritic" (PhD diss., Yale University, 1982), 154–56; Carl Martin Follingstad, *Deictic Viewpoint in Biblical Hebrew Text: A Syntagmatic and Paradigmatic Analysis of the Particle* כי (Dallas: SIL International, 2001), 156–57, 290–92; 563–66; GKC, §163*c*; *HALOT*, s.v. "כִּי־אִם"; BDB, s.v. "כִּי אִם־"; Wilhem Gesenius, *Hebräisches und Aramäisches Handwörterbuch über das Alte Testament*, s.v. "כִּי אִם." Follingstad (156–57, 563–66) argues that "exceptive" is not the most accurate description of כי אם, but it should rather be regarded as signaling "exhaustive-listing focus," functionally similar to, though not identical with, the English phrase "but only." This description has the benefit of being able to account for most if not all uses of the collocation (when functioning as a collocation, rather than two independent particles).

19. John William Wevers, *Notes on the Greek Text of Genesis*, SCS 35 (Atlanta: Scholars Press, 1993), 542: "[The Genesis translator] understood this rightly as ἐὰν μή 'except, unless.'"

> Now, I know that pharaoh, king of Egypt, will not give you up to go, *ean mē* with a mighty hand.
>
> ואני ידעתי כי לא־יתן אתכם מלך מצרים להלך ולא ביד חזקה
> And I know that the king of Egypt will not let you go—and not with a strong hand.

Similar to Gen 32:26, ἐὰν μή is preceded by an evocative utterance ("pharaoh will not give you up to go") that the recipient will process as an absolute claim. The DM then signals a counter to the truth-propositional content of the preceding: If a mighty hand is involved, then pharaoh *will* give you up. The reader must reassess their mental representation of the discourse and restructure it with the exceptive clause and its effect on the utterance in mind. The reader comes away from the text with a sense of how utterly committed the pharaoh will be to keeping the people of Israel in Egypt, owing to the evocative claim that was first processed as an absolute; moreover, the reader's attention is drawn to the information conveyed by the exceptive clause, regarding it as the most salient part of the utterance. This works well in the context. In the following verse, the theme of "a mighty hand" is continued. The Lord reveals that he is the one who will make the possible event, that which is contingent upon the realization of the exception, a reality: "And when I stretch out my hand, I will strike the Egyptians with all of my wonders that I will perform among them, and after these things, he will send you out."

The MT's ולא ביד חזקה is unclear, but it seems to differ notably from the Greek.[20] The Hebrew text does not appear to convey an exceptive relation.[21] Rather, ולא ביד חזקה communicates the hopelessness of Moses convincing the pharaoh to send the people away.[22] Assuming the LXX translator's source was similar to MT Exod 3:19, this instance of ἐὰν μή evinces a translator who not only rendered the text into idiomatic Greek despite the lack of any lexical motivation (in no way can ἐάν be regarded as an equivalent to conjunctive *vav*) but who also, it would seem, translated with an eye as to what was contextually appropriate. As Anwar Tjen

---

20. Consider just a few of the different ways this clause is translated: "not even under force" (NET), "no, not by a mighty hand" (KJV), "unless compelled by a mighty hand" (NRSV; see also HCSB, ESV, Nouvelle Edition de Genève, Schlachter).

21. Though see the final discussion below for this possibility.

22. I.e., "The king will not let you go—not (even) with a strong hand."

writes concerning this issue, "Overall, the LXX rendering … fits the context very well here."[23] As a result, one may observe two different meanings arising out of the two texts. In the LXX, the exception is given, providing a counter to the previous claim and preparing the reader for 3:20. In the MT, depending on one's interpretation, verse 19 either speaks about the hopelessness of the situation with regard to the strong hand of man, which verse 20 answers with YHWH stretching out *his* hand, or verse 19 presents the situation from pharaoh's inner viewpoint.[24] Granted, it is possible, as Alain Le Boulluec and Pierre Sandevoir suggest, that the LXX translator was influenced by other uses of ביד חזקה and בחזק יד, where the collocation clearly refers to divine power, and harmonized this occurrence.[25] Even so, if the *Vorlage* mirrored the text of the MT, the resultant translation and its appropriateness to the context can only be explained by a translator who was cognizant of the surrounding discourse and was willing to translate according to his understanding and interpretation of it.

Two other possible explanations bear mentioning. First, in one manuscript, 4Q13 (4QExod[b]), the Hebrew reads כי אם ביד חזקה rather than ולא ביד חזקה. Regarding this manuscript, Frank Moore Cross writes, "We must conclude that 4QExod[b] is a collateral witness to the textual family which provided the *Vorlage* of the Old Greek translation."[26] Despite Cross's confidence, without any further textual evidence, it is difficult to make such a firm claim. However, the possibility that the Greek translator's *Vorlage* mirrored 4Q13 rather than the MT must be considered. Second, there are two occurrences in the MT, 2 Sam 13:26 and 2 Kgs 5:17, where the text attests to וָלֹא and seems to indicate at least a negated conditional if not an

---

23. Tjen, *On Conditionals*, 102. So also John William Wevers, *Notes on the Greek Text of Exodus*, SCS 30 (Atlanta: Scholars Press, 1990), 37.

24. John I. Durham, *Exodus*, WBC 3 (Waco, TX: Word, 1992), 40: "The Pharaoh will have no thought of granting such a wish and could not even be forced to do so by any power men could muster. Thus will Yahweh bring his power into action." Or, the narrator is providing the reader insight into pharaoh's perspective, making the reader feel "the full impress of the storyteller's ironic emphasis on Pharaoh's blind obstinacy" (Peter Addinall, "Exodus III 19B and the Interpretation of Biblical Narrative," *VT* 49 [1999]: 297).

25. They provide the references 6:1; 13:3, 9, 14, 16 in Alain Le Boulluec and Pierre Sandevoir, *L'Exode*, Bd'A 2 (Paris: Cerf, 1989), 94.

26. Cross, "4QExodb," in *Qumran Cave 4: VII, Genesis to Numbers*, ed. Eugene Ulrich and Frank Moore Cross, DJD XII (Oxford: Clarendon, 1994), 84.

exceptive relation.[27] It is at least possible, though unlikely, that the translator read וְלֹא here as וְלֻא, understood the rare וְלֻא as an exceptive marker, and thus rendered the text accordingly.[28]

In 1 Kgdms 27:1, David realizes that he will fall into Saul's hands soon. However, he does see a possible circumstance that would keep such an event from happening.

> Καὶ εἶπεν Δαυιδ ἐν τῇ καρδίᾳ αὐτοῦ λέγων Νῦν προστεθήσομαι ἐν ἡμέρᾳ μιᾷ εἰς χεῖρας Σαουλ, καὶ οὐκ ἔστιν μοι ἀγαθόν, ἐὰν μὴ σωθῶ εἰς γῆν ἀλλοφύλων καὶ ἀνῇ Σαουλ τοῦ ζητεῖν με εἰς πᾶν ὅριον Ισραηλ, καὶ σωθήσομαι ἐκ χειρὸς αὐτοῦ.
> And David thought, "I will now be added into Saul's hands in one day, and there is nothing good for me, *ean mē* I deliver myself into the land of foreigners and Saul gives up seeking me inside every border of Israel, and I will be saved from his hand."

> ויאמר דוד אל־לבו עתה אספה יום־אחד ביד־שאול אין־לי טוב כי המלט אמלט אל־ארץ פלשתים ונואש ממני שאול לבקשני עוד בכל־גבול ישראל ונמלטתי מידו
> And David thought, "Now, I will be swept away one day by the hand of Saul. There is no good for me, but I will escape to the land of the Philistines. And Saul will cease searching for me any longer in all the territory of Israel, and I will escape from his hand."

The DM signals to the reader that the content following provides the exception, the answer, to the problem just posed. The exceptive counters the truth-propositional content of the preceding and modalizes the mental representation: David may or may not fall into Saul's hands; it depends on whether he escapes to a foreign land. The gravity of the situation is expressed by the strong claim ("I will now be added into Saul's hands … and there is nothing good for me"), which the reader first processes as absolute. What David regards as the most salient information, the exception that he will find deliverance from Saul if he escapes to a foreign land, is highlighted by nature of its placement after the claim it counters.

---

27. See *HALOT*, s.v. "לֹא" (§12); Gesenius, *Hebräisches und Aramäisches Handwörterbuch*, s.v. "לֹא" (§4).

28. Gesenius wonders whether וְלֹא may be able to convey an exceptive relation and cites this verse. Gesenius, *Hebräisches und Aramäisches Handwörterbuch*, s.v. "לֹא." This is argued by Jean Louis Ska, though not decisively ("Note sur la traduction de *welō'* en Exode III 19b," *VT* 44 [1994]: 60–65).

The underlying Hebrew, if matching the MT, contains a כי where the Greek translator used ἐὰν μή. This is not what one would normally expect. The exceptive DM does not quantitatively represent כי, and crucially, it does not qualitatively represent it either.[29] Thus, it cannot be said that ἐὰν μή was lexically motivated by כי. That is not to say that ἐὰν μή is a bad rendering, especially given the context, but for the translator to choose ἐὰν μή here required more than simply choosing something to represent כי. The translation demonstrates an awareness of the broader context and an interpretation of the relations between propositions.[30] The translator did not disregard כי, as a subordinating collocation that draws attention to its host utterance is used, but neither did the translator feel the need to use a stereotyped or lexically equivalent rendering.[31]

A slightly different example may be observed in Esth 6:6. Here, King Artaxerxes asks Haman what to do for someone he wants to honor. The reader is then given a glimpse into Haman's thinking, who is convinced that the king intends on honoring him.

εἶπεν δὲ ὁ βασιλεὺς τῷ Ἁμάν Τί ποιήσω τῷ ἀνθρώπῳ, ὃν ἐγὼ θέλω δοξάσαι; εἶπεν δὲ ἐν ἑαυτῷ ὁ Ἁμάν Τίνα θέλει ὁ βασιλεὺς δοξάσαι εἰ μὴ ἐμέ;

29. Although it has been demonstrated that כי following a negated clause can signal a counterstatement or carry an adversative force (see Christian S. Locatell, "Grammatical Polysemy in the Hebrew Bible: A Cognitive Linguistic Approach to כי" [PhD diss., University of Stellenbosch, 2017], §9.1.2.4; Follingstad, *Deictic Viewpoint*, 156–57, 280–81; Bandstra, "Syntax of Particle 'KY,'" 149–58; *BHRG*, 303; Tjen, *On Conditionals*, 11; Aejmelaeus, "Function and Interpretation of כי," 175–76), this function is by no means the most typical of כי (Follingstad [412] observes that adversative כי accounts for only 6 percent of all occurrences of the DM in Joshua–2 Kings and Isa 1–39. Locatell [257] also cites a 6 percent statistic for adversative כי. Bandstra [149], in his investigation of כי in the Pentateuch and Psalms [1,480 occurrences of כי], states that adversative כי only occurs in 101 instances [6.8 percent]) nor is it equivalent to signaling an exceptive relation. As Follingstad (156–57, 290–92; 563–66) and Bandstra (154–56) both demonstrate, "exceptive כי" only occurs in the כי אם construction.

30. Anneli Aejmelaeus recognizes this at least to a certain extent. She writes, "It is quite obvious that the translator could distinguish the temporal and adversative cases of כי—the rendering ἐὰν μή in 1 Sam 27:1 also speaks for this" ("The Septuagint of 1 Samuel," in *On the Trail of the Septuagint Translators*, 132).

31. The highlighting effect of ἐὰν μή does mirror well the cognitive effects of Follingstad's assertive polar focus category for כי in contexts such as this. See Follingstad, *Deictic Viewpoint*, 156–57, 569–79. Also, Follingstad (631) places the כי in 1 Kgdms 27:1 in this category.

Now, the king said the Haman, "What should I do for the man whom I want to honor?" But Haman thought to himself, "Whom does the king wish to honor *ei me* me?!"

ויבוא המן ויאמר לו המלך מה־לעשות באיש אשר המלך חפץ ביקרו ויאמר המן בלבו למי יחפץ המלך לעשות יקר יותר ממני
And Haman entered, and the king said to him, "What to do for the man whom the king wishes to honor?" And Haman thought, "Whom does the king wish to honor more than me?"

Two differences are immediately observable. First, a question precedes the DM rather than an assertion. Second, there is no modalizing effect on the mental representation as a result of processing the exceptive clause (the resulting mental representation does not envision the king as maybe honoring a man). Both of these will be discussed in turn.

With regard to the first difference, the effect of the exceptive's interaction with a preceding interrogative would appear to be to require the reader to fill in "No one!" before "εἰ μὴ ἐμέ." Note that, if the interrogative were not joined to an exceptive, a simple question would be asked: Whom does the king wish to honor? It is by virtue of the exceptive relation that the interrogative is not a simple request for information. Rather, it is transformed to imply that there is, in fact, no one (other than Haman) that the king would want to honor. In this case, then, the DM does not counter the truth-propositional content of a preceding assertion as in earlier examples but rather *of the implication that arises*.[32] Thus, though this example occurs in a different kind of context, the core function is the same as what has been observed in the previous examples: εἰ/ἐὰν μή signals a counter to truth-propositional content.

Concerning the second difference, the lack of a modalizing effect, this may come down to an issue of scope. Whereas the other occurrences of the DM have introduced dependent clauses that provide exceptions to the event or action of the preceding claim, this use of εἰ μή occurs with a narrower scope, introducing a noun phrase that does not provide an exception to the verbal event but rather to the object of it. As was consistently

32. Recall the discussion in §1.2.2.4. Discourse markers effect a relation between their host utterances and information within the recipient's mental representation. Thus, that information may originate in the explicit text or may come from other sources, such as implications and assumptions.

seen above, the natural effect of an exception applied to a verb phrase is to create a condition, which in turn modalizes the verb. The natural effect of an exception applied to a nominal element, even an implied one, will not be the same.[33] With this scope, the effect of the exception is to provide a counter to an established set. In this case, it is the implied all-encompassing set "no one." There is no person whom the king would want to honor. Thus, Haman, believing that the king would, in fact, want to honor him, must introduce himself as excepted from that set. By using εἰ μὴ ἐμέ, it is communicated that the referent of ἐμέ, though a member of the previously mentioned set, has been excepted. The effect on the reader's mental representation of the discourse is largely the same as the other instances of εἰ/ἐὰν μή, save for the modalizing effect. Upon encountering εἰ μή, the reader understands that they must fill out the utterance with the implied "no one!" and then, once the exception is processed, reassesses the mental representation, realizing that it is inadequate for the direction the communication has taken. The reader thus restructures the mental representation to account for the exceptive's effect on the utterance as a whole. Additionally, as with many of the previous examples, the claim preceding the exceptive clause is evocative. In this context, it accurately portrays Haman's high opinion of himself. As with every other occurrence of εἰ/ἐὰν μή examined thus far, the pragmatic effect of the postposed exceptive DM is to highlight it, thereby drawing the reader's attention to what Haman considered to be the most salient information and how it relates to the communication as a whole.[34]

Assuming the translator's *Vorlage* reflected the MT here, the Greek makes a contextually appropriate, though lexically unmotivated, move that is not mirrored in the Hebrew text. Haman's thought, "Whom does

33. This may be observed in English by the different DMs used based on what is being excepted. "Unless," which signals an exceptive conditional clause (= "except if"), is only used to counter verb phrases. Owing to this, it will never occur at the word level. (In English, "unless" and "except if" are not entirely coextensive [though largely so].) However, for our purposes here, the distinction is immaterial. For a discussion on the two DMs, see Dancygier and Sweetser, *Mental Spaces*, 193–200. "Except," on the other hand, may occur at any level of the discourse, as long as there is not a conditional element within the exception (if there is, "unless" will be used or "except if," but the latter is fairly rare). In English, then, the natural effects that arise from an exception's interaction with its context are uniquely paired with different DMs.

34. Regarding how this occurrence of εἰ μή differs from a similar utterance in Esth 5:12, see the discussion and description of ἀλλ᾽ ἤ in ch. 5 and how it differs from exceptives but also shares overlap with them.

the king wish to honor more than me?" directs the reader down a different mental processing route. There is no exception, no counter to the truth-propositional content of the preceding. Instead, the utterance implies that there are or may be others the king would like to honor, but Haman is the one whom the king wishes to honor the most. The underlying Hebrew, יותר ממני, is a comparative construction, not an exceptive one, and the translator could have rendered it into Greek as such. The fact that the translator did not, barring a difference in the source text, evinces an interpretive move that results in painting a slightly more arrogant picture of Haman than is presented in the Hebrew text.

The last LXX example comes from Dan 2:11. Here, the Chaldeans are responding to Nebuchadnezzar's earlier statement in verse 9 that if they are able to tell him what vision he saw during the night, then he will know that they are able to disclose its meaning to him.

> καὶ ὁ λόγος, ὃν ζητεῖς, βασιλεῦ, βαρύς ἐστι καὶ ἐπίδοξος, καὶ οὐδείς ἐστιν, ὅς δηλώσει ταῦτα, εἰ μή τις ἄγγελος, οὗ οὐκ ἔστι κατοικητήριον μετὰ πάσης σαρκός· ὅθεν οὐκ ἐνδέχεται γενέσθαι καθάπερ οἴει.
> And the thing that you are seeking, O king, is heavy and glorious, and there is no one who will make these things clear *ei me* some angel, whose dwelling place is not with any flesh. Therefore, it is not possible that it happen, as you suppose.

> ומלתא די־מלכה שאל יקירה ואחרן לא איתי די יחונה קדם מלכא להן אלהין די מדרהון עם־בשרא לא איתוהי
> And the thing that the king is asking is difficult, and there is no one who will declare it to the king except the gods, whose dwelling is not with flesh.

The Chaldeans are not able to accomplish what Nebuchadnezzar desires, and they are convinced that there is no one who could meet the king's standard. After communicating this to the king, they introduce the exceptive: "εἰ μή some angel."[35] Like the previous example, a set is first negated ("there is no one") and then a member of that set ("some angel") is introduced as an exception. The DM signals that the content it governs counters the truth-propositional content of the preceding evocative claim. There is, in fact, someone who could do what the king is asking. There is an argumentative purpose in the Chaldeans' presentation. The

35. Regarding the difference in the Theodotionic text, which reads ἀλλ' ἢ θεοί rather than εἰ μή τις ἄγγελος, see the discussion on ἀλλ' ἤ in ch. 5.

exceptive clause following the statement it modifies requires the king to reassess and restructure his mental representation of the discourse. This, in turn, draws his attention to the new information, which communicates that only an other-worldly being could do what the king has asked. By highlighting the information contained within the exceptive clause over against its preceding context, a certain implicature is achieved. The Chaldeans are not suggesting that the king go find an angel to answer his query, rather they are using a pragmatically and rhetorically motivated construction to imply that his request is absurd. This implicature would have been achieved even if the exceptive clause preceded the statement it modified ("Except for some angel, there is no one who will make these things clear."), but the effect of the postposed exceptive clause to allow the evocative "there is no one who will declare it!" be processed and to force a correction to one's mental representation is a much more rhetorically charged method for communicating the idea that the king is preposterously asking the impossible.[36]

### 3.4.2. A Cognitive-Functional Description of εἰ/ἐὰν μή

Based on what has been observed in the LXX, the findings in the papyri are confirmed but also built upon. First, εἰ/ἐὰν μή is not restricted to introducing clauses. Second, when εἰ/ἐὰν μή occurs with a narrow scope, it does not have the effect of modalizing the prior assertion, but rather introduces an excepted member of a previously asserted set. Lastly, it is important to note that the contextual effects are just that—contextual effects. Modalizing prior content and introducing an excepted member of an asserted set are not necessary conditions for the use of εἰ/ἐὰν μή, rather they are effects that naturally arise out of the typical contexts in which the DM occurs. The core pragmatic function of the DM is to introduce an utterance that counters the truth-propositional content of an assertion. This is why one can sometimes find instances of εἰ/ἐὰν μή in which no modalizing seems to take place in the mental representation nor is there an excepted member of a set being introduced (e.g., Ps 105:23 [106:23 MT])[37]—the truth-propositional content of some piece of information within the

36. With regard to the underlying Aramaic, the translator qualitatively represents להן.

37. καὶ εἶπεν τοῦ ἐξολεθρεῦσαι αὐτούς, εἰ μὴ Μωυσῆς ὁ ἐκλεκτὸς αὐτοῦ ἔστη ἐν τῇ θραύσει ἐνώπιον αὐτοῦ τοῦ ἀποστρέψαι τὴν ὀργὴν αὐτοῦ τοῦ μὴ ἐξολεθρεῦσαι. "He spoke

mental representation is countered, but the interaction with the context does not result in any of the typical effects. Thus, postposed εἰ/ἐὰν μή may be described as follows.

The DM εἰ/ἐὰν μή functions within the cognitive domain and signals an exception, informing the reader that the DM's host utterance is relevant in that it counters the truth-propositional content of recently acquired information in the reader's mental representation (typically, the utterance to which εἰ/ἐὰν μή is subordinate). The natural effect of the DM, as a result of its placement, is to instruct the reader to correct and "fix"—to restructure—the mental representation of the discourse. When the DM occurs with a moderate scope, the previously processed information is typically modalized, resulting in its truth-propositional content being viewed as contingent on whether the material introduced by εἰ/ἐὰν μή is realized. When the DM occurs with a narrow scope, it typically introduces an excepted member of a previously asserted set, thus countering the truth-propositional content of previously processed information. The postposing of the DM results in an extra processing requirement that has the natural effect of highlighting the exception and drawing the reader's attention to it and its relation to the communicative act. In addition, postposed εἰ/ἐὰν μή is uniquely suited to providing exceptions to evocative or counterexpectational claims. Owing to the interaction between the DM and the evocative claim, there is a strong rhetorical force that arises from such a construction and may be a further factor, in addition to the pragmatics, in the choice to use it.

That εἰ/ἐὰν μή marks exception is not a new insight. However, the pragmatics of exception are rarely discussed. Rarer still is a discussion on the pragmatics of postposing the exceptive clause. Runge has made the most significant contribution, providing a detailed discussion of εἰ/ἐὰν μή. Regarding the interaction between the exceptive and a negated set or an interrogative, he writes:

> The negation serves to remove all possible candidates from the data set, essentially wiping the slate clean by negation (e.g., *no one* can do X = X cannot be done by *anyone*). The interrogative asks a question that expects a negative answer (e.g., "Who can do this?" "No one"). In both cases, this protasis has the effect of predicating a set of items that will

---

in order to destroy them—except Moses, his chosen one, stood in the destruction before him to turn his wrath away so as not to destroy."

> be completely removed from consideration. This is where the exceptive/restrictive apodosis comes in. One member from this negated set is presented as the exception. Only after reading the apodosis does the reader realize that the totality of the initial protasis is not the complete story. There is one item singled out for consideration.... The original set contains all of the potential members that could fill in the blank. Negating this entire set temporarily removes all of the members from consideration. Finally we reach the exceptive element that adds back one member ... from the original set. This one item could have just as easily been stated in a simple affirmative statement.... The effect of creating a set removing all members of the set, and then adding one member back is to attract additional attention to the excepted item, attention that it would not otherwise have received.[38]

Just as was observed above, a set is negated (e.g., Dan 2:11, "There is no one who will make these things clear"), which completely removes everything that comprises the set from consideration. Then, an element is introduced ("εἰ μή some angel") that would have been included in the original set of "no one," thus drawing the reader's attention to its exclusion from the negated set.[39] Granted, Runge does not mention the frequent modalizing contextual effect of εἰ/ἐὰν μή that has been observed in the LXX and papyri, but he is concerned with the New Testament corpus, in which the DM seems to signal exceptions to nonverbal elements (i.e., typical contexts of set-membership type exception) more frequently. In addition, though he does not speak of the DM's core pragmatic function explicitly in terms of countering truth-propositional content, it seems that is nonetheless what he observes in the New Testament. Consider his remarks on Mark 6:4–5: "The negated statements in v. 4 and v. 5 *are not entirely true*; exceptions to each statement are added in the apodosis.... The statements are essentially incomplete until one reads the apodoses; *it is only then that they are accurate*."[40] Further, his comments on 2 Tim 2:5: "The apodosis provides

38. *DGGNT*, 85–86.

39. There are examples in the LXX of an interrogative and an exceptive (as was observed above in Esth 6:6), though they are much fewer than a negation and an exceptive. See Gen 3:11; Lev 25:20; Deut 32:30; 1 Macc 3:53; Amos 3:3, 4. There are a handful of examples in the LXX and papyri of a positive statement preceding an exceptive (e.g., P.Cair.Zen.3.59304; P.Lond.7.1977; P.Mich.1.56; P.Erasm.1.1; Gen 42:37; Deut 32:27; Pss 105:23; 136:6). These are atypical in their construction, but there does not seem to be any functional difference from the typical [NEG + εἰ/ἐὰν μή].

40. *DGGNT*, 87, emphasis added.

the restriction *that makes the counterpoint true*."[41] Finally, his discussion of Rom 7:7: "The statement that Paul 'did not know sin' *is not completely true*. He did indeed know sin, and he knew it through of the law.... Similarly, his statement about not knowing covetousness *is not entirely true apart from the apodosis*."[42]

Outside of biblical studies, insightful cross-linguistic work on exceptives has been produced that further illuminates what we observe in Koine Greek. Isabel Pérez-Jiménez and Norberto Moreno-Quibén, based on their work on Spanish exceptives, discuss the exceptive DM's relation to the information it connects. They write:

> [Connected exceptives] operate semantically at the subsentential level.[43] They operate on universal quantifier phrases, restricting their domain of quantification. The complement of the exceptive marker denotes a set of entities that must be subtracted from the domain of quantification of the universal quantifier in order for the proposition denoted by the whole sentence to be true.[44]

The scope is narrow (subsentential) and introduces an excepted member of a set that counters the truth-propositional content of the previously processed information. This matches the nonverbal exceptive DMs that were observed in the LXX and also corresponds to Runge's claims with regard to εἰ/ἐὰν μή in the New Testament. In addition, Pérez-Jiménez

41. *DGGNT*, 89, emphasis added.

42. *DGGNT*, 89, emphasis added.

43. Isabel Pérez-Jiménez and Norberto Moreno-Quibén, among others, differentiate between "connected exceptives" and "free exceptives." Free exceptives differ from connected exceptives in that they "operate semantically at the clause level by introducing exceptions to generality claims" ("On the Syntax of *Exceptions*: Evidence from Spanish," *Lingua* 122 [2012]: 585). In simple terms, if the DM's host utterance is a noun phrase, it is a connected exceptive; if the host utterance is adverbial in nature, e.g., a prepositional phrase, it is a free exceptive. Apart from the slight difference in scope and syntactic requirements, the use and function of the two types of exceptives are identical, and thus the distinction between the two is immaterial. This seems to be the opinion of Friederike Moltmann as well. She begins her investigation of exceptives by stating, "In the following, I will assume that connected and free [exceptive phrases] have essentially the same semantics, though they involve different syntactic structures as the basis for their interpretation." ("Exception Sentences and Polyadic Quantification," *Linguistics and Philosophy* 18 [1995]: 225).

44. Pérez-Jiménez and Moreno-Quibén, "On the Syntax of *Exceptions*," 585, 590.

and Moreno-Quibén observe that, prototypically, connected exceptives signal relations between their host utterances and universal quantifier phrases, such as "everyone" or "no one."[45] This tendency matches Runge's description of exceptives in the New Testament and was observed in both examples of connected exceptives in the LXX data, Esth 6:6 and Dan 2:11.

Friederike Moltmann has also contributed to scholarship on exceptives that correct nominal and phrasal elements. First, she recognizes the truth-propositional countering function of exceptives as their first basic property. She states:

> The first basic semantic property of exception constructions is that they carry what I call the "**negative condition**"; that is, simply, the exceptions have to be exceptions. More precisely, applying the predicate to the exceptions should yield the opposite truth value from applying the predicate to nonexceptions.[46]

She also discusses the issue of set inclusion and writes, "The second basic semantic property of [exceptive phrases] is that the entities that are specified as the exceptions must fall under the restriction of the associated quantifier."[47] She further argues that the material corrected by the exceptive must denote a universal or negative universal quantifier such as "ever, all, or no" and that the exceptive's host utterance must be a unique set.[48] Again, this matches what was seen in Esther and Daniel.

With respect to clause-level exceptions, Moltmann treats "unless" and "except if" clauses similarly to exceptions with a narrow scope, in that she maintains an exception is being made to a universal quantifier set. A brief summary of the argument will have to suffice, as she relies primarily on symbolic logic to make her case, which is out of the linguistic purview of this investigation. She posits an epistemic information state that comprises "a set of facts which represent the current information shared by speaker and addressee."[49] A given proposition will hold based on the information available in that information state. Moltmann then asserts the property

45. Pérez-Jiménez and Moreno-Quibén, "On the Syntax of *Exceptions*," 585–86.

46. Moltmann, "Exception Sentences," 225, emphasis original.

47. Moltmann, "Exception Sentences," 226. See also her discussion on 238–39.

48. Moltmann, "Exception Sentences," 227, 234–35.

49. Moltmann, "Exception Sentences," 257. This is essentially the same concept as what was briefly mentioned in §1.2.2.4 regarding shared knowledge and assumptions between communicator and recipient.

of persistence: "A proposition p is persistent if and only if the following holds: If p is true in an information state s, then p is true in every extension of s."[50] In a sense, a proposition that is persistent creates a universal quantifier, in that the proposition holds and is true in any extension of the information state. Thus, for Moltmann, "unless" (and "except if") clauses "act as [exceptive phrases] to this quantifier."[51] When an "unless" clause is applied to a persistent proposition, she argues that "it takes away the extensions of [the information state] at which [the unless clause] holds."[52] Whether set theory does equally apply to nonverbal and verbal exceptives is ultimately not the most important point.[53] What is crucial to understand is that, by taking away the extensions of the information state, an exception to a whole sentence cancels the persistence of the proposition, thereby rendering it *not necessarily true* or, in other words, modalizing it, as was observed in the examples from the papyri and LXX.

The highlighting effect of a postposed exceptive has also been recognized by others. For instance, Barbara Dancygier and Eve Sweetser write, "*Unless*, like *if*, is useful in exploring trains of thought; in particular, it has special utility in highlighting exceptional possibilities amid larger contrary generalizations."[54] As previously discussed, this highlighting effect is realized owing to the extra processing requirement of postposed exceptives,

---

50. Moltmann, "Exception Sentences," 257.

51. Moltmann, "Exception Sentences," 257.

52. Moltmann, "Exception Sentences," 257.

53. While I do find Moltmann's argument convincing to a certain extent, the inner logic of the concept of exception is not identical with the effect of an exceptive on a recipient's processing of the discourse. It thus seems to me that it is more productive to investigate and explain how humans process exceptions than the logical theory behind them, which may not even be subconsciously realized by the recipient processing the utterance.

54. Dancygier and Sweetser, *Mental Spaces*, 185, emphasis original. Dancygier and Sweetser also claim that "unless" clauses set up marked space that contains abnormal alternatives that are likely an afterthought (186). This, however, is based on the context of the examples used and is not an inherent feature of "unless" (or, at least, prosodically unmarked "unless"). That is to say, the value of exceptions differs based on the surrounding information structure. Typically, the exception that follows the assertion it corrects comprises the focal information, as observed in this chapter. However, in certain contexts, at least in English, where the absolute claim contains the focal information and the exception contains the old, given information, the exceptive structure allows for a strong absolute claim that is subsequently "toned down" by the reassertion of the given information in a postposed exceptive clause.

as they require a restructuring of the recipient's mental representation. Dancygier and Sweetser even note that preposed "unless" clauses (though this is applicable to any exceptive) are often used because "it is easier for readers or listeners to process the negative stance and even to process it counterfactually; an initial distanced unless-clause is a clear notice that they no longer have to compare with the previous network for contradictions in stance towards the same material."[55] This ease of processing that naturally does not grab the recipient's attention exists in stark contrast to the high processing cost of postposed exceptives that naturally does grab the recipient's attention.[56]

With regard to the highlighting effect of postposed εἰ/ἐὰν μή in particular, Runge provides the following analogy in his discussion on the collocation in Matt. 12:24 ("He does not cast out demons εἰ μή by Beelzebul, the ruler of demons"):

> This rhetorical process is analogous to having a table full of items, sweeping all of them onto the floor, and then placing the one item you are interested in back onto the table all by itself. You could have simply pointed to the item and said, "This is the one I am interested in." But sweeping every item onto the floor has a dramatic effect, on top of making a mess! Removing everything and then adding back the important item that was already there attracts far more attention to it than just pointing to it on the table. The same holds for negation + exception/restriction. The same propositional content could have been more easily communicated using a positive statement: "This one casts out demons by Beezebul, the ruler of demons." Saying that he does not cast out demons (which by itself is untrue) and then

55. Dancygier and Sweetser, *Mental Spaces*, 199.

56. This is an issue of iconic ordering and markedness. According to Dik, the iconicity principal stipulates that "Clauses should preferably be ordered in accordance with the conceptual or temporal relations which obtain between the facts or States of Affairs which they designate" (*TFG 2*, 134). It would appear that postposed exceptions, like conditionals (see *TFG 1*, 400; *TFG 2*, 133–34), are conceptually prior to the information they modify. This seems evident given that preposed exceptives do not force a restructuring of the mental representation but postposed exceptives do by countering the truth-propositional content of previously processed information. Therefore, because exceptives should come before the content they modify, according to the iconicity principle, when they do not, it results in a marked ordering that necessarily draws the recipient's attention.

> adding the means by which he does do it effectively highlights the excepted element.[57]

His observations in the New Testament further confirm what was observed in the examples above. The function of εἰ/ἐὰν μή to signal a counter to truth-propositional content and the highlighting effect that naturally arises from postposing an exceptive clause are clearly demonstrated in both early Koine and the New Testament literature.[58]

In this section, I have provided a description of εἰ/ἐὰν μή in early Koine that finds support in wider linguistic research. Overall, my research confirms the traditional treatment of the collocation, though it does offer a more precise linguistic understanding of its core pragmatic function than is normally found. In addition, I have demonstrated that there are typical and predictable contextual effects that arise as the reader processes the whole utterance, namely modalizing the verbal event prior to the DM or signaling an exception to a prior set, depending on the scope of the DM.

### 3.4.3. εἰ/ἐὰν μή and LXX Translation Technique

In the majority of occurrences, εἰ/ἐὰν μή in the LXX qualitatively represents an element of the underlying Hebrew; כי אם and אם־לא alone account for twenty-five of the thirty-nine occurrences of postposed εἰ/ἐὰν μή in the

57. *DGGNT*, 84.

58. One may ask how εἰ/ἐὰν μή, if it signals a counter to truth-propositional content, can interact with information that is counterfactual or in which the mood of the countered proposition is *irrealis* (and thus not making a truth claim). Examples of this are rare, but P.Mich. 1.56 (251–248 BCE) contains an example of a counterfactual followed by εἰ μή, and P.Lond. 7.1977 (253 BCE) contains an example of an *irrealis* proposition followed by the collocation. Based on Wakker's work on Greek conditionals (see Wakker, *Conditions and Conditionals*, 212–14, for a discussion of negated conditionals that follow counterfactuals), these are not occurrences of the exceptive DM but rather of the individual conditional and negative particles. However, if one wanted to maintain that these are instances of the DM, then I would suggest that whereas truth-propositional content is countered in [*realis* + εἰ/ἐὰν μή], in [*irrealis*/counterfactual + εἰ/ἐὰν(?) μή], the DM signals that its host utterance cancels out the countered information entirely. Either way, Wakker's comment on one of the purposes of using εἰ μή in this way mirrors well the effect of the DM observed throughout this chapter: "As events that do not take place have significance only in comparison to what does happen, it makes what actually happens [the content of the εἰ μή clause] stand out in sharper relief" (214).

translated books of the LXX.[59] However, if one were to stop there in their description, that the majority of εἰ/ἐὰν μή simply mirrors functionally synonymous constructions in the Hebrew (and, in the case of אם־לא, lexically represents), the more interesting and important point would be missed. Despite the functional equivalence with and the translational fittingness of the Greek DM, to say that εἰ/ἐὰν μή is only a qualitative representation of the Hebrew markers is reductionistic. One may observe this most clearly with regard to כי אם. As discussed with regard to Gen 32:26, the collocation is not completely coextensive with any one Greek DM.[60] Additionally, its interactions with various types of contexts allows for the realization of different (though related) relations between the linked pieces of information, such as emphatic, corrective, exceptive, restrictive, or if the two particles are acting independently of each other, the whole range of functions of כי and אם.[61] The translator thus had a plethora of options available to them for functionally and formally representing the Hebrew such as μήν/δή, ἀλλά, εἰ/ἐὰν μή, ἀλλ᾽ ἤ, ὅτι/διότι εἰ/ἐάν, and εἰ/ἐὰν γάρ. However, in order to employ any one of these options, aside from literal representation of the individual lexemes, it would have been necessary that the translator determine the Hebrew collocation's function in its context, which of course required an awareness of the surrounding context on the part of the translator and an assessment of the communicative intent of the discourse. Therefore, it is not enough to say that a translator who uses εἰ/ἐὰν μή to render exceptive כי אם is appropriately qualitatively representing the underlying Hebrew. While that is certainly true, there is much more to it that ought to be recognized. Even when the Hebrew could not reasonably be interpreted any other way than as an exceptive marker, the translator who renders it as such evinces, at the very least, the ability and understanding to look to the immediate context in order to determine how to translate כי אם (if they did not, then each member of the collocation would be rendered literally, e.g., ὅτι εἰ/ἐάν).

Though comprising only a handful of occurrences, the instances in which postposed εἰ/ἐὰν μή is used despite lexical motivation, such as was

59. Thirteen and twelve, respectively.

60. See also n. 32 in ch. 5.

61. See *HALOT*, s.v. "כִּי־אִם"; BDB, s.v. "כִּי אִם־"; Gesenius, *Hebräisches und Aramäisches Handwörterbuch*, s.v. "כִּי אִם". Traditionally, these have been considered separate functions of כי אם but see n. 18 for a brief discussion and reference to Follingstad's work on the DM, which posits a core pragmatic function for the collocation.

observed in Exod 3:19 and Esth 6:6, may provide glimpses into translators who were willing to translate according to their own interpretation of the relations between propositions, with an eye to the broader context, when it suited them to do so.[62] Even in a case such as 1 Sam 27:1, though כי occurring after negated content may signal a counter to the preceding claim, it is not enough to simply state that the translator was able to distinguish this function of כי.[63] The translator had a choice before them and had to make a decision. Thus, even small pieces of data such as this evince translation work informed and motivated by an awareness of the wider context.

In the end, the occurrences of εἰ/ἐὰν μή require one not only to describe what the end product looks like but to also seriously consider how the translation came to be. Whether motivated by a collocation such as כי אם, a particle such as כי, or not lexically motivated at all, the translator had choices available to them based on their understanding of the flow of the discourse.[64] Because of this, the Septuagintalist ought to be encouraged when describing the ad-hoc "method" of the translators to also keep in mind that the translators were not necessarily ignorant of the broader discourse and were willing and able to translate according to their understanding and interpretation of it.

### 3.5. εἰ/ἐὰν μή in the Twelve

There are only four postposed instances of ἐὰν μή in the Twelve (there are no postposed εἰ μή). They occur in Amos 3:3, 4, 7; and Mic 3:8.[65] Amos 3:3 and 4 qualitatively represent the underlying Hebrew בלתי. Amos 3:7 renders כי אם. Micah 3:8, however, is the most interesting occurrence. In the preceding verses, the Lord is pronouncing judgment on false prophets who lead his people astray.

---

62. Other occurrences of nonlexically motivated εἰ/ἐὰν μή may be found in Gen 3:11 and Mic 3:8. Mic 3:8 will be discussed in §3.5.

63. Such is as much as Aejmelaeus says on the matter: "It is quite obvious that the translator could distinguish the temporal and adversative cases of כי—the rendering ἐὰν μή in 1 Sam 27:1 also speaks for this" (Aejmelaeus, "Septuagint of 1 Samuel," 132).

64. This is not to say, of course, that there is not occasional interference from the source text or that the translators did not experience difficulty in understanding and rendering their source text. This certainly does happen and may be clearly seen in instances such as Job 22:20 and Eccl 8:15. Instances such as these are to be expected, but they are the rare exceptions to what has been observed throughout the LXX.

65. Mal 3:10 is not included here as the ἐὰν μή is introducing an oath.

(3:7) And the ones who see dreams will be disgraced, and the diviners will be ridiculed, and they all will speak against them, for there will be no one who listens to them.

(3:8) ἐὰν μὴ ἐγὼ ἐμπλήσω ἰσχὺν ἐν πνεύματι κυρίου καὶ κρίματος καὶ δυναστείας τοῦ ἀπαγγεῖλαι τῷ Ιακωβ ἀσεβείας αὐτοῦ καὶ τῷ Ισραηλ ἁμαρτίας αὐτοῦ.
*ean mē* I fill strength[66] in the spirit of the Lord and of judgment and of lordship to proclaim to Jacob his impious acts and to Israel his sins.

ואולם אנכי מלאתי כח את־רוח יהוה ומשפט וגבורה להגיד ליעקב פשעו ולישראל חטאתו
However, I am filled with strength, namely, with the spirit of YHWH, with judgment, and with might, in order to declare to Jacob his transgression and to Israel his sin.

The underlying Hebrew אולם only occurs here in the Twelve, so it is difficult to know with certainty how the translator understood the particle. Granting that they likely did not regard it as an exceptive, it is odd that they render ואולם with ἐὰν μή, as the two signal rather different relations. In attempting to understand the resultant Greek text, then, there are three possible functions of ἐὰν μή in this instance: Oath formula/affirmation, negated conditional "if not," or postposed exceptive.[67] These will each be addressed in turn.

---

66. It is difficult to understand exactly what is being communicated by ἐγὼ ἐμπλήσω ἰσχύν. Some have rendered it similar to the Hebrew "I am filled with strength" or "I will strengthen myself" (Brenton; W. Edward Glenny, *Micah: A Commentary Based on Micah in Codex Vaticanus*, Septuagint Commentary Series [Leiden: Brill, 2015], 83), but this meaning is alien to the active form of ἐμπίπλημι and would also require ἰσχύν to be in the genitive rather than the accusative (I can find no construction in the LXX or New Testament in which "to be filled with X" is communicated by [ἐμπίπλημι + acc.] instead of [ἐμπίπλημι + gen.]). The accusative that follows ἐμπιπλημι is always the thing being filled. Thus, the resultant meaning of this construction would seem to be that ἰσχύν is being filled up, which is sufficiently nebulous. (Muraoka's entry "to have/take one's fill" for ἐπίπλημι seems more motivated by this occurrence, to try to make sense of it, than by the semantics of the word itself. The other few examples he provides are perfectly normal usages of the verb. *GELS*, s.v. "ἐμπίμπλημι.")

67. For oath formula, see *GELS*, s.v. "ἐάν"; see also Brenton, which renders the collocation as "surely." For negated conditional, see NETS and LES, which render the collocation as "Otherwise" (either this or the translations were influenced by the underlying Hebrew). This seems to also be where Glenny falls, though his rendering of

The first option, oath formula/affirmation, would most likely result in one regarding 3:8 as the prophet Micah's own speech rather than as a continuation of the Lord's pronouncement of judgment. Thus:

> (3:7) And the ones who see dreams will be disgraced, and the diviners will be ridiculed, and they all will speak against them, for there will be no one who listens to them. (8) Surely I will fill strength in the spirit of the Lord and of judgment and of lordship to proclaim to Jacob his impious acts and to Israel his sins.

One immediately wonders, though, how this is an oath. First, the exclamatory formula ζῇ κύριος or ζῶ ἐγώ preceding the oath, as in 4 Kgdms 5:20 and Ezek 17:16, 19, is missing. Granted, the exclamatory formula is likely not necessary, but its absence does not help the argument that ἐὰν μή be regarded as signaling an oath.[68] Second, and more importantly, nothing is being sworn. Verse 8 is not an oath. If anything, whether understood as signaling an oath or affirmation, one would expect a particle of affirmation here such as μήν or δή (μήν does appear in the Lucianic recension, in fact), but there is nothing inherent to the verse that suggests an oath or an affirmation is being made. Thus, the suggestion that ἐὰν μή is functioning in such a way here seems unlikely.[69]

It could be the case that the collocation is simply a negated conditional with an elided phrase (e.g., "Otherwise …" or "If not …"). This happens fairly frequently with εἰ/ἐὰν μή. However, when this occurs, the typical constructions are εἰ δὲ μή, καὶ εἰ μή, and καὶ ἐὰν μή, not εἰ/ἐὰν μή alone.[70] Thus, at its onset, this interpretation seems unlikely. Moreover, one must

---

the collocation as "however" goes beyond what ἐὰν μή signals. See W. Edward Glenny, *Micah: A Commentary Based on Micah in Codex Vaticanus*, Septuagint Commentary Series (Leiden: Brill, 2015), 83. For a postposed exceptive, see LXX.D, which regards 3:7–8 as one sentence and renders ἐὰν μή with "es sei denn" ("unless").

68. E.g., Mal 3:10b, wherein it is clear that an oath is being made: ἐπισκέψασθε δὴ ἐν τούτῳ, λέγει κύριος παντοκράτωρ, ἐὰν μὴ ἀνοίξω ὑμῖν τοὺς καταρράκτας τοῦ οὐρανοῦ καὶ ἐκχεῶ ὑμῖν τὴν εὐλογίαν μου ἕως τοῦ ἱκανωθῆναι· "'Indeed, carefully observe in this,' says the Lord Almighty, 'I will surely open the floodgates of heaven for you and pour out my blessing on you until you are satisfied.'"

69. Glenny writes, "That understanding fits well with the introduction of Micah's resolution to prophesy in the verse, but it does not communicate the contrast between the false prophets and Micah" (Glenny, *Micah*, 83).

70. εἰ δὲ μή: Gen 18:21; 24:49; Exod 32:32; 1 Kgdms 19:17; 2 Kgdms 17:6; 1 Macc 15:31; Sir 5:12; 29:6; Jer 47:5; Dan 3:15. καὶ εἰ μή: Judg 9:15, 20 (twice); 1 Kgdms

ask what potential event is being negated by ἐὰν μή. Contextually, reading ἐὰν μή as a negated conditional with an elided phrase is not coherent, as it would convey the idea that if the false prophets are not disgraced and ridiculed or if the people do not speak against the prophets and do listen to them, then the events of 3:8 will occur. Even given the ambiguous semantics of verse 8, this does not seem to be the purpose of the communication or what makes verse 8 relevant to the discourse.[71] Based, then, on both the lack of a typical construction and the contextual difficulty of making sense of such a reading, ἐὰν μή is likely not meant to be understood here as a negated conditional with an elided phrase.

Lastly, ἐὰν μή may be functioning here as an exceptive marker, signaling a counter to the preceding content. Reading ἐὰν μή in this way significantly alters the communicative intent of LXX Mic 3:8 from its Hebrew source:

> (3:7) And the ones who see dreams will be disgraced, and the diviners will be ridiculed, and they all will speak against them, for there will be no one who listens to them (8) unless I fill strength in the spirit of the Lord and of judgment and of lordship to proclaim to Jacob his impious acts and to Israel his sins.

In this reading, Micah is not the speaker of 3:8; rather, the Lord is continuing his speech from verse 7. LXX.D understands the text in the same way, stating, "In our rendering of the LXX, it is not, as in the MT, the prophet who is speaking, but rather God."[72] Thus, the resulting communication, though the meaning of "I fill strength" is unclear, focuses on the Lord as the force behind true prophets. All of the events of verse 7 will take place; the only exception to this is if the Lord were to act in such a way as to effect a change in the false prophets. The overall rhetorical force of verses 7–8, then, seems to be to convey the idea not that the Lord may effect such a change in the false prophets, but rather that the Lord himself is the one who legitimizes prophets and that he has never been the energizing force behind these prophets, thus disenfranchising them completely. I

---

20:15; 2 Kgdms 13:26; 4 Kgdms 5:17; Sir 12:2; Jer 31:27. καὶ ἐὰν μή: 1 Kgdms 6:9; 20:9; 4 Kgdms 2:10.

71. For the ambiguous semantics, see n. 66 above.

72. German original: "In unserer Wiedergabe der LXX ist nicht, wie im MT, der Prophet der Ich-Sprecher, sondern Gott" (LXX.D 2:2372).

admit that 3:8 is unclear, but the reading suggested here is stronger than the other two interpretations.[73] In fact, the largest hindrance to this reading is the punctuation in the Göttingen LXX and in R-H, which place a full stop at the end of 3:7. Given that the punctuation is not original to the Greek text, I suggest, based on the above discussion, that the most likely and defensible function of *ἐὰν μή* in LXX Mic 3:8 is as an exceptive DM.[74]

The uses of *ἐὰν μή* do not tell us much, but they may provide some small insights into the translator of the Twelve. First, בלתי, which is rendered by *ἐὰν μή* in Amos 3:3, 4, also appears in Hos 13:4. In this instance, it is translated by the rather rare preposition *πάρεξ*. While one may wish to see this as evidence for a different translator, it is possible that *πάρεξ* was simply preferred by the translator for exceptions of set members (Hos 13:4: "there is no one who saves except me") and *ἐὰν μή* was preferred for moderate-scope exceptions. Without more data, it is impossible to have any more certainty. However, the translation of כי אם with *ἐὰν μή* in Amos 3:7 does tell us a bit more. First, it informs us that the translator was aware of context. As previously discussed, כי אם can be properly rendered into Greek by different means depending on how the Hebrew collocation is interacting with a given context.[75] In order to translate כי אם with *ἐὰν μή*, it required at least enough awareness of the movement of the discourse to understand that it was signaling an exception. Second, this is all the more informative as postposed כי אם is also rendered in the Twelve by *ἀλλά* (Amos 8:11), *ἀλλ' ἤ* (Mic 6:8; Zech 4:6), and *διότι* (Hos 9:12; Amos 5:22).[76] The translator was seemingly aware of how the Hebrew DM can allow for the realization of different (though related) relations and was able to translate according to their interpretation of the DM within its context. Even though small, the data do contribute to a developing picture of the translator of the Twelve as one who was aware of more than the most immediate

73. Renaud's description of the oddities in LXX Mic 3:8 is introduced by the relevant admission and lament, "But the whole sentence is very difficult in Greek." See B. Renaud, *La Formation du Livre de Michée: Tradition et Actualisation*, Études bibliques (Pendé: Gabalda et Cie, 1977), 131–32: "Mais toute la phrase est très difficile en grec."

74. One may do well to consider whether the explanation I have put forth here would even be necessary if the Greek texts had been punctuated differently. Indeed, if one ignores the punctuation, it seems to me that the reading LXX.D and I suggest is the most natural way to read Mic 3:7–8.

75. See p. 113 (particularly n. 18) and p. 129.

76. *ἀλλά* and *ἀλλ' ἤ* are discussed in more detail below in chs. 4 and 5, respectively.

context and made decisions in their translation based on that awareness in order to faithfully convey their interpretation of the *Vorlage*.[77]

## 3.6. Conclusion

When εἰ/ἐὰν μή functions as a DM, it signals to the reader that the following information is an exception, a counter, to the truth-propositional content of the recently processed information in the reader's mental representation. This is a necessary pragmatic feature for a language to have, given that asyndeton would be too underencoded for a reader to provide the exceptive relation on their own. Thus, εἰ/ἐὰν μή not only aids readers in the processing task but wholly directs them in their processing effort as to how they should integrate what follows the DM into their mental representation. When the exceptive clause is postposed, it requires the reader to slow down the construction of their mental representation of the discourse and to fix what had previously been processed to reflect its relation to the newly processed exception. The effect of forcing the reader through this mental route is to draw attention to the correcting element, thus highlighting it and its relation to the communicative act as a whole. In this way, the information that tends to occur in postposed exceptive clauses is that which is considered by the speaker or author as most salient in relation to the entire communication.[78] Lastly, the DM interacts with different contexts in a predictable manner. When occurring with a moderate scope, a contextual effect arises by which the previous claim, which would have been processed as an absolute, is modalized. When occurring with a narrow scope, the effect is to introduce an excepted member of a previously established set.

The use of εἰ/ἐὰν μή in the LXX, even when lexically motivated (in most cases), attests to translators who translated according to their

77. One may ask why postposed exceptive ἐὰν μή occurs only in Amos and Micah. It should be remembered, however, that there are only thirty-nine occurrences of postposed DM εἰ/ἐὰν μή in the entirety of the translated books of the LXX. Four out of thirty-nine is more than 10 percent of all occurrences. What we have here is, in fact, an abundance!

78. Granted, without audio recordings, this must be a tentative claim to a certain extent. Even in English there are prosodic cues that signal when a postposed exceptive is not introducing the most salient information. On the whole, however, the claim holds.

interpretation and understanding of the wider context and the relevant relations between propositions. When not lexically motivated, this attestation is magnified, revealing translators who, whether because they preferred their own interpretations, because they did not understand their source text and sought other means of making sense of it, or because they were making explicit what was implicit in their *Vorlagen*, were willing to create texts that guided their readers on mental routes that reflected their own contextual understandings. It is also important to note that, even when lexically motivated, postposed εἰ/ἐὰν μή does not reliably guide one back to the underlying Hebrew.[79] According to the data investigated, the DM could be rendering אם לא, לולי, להן, הן לא, בלתי אם, בלתי, or כי אם. In most cases, when postposed εἰ/ἐὰν μή is lexically motivated more than once in a book (as in Genesis, Leviticus, Deuteronomy, 3 Kingdoms, and the Twelve), it renders more than one of these Hebrew DMs, rather than consistently rendering only one lexeme or collocation.[80] This is not to say that the Hebrew is at times misrepresented. On the contrary, in each of these cases the translators are using a DM that signals a similar processing route to the reader as the DM used in the Hebrew. However, it should be noted that, though the Hebrew often witnesses to different exceptive DMs, these translators decided to use one rather than matching each Hebrew DM with its own dedicated translation in Greek.

With regard to the work of the translator of the Twelve, there is not enough data to inform much of an opinion. However, their ability to appropriately render כי אם in Amos 3:7 and their flexibility in rendering ואולם in Mic 3:8 may attest at least to some contextual awareness. Specifically with regard to ואולם, the Greek and Hebrew do not match lexically nor pragmatically. As there is no linguistic reason to render ואולם with ἐὰν μή, it would seem that the translator understood the Lord to be the speaker, asserting himself as the energizing force behind valid prophets, and that this reading of the text influenced the translator's choice of DM.

---

79. Except when used as a Hebraistic oath formula (in most cases), which seems to consistently render אם לא.

80. The exceptions to this are Nehemiah (two εἰ μή for כי אם) and Ecclesiastes (three εἰ μή for כי אם).

# 4

# ἀλλά

There is a general consensus among grammarians and lexicographers on the core function of ἀλλά: it is primarily regarded as a marker of adversative relations or opposition. For example, J. D. Denniston writes, "General use, as an adversative connecting particle. The adversative force of ἀλλά is usually strong (eliminative or objecting): less frequently, the particle is employed as a weaker (balancing) adversative."[1] Likewise, BDAG states, "Generally adversative particle ... indicating a difference with or contrast to what precedes, in the case of individual clauses as well as whole sentences."[2] The consensus ends, though, in those instances where ἀλλά does not appear to be functioning as an adversative. This is especially problematic as nonadversative ἀλλά is inexplicable and far more prevalent than one would expect if the core function of the DM is to mark adversative relations. Thus, multiple and various explanations are given for its nonadversative uses. Frequently, ἀλλά is described as a marker of emphasis.[3] Sometimes, it is regarded as signaling an exception, like εἰ/ἐὰν μή.[4] Some instances of nonadversative ἀλλά are even taken to be mark-

---

1. Denniston, *Particles*, 1. See also Smyth, §2775; Winer, *New Testament Greek*, 551–52; Moulton and Turner, *Grammar*, 329–30; Abel, *Grammaire du Grec Biblique*, 346; Green, *Grammar of the Greek Testament*, §404; Dana and Mantey, *Manual Grammar*, §211; Wallace, *Greek Grammar*, 671; Young, *New Testament Greek*, 180.

2. BDAG, s.v. "ἀλλά." See also LSJ, s.v. "ἀλλά"; L-N, §89.125; *GELS*, s.v. "ἀλλά"; Danker, *Greek-English Lexicon*, s.v. "ἀλλά."

3. E.g., Young, *New Testament Greek*, 181; Smyth, §2782; Moulton and Turner, *Grammar*, 330; Porter, *Idioms*, 205–6; Wallace, *Greek Grammar*, 673; Dana and Mantey, *Manual Grammar*, 240; Danker, *Greek-English Lexicon*, s.v. "ἀλλά"; L-N, §91.11.

4. E.g., Smyth, §2777; Margaret E. Thrall, *Greek Particles in the New Testament: Linguistic and Exegetical Studies*, NTTS 3 (Leiden: Brill, 1962), 18–19; Dana and Mantey, *Manual Grammar*, 240; Moulton and Turner, *Grammar*, 330; Young, *New*

ers of continuity.[5] Similar to these are occurrences that are regarded as markers of transition from one topic to another or to a new aspect of the current topic.[6]

In what follows, I examine a representative sample of the DM's occurrences in the papyri and LXX to discern whether ἀλλά truly does exhibit a plethora of unrelated functions, at least in this period of the language, or if, perhaps, a core function or polysemic network of functions can be posited that tie its uses together. This will then allow for a discussion of the significance of ἀλλά to the study of translation technique in LXX.

## 4.1. The Use of ἀλλά in the Papyri

### 4.1.1. P.Tebt. 3.1.786 (138 BCE)

A group of farmers in Oxyrhyncha who worked for the crown were apparently having trouble with unjust taxes and intruders on their threshing-floor. In this letter to Phanias, an official and the overseer of the revenues, they request his help in putting a stop to these problems.

> (20) *ἀξιοῦμέν σε, ἐὰν φαίνηται, ἀντιλαβόμενον ἡμῶν καὶ τῶν βασιλικῶν συντάξαι γράψαι Δημητρίωι καὶ Στεφάνωι τοῖς ἐπιστάταις κα[τα]κολουθήσαντα\ς/ τοῖς (25) προγεγραμ[μένοις] μηθενὶ καθ' ὁντινοῦ[ν] τρό[π]ον \ἐπιτρέπειν/ παραλογεύειν ἡμᾶς (30) μηδ' [ε]ἰσβιάζεσθαι εἰς τὰς ἅλως ἀλλὰ τοὺς τοιούτους ἐκπέμπειν ἐπὶ σὲ κατὰ μηθὲν συνα̣π̣ενεχθέντας, ὅπως δια̣λ̣ά̣β̣ης περὶ αὐτῶν κατὰ τὸ φανερόν.*
>
> (20) We ask you, if it seems good, to come to our aid and that of the crown revenues by ordering a letter to be written to Demetrios and Stephanos, (25) the magistrates that, complying with the above, they should not allow anyone in any way to extort us nor to force their way onto the threshing (30) floors *alla* that they should send away such ones to you, not being eliminated in any way, so that you may pass judgment on them publicly.

*Testament Greek*, 181; Mayser, *Grammatik*, 118–19; Danker, *Greek-English Lexicon*, s.v. "ἀλλά." Denniston mentions this possible usage, but his discussion of it reveals a reticence to accept it as a function of the particle. Denniston, *Particles*, 3–4.

5. Chamberlain, *Grammar of the Greek New Testament*, 150–51; L-N, §89.96.

6. Green, *Grammar of the Greek Testament*, §404; Denniston, *Particles*, 21–22; Moulton and Turner, *Grammar*, 330; Young, *New Testament Greek*, 181; L-N, §91.2.

The farmers first state what they want Demetrios and Stephanos *not* to do: allow anyone to extort them or force their way onto the threshing floors. This is then followed by a proposition detailing what Demetrios and Stephanos *should* do: send these people to Phanias so he may pass judgment on them publicly. The particle ἀλλά occurs between these two statements: not do X ἀλλά do Y.[7] This is a clear instance of a typical use and context of use of ἀλλά—what one may consider an example of so-called adversative ἀλλά. However, it may be asked whether "adversative" is the best descriptor. The notion of opposition is more properly related to the overall construction [NEG > POS] wherein a positive clause is connected to a preceding negated clause and the two are addressing the same overarching issue. Presumably καί, δέ, or even asyndeton could have been used here, bringing their own pragmatic constraints to the text, and an adversative relation would still be felt. This is similar to the discussions in chapter 2 on δέ and contrast. Opposition would be present with or without ἀλλά because it arises from the semantics of the particular context. Opposition is inherent to the utterance itself when a negated clause and a positive clause that provide alternate courses of action are juxtaposed. Thus, ἀλλά likely signals a more specific pragmatic constraint that uniquely sets it apart from other viable options (καί, δέ, Ø). The relation that ἀλλά signals may be better described as corrective. The reader is instructed to build their mental representation by regarding what follows the DM as a correction to previously processed information: "not to allow anyone to extort us nor to force his way *but/rather/instead* to send away such ones." Thus, unlike εἰ/ἐὰν μή, which is also a corrective, ἀλλά does not have the requirement that its host utterance counter truth-propositional content. Instead, ἀλλά signals a broader corrective that serves to realign the reader's mental representation according to the author's purposes. The material preceding ἀλλά is still both relevant and salient—the authors do not want Demetrios and Stephanos to allow officials to do those actions—but by using ἀλλά to signal a correction, the preceding negated act is understood to be supplanted by the act to send such people away. The result of this is that the authors have led their reader down a particular mental path that regards the two requests as intrinsically tied together by being mutually exclusive options ("do not do X instead do Y"). While the reader may have been able to travel this mental path without an explicit corrective marker, such is not

7. The DM is occurring with a low moderate scope, connecting the two clauses headed by the infinitives ἐπιτρέπειν and ἐκπέμπειν.

a foregone reading of the text without ἀλλά. The authors ensure the mental route is taken by guiding the reader with ἀλλά.

### 4.1.2. P.Cair.Zen. 1.59041 (257 BCE)

The beginning of this letter is fragmentary and so some of the context is lost, but it concerns a tax collector who had been arrested (presumably wrongly). The author writes to Zenon to explain the situation.[8]

> ἀ̣κ̣ο̣ύσας δὲ [π]αρ' ἡμ̣[ῶν ὅτι] οὐκ ἔστιν [Δ]ι̣ο̣σ̣κουρίδου ὑπηρέτης, ἀλλὰ ἡμέτερος ἦ̣ν̣ λογευτής, ν̣ῦ̣ν̣ δὲ Ἀθηνοδώρου τοῦ ἐγλαβόντος Μέμφιν, ἅμα δὲ καὶ μαινόμενος ὅτι οὐκ ἠβούλετο αἰτούμεν[ος] ἀργύριον δοῦναι \ προσήγγειλ̣ε̣ν αὐτὸν/ ⟦ἀπήγαγεν [α]ὐτὸν⟧ Νικάνορι \καὶ ἀπήγαγε[ν]./
> Now, after hearing from us that the man is not a servant of Dioskouridos (*alla* he was my tax collector and now [he works] for Athenodoros who receives taxes in Memphis)[9] and also at the same time being enraged because the one who was asked did not want to provide the silver, he denounced the man to Nikanor and arrested him.

Similar to the previous example, ἀλλά occurs here in a [NEG X ἀλλά Y] construction, where ἀλλά introduces a correction to a preceding statement: "the man is not a servant of Dioskouridos, *but/rather* he was my tax-collector and now works for Athenodoros." As discussed previously, though opposition is present, an adversative relation would be felt regardless, whether the DM was ἀλλά, καί, or δέ, owing to what is explicitly communicated in context. The DM could have even been left out, and an adversative relationship would have still been retrievable: "The man is not a servant of Diskouridos; he was my tax collector." Of course, if left to asyndeton, the reader must be able to supply any relevant relation beyond that of contextual opposition, and this risks miscommunication. Thus, ἀλλά must narrow the reader's processing options in some way if it is to be of communicative use. The utterance as a whole makes the most sense

8. For a little more on the context, see Edgar, *P.Cair.Zen*, 66.

9. It is unclear what is meant by τοῦ ἐγλαβόντος Μέμφιν. My translation assumes that the intended meaning of the participle is to describe Athenodoros as a tax-collector for whom other tax-collectors work. Regarding the confusion of γ for κ (ἐκλαβόντος), see Francis Thomas Gignac, *A Grammar of the Greek Papyri of the Roman and Byzantine Periods, Vol. 1: Phonology* (Milan: Istituto Editoriale Cisalpino—La Goliardica, 1976), 63.

if ἀλλά is corrective, signaling that what follows corrects the preceding by replacing the incorrect employment with an accurate employment history. Inherently, there is an element of opposition to correction, which is likely why ἀλλά is so frequently found in adversative contexts, but the focus of a corrective relation is on the explicit pragmatic constraint to regard what follows as a correction to previously processed information.[10]

However, this instance of ἀλλά is more complicated than it first appears and does differ from the previous example. The ἀλλά in example 1 links two infinitive clauses together that operate on the same plane of discourse. There, the DM corrects material as it is explicitly stated in the text. In the present example, though, ἀλλά corrects information arising from the textual material but not quite as it is stated in the text. The material that precedes the DM is an object clause ("that the man is not a servant of Dioskouridos), but ἀλλά introduces two independent sentences. What's more, these sentences function in the discourse as an aside, as background information. The DM's host utterance—ἀλλὰ ἡμέτερος ἦ̣ν̣ λογευτής, ν̣ῦ̣ν̣ δὲ Ἀθηνοδώρου τοῦ ἐγλαβόντος Μέμφιν—is not a part of the narrative of the letter. It could be removed and the letter would flow just as well, narrating the events that took place. In other words, the purpose of the ἀλλά clause is not to convey what the man heard instead—such is immaterial to the sentence as a whole within the context of the narrative—but to provide this information to Zenon, who is reading the letter. Thus, the ἀλλά here does not correct the explicitly stated object clause, that is, "hearing that the man is not a servant of Dioskouridos but rather hearing that he was my tax collector." Instead, its use assumes that the information "He is not a servant of Dioskouridos" is present in Zenon's mental representation as discrete information that can be corrected outside of the grammatical context of the letter as an independent statement.

### 4.1.3. P.Mich. 1.23 (257 BCE)

Aristeides writes to Zenon about his nomination by his fellow citizens as the commissary of grain. This is not a job that he wants or for which he feels qualified.

10. Consider the difference in English between "but" and "instead" or "rather." While "but" can be used in practically any context suitable to "instead" and "rather," owing to its more general pragmatic constraints (see the discussion of example 4 below), "instead" and "rather" are used to explicitly indicate correction or replacement.

(1) Ἀριστείδης Ζήνωνι χαίρειν. {καλῶς ἂν ἔχοι} εἰ ἔρρωσαι καὶ τὰ λοιπά σοί ἐστι πάντα κατὰ γνώμην, ἔχοιμι ἂν τοῖς θεοῖς πολλὴν χάριν· ἔρρωμ[αι] δὲ καὶ αὐτός. συμβέβηκέν μοι ὑπὸ τῶν πολιτῶν προβεβλῆσθαί με σίτου ἐγδοχέα[11] οὔπω ὄντι μοι τῶν ἐτῶν οὐδὲ γινομένης μοι τῆς λειτουργίας ταύτης, ἀλλὰ διὰ φθονερίαν τινές [με προέβαλλον].
(1) Aristeides to Zenon. Greetings. If you are well and everything else is in accordance with your wishes, I would give much thanks to the gods. I am also well. It has fallen to my lot to be proposed by the citizens as receiver of grain, not yet being of age nor due for this public service, *alla* certain persons proposed me because of envy.

In this instance, none of the options provided by grammars and lexica (adversative, exceptive, transitional, continuative, and emphatic) are able to pinpoint what is communicated by the DM. This is due in part to the lack of an obvious connection between the propositions connected by ἀλλά. However, recall the discussion from §1.2.2.4. A DM guides the reader in how to process its host utterance in relation *to the mental representation under construction*. The explicit linguistic components of a discourse are not the only elements that are stored in the reader's mental representation. Elements such as the movement of the discourse, implications, implicatures, assumptions, and the reader's encyclopedic knowledge are a part of the mental representation that the reader is in the process of constructing. Thus, in this case, it appears that ἀλλά is connecting its host utterance to information drawn from an implication that arises from processing the previous material. By stating that he is not of age nor due for the public service, Aristeides implies that he should have never been proposed for this office in the first place. The DM's host utterance corrects the implication, communicating that, despite his unsuitability, he was proposed for the office by certain persons with something against him. To introduce this correction to the natural implication of his lack of qualifications, he uses ἀλλά, signaling that what follows offers a corrective to the preceding implication. Unlike example 1, where the reader could have inferred the corrective relation even without ἀλλά, the context here does not lend itself to a corrective interpretation. The DM is necessary.

This instance of ἀλλά would likely fall under the traditional "adversative" label, but such nomenclature leaves something to be desired.

11. ἐγδοχέα is a spelling variation of ἐκδοχέα. On the interchange of γ and κ, see n. 9 above.

The information following ἀλλά is relevant not because of opposition between it and the implication but because it informs the reader of how the current events have come about despite the implication that Aristeides should not have been put forward for the position to begin with. Thus, by using ἀλλά, the author sets up his reader to incorporate the DM's host utterance into their mental representation of the discourse as a corrective to this information.

### 4.1.4. P.Col. 4.66 (256/255 BCE)

The author of this letter writes to Zenon about his mistreatment at the hands of some of Zenon's associates.[12] The content of the letter clearly indicates that the author was not a Greek and that this is a factor in the current trouble he faces.[13] He requests that Zenon instruct his associates to treat him fairly.

> *ἐγὼ δὲ καὶ θέρος καὶ χẹιμῶνα ἐν τῶι πόνωι γίνομαι. ὁ δέ μοι συντάσσει ὄξος λαμβάνειν εἰς̣ ọψώνιον. ἀλλὰ κατεγνώκασίν μου ὅτι εἰμὶ βάρβαρος. δέομαι οὖν σου (20) \εἴ σοι δοκεῖ/ συντάξαι αὐτοῖς ὅπως τὰ ὀφειλόμενα κομίσωμαι καὶ τοῦ λοιποῦ εὐτάκτωσίν μοι ἵνα μὴ τῶι λιμῶι παραπόλωμαι ὅτι οὐκ ἐπίστ̣αμαι ἑλληνίζειν.*
>
> Now, I am also in difficulty both summer and winter. And he orders me to accept poor wine for salary. *Alla*, they have treated me with scorn because I am a "barbarian." I beg you therefore, if it seems good to you, to give (20) them orders that I am to obtain what is owed and that in the future they pay me in full, in order that I may not perish of hunger because I do not know how to act the Hellene.

As an attempt is made to discern what ἀλλά signals and what its core function is, it is important to note that this occurrence of ἀλλά differs from the above examples in that (1) it is not preceded by a negated clause (or a negated implication) and (2) no adversative element may be felt.

The salient relation between the mental representation and the utterance introduced by ἀλλά is not immediately clear. This may be an instance in which one is tempted to regard ἀλλά as an emphatic particle, since the

12. The author is unknown.

13. John L. White takes the mention of camels earlier in the letter to suggest that the author "was an Arab" (*Light from Ancient Letters* [Philadelphia: Fortress, 1986], 47).

traditional adversative understanding does not fit. This would result in the host utterance being read as a confirmation of the preceding content: "And he orders me to accept poor wine for a salary. *Indeed*, they have treated me with scorn because I am a 'barbarian.'" It is not clear how an emphatic reading is relevant or coherent. Even if such a reading could be argued as coherent, it does leave one wondering why clear emphatic particles, such as *μήν* or *δή*, were not used. More importantly, before such a reading could be accepted, this postulated function for *ἀλλά* would need to be demonstrated in some other occurrences of it and, crucially, would need to be somehow related to its more frequent and productive uses (i.e., uses that exemplify a prototypical core) that are clearly not emphatic.

I suggest that *ἀλλά* is signaling a corrective relation, as it has done in the above three examples. In this case, however, rather than signaling a correction to explicit content within the preceding proposition or to an implication that arises from what preceded, it appears to be signaling that what follows is a correction to any other possible assumption Zenon may have as to why the author is being treated with scorn. The author wants Zenon to know that he is being treated poorly because of his ethnicity and not for any other reason. In order to communicate this, he could simply place the two propositions side by side, but this would leave the relation implicit. By using *ἀλλά*, he explicitly guides his reader to understand what follows as a corrective. Since there is nothing textual nor an implication for the proposition to correct, though, the corrected element must be something else in the reader's mental representation—in this case, a presumed incorrect assumption regarding the situation that could have arisen from his reading of the text and his knowledge of the people involved. It may even be the case that by using *ἀλλά* the recipient is invited to realize or manifest the assumption. That is, rather than presuming the recipient has, in fact, made an assumption, the use of *ἀλλά* forces the assumption to be realized in order to accommodate the rhetorical purpose.

This is similar to how the DM "but" is used in English. As discussed in chapter 1, Blakemore has argued that "but" encodes a procedural constraint that activates "an inference that results in the contradiction and elimination of an assumption," even if the speaker is only presuming the intended recipient holds that assumption.[14] This was demonstrated by the

14. See ch. 1. Blakemore, *Relevance and Linguistic Meaning*, 100, but see Blakemore's entire discussion in 89–115.

sentence, "I enjoy books by Brandon Sanderson, but I am not a Mormon." Moreover, the assumption does not even have to be derivable from the linguistic context but can simply be presumed by the speaker to be held by the recipient. Blakemore demonstrates this with the example of Person A giving Person B a glass of whiskey and Person B saying, "But I don't drink."[15] From a cognitive perspective, then, there is no reason that ἀλλά cannot signal a corrective to an assumption that the author presumes the reader may hold. Since it is to the reader's mental representation that ἀλλά signals a correction, it should not matter whether the stored information was an assumption, an implication, or derived from explicit material.

This explanation is more satisfying than positing any of the plethora of meanings often attributed to ἀλλά in nonadversative contexts. Positing a corrective function has the strength of being more in line with what has been observed thus far with ἀλλά than any other possible function. In addition, one should expect the DM's core function, signaling a corrective, to be applicable in various contexts of use.

### 4.1.5. P.Mich. 18.774 (194/193 BCE)

In this letter, a goldsmith named Menches writes to Protarchos, an official. Two men, a tax collector and police officer, recently attacked Menches and took a lump of silver that he had under contract. Menches now finds himself in a precarious position and requests help in reclaiming the silver.

> (25) ἐγὼ δὲ περισπώμενος ὑπὸ τοῦ κυρίου τοῦ ἀργυρίου οὐ δύναμαι ἐκδημῆσαι <u>ἀλλὰ</u> (30) καταφθείρομαι ἀργῶν. ὅπως οὖν δύνωμαι τ̣ὰ εἰς τ̣ὸ βασιλικὸν τέλη ἀναπληροῦν, ἀξιῶ σε δεόμενος μεταπεμψάμενον αὐτοὺς ἐπαναγκάσαι ἀποδοῦναί μοι τὸ ἀργύριον. (35) τούτου γὰρ γενομένου ὢν ὑποτελὴς οὐκ ἀδικηθήσομαι <u>ἀλλὰ</u> τεύξομαι βοηθείας. εὐτύχει.
> (25) Now, since I am being overburdened by the owner of the silver, I am not able to leave town *alla* I am being destroyed from being idle. Therefore, in (30) order that I be able to pay the taxes owed to the royal bank in full, I ask and beseech you to send for them and to force them to give back the silver to me. For, when this happens, I being one who is

15. Blakemore, *Relevance and Linguistic Meaning*, 105. Granted, the assumption is presumed to be held based on the situational context, but the point remains that DMs relate information to the mental representation being constructed by the recipient and this allows assumptions to be that to which a DM relates.

> subject to taxes, I will (35) not be done injustice *alla* I will have received help. Farewell.

Similar to example 4, the first occurrence of ἀλλά ("I am not able to leave town ἀλλά I am being destroyed from being idle") seems to signal a correction to a presumed assumption. Upon reading "I am not able to leave town," the recipient may assume that, despite the unfortunate circumstances, at least Menches (the author) is still able to work and make a living. However, there is another issue at hand. The silver Menches had under contract was taken from him, and he cannot go about his work without it. Thus, to remind his reader of this, the author uses ἀλλά, signaling that a correction is being made to the mental representation: "I am not able to leave town, *but* (*that does not mean I am able to work*) I am being destroyed from being idle!" The salient relation between the mental representation and the correction is not so much one of opposition or contrast (in this case, semantically, it would be difficult even to pin down any explicit opposition or contrast); rather, the issue is that the material following ἀλλά offers a correction to a possible assumption the reader may make. Note, too, that the DM's interaction with this kind of context, that is, correcting an assumption, brings to bear a slightly different "feel" to the corrective relation than what is normally expected with ἀλλά. In what is a typical kind of occurrence of ἀλλά, the DM is preceded by a negated clause, followed by a positive assertion (the construction [NEG ἀλλά POS]), and the particle's host utterance corrects *and replaces* information in the mental representation that originates from the explicit textual material preceding the particle.[16] This is why glosses like "rather" and "instead" are so fitting for ἀλλά, since interclausal "rather" and "instead" typically occur in [NEG particle POS] constructions and signal a correction that *replaces* information originating in the preceding textual material, for example, "I do not want to go to school, rather/instead I want to go to the movies." In this example, what the speaker wants to do (go to the movies) replaces what they do not want to do (go to school). In the instance of ἀλλά under discussion, however, glosses such as "rather" and "instead" are unsuitable translations. It would not be clear what is being communicated by "Now, since I am being overburdened by the master of the silver, I am not able to leave town, *rather/instead* I am being destroyed from being idle." The

16. This usage may be observed in examples 1 and 2 above.

unsuitability of "rather" and "instead" is due to the fact that the DM's host utterance, while it is a correction, does not *replace* anything in the reader's mental representation. This is not to say that ἀλλά is exhibiting a different function. As discussed in §1.2.2, the slightly different meanings that one may observe in a DM are not necessarily evidence of divergent semantics; instead, they may simply be the result of how the DM's core function interacts with different types of contexts. Thus, in this example, ἀλλά can still be seen to signal its core corrective constraint; its interaction with the context results in the correction not being one of replacement, though, but one that counters the reader's incorrect assumption by realigning the reader to the issue at hand. Note that, had ἀλλά not occurred, the overall contribution of the clauses to the letter's discourse may have remained the same, but the reader would not have been led to correct a presumed assumption nor would the relation between the two sentences be immediately clear and retrievable.

The second instance of ἀλλά ("I ... will not be done injustice ἀλλά I will have received help"), is more typical of what one normally encounters with the DM. It is occurring in a [NEG ἀλλά POS] construction, in which the particle introduces a correction to information that is explicitly communicated in the preceding clause. The interaction of the DM's corrective constraint with this type of context results in the reader understanding the host utterance to be the positive corollary to what was previously negated. In other words, the information communicated in the DM's host utterance provides a positive replacement for the canceled event—Menches will not be done injustice, *instead* he will have received help. Interestingly, a different DM could have been used here, such as καί: τούτου γὰρ γενομένου ὢν ὑποτελὴς οὐκ ἀδικηθήσομαι καὶ τεύξομαι βοηθείας—"For, when this is happens, I, being one who is subject to taxes, will not be done injustice, and I will have received help." The overall meaning is the same, but the pragmatic relation between propositions has changed, which alters how the reader processes the discourse and affects the nature of the rhetoric. By using ἀλλά, the reader is led to regard the two clauses as binary options. Receiving help is understood as a correction to being done injustice and, in this way, as that which *ought* to happen instead. On the other hand, καί signals a simple continuative, additive relation that does not explicitly lead the reader to view its host utterance as the proper resulting action that happens in place of being done injustice. Thus, there is pragmatic and rhetorical purpose in using ἀλλά here. By using the connective, the author constrains the reader to view events as a binary, the second as a correction to the first, detailing what should happen instead of, or in place of, the potential first event. The DM's host utterance is portrayed as communicating the positive event that corrects and takes the place of the negated event—receiving help happens in place of being done injustice. Note that the negated clause is still true, Menches will not be done injustice. It is the potential event of *being done injustice* to which ἀλλά signals a correction. Note also that the traditional label "adversative ἀλλά" leaves something to be desired here, as it does not fully explain what the particle is signaling and how the information in its host utterance relates to the information in the reader's mental representation of the text.

### 4.1.6. P.Tebt. 1.105 (103 BCE)

This is a contract between Ptolemaios and Horion concerning the lease of land from Horion to Ptolemaios. It details for the parties involved what is expected during the contracted period.

> βεβαιώτω δὲ Ὡρίων Πτολεμαίωι καὶ τοῖς παρ' αὑτοῦ τὴν μίσθωσιν κα[ὶ] τὰ ἐκ τῆς (30) [γῆς] [γεν]ήματα ἐκκαρπίσασθαι ἐπὶ τοῖς διηγορευμένοις τὸν συγγεγραμμένον χρόνον καὶ ὃν ἂν δέηι ἐπὶ τ̣ο̣ύ̣[τωι,] [καὶ μ]ὴ ἐ[ξέστω αὐ]τῶι ἑτέροις μεταμισθοῦν μηδ' ἐγβάλλειν τὸν Πτολεμαῖον πρὸ τοῦ χρόνου μηδὲ κωλύ[ειν] [μη]δὲ τοὺς [παρ' α]ὑτοῦ κατεργαζ[ο]μένους τὴν γῆν μηδὲ ποτίζοντας κατ' ἔτος τὸν σπόρον εἰς φύλλον, <u>ἀλλ̣ὰ̣</u> καὶ ἀ[πο-][δότ]ω Πτολεμαίωι ἐν τῶι διωρισμένωι χρόνωι τὰ εἰς τὴν χερσοκοπίαν λοιπὰ χαλκοῦ τάλαντα δύο καθότι π̣ρ̣[όκειται.]
>
> Horion must guarantee to Ptolemaios and those from him the lease and (30) the produce of the land upon the terms for the contracted time and for whatever may be necessary upon this, and he is not permitted to lease the land to others or expel Ptolemaios before this time or hinder him or those from him from tilling the ground or watering the crop each year, *alla* he must also pay Ptolemaios within the declared time the remaining two talents of bronze for the breaking up of the dry land, as is mentioned above.

The contract first states what Horion is not permitted to do, namely, lease the land to others, expel Ptolemaios, or hinder his work, and then what Horion must do: Give Ptolemaios the remaining two bronze talents within the appointed time. These two complementary parts of the contract are joined together by ἀλλά. Similar to some of the examples above (1, 2, and 5 [second occurrence]), ἀλλά occurs in a [NEG ἀλλά POS] construction, and to a certain extent, a similar corrective/replacement force can be felt:

The host utterance provides the positive action that Horion is meant to undertake—remuneration—in place of the canceled actions he is not to undertake—leasing the land, expelling Ptolemaios, and hindering Ptolemaios. However, the adverbial *καί* after *ἀλλά* works against reading the host utterance as a replacement or at least renders it an atypical kind of replacement. The adverbial *καί* would seem to guide the reader to understand the utterance introduced by *ἀλλά* to be an addition to the preceding. In this way, *ἀλλὰ καί* together would signal a correction not to preceding textual material but to an assumption that all of the requirements have been given—similar to English's "what's more." That this is the case is ostensibly confirmed by what immediately follows in the letter:

> [ἐὰν δ]ὲ αὐτοὺς μὴ βεβαιοῖ καθὰ γέγραπται ἢ ἄλλο τι παρασυγγραφῆι τῶν (35) προγεγραμμένων ἀποτεισάτω Ὡρίω[ν] Πτ[ολε]μαίῳ ἐπίτιμον χαλκοῦ τάλαντα τριάκοντα καὶ τοῦ μὴ ἀποδοῦναι τὸν εἰς τὴν χερσοκοπίαν χαλκὸν ἡμ[ιόλιον] \καὶ τὸ βλάβος/
> Now, if he should not guarantee them as it is written or breaks contract (35) with respect to anything mentioned above, Horion must pay Ptolemaios a penalty of thirty bronze talents and, for not paying the copper money for the breaking up of the land, one and a half times (the cost) plus the damage.

The consequences for Horion are divided into two: first, the consequence for not fulfilling what was guaranteed and, second, the consequence for failing to pay Ptolemaios for breaking up the land. The two are treated separately, following from the instructions for Horion where they are presented separately. Since the payment for Ptolemaios's work on the land is a distinct part of the agreement that incurs its own consequences if not fulfilled, it makes sense to separate it from the other instructions.[17] By using *ἀλλά* (+ *καί*) to introduce it, the reader is encouraged to correct an assumption (or to manifest an assumption and then correct it) that the preceding are the only instructions for Horion. The reader is then prepared to process correctly another distinct instruction that has its own consequences should it not be carried out.[18]

---

17. Presumably, δέ is not used here as it would indicate too strong a break. Note that δέ is used at the beginning of the details of Horion's commitments (βεβαιώτω δὲ Ὡρίων) and then again to introduce the consequences should Horion not fulfill his commitments ([ἐὰν δ]ὲ αὐτοὺς μὴ βεβαιοῖ).

18. This, then, is similar to the fairly common construction [οὐ μόνον X ἀλλὰ καί Y].

### 4.1.7. The Function of ἀλλά as Evinced in the Papyri

In light of the representative sample examined above, a corrective function can be posited for ἀλλά that suitably covers each instance of use. The DM signals a corrective to a presumed piece of information in the recipient's mental representation of the text, which, once processed, realigns the recipient's mental representation according to the author's purposes. The corrected information may originate in the explicit textual communication, in an assumption the author presumes the reader may have, or in an implication that arises from the material preceding the particle. In no instance was there a need to find an alternative explanation for the DM's use. One can observe in each occurrence of ἀλλά above a core function of instructing the reader to regard its host utterance as a corrective to prior information. When occurring in the construction [NEG ἀλλά POS] and correcting information that originates in the explicit textual material (as opposed to an implication or assumption), opposition arises owing to the negation of one item of a set and the positive assertion of an item from an alternative set. As a result in such contexts, the correcting set signaled by ἀλλά is felt to replace the negated (canceled) set. This is a natural outworking of the semantics of the surrounding context and the DM's corrective function.

## 4.2. The Use of ἀλλά in the LXX

In this section, I investigate a representative sample of ἀλλά taken from the LXX Pentateuch. There are sixty occurrences of the DM in the Pentateuch.[19]

### 4.2.1. Examples from the LXX

In Gen 19:2, two angels visit Sodom and encounter Lot at the city gate. He invites them to his home for the night, but they decline.

> καὶ εἶπεν Ἰδού, κύριοι, ἐκκλίνατε εἰς τὸν οἶκον τοῦ παιδὸς ὑμῶν καὶ καταλύσατε καὶ νίψασθε τοὺς πόδας ὑμῶν, καὶ ὀρθρίσαντες ἀπελεύσεσθε εἰς τὴν ὁδὸν ὑμῶν. εἶπαν δέ Οὐχί, ἀλλ᾽ ἐν τῇ πλατείᾳ καταλύσομεν.

19. Genesis: twenty-two times; Exodus: nine times; Leviticus: six times; Numbers: ten times; Deuteronomy: thirteen times. The collocation ἀλλ᾽ ἤ is not included.

> And he said, "Listen, sirs! Turn aside into the house of your servant, rest, and wash your feet. When you rise early in the morning, you will depart on your way." But they said, "No, *alla* we will rest in the street."

> ויאמר הנה נא־אדני סורו נא אל־בית עבדכם ולינו ורחצו רגליכם והשכמתם והלכתם לדרככם ויאמרו לא כי ברחוב נלין
> And he said, "Please listen, sirs! Turn aside to your servant's house, stay overnight, and wash your feet. You may rise early in the morning and go on your way." But they said, "No, rather we will stay overnight in the street."

The angels' answer to Lot, Οὐχί, ἀλλ' ἐν τῇ πλατείᾳ καταλύσομεν, exhibits what is mostly typical of what one would expect with ἀλλά. It appears in a [NEG ἀλλά POS] construction—the only atypical feature being that the negated clause is assumed—and the host utterance serves as a corrective replacement to information that originated in the assumed counter Lot's request ("No, [we will not stay in your house])." *Instead of* resting at Lot's house, they will rest in the street. The DM signals that this correction to prior content is being made, and the interaction between it and the context results in a sense of replacement—the angels' resting in the street will happen in place of their resting at Lot's. An example such as this may be the most fitting of the label "adversative ἀλλά," owing to how the DM's host utterance counters and replaces the prior information. However, such opposition arises naturally by means of negating the prior information and then asserting a positive statement that contrasts with it. Moreover, replacement is felt by virtue of the vacuum that is created when an event is negated and then followed by ἀλλά. In such contexts, it is typically the case that the DM's host utterance fills the spot left by the prior negation. The particle does not always occur in such contexts, but insofar as has been observed up to this point, it always carries a general corrective constraint. Thus, though this may be a fitting example of so-called adversative ἀλλά, we ought to understand such not as a defining function of ἀλλά but rather as a particular usage of the corrective marker in specific types of contexts.

The translation of the underlying Hebrew is both fitting and informative. Here, ἀλλά represents the particle כי. Certainly, ἀλλά is not normally regarded as a qualitative equivalent to כי (particles such as ὅτι and διότι would typically be more appropriate), but in this case, it ought to be regarded as such. The Hebrew DM כי is polysemous, and its functions can be difficult to describe and relate to one another.[20] However, there is reason and consensus enough to regard כי in certain contexts as a marker of content that counters and replaces prior information. When כי follows לא, as it does here, Carl Follingstad argues that it marks counterassertive polar focus. He writes, "In this case, the addressee has denied or challenged an original assertion by the speaker in some way, so the speaker first denies (with לא), then positively asserts (with כי) a proposition relative to the contradiction."[21] This use of כי, in this type of context, is confirmed by Barry Bandstra as well, who even cites Gen 19:2 as an example.[22] What one may observe in LXX Gen 19:2, then, is a translator rendering כי with

20. Three works in recent years have noted the difficulties in understanding the function of כי and have attempted linguistic descriptions of it. First, Bandstra concludes that it is a syntactic relator particle that joins two clauses in a dependency relation and details various semantic functions that arise based on the כי-clause's position in its sentence and on its interaction with the context. In noting the difficulties of כי, he writes, "Particle ky has a remarkable breadth of usage in Biblical Hebrew.... It is as common as it is elusive and enigmatic" (Bandstra, "Syntax of Particle 'KY,'" 1). Second, Follingstad, approaches כי from the perspective of mental space theory and regards the DM as a discourse deictic particle that may be used as a complementizer, a focus particle, or an epistemic modal particle. He also notes the difficulty of the particle: "כי is without doubt the key problem in the BH [Biblical Hebrew] particle system, a system itself not without importance. Occasionally, the particle is seemingly so difficult to interpret that it inspires excision" (Follingstad, *Deictic Viewpoint*, 2). Lastly, Locatell takes a cognitive linguistic approach and incorporates insights from mental space theory, grammaticalization, linguistic typology, and prototype theory. He posits that causal כי is its most prototypical use (which itself is internally complex) and then eight further uses: "in order of prototypicality:... complementizer, conditional, temporal, adversative, discourse marker of continuation/elaboration, concessive, purpose/result, exceptive/restrictive/negative conditional, and apodosis marker of a conditional clause" (Locatell, "Grammatical Polysemy in the Hebrew Bible," 287).

21. Follingstad, *Deictic Viewpoint*, 157. So also Aejmelaeus, "Function and Interpretation of כי," 175–76; Joüon, §172*c*.

22. Bandstra, "Syntax of Particle 'KY,'" 152. Bandstra labels this use of the particle as "adversative כי." However, consider Follingstad's comment on such a label: "From the point of view of the traditional BH grammatical analysis of כי, [the occurrence of כי in 1Sam 15:35] is a typical 'adversative' clause.... However, a more schematic and insightful analysis of כי is as a marker of '(assertive) polar focus.' This type of focus asserts a positive polar value relative to an explicitly stated or contextually implied counter-presupposition which the speaker/narrator assumes the hearer/reader has in mind in that context. Polar focus is more involved than any 'adversative' 'but' meaning, which in any case can be marked **without** כי by -ו 'and' and a preposed noun, for example" (Follingstad, *Deictic Viewpoint*, 157 [emphasis original]).

a contextually sensitive qualitative translation. Under normal circumstances, there would be no reason to render כי with ἀλλά. However, in this particular context, ἀλλά is, in actuality, a better translation than any of the Greek particles that typically render כי. Such a translation is only possible, at the least, by attention to context and, possibly, also by an awareness of the corrective function of כי in a [NEG כי POS] construction.[23] It is also worth noting that in order to use ἀλλά, the translator had to have some idea of what was about to be communicated. Moreover, they had to make the decision, based on their reading of the text, of how the DM's host utterance ought to be related to the discourse.

The next example of ἀλλά is found in Gen 20:12. In this verse, Abraham is speaking with Abimelech, who has just been informed that Sarah is Abraham's wife. Abimelech confronted Abraham, asking him why he would deceive him. Abraham responds:

> (20:11) And Abraham said, "For, I said 'There is, then, no piety in this place, and they will kill me because of my wife.'
>
> (20:12) *καὶ γὰρ ἀληθῶς ἀδελφή μού ἐστιν ἐκ πατρός, <u>ἀλλ'</u> οὐκ ἐκ μητρός· ἐγενήθη δέ μοι εἰς γυναῖκα.*
> For, she also is truly my sister by father, *alla* not by mother. And she became my wife."
>
> וגם־אמנה אחתי בת־אבי הוא אך לא בת־אמי ותהי־לי לאשה
> And, truly, she is also my sister; she is the daughter of my father—only not the daughter of my mother. And she became my wife.

Similar to the occurrences of ἀλλά in papyri examples 4 and 5 above, the particle in 20:12 signals a correction to an assumption, namely, that Sarah is Abraham's full-blooded sister. Such would be the natural assumption for the hearer or reader to make upon processing the statement *καὶ γὰρ*

23. So also Wevers, who writes on this instance, "In their reply οὐχί is followed by a כי clause in the Hebrew. [The translator] interpreted this contextually as an adversative particle, ἀλλ'" (Wevers, *Genesis*, 266). This is not surprising for the translator of Genesis. As Mark W. Scarlata writes, "Although the translator of Genesis closely adhered to the Hebrew text, his linguistic skills are demonstrated through his semantic differentiation and his ability to use a variety of Greek terms or expressions depending on contextual demands" ("Genesis," in Aitken, *T&T Clark Companion to the Septuagint*, 16–17).

ἀληθῶς ἀδελφή μού ἐστιν ἐκ πατρός. By using ἀλλά, Abraham alerts his recipient that a correction is forthcoming, and once the particle's host utterance has been processed with this procedural instruction in mind, it is clear that the corrected information is the potential assumption that Sarah is a full-blooded sibling to Abraham. It is important to note how the same core corrective function may be observed here as in Gen 19:2 despite the fact that there is no sense of replacement. The host utterance οὐκ ἐκ μητρός does not replace the corrected information, rather it simply offers a corrective to it.[24] The two occurrences of ἀλλά both signal correction, but that constraint interacts with their respective contexts in slightly different ways.

This is the only instance in LXX Genesis in which ἀλλά is used in place of אך. The two are certainly not qualitatively equivalent, and in this context, an adverb such as μόνον could have been used to represent both the text and the meaning of the underlying Hebrew.[25] Assuming, then, that the translator's *Vorlage* did contain the adverb אך, it would seem that they were not concerned with guiding their reader back to the Hebrew, since ἀλλά in no way can be said to do so in this instance.[26] Rather, the translator appears to have been concerned with providing a contextually appropriate rendering of their source text. Thus, this evinces a contextual awareness on the part of the Genesis translator, as ἀλλά would not have been motivated otherwise.

The DM also occurs in Exod 10:25. Here, the pharaoh has agreed to let the Hebrews go in order to worship the Lord in the wilderness. His one

---

24. This is why the English translation "instead" works well in Gen 19:2 but not in Gen 20:12, as it explicitly signals replacement.

25. Though Hebrew lexica include subentries (normally final or near-final) for the few occurrences of supposedly adversative אך (*HALOT*, s.v. "אַךְ"; BDB, s.v. "אַךְ"; Gesenius, *Hebräisches und Aramäisches Handwörterbuch*, s.v. "אַךְ"), Hebrew grammarians make no mention of such a function (see *BHRG*; Ronald J. Williams, *Williams' Hebrew Syntax*, rev. and exp. John C. Beckman, 3rd ed. [Toronto: University of Toronto Press, 2007]; *IBHS* [though Waltke and O'Connor use the gloss "but" occasionally, they are clear that the particle is a restricting adverb, not an adversative; see §39.3.5d.]; Joüon; GKC; Bill T. Arnold and John H. Choi, *A Guide to Biblical Hebrew Syntax* [Cambridge: Cambridge University Press, 2008]). The Hebrew lexica, it would seem, are attempting to account for those few instances in which a disjunction or adversative sense is overt contextually, though the limitative force of אך is sufficient explanation for its use.

26. According to Dines, the Genesis translator was using a text "very similar to (though not always identical with) the later MT" (Dines, *Septuagint*, 14).

stipulation is that their sheep and cattle be left behind. Moses, however, debates this.

> (10:24) And pharaoh called Moses and Aaron saying, "Go! Serve the Lord your God. Only leave the sheep and cattle. And let your women and children depart with you."
>
> (10:25) καὶ εἶπεν Μωυσῆς Ἀλλὰ καὶ σὺ δώσεις ἡμῖν ὁλοκαυτώματα καὶ θυσίας, ἃ ποιήσομεν κυρίῳ τῷ θεῷ ἡμῶν,
> And Moses said, "*Alla* you will also give us burnt offerings and sacrifices, which we will make to the Lord our God;
>
> (10:26) our animals will also go with us, and we will not not leave behind a hoof. For, we will take from them to serve the Lord our God. We do not know how we might serve the Lord our God until we arrive there."
>
> ויאמר משה גם־אתה תתן בידנו זבחים ועלות ועשינו ליהוה אלהינו
> And Moses said, "You will also give sacrifices and burnt offerings into our hand so that we might present them to YHWH our God."

This occurrence of ἀλλά differs significantly from the others examined in that it is speech-initial. The information to which it signals a correction must either originate in preceding textual material *outside of* its discourse context (Moses's speech) or in implied or assumed information presumed to be cognitively active in the mind of the interlocutor. The latter is the case here. There is an implicit assumption made by the pharaoh that the Hebrews will be able to perform their cultic duties without their animals. By using ἀλλά, the host utterance is portrayed as a corrective to that assumption: The Hebrews cannot sacrifice without their animals, so the pharaoh must be willing to supply them.[27] This occurrence is all the more interesting given the rhetoric in play. Moses does not actually believe that the pharaoh will provide offerings for the Hebrews; this is made clear in 10:26, where he drops the pretense. Thus, it appears in verse 25 that Moses is portrayed as being impudent; he signals his utterance as a corrective to pharaoh's incorrect assumption and then

27. Wevers comments, "The sense of Exod lies in the understanding of δώσεις as 'but also you must grant us,' i.e. a cultic journey without the accoutrements of sacrifice is meaningless" (Wevers, *Exodus*, 158).

positively asserts that, since they cannot sacrifice without their animals, pharaoh must be providing them.[28]

Regarding the particle's relationship to the underlying Hebrew, it would seem that ἀλλά was used despite the lack of an equivalent in the *Vorlage*.[29] Instead, ἀλλά was apparently motivated by the communicative desire to explicitly guide the reader to process Moses's response as a corrective. If the translator had no conception of the wider context, ἀλλά would not have been used here, as its appearance is necessarily motivated by an awareness of the discourse and a contextually based decision of how the pieces of information ought to be related. In addition, if the translator were concerned with guiding the reader back to the Hebrew text, then there would have been every reason not to use ἀλλά. The text would still make sense without it. In the end, what one may observe here is the work of a diligent translator who was willing to render his *Vorlage* into good Greek style, even when his choices were not lexically motivated. This fits with the character of the Exodus translator as described by Aejmelaeus. She writes:

> He was free enough to add and omit words and grammatical items, but he obviously did not do so out of indifference or negligence.... The translator of Exodus may thus be characterized as a competent translator, mindful of genuine Greek expressions, free in his relationship to the original, but still exact in reproducing his original relatively faithfully.[30]

In Lev 27:16–21, the laws regarding a field that has been consecrated are detailed. Verses 20–21 specifically deal with what may happen if a man does not redeem the field and decides to sell it.

> (27:20) "Now, if he does not redeem the field and sells it to another man, he may no longer redeem it,

> (27:21) <u>ἀλλ'</u> ἔσται ὁ ἀγρὸς ἐξεληλυθυίας τῆς ἀφέσεως ἅγιος τῷ κυρίῳ ὥσπερ ἡ γῆ ἡ ἀφωρισμένη· τῷ ἱερεῖ ἔσται κατάσχεσις.

28. In colloquial English, this may be represented by something like, "*Well then, I guess* you are giving us burnt offerings and sacrifices!"

29. Larry J. Perkins ("Exodus: To the Reader," NETS, 43) states that the Exodus translator followed a text quite similar to the MT.

30. Aejmelaeus, "What Can We Know?," 92.

> *alla* the field will be, when the release has expired, holy to the Lord just as the land set aside; it will be a possession for the priest."
>
> והיה השדה בצאתו ביבל קדש ליהוה כשדה החרם לכהן תהיה אחזתו
> And the field will be, when it reverts in Jubilee, consecrated to YHWH, as a devoted field; his possession will belong to the priest.

By using ἀλλά, the author guides the reader down a mental pathway that results in a specific mental representation. Verse 20 is not the last word on the subject. The man may no longer redeem the land, but there is more to say about what will happen to it. Instead of the land being redeemable, it will be given to the priest. The DM explicitly signals this corrective relation, instructing the reader to regard the information communicated in 27:21 as the positive correction, or in this context, corrective replacement, to the negated prior information. Thus, ἀλλά connects the pieces of information detailing what will not and what will happen to land that is not redeemed, signaling a corrective relation between the negated assertion and positive claim.

The Hebrew text of verse 21 begins with והיה, which could have been qualitatively rendered into Greek by καὶ ἔσται. That the translator did not render *vav* with καί is notable, especially given that they do so with most occurrences of והיה (or they choose asyndeton, which is more typical in Lev 27). What is more notable, though, is that they chose to use ἀλλά, a particle that is certainly not lexically motivated by *vav*. The motivation to use ἀλλά seems to have come from the translator's own understanding of how the text fit together and should be processed. This understanding and the subsequent decision to use ἀλλά would not be possible unless the translator knew what was about to be communicated as well as how it related to the preceding information.

Numbers 14 recounts Israel's complaints against the Lord upon hearing the terrifying report of the ten spies sent into Canaan. The Lord responds to Moses and threatens to destroy the people. Moses then pleads with the Lord to forgive them. In 14:20, the Lord relents, but there are still consequences for the people who did not believe him.

> (14:20) And the Lord said to Moses, "I am merciful to them according to your word,
>
> (14:21) <u>ἀλλὰ</u> ζῶ ἐγὼ καὶ ζῶν τὸ ὄνομά μου, καὶ ἐμπλήσει ἡ δόξα κυρίου πᾶσαν τὴν γῆν,

*alla* I live and my name is living, and the glory of the Lord will fill all the earth.

(14:22–23a) Since all the people who saw my glory and the signs that I did in Egypt and in this wilderness and tested me this tenth time and did not listen to my voice, they will surely not see the land that I swore to their fathers."

ואולם חי־אני וימלא כבוד־יהוה את־כל־הארץ
However, as I live, the glory of YHWH will fill all the earth.

Upon reading verse 20, one may think that there is nothing more to be said on the matter, that the Lord's mercy precludes any sort of act against the people. This would be a natural assumption, and it is because of this that ἀλλά works so well in 14:21. It signals a corrective to the assumption, a counter stating that, even in his mercy, the Lord will punish those who did not trust him. Note that the corrected information is not derived from explicit textual material. It cannot be said that the corrective signaled by ἀλλά counters the previous content "I am merciful to them according to your word." Instead, it corrects the presumed assumption that one will likely make upon processing that prior content. Since this is the context in which ἀλλά occurs here, the core corrective constraint is clearly felt but there is no sense of replacement. This is because the correcting information does not relate to the corrected information in that way.

This is one occurrence in which ἀλλά qualitatively represents the underlying Hebrew. The Hebrew text witnesses to ואולם, which is suitably rendered by ἀλλά.[31] It lacks quantitative equivalence, as *vav* is not represented in the Greek, however this is likely due to having to choose between καί and ἀλλά, as καὶ ἀλλά would be incoherent.[32]

---

31. Contra Aejmelaeus, *Parataxis in the Septuagint*, 62, who writes, "This translation may be considered to spring from the context rather than from a correct understanding of the rare word אולם." I agree that the translation springs from the context but I see no reason to doubt lexical motivation as well.

32. καὶ ἀλλά would require καί to function as a conjunction (unlike ἀλλὰ καί, wherein it functions as an adverb), and while a meaningful collocation of two conjunctions is not unheard of, καὶ ἀλλά is not one. John William Wevers (*Notes on the Greek Text of Numbers*, SCS 46 [Atlanta: Scholars Press, 1998], 222) puts forth a different explanation, suggesting that the translator of Numbers did not recognize the initial ו.

One final example may be found in Deut 7:5. Moses is giving instructions to the people of Israel regarding how they are to interact with the inhabitants of the land.

> (7:2–4) And the Lord your God will deliver them into your hands, and you will strike them. You will destroy them with destruction. You will not make a covenant with them nor will you have mercy on them nor will you intermarry with them. You will not give your daughter to his son, and you will not take his daughter for your son. For, she will mislead your son from you, and he will serve other gods. The Lord will be angered with wrath toward you, and he will completely and swiftly destroy you.
>
> (7:5) <u>ἀλλ᾽</u> οὕτως ποιήσετε αὐτοῖς· τοὺς βωμοὺς αὐτῶν καθελεῖτε καὶ τὰς στήλας αὐτῶν συντρίψετε καὶ τὰ ἄλση αὐτῶν ἐκκόψετε καὶ τὰ γλυπτὰ τῶν θεῶν αὐτῶν κατακαύσετε πυρί·
> *Alla*, you will act in this way to them: You will destroy their altars, and you will break their monuments. You will cut down their sacred groves, and you will burn their carved idols with fire.
>
> כי־אם־כה תעשו להם מזבחתיהם תתצו ומצבתם תשברו ואשירהם תגדעון ופסיליהם תשרפון באש
> Instead, thus will you do to them: You will tear down their altars, and you will break their pillars. You will cut their Asherah poles to pieces, and you will burn their idols with fire.

The information that is corrected originates from preceding explicit textual material; however, unlike previous examples, the textual material does not directly precede ἀλλά, rather it is found a couple of lines earlier. The DM's host utterance instructs the Israelites as to what they *will* do (destroy altars, break monuments, cut down sacred groves, and burn idols). Owing to ἀλλά, this is portrayed as a corrective to the instructions in 7:2–3 that detail what they will *not* do (make a covenant, have mercy, and intermarry). The intervening material of 7:4 is an explanatory digression, signaled by γάρ, that underpins the instruction to not intermarry. As this is an instance of [NEG … ἀλλά POS] in which the corrected information originates in the textual material, there is a felt effect of replacement, that is, the resulting communication is: You will not make a covenant with, have mercy on, or intermarry with them, *instead of/in place of these things* you will destroy, break, cut down, and burn. It is important to note that the corrected information is not any less relevant or salient than what corrects (and replaces) it; the instructions of what not to do are equally important to the instructions of what to do. Note also that it is not the actual instructions that are replaced. They remain in full-force and are not canceled out—the Israelites are not to make any covenants, have mercy, or intermarry. However, by using ἀλλά to instruct the hearer/reader to process a positive assertion as a corrective to information derived from negated assertions, the corrected information is retroactively portrayed as having created a vacuum that needed to be filled. That is to say, upon processing ἀλλά and its host utterance, the hearer/reader regards the realization of the negated instructions, *not* doing something, as having left a hole that needed to be filled by the realization of a subsequent positive instruction to do something else instead. It is the filling of that void with the positive illocutionary correction that results in the replacement effect. By using ἀλλά, the explicit relation is created and the recipient is led down a specific mental pathway.

The MT witnesses to כי־אם for the underlying motivating marker. On the one hand, ἀλλά works well as a rendering of כי־אם, as a corrective relation may be realized in certain contexts in which כי־אם is used.[33] On the other hand, though, ἀλλά does not quantitatively represent the underlying Hebrew. In addition, this is the only instance in which the translator of Deuteronomy translates כי־אם with ἀλλά.[34] Thus, it cannot be said that ἀλλά guides the reader back to the underlying Hebrew. There would no way for a reader or hearer to know whether the underlying Hebrew had conjunctive *vav*, כי־אם, asyndeton, or כי. Moreover, because כי־אם can signal a corrective relation, an exceptive relation, or a causal-conditional, the translator had to make a decision as to how they would render it into Greek. This would require an awareness of what was being communicated within the context. In order to use ἀλλά, the translator must have had an awareness not only of what they had translated but also of what was coming up in the text and how it ought to be related to the previously communicated information.

### 4.2.2. A Cognitive-Functional Description of ἀλλά

The function of ἀλλά observed in the LXX Pentateuch matches and confirms the earlier description of the DM's use in the papyri. The DM

33. Follingstad, *Deictic Viewpoint*, 156–57, 290–92; 563–66; *HALOT*, s.v. "כִּי־אִם"; BDB, s.v. "כִּי אִם"; Gesenius, *Hebräisches und Aramäisches Handwörterbuch*, s.v. "כִּי אִם."

34. Elsewhere ἀλλ᾽ ἤ (10:12; 12:5, 14, 18; 16:6) and καὶ ἔσται (11:22) are used.

consistently exhibits one core function: It signals a corrective, a realignment, to a presumed piece of active information in the recipient's mental representation. Sometimes the information being corrected will originate in the textual material, sometimes it is an implication of the proposition preceding ἀλλά, and sometimes it is an assumption that the communicator presumes the recipient has made or, possibly, invites the recipient to make. Discerning what is being corrected is a matter of context and relevance.[35] The recipient will subconsciously look for the most obvious element that takes the least processing effort to view as being corrected.[36] Just as in the papyri, because this single constraint was consistently observed, there was no reason to posit multiple unrelated functions for the particle. In every case, one is able to observe the core function of ἀλλά.

The DM occurs with a moderate scope. It seems to prefer the sentence as its host utterance, though it does occur with phrases as well. However, instances in which the DM occurs with a phrase could be categorized as sentence-level, given that the old information, that which would normally

35. Examples of this have been seen throughout this chapter, but the A text of Judg 19:28 so clearly demonstrates this that it deserves mention here. In 19:26, a man's concubine falls down at her master's door after being raped by a group of men. In the morning, the master wakes up and finds her at his door. The first half of Judg 19:28 then says: καὶ εἶπεν πρὸς αὐτήν Ἀνάστηθι καὶ ἀπέλθωμεν· καὶ οὐκ ἀπεκρίθη αὐτῷ, ἀλλὰ τεθνήκει. 'He said to her, "Get up! Let's go!" But she did not answer him, ἀλλά she had died.' Note that this is a plus in the Greek text. It may have been motivated by an underlying Hebrew text that differs from that of the MT, but we cannot know with certainty. However, given that the B text has ὅτι ἦν νεκρά "because she was dead" instead, it is not unreasonable to posit the possibility of an underlying כי here (so *BHK*), given that כי could motivate both ὅτι and ἀλλά and given that the B text typically stuck closer to the MT (Philip E. Satterthwaite, "Judges," in Aitken, *T&T Clark Companion to the Septuagint*, 103–5). Semantically, the DM's host utterance relates to the preceding by providing an explanation for why the woman did not answer, hence the B text's straightforward ὅτι. This semantic relation is not lost in the A text, but it is processed differently. The ἀλλά signals a correction, but to what? It is not to information originating in the explicit textual material—the pluperfect τεθνήκει is not an action that the woman performed instead of answering. Rather, it is an action that was done prior to the opportunity to answer and explains why she did not answer. Thus, the ἀλλά signals a correction to a potential assumption in the reader's mental representation of the story thus far: that the woman is still alive and thus able to answer. In this way, ἀλλά signals something to the effect of: "She did not answer; *but she could not as* she had died."

36. This is an insight drawn from relevance theory. See Blass, *Relevance Relations in Discourse*, 43–64; Blakemore, *Relevance and Linguistic Meaning*, 61–71.

be repeated, has been elided.[37] In any case, there does not seem to be a meaningful difference between the two other than the fact that occurrences with a phrasal host utterance are naturally suited to the [NEG *ἀλλά* POS] construction wherein information originating from the textual material is corrected.

Historically, *ἀλλά* has been regarded primarily as an adversative particle.[38] However, one of the repeated observations throughout this chapter has been that *ἀλλά* frequently cannot be categorized as an adversative but that it always maintains its corrective-marking function. If the historical position is reconsidered and *ἀλλά* is regarded as a corrective marker rather than an adversative, these observations fall into place. Owing to the DM's corrective-marking pragmatics, *ἀλλά* naturally and frequently connects propositions between which an adversative reading arises, but this is due to the semantics of the context rather than the constraints of the particle. These types of contexts, which are typically [NEG *ἀλλά* POS] constructions in which *ἀλλά* tends to signal a correction to information originating in the explicit textual material, are typical and frequent for the particle. It would seem that the historical adversative category was derived from these occurrences but focused on the adversative semantics of the context rather than the corrective pragmatics of the DM that can be observed not only in these kinds of contexts but others as well (and thus has more explanatory power than the adversative label). In fact, if this is how *ἀλλά* was regarded historically, it is likely that this understanding is what gave rise to a multiplicity of functions being posited for the particle. That is to say, the adversative constraint works well enough in many contexts, but once *ἀλλά* occurs in a different context, such as signaling a correction to an element of the mental representation not explicitly derived from the textual material or in a [POS *ἀλλά* POS] construction, the particle often cannot be viewed as adversative. Thus, the traditional Greek grammarians and lexica had to seek other avenues of explanation. Rather than having one particle with one core constraint that accounted for most if not all of its occurrences, a plethora of homonyms, effectively, was postulated. If, on the other hand, the corrective

---

37. E.g., Gen 20:12: *καὶ γὰρ ἀληθῶς ἀδελφή μού ἐστιν ἐκ πατρός, ἀλλ' οὐκ ἐκ μητρός*. "For, she also is truly my sister by father, but (she is) not (my sister) by mother." Also, PSI 4.356: *οὐθεὶς οὖν ἐν τοῖς τόποις πωλεῖ πρὸς σῖτον, ἀλλὰ πρὸς ἀργύριον*. "So, no one in the places is selling for wheat but (they are selling) for silver."

38. See the grammars and lexica cited in nn. 1 and 2, respectively.

function is viewed as the core pragmatic constraint of ἀλλά, there is no need to posit multiple unrelated meanings. Instead, regarding the DM as marking a corrective clarifies its use in different contexts by allowing one to see its core constraint as the consistent motivation behind its use. Thus, ἀλλά is not adversative, it is not transitional, it is not continuative, it is not emphatic, and it is not exceptive. Granted, one could reasonably posit polysemy for the adversative sense, arguing that adversative ἀλλά is a use that is so prevalent because of its frequency in [NEG ἀλλά POS] contexts that it became conventionalized and should be regarded as a distinct function. Even then, a straight line can still be drawn from the DM's corrective function to adversative. Given this, it seems best to understand that the DM simply instructs the recipient to regard its host utterance as a correction to an active element presumed to be in the recipient's mental representation.

This core pragmatic function of ἀλλά to signal a correction has been observed by others as well. Runge, focusing primarily on [NEG ἀλλά POS] constructions in which the corrected information mirrors the preceding textual material, writes, "If we take the traditional idea of 'adversative,' this particle does more than just indicate contrast. This holds true even if the preceding element is positive rather than negative. It provides a corrective to whatever it stands in contrast with."[39] Runge also uses replacement language to describe what ἀλλά signals. For example, he states, "The clause element introduced by ἀλλά either replaces or corrects some aspect of what precedes."[40] However, as has been observed above, signaling a replacement is not a function of ἀλλά but is rather a side effect of the corrective's interaction with a [NEG ἀλλά POS] context in which explicit textual material is corrected.[41] Rick Brannan, who focuses primarily on nonnegative contexts, also regards the particle as a corrective marker (though, like Runge, he does

39. *DGGNT*, 93. Runge seemingly maintains the "adversative" label, but his discussion clearly indicates that he regards the particle as a corrective marker. Whether correction is a type of adversative relation is up for discussion, but it will largely depend on how one defines adversative relations.

40. *DGGNT*, 93. In the following pages, Runge works through examples of ἀλλά from the New Testament, describing it with both correction and replacement language. See also Runge, "Teaching Them What Not to Do: The Nuances of Negation in the Greek New Testament," paper presented at the Annual Meeting of the Evangelical Theological Society, San Francisco, November 2007, https://tinyurl.com/SBL0414a, 9–11.

41. The replacement side effect arises in examples 1, 2, 5, 6, and Gen 19:2 above.

use replacement language).[42] Concerning the plethora of functions normally attributed to the DM, he rightly states, "One must understand the function of ἀλλά, not simply substitute sense-derived glosses, in order to understand what a particular passage communicates."[43] Regarding its function, Brannan writes, "ἀλλά involves correction or replacement. The second item either corrects or replaces the first. 'Correction' is when the second item sharpens, redirects or clarifies the first item. 'Replacement' is when the second item wipes the first item off of the table and replaces it completely."[44] He also explicitly argues against the traditional idea that ἀλλά is an adversative:

> Upon an examination of every instance of ἀλλά in the New Testament and the Apostolic Fathers, one learns that the vast majority of instances

42. The one New Testament example that Brannan describes with replacement language, Mark 11:31–32 (Καὶ διελογίζοντο πρὸς ἑαυτοὺς λέγοντες· ἐὰν εἴπωμεν· ἐξ οὐρανοῦ, ἐρεῖ· διὰ τί οὖν οὐκ ἐπιστεύσατε αὐτῷ; ἀλλ' εἴπωμεν· ἐξ ἀνθρώπων;—ἐφοβοῦντο τὸν ὄχλον· ἅπαντες γὰρ εἶχον τὸν Ἰωάννην ὄντως ὅτι προφήτης ἦν), is problematic. Based on what I have observed in the papyri and LXX, this use of ἀλλά is unusual, as one would normally expect to find ἐὰν δέ instead. This is confirmed by Matthew's and Luke's accounts of the scene, both of which use ἐὰν δέ (Matt 21:26; Luke 20:6). The DM's appearance in Mark 11:32 may be due to an author who was a second-language speaker (see the brief discussion in M. Eugene Boring, *Mark: A Commentary*, NTL [Louisville: Westminster John Knox, 2006], 23–24). This is not to say that ἀλλά does not signal a corrective relation. It does (correcting the presumed assumption that the other option provided must therefore be the answer they choose). It is simply an unidiomatic use in an atypical context. However, the relation, or even felt effect, between the two utterances cannot be one of replacement. Ἀλλ' εἴπωμεν· ἐξ ἀνθρώπων does not replace ἐὰν εἴπωμεν· ἐξ οὐρανοῦ, ἐρεῖ· διὰ τί οὖν οὐκ ἐπιστεύσατε αὐτῷ. It is the other option provided, and the religious leaders are considering both. The reason replacement language works well for many occurrences of ἀλλά is because of the vacuum that is created by canceling out a proposition and by immediately introducing a positive assertion. E.g., John 3:16c: ἵνα πᾶς ὁ πιστεύων εἰς αὐτὸν μὴ ἀπόληται ἀλλ' ἔχῃ ζωὴν αἰώνιον. The first clause cancels out a potential event, and when ἀλλά is used to introduce the positive corrective, the felt effect is that a vacuum was created by canceling out the first event and the positive assertion *fills in* or *replaces* the canceled event. These contextual effects are not present in Mark 11:31–32.

43. Rick Brannan, "The Discourse Function of ἀλλά in Non-Negative Contexts," in *Discourse Studies and Biblical Interpretation: A Festschrift in Honor of Stephen H. Levinsohn*, ed. Steven E. Runge (Bellingham WA: Logos Bible Software, 2011), 265.

44. Brannan, "Discourse Function of ἀλλά," 265. Though, regarding replacement, it is not the second item that wipes the first item off the table. Rather, it is the negative operator that occurs in the first half of the [NEG ἀλλά POS] construction.

> of ἀλλά in these corpora (approximately 80%) involve the comparison of two items (phrases, clauses or otherwise), one of which uses a negator. It is this larger context that is "adversative"; ἀλλά itself does not create the adversity or contrast. It is more proper in such instances to speak of ἀλλά as being used in adversative contexts. But ἀλλά is used in other contexts as well, as the standard lexicons and grammars readily display.[45]

Brannan's point is well made and further confirms what was observed in the papyri and LXX. Thus, based on the work of Runge and Brannan, it appears that the core discourse-pragmatic function of ἀλλά evinced in early Koine, signaling a correction, is also its function in the Koine of the first century CE.

Jakob Heckert investigated the use of ἀλλά in the Pastoral Epistles and concludes:

> The basic function of ἀλλά is contrast although in each of its occurrences the context determines the specific use of the conjunction. Thus, when a negative marker *precedes* ἀλλά, the second conjunct replaces a rejected proposition; when a negative marker *follows* ἀλλά the expectations raised by the preceding conjunct are denied; and when a negative marker is absent, the second proposition corrects the expectations initiated by the first one.[46]

Though he uses the language of "contrast," Heckert does see a core function that is present in each of the DM's uses. As I have discussed throughout this chapter, I do not find "contrast" or "adversative" to be the most helpful descriptor for the core pragmatic function of ἀλλά, as they are semantic categories that are dependent upon the semantics of the surrounding context.[47] That said, if Heckert's language was changed from "contrast" to "corrective" or "realignment marker" then our descriptions of the particle would share extensive overlap. This is due, first, to his understanding that ἀλλά may correct expectations (and assumptions) and, second, to his

45. Brannan, "Discourse Function of ἀλλά," 264–65.

46. Heckert, *Discourse Function*, §2.6.

47. So also Robertson, who states, "Like δέ the thing introduced by ἀλλά is something new, but not essentially in contrast" (Robertson, *Grammar*, 1185). Regarding "adversative particles," he even writes, "It should be stated again that not all of these conjunctions mean contrast (antithesis) or opposition, but the context makes the matter clear" (1186).

regard for the particle's interaction with different contexts as a determinative factor in how its core function is realized.[48]

Several classicists have also described the function of ἀλλά in discourse-pragmatic terms. Drummen examined discourse-initial ἀλλά in a selection of comedies and tragedies. Even given that the instances Drummen investigated occurred at the beginnings of speeches and responses in dialogues, she also ascribes a corrective-marking function to the DM.[49] In addition, she observes the use of ἀλλά to correct nontextual material. She states, "In all cases investigated, the function of turn-initial ἀλλά can be interpreted as marking a correction of the preceding words or actions. The corrected (substituted) element is either an explicitly stated element, a presupposed element, an implication, or the discourse topic."[50] Drummen also helpfully discusses how the particle has one core function, rather than a plethora of unrelated meanings, that can interact with various contexts differently:

> Now it is hard to believe that the very same particle could express disagreement as well as agreement, and a strong break-off as well as a gentle transition, unless these opposite interpretations are not inherent in the meaning of ἀλλά, but rather arise from the different contexts with which ἀλλά is compatible. Still if ἀλλά has some meaning of its own at all, I believe this compatibility has to exist because of some similarity between these contexts.… In other words, I believe the particle has only one basic function, viz. the marking of corrections. This function may lead to several possible interpretations, depending on the context.[51]

To a certain extent, Drummen builds on the claims of Louis Basset, as he advocates for discerning a core function (which he views as corrective

48. Heckert, *Discourse Function*, 18.

49. In a more recent publication, Drummen investigates a wider variety of occurrences of ἀλλά and arrives at the same conclusions (Bonifazi, Drummen, and de Kreij, *Particles in Ancient Greek Discourse*, §III.2.2.6).

50. Annemieke Drummen, "Discourse Cohesion in Dialogue: Turn-Initial ΑΛΛΑ in Greek Drama," in Bakker and Wakker, *Discourse Cohesion in Ancient Greek*, 152. Regarding a correction to a discourse topic, there are no clear examples of this in the Pentateuch and the Twelve, though I do think it is possible that the instances of ἀλλά in Gen 34:31 and Num 14:9 are functioning in this way.

51. Drummen, "Discourse Cohesion in Dialogue," 140.

rather than adversative) for the DM over against attributing the typical, numerous semantic senses to it.[52] He writes:

> The search for a unitary description must, however, also allow one to give an account for the diversity of uses.... A single meaning, which must be defined, is at the base of all the uses. The differences between them come from the different linguistic objects that the conjunction ἀλλά can coordinate. It is therefore not about differences of sense, as the suggested distinctions of use *eliminatives*, *adversatives*, *progressives*. It is about, in fact, differences of syntactic or pragmatic significance.[53]

I have claimed the same throughout this section. Basset also provides four categories, from which Drummen developed her four, for how ἀλλά interacts with its context: to change the theme of a discourse, to invalidate a presupposition, to invalidate what was posed, or to invalidate an implication.[54] This further confirms what was observed and claimed with regard to the DM's use in the papyri and LXX.

In his study of particle usage in Herodotus, S. R. Slings regards ἀλλά as "a replacing adversative particle."[55] This is in keeping with the occurrences of ἀλλά in the LXX and papyri, as its use does frequently result in a sense of replacement and contrast. However, even though he uses "replacement" language, Slings does note that the DM's use is not restricted to replacing and can function to signal a denial of an expectation.[56] Like Drummen and Basset, he also observes its use with a

52. Basset, "'Αλλ' ἐξόλοισθ' αὐτῳ κοαξ: Réexamen des emplois de ἀλλά à la lumière de l'énonciation dans *Les Grenouilles* d'Aristophane," in *New Approaches to Greek Particles: Proceedings of the Colloquium Held in Amsterdam, January 4–6, 1996, to Honour C. J. Ruijgh on the Occasion of His Retirement*, ed. Albert Rijksbaron, ASCP 7 (Amsterdam: Gieben, 1997), 97.

53. Basset, "'Αλλ' ἐξόλοισθ' αὐτῳ κοαξ," 77: "La recherche d'une description unitaire doit cependant permettre de rendre compte aussi de la diversité des emplois.... Une signification unique, qu'il faut définir, est à la base de tous les emplois. Les différences entre ceux-ci viennent des différents objets linguistiques que peut coordonner la conjonction X. Il ne s'agit donc pas de différences de sens, comme le suggèrent les distinctions d'emplois *éliminatifs*, *adversatifs*, *progressifs*. Il s'agit en fait de différences de portée syntaxique ou pragmatique."

54. Basset, "'Αλλ' ἐξόλοισθ' αὐτῳ κοαξ," 82.

55. Slings, "Adversative Relators between PUSH and POP," in Rijksbaron, *New Approaches to Greek Particles*, 107.

56. Slings, "Adversative Relators between PUSH and POP," 107, 111–12.

discourse-level scope in order to, in his words, "replace one Discourse Topic with another."[57] While I would advocate for the language of "corrective," since it better subsumes the various uses of ἀλλά within different contexts, it is evident that what Slings observed in Herodotus corresponds to how ἀλλά is used in early Koine.

Lastly, Sicking investigated occurrences of ἀλλά in Lysias 1 and 12. He was also dissatisfied with how ἀλλά tended to be categorized and thus sought to provide a unified description for the DM.[58] Sicking observed that ἀλλά could occur in contexts of a correct predication replacing an incorrect one, of an elimination of a suggestion that could be raised by the material preceding ἀλλά, and of a conversational move from one topic to another.[59] Despite the variety of contextual features, he found that ἀλλά could always be seen to exhibit one core function. He concludes:

> For ἀλλά we find, besides a use often characterized as *adversative*, one of *breaking off* [i.e., changes of discourse topic]. The common factor between the two can be identified if it is accepted that in "*a ἀλλά b*" the hearer is invited to replace *a* with *b*. In "*οὐκ a ἀλλά b*" (or "*a ἀλλ᾽ οὐ b*") there is envisaged a *complete* substitution of *b* for *a*, in "*a ἀλλά b*" a *partial* substitution is intended, for instance of *b* for a connotation, implication or suggestion contained in *a*, as in "short but stout," "slight but valiant," "brief but intense" or "poor but honest."[60]

Thus, Sicking understands ἀλλά to have core one function, substitution, that interacts with various constructions in slightly different yet similar ways. In addition, it is not only the textual material preceding ἀλλά that

57. Slings, "Adversative Relators between PUSH and POP," 109.

58. See Sicking, "Devices for Text Articulation," 36.

59. Sicking, "Devices for Text Articulation," 36–39.

60. Sicking, "Devices for Text Articulation," 49. Sicking also argues against the traditional adversative understanding of ἀλλά, stating that "ἀλλά is primarily a matter of presentation rather than of oppositions existing in fact" (50). He goes on to show that in [POS ἀλλά POS], even where there is semantic opposition, καί could easily be substituted for ἀλλά. Regarding [NEG ἀλλά POS], though καί cannot be substituted, he states that the opposition arises from the semantic context ("a relation of contradiction in fact obtains; not, however, between the two complete statements linked by ἀλλά, but between *b* and the denial of *a* or, what amounts to the same thing, between *b* and *a* divorced of the negation which in this context goes with it" [50]) and that the contextual mutual exclusion is what hinders καί from being able to be substituted for ἀλλά.

he sees as being substituted, but connotations, implications, suggestions, and discourse topics as well. This is exactly what one can see ἀλλά signaling—and in these same types of constructions and contexts—in early Koine. Note, too, how Sicking pairs the construction "οὐκ a ἀλλά b" with "complete substitution," which is precisely what was observed in the LXX and papyri (what I categorized as [NEG ἀλλά POS]).[61] Nevertheless, I do believe Sicking's description would be improved by using the language of correction rather than substitution, which is more-or-less in keeping with the "replacement" language of some of the other scholars mentioned above. Understanding ἀλλά as a marker of correction, rather than replacement or substitution, allows for the most unified description of the DM's function. The problematic aspect of "substitution" is the same as that of "replacement," in that as soon as one attempts to describe the nonsubstituting occurrences of ἀλλά, the terminology is found wanting. Sicking is forced to use modifiers such as "complete" and "partial" in order to keep the description of ἀλλά limited to one term. Moreover, how exactly the nonsubstituting occurrences do exhibit even partial substitution is difficult to discern. Often, there is no element of replacement or substitution communicated or felt. However, this is not a problem if one regards ἀλλά as a corrective marker rather than as substitutive.

It should be noted that while my description of ἀλλά is largely equivalent to those provided by the scholars above, there are two differences. First, as has already been discussed, is the issue of replacement language. "Replacement" and "substitution" are labels that describe the side effect of the correction ἀλλά signals in a specific (albeit frequently occurring) context.[62] However, because replacement/substitution is a felt effect of contextual features and cannot be used to categorize occurrences of ἀλλά

61. Regarding "*a* ἀλλ' οὐ *b*" or [POS ἀλλά NEG], there is too little data to corroborate Sicking's claim. In the LXX Pentateuch and the Twelve, I found only four instances of [POS ἀλλά NEG]. Two of them, Gen 20:12 and Exod 8:28, would seem to fall into Sicking's "complete substitution" category, but the other two, Num 14:9 and Deut 28:65, definitely do not (the former signaling a correction to an implication or the discourse topic, the latter seemingly signaling a correction to an assumption). With respect to the papyri, I have not yet observed an instance of [POS ἀλλά NEG].

62. This kind of effect was encountered by Hansen as well in her study on French discourse particles. She describes some senses "as 'side effects' or implicatures of the interaction between the particles in question and the contexts in which they occur, rather than as coded features of the particles themselves" (Hansen, *Function of Discourse Particles*, 88). See also the discussion in §1.2.2.

outside of one specific context, it is not a helpful label when attempting to describe a core function of the particle that can account for all of its occurrences.[63] Second, in addition to the primary claim concerning the function of ἀλλά, some of the scholars also assert that the DM focuses the recipient's attention on the correction. Runge and Brannan argue that ἀλλά highlights the information it introduces, placing more attention on the correction than it would have received in a less complex formulation.[64] Similarly, Sicking states that ἀλλά replaces the preceding material with material that is "nearer to the heart of the speaker's concerns."[65] While there are many examples that would seemingly corroborate these claims, there are too many occurrences wherein this cannot be the case. For example, consider Gen 40:23; Exod 16:19–20a; and Lev 11:20–21:

Genesis 40:23
οὐκ ἐμνήσθη δὲ ὁ ἀρχιοινοχόος τοῦ Ἰωσήφ, ἀλλ' ἐπελάθετο αὐτοῦ.
But the chief cupbearer did not remember Joseph, rather (*all'*) he forgot him.

Exodus 16:19–20a
(16:19) εἶπεν δὲ Μωυσῆς πρὸς αὐτούς Μηδεὶς καταλιπέτω εἰς τὸ πρωὶ ἀπ' αὐτοῦ, (20) καὶ οὐκ εἰσήκουσαν Μωυσῇ, ἀλλὰ κατέλιπόν τινες ἀπ' αὐτοῦ εἰς τὸ πρωί·
Now, Moses said to them, "Let no one leave any of it for the morning." But they did not listen to Moses, rather (*alla*) they left some of it for the morning.

Leviticus 11:20–21
(11:20) καὶ πάντα τὰ ἑρπετὰ τῶν πετεινῶν, ἃ πορεύεται ἐπὶ τεσσάρων, βδελύγματά ἐστιν ὑμῖν. (21) Ἀλλὰ ταῦτα φάγεσθε ἀπὸ τῶν ἑρπετῶν τῶν πετεινῶν, ἃ πορεύεται ἐπὶ τεσσάρων· ἃ ἔχει σκέλη ἀνώτερον τῶν ποδῶν αὐτοῦ πηδᾶν ἐν αὐτοῖς ἐπὶ τῆς γῆς.

---

63. Granted, it is possible that ἀλλά is polysemous, i.e., that it has two related but distinct functions: correcting and replacing (see the discussion in §1.2.2.1). However, given that the corrective function can easily be viewed as the single constraint in all instances of use, with replacement a felt effect from interaction with a certain kind of context, it seems best to me to regard ἀλλά as monosemous, though I remain open to the real possibility that the replacement side effect had become conventionalized and thus its own distinct function.

64. *DGGNT*, 93–94, 96–97; Brannan, "Discourse Function of ἀλλά," 265.

65. Sicking, "Devices for Text Articulation," 50.

> And all the creeping things that are able to fly, the things that walk on all fours, they are an abomination to you. But (*Alla*) you will eat these from the creeping things that are able to fly, the things that walk on all fours: the things that have legs above their feet with which [they jump?] on the ground.

In Gen 40:23, the reader is, for all intents and purposes, faced with a tautology. The material that ἀλλά introduces adds nothing of informational value other than being portrayed as a corrective that positively asserts an action (forgetting) that occurs in place of the negated opposite (remembering). There is nothing about the information introduced by ἀλλά that draws the reader's attention or is nearer to the heart of the speaker's concerns any more than what precedes ἀλλά. The same can be said of Exod 16:20. In addition, one could argue that the material directly preceding ἀλλά ("But they did not listen to Moses") would draw the reader's attention more than the correction, as it is entirely new information and the correction is nothing more than a positive restatement of Moses's words. At the very least, the material preceding ἀλλά maintains its relevance and cannot be said to be *less* at the heart of the speaker's concerns than the correction.[66] In Lev 11:21, again the information being corrected is just as relevant and just as salient as the correction itself. The material of verse 21 is not highlighted relative to verse 20; both provide information that is central to what the speaker is communicating. In the end, a correction is not necessarily highlighted relative to the information it is correcting. A correction is simply a particular way of portraying the relationship between two pieces of information. Granted, the claim that ἀλλά highlights its host utterance or introduces information that is nearer to the heart of the speaker's concerns is an understandable one. In fact, it is likely the case that in the vast majority of occurrences, the DM's host utterance does convey more salient information than the material being corrected. However, I would argue that this is due to the nature of how information naturally tends to be conveyed, with the communicator typically either starting with given information and then proceeding to new, salient information or ordering the communication iconically.[67] Thus, whether given

---

66. Regarding material preceding ἀλλά, at least in [NEG ἀλλά POS] constructions, Levinsohn states, "When ἀλλά links a negative characteristic or proposition with a positive one, the negative part usually retains its relevance" (*DFNTG*, 115).

67. On moving from given to new information, see *TFG 1*, 11; *DGGNT*, 187–88; Chafe, "Cognitive Constraints," 36–37; Heidi Wind Cowles, "The Psychology

information is reasserted or negated and lays the groundwork for the ἀλλά clause or the communication is ordered iconically, ἀλλά is not highlighting its host utterance; rather, the information contained within the host utterance, generally speaking, will naturally be the most salient.[68]

In LXX scholarship, Le Moigne has investigated the use of ἀλλά in Isaiah. Le Moigne posits a number of different usages of the DM, separating them into two groups: Minority uses—ἀλλά with a volitive (either before or in the host utterance), ἀλλά introducing an objection, ἀλλά meaning "at least"—and majority uses—ἀλλά after negation, and ἀλλά expressing a

---

of Information Structure," in *The Expression of Information Structure,* ed. Manfred Krifka and Renate Musan, Expression of Cognitive Categories 5 (Berlin: de Gruyter, 2012), 289–90. (Chafe and Cowles relate their comments primarily to subject-predicate/topic-comment ordering, but the principles discussed are applicable and may be extended to larger discourse units.) On the iconicity principle and iconic sequencing, see n. 57 in ch. 3; and *TFG 2*, 132–35, 435–36; Willy van Langendonck, "Iconicity," in Geeraerts and Cuyckens, *Oxford Handbook of Cognitive Linguistics*, 407–13; Langacker, *Cognitive Grammar*, 490 ("natural path"); Brown and Yule, *Discourse Analysis*, §4.3.5 ("natural order").

68. Though a negated clause does assert a new relation, the content is typically derived entirely from given or known information, e.g., A: "Did you go to the store?" B: "No, I did not go to the store." The negated relation is new, but the content has been repeated. Negated clauses tend to be given to such an extent that, usually, a negative operator ("No") can be provided and the actual clause left unstated. Similarly, Talmy Givón writes, "Negative sentences must be *more presuppositional* than their corresponding affirmatives, since subject and object nouns tend to be *more definite* in them. In other words, when a speaker utters a negative sentence in discourse, he *assumes more* about what the hearer knows than when he utters an affirmative" (*On Understanding Grammar*, Perspectives in Neurolinguistics and Psycholinguistics [New York: Academic Press, 1979], 103, emphasis original). Thus, a negated clause will assert some element of new information, but it is a method of communicating that, by its nature, is more presuppositional. Because of this, it is likely that an ἀλλά preceded by a negated clause will naturally introduce more salient information than the negated clause, simply owing to the types of information typically contained in negated clauses and ἀλλά clauses. This is even more evident with the textual material correcting [NEG ἀλλά POS] construction and its replacement side effect. Since replacement is a type of focus relation (see *TFG 1*, 332–33), one would expect it to follow the information it is correcting. Examples of reasserted or negated given information are Gen 19:2; 20:12; Deut 7:8; examples of iconic ordering are Gen 32:28, 40:14, 15; Lev 27:21. This highlighting is also due to the content of the correction. It is not only connected to the mental representation via a newly asserted relation (correction), but also tends to be comprised of much newer information relative to the preceding assertion.

synonymy.[69] While there may be exegetical value to such categorization, it is a system of categorization that is based entirely on different types of context in which the particle appears rather than the particle's function. The DM is thus presented as having multiple discrete meanings that are disconnected and highly contextual; it does not consider the pragmatics of the particle itself and how it may guide the reader in their processing of information. At the same time, Le Moigne does provide helpful insight into the translator and how they engaged with their *Vorlage*. This will be returned to below.

In the end, the observations the above scholars make on the use of ἀλλά in Classical Greek, the New Testament, and the Apostolic Fathers corroborate the claims I have made in this chapter. Namely, I have argued that "adversative" does not adequately describe the core function of ἀλλά, that the plethora of functions attributed to the DM are motivated by a lack of clarity about how ἀλλά pragmatically instructs the reader to process information, and that ἀλλά is best described as a corrective marker, that is, it is used to instruct the recipient to regard the DM's host utterance as a correction to some element within his or her mental representation for the purpose of realigning the mental representation. In addition, the fact that one may observe this same function in Classical Greek and the Koine of the New Testament and Apostolic Fathers more-or-less necessitates that it also be the function of the DM in the period intervening and therefore also indicates that ἀλλά was communicatively stable during this rather long period. Thus, ἀλλά may be described as follows.

The DM ἀλλά functions within the cognitive domain and instructs the recipient to process a corrective relation holding between two pieces of information. That is, the recipient is instructed to regard the information introduced by the particle as a corrective to some element within their mental representation of the discourse for the purpose of realigning it according to the communicator's concerns. The information being corrected may be textually based, an assumption, an implication, or a discourse topic—whatever is most manifest and relevant to the recipient upon processing the correction and integrating it into the mental representation (i.e., takes the least amount

69. Le Moigne, "Le livre d'Ésaïe dans la Septante," ch. 7 §A (minority uses); ch. 7 §B.1 (majority uses). Le Moigne considers ἀλλά expressing a synonymy as "a pivot for lexical repetitions" (Le Moigne, "Le livre d'Ésaïe dans la Septante, ch. 7 §B.2.a), double expressions (the positive statement of what something is after a statement of what it is not; ch. 7 §B.2.b), and ἀλλά at the center of a chiasm (ch. 7 §B.2.c).

of processing effort). Frequently, ἀλλά occurs in [NEG ἀλλά POS] constructions wherein its host utterance corrects information that originated in the explicit textual material preceding the particle. In so doing, the correcting material fills the void left by the negated assertion, thereby acting as a replacement to the preceding information. In the data investigated here, the particle appears to occur primarily with a moderate scope.[70]

### 4.2.3. ἀλλά and LXX Translation Technique

In the corpora examined thus far, ἀλλά almost always provides evidence of translators who were making contextually aware decisions of how to render their Hebrew *Vorlagen* into Greek. Out of all of the occurrences of ἀλλά in the LXX Pentateuch, only in two could one argue for lexical motivation without any need for an awareness of the flow of the discourse, Gen 48:19 and Num 14:21, where the MT reads ואולם. Elsewhere, even

70. One further point bears mentioning. The idea that ἀλλά can signal an exceptive relation is a prolific one (see n. 4 above). The only instance of the DM I have found for which one could mount a convincing argument for an exceptive reading is in P.Cair.Zen. 3.59494 (mid third century BCE): οὐ γὰρ ἔχομεν οὐθένα κύριον ἀλλὰ σέ, "For we have no master ἀλλά you." It is worth noting that there have been grammarians opposed to this idea. Denniston, e.g., posits the category but his discussion reveals hesitation to fully accept it (note, too, his important point that many grammarians seem to miss: "Passages in which some form of ἄλλος precedes have been cited as parallel [to exceptive ἀλλά], but are really not so: ἄλλος makes the ἀλλά normal, 'no one else, but'"; Denniston, *Particles*, 3–4). Winer (*New Testament Greek*, 566) is strongly against the notion. He states that ἀλλά never stands for εἰ μή and, with regard to whether there was an interchange of meaning between ἀλλά and εἰ μή, he writes, "There is no sufficient reason for believing that this interchange exists in the N.T." Lastly, Jannaris allows an exceptive function for ἀλλά, but only in Attic and only occasionally; he states that during the Hellenistic period there was interchange and rivalry between particles and that "ἀλλά was ultimately forced to retreat and leave a considerable part of its adversative functions to its exceptive rivals" (Jannaris, *Greek Grammar*, 407). I am inclined to follow Winer and Jannaris and not regard ἀλλά as able to mark exception in Koine, save, perhaps, for the odd archaism. However, I think it is most likely that there are a few occurrences wherein ἀλλά looks exceptive because it can *technically* stand in such a context owing to its corrective constraint. Exceptives are, it seems to me, a subcategory of correctives. They signal a correction to prior information in very specific contexts. Thus, in order to be used, an exceptive marker requires certain contextual constraints. A member of the superordinate category "corrective," however, could arguably stand in a context in which an exceptive would be acceptable (and perhaps preferable!).

though ἀλλά does render כי־אם seven times and may be pragmatically synonymous with the collocation, כי־אם can effect a corrective relation, an exceptive relation, or a causal/strengthening relation that begins with a conditional frame.[71] Thus, the translator had to decide, based on his understanding of what was being communicated in context and how the pieces of information were related, how to best render the meaning of the Hebrew. This is especially significant in light of the instances of כי־אם investigated and noted in §3.1. It was observed that these same translators would often render the Hebrew collocation with εἰ/ἐὰν μή when an exceptive constraint was the most natural reading of the Hebrew. In just these occurrences of כי־אם, then, an approach to translation technique is needed that focuses not only on representation of the underlying lexeme but also takes into consideration how the translators built their own mental representations of the discourse and translated accordingly. This is also true for those occurrences where the underlying Hebrew witnesses to a corrective כי. The fittingness of ἀλλά in these contexts despite the lack of clear lexical motivation should not be overlooked. The translators had to make a decision as to how they would render כי. When they chose ἀλλά, it was due to contextual features of which they must have been aware. Also interesting are those occurrences where there is not only lexical mismatch but also pragmatic mismatch, where ἀλλά renders conjunctive ו or ואם or אך or ואך or רק or asyndeton.[72] These would also seem to point to translators who were interpreting their source texts and trying to determine the best way to relate information and piece the discourse together. Lee makes this point when discussing the use of ἀλλά in Gen 34:31, which renders, of all things, the Hebrew interrogative particle. Lee writes, "The choice of ἀλλά where the original has ה- may seem strange; but in fact the translator has chosen an idiomatic use of ἀλλά introducing a question 'following a rejected suggestion or supposition.'"[73]

71. Gen 15:4; 32:28; 35:10; 40:14; Num 10:30; 35:33; Deut 7:5. See the discussion on כי־אם on pp. 113 and 129.

72. ו sixteen times: Gen 17:5; 40:23; 45:1; 47:30; 48:19; Exod 3:22; 9:2; 16:20; 21:13; Lev 26:23, 27; 27:21; Num 13:34; Deut 1:28; 9:4; 28:65. ואם once: Lev 26:15. אך thrice: Gen 20:12; Num 14:9; Lev 11:21. ואך once: Num 22:20. רק thrice: Exod 8:28 (24 MT); Num 20:19; Deut 20:20. Asyndeton eleven times: Gen 21:23; 34:31; 38:23; 42:34; 44:26; Exod 10:25; 23:5; 32:18; Lev 27:29; Num 13:31; 14:14.

73. Lee, *Greek of the Pentateuch*, 153–54. Lee offers the very appropriate gloss "Well, if not that" for this instance of ἀλλά.

Le Moigne provides similar insights when investigating the translator of LXX Isaiah, who makes good use of ἀλλά. For example, he rightly notes the use of ἀλλά in Isa 49:15 in place of the MT's *vav* (introducing an apodosis) as idiomatic Greek that also represents the translator's desire to preserve the force of the passage, even though it requires that they do not qualitatively represent the underlying Hebrew.[74] In another example, Le Moigne demonstrates that the translator regarded a [NEG X POS] construction in Isa 50:7 as containing synonymous propositions and so used ἀλλά in order to focus on that relation rather than the causal relation conveyed by the underlying עַל־כֵּן.[75] The overall meaning is similar, and the synonymy between the propositions is not necessarily absent in the Hebrew. But the reader is led down an alternate mental pathway resulting in a slightly different mental representation of the text. Thus, just as was observed above in the Pentateuch, the translator of LXX Isaiah made decisions based not on how to formally represent the underlying Hebrew but on how to represent how they read the text. These decisions were necessarily contextual and provide insight into the translator's own interpretation of these passages.

In the end, it is enough to say that describing the motivation behind ἀλλά is not a simple matter of whether or not it was lexically motivated. Almost always, its use required both an awareness of the flow of the discourse and a decision by the translator as to how they would relate the information. Often, this results in a faithful rendering of the Hebrew, even if not exhibiting pure lexical equivalence. Sometimes, it results in guiding the reader down a different mental pathway than the Hebrew. In either case, the translators could not have used ἀλλά without contextual motivation, as the underlying Hebrew lexeme or collocation alone would rarely require it as a rendering.

---

74. εἰ δὲ καὶ ἐπιλάθοιτο ταῦτα γυνή, ἀλλ' ἐγὼ οὐκ ἐπιλήσομαί σου, εἶπεν κύριος, "'Even if a woman could forget these, *nevertheless/regardless* [ἀλλά] I will not forget you!' says the Lord." The ἀλλά effectively cuts off the implication of the preceding (Le Moigne, "Le livre d'Ésaïe dans la Septante," ch. 7 §A.3).

75. καὶ κύριος βοηθός μου ἐγενήθη, διὰ τοῦτο οὐκ ἐνετράπην, ἀλλὰ ἔθηκα τὸ πρόσωπόν μου ὡς στερεὰν πέτραν καὶ ἔγνων ὅτι οὐ μὴ αἰσχυνθῶ, "The Lord became my helper. Because of this, I was not put to shame. *Rather* [ἀλλά], I set my face as a solid rock, and I realized that I will never be dishonored" (Le Moigne, "Le livre d'Ésaïe dans la Septante," ch. 7 §B.1).

### 4.3. ἀλλά in the Twelve

There are only three occurrences of ἀλλά in the Twelve.[76] Each one will be discussed in turn. The first occurs in Amos 8:11. In this chapter, the Lord is pronouncing his judgment on the people of Israel because of their oppression of the poor.

> ἰδοὺ ἡμέραι ἔρχονται, λέγει κύριος, καὶ ἐξαποστελῶ λιμὸν ἐπὶ τὴν γῆν, οὐ λιμὸν ἄρτου οὐδὲ δίψαν ὕδατος, <u>ἀλλὰ</u> λιμὸν τοῦ ἀκοῦσαι λόγον κυρίου·
> "Pay attention! Days are coming," says the Lord, "and I will send a famine on the land! Not a famine of bread nor a thirst of water, *alla* a famine of hearing the word of the Lord!"

> הנה ימים באים נאם אדני יהוה והשלחתי רעב בארץ לא־רעב ללחם ולא־צמא למים כי אם־לשמע את דברי יהוה
> "Pay attention! Days are coming," says the Lord YHWH, "when I will send a famine into the land! Not a hunger for bread nor a thirst for water, but rather for hearing the word of YHWH!"

The DM stands in a [NEG ἀλλά POS] construction and corrects information that originated in the preceding textual material. As such, there is a sense of replacement, in that the Lord will not send a famine of bread or water *but rather/instead* a famine of hearing the word of the Lord. The famine of hearing occurs in place of, or instead of, the kind of famine one would normally expect. The negated information is true and maintains its relevance; the corrective simply counters the effect of the negated information, communicating what kind of famine it will not be, and provides the positive other side of the coin, communicating what kind of a famine it *will* be.

The attested underlying Hebrew here is כי אם. As previously discussed, ἀλλά is often qualitatively equivalent to כי אם, but that does not therefore point to a translator who read the Hebrew collocation and used ἀλλά without a second thought.[77] When faced with a particular occurrence of כי אם, a translator had to determine its function within its context before they could decide how to best translate it. Indeed, elsewhere in the Twelve, the translator renders the collocation with ἐὰν μή (Amos 3:7), ἀλλ᾽ ἤ (Mic 6:8;

76. Not including occurrences of ἀλλ᾽ ἤ.
77. See p. 160.

Zech 4:6), and διότι (Hos 9:12; Amos 5:22). Moreover, כי אם could arguably also be rendered, depending on its context of use, by various other particles, such as μήν/δή, ὅτι/δίοτι εἰ/ἐάν, and εἰ/ἐὰν γάρ. Thus, at the least, this instance evinces a translator who was not only aware of the most immediate context but who considered and determined how the connected pieces of information related to each other.

The second instance of ἀλλά is in Mal 2:9. The Lord is speaking to his priests, condemning them for turning away from his ways.

> *καὶ ἐγὼ δέδωκα ὑμᾶς ἐξουδενωμένους καὶ παρειμένους εἰς πάντα τὰ ἔθνη, ἀνθ' ὧν ὑμεῖς οὐκ ἐφυλάξασθε τὰς ὁδούς μου, <u>ἀλλὰ</u> ἐλαμβάνετε πρόσωπα ἐν νόμῳ.*
> And I have given you, scorned and weakened, into all the nations, because you did not keep my ways, *alla* you were showing partiality in the law.

> וגם־אני נתתי אתכם נבזים ושפלים לכל־העם כפי אשר אינכם שמרים את־דרכי ונשאים פנים בתורה
> And I have even given you, despised and devalued, to all peoples inasmuch as you were not keeping my ways but were showing partiality in instruction.

The DM instructs the recipient to regard "you were showing partiality in the law" as a corrective to some previously processed material. Given the context and the [NEG ἀλλά POS] construction, it is clear that the information being corrected is drawn straight from the preceding text. Thus, the correction, showing partiality, is viewed as the positive counterpart or converse that did occur *instead of* the negated preceding action, keeping the Lord's ways.[78]

Regarding the underlying Hebrew, ἀλλά has rendered conjunctive *vav*. Normally, καί would be expected. However, [NEG καί POS] is not a construction that is used in Greek for contrastive contexts. Thus, as far

78. So also Vianès, who writes, "The Greek, by translating the coordinator *we*- with ἀλλά ('but'), understands this as an act of favoritism that is opposed to keeping the paths of the Lord." French original: "Le grec en traduisant par *allá* ('mais') la coordination *we*- comprend cela comme un acte de favoritisme qu'il oppose au fait de garder les chemins du Seigneur." Laurence Vianès, *Les Douze Prophètes: Malachie*, Bd'A 23.12 (Paris: Cerf, 2011), 124.

as Greek idiom is concerned, ἀλλά is the most natural choice.[79] In order to appropriately render *vav* with ἀλλά, though, the translator did have to know that the second half of a contrastive pair was coming up in their text. Thus, this occurrence does, to at least a small extent, point to a translator who was aware of more than the most immediate context and more than the information unit in front of them. Rather, at the least, they had to consider the communicative act as a whole.

The final ἀλλά occurs a few verses later in Mal 2:16. The Lord is now speaking against Judah, warning them against their unfaithfulness.

> (2:15b) "And you all said, 'What else does God want apart from offspring?' And be guarded in your spirit, and do not forsake the wife of your youth.
>
> (16) <u>ἀλλὰ</u> ἐὰν μισήσας ἐξαποστείλῃς, λέγει κύριος ὁ θεὸς τοῦ Ισραηλ, καὶ καλύψει ἀσέβεια ἐπὶ τὰ ἐνδύματα αὐτοῦ, λέγει κύριος παντοκράτωρ. καὶ φυλάξασθε ἐν τῷ πνεύματι ὑμῶν καὶ οὐ μὴ ἐγκαταλίπητε.
> *Alla* if you hate her and send her away," says the Lord God of Israel, "then impiety will cover over his garments," says the Lord Almighty. "And be guarded in your spirit and do not ever forsake her."
>
> כי־שנא שלח אמר יהוה אלהי ישראל וכסה חמס על־לבושו אמר יהוה צבאות ונשמרתם ברוחכם ולא תבגדו
> "For, he hates to send," says YHWH God of Israel, "And violence covers over his clothes," says YHWH of Hosts, "So, you will be on guard in your spirit, and do not act unfaithfully."

It would seem that the Lord's concern is to make certain that the people of Judah understand the gravity of the situation. After charging them not to forsake the wife of their youth, he provides a corrective that counters the presumed assumption that forsaking the wife of one's youth would not result in suffering consequences. Without ἀλλά, such a relation between verse 16 and the information within the mental representation would not be impossible, but it would not be the only way to process the information and perhaps not even the most natural. The DM ἀλλά explicitly instructs and constrains the recipient in his or her processing of the information to view the host utterance as a corrective.

---

79. See Stephen H. Levinsohn, "Self-Instruction Materials on Non-narrative Discourse Analysis," 29–30.

The issue of what the translator was rendering is a complicated one. Not only is the text of the MT difficult to understand, if not corrupt, but there is also a divergent textual tradition witnessed at Qumran.[80] First, regarding the MT, it witnesses to כי. Since ἀλλά does signal a similar constraint as כי when the Hebrew DM occurs in particular contexts, it is at least possible that the translator understood the discourse in this way and used ἀλλά accordingly. Of course, ἀλλά is not the first choice that comes to mind when כי is encountered, so this would evince a translator who was considering the context and making a decision based on their interpretation of the whole communication. In 4Q76 (4QXII[a]), however, 2:16 begins כי אם שנתה שלח. This, it would seem, is more likely to reflect the text that the translator of the Twelve was reading. Not only does it contain אם, which would motivate the use of ἐάν, but it also has the second-person singular verb שנתה, which, though rendered by a participle in the Greek, does correspond in person and number to the indicative verb ἐξαποστείλῃς. If the translator was reading a text similar to 4Q76, then, his translation reveals an understanding of כי as a corrective, thus fitting with one of Follingstad's categories for כי, and אם as a conditional particle.[81] This provides an important insight into the capability of the translator. The collocation כי אם, depending on the context in which it is found, may produce an exceptive relation, a corrective relation, or may not be functioning as a set phrase at all.[82] Thus, if a translator were to encounter an occurrence of כי אם, they would have to decide, based on the broader context, how to render it. Granted, one may argue that the translation in Mal 2:16 evinces a translator who was translating word for word without any awareness of the context. However, elsewhere, one sees evidence that the translator of the Twelve did, in fact, appreciate the polysemy of כי אם. As mentioned in §3.5, the collocation is rendered, fittingly, by ἐὰν μή. In Amos 8:11, discussed above, כי אם is represented, quite rightly, with ἀλλά. In the few other occurrences of the collocation, it is also rendered by διότι καὶ ἐάν (Hos 9:12), διότι ἐάν (Amos 5:22), and ἀλλ᾽ ἤ (Mic 6:8; Zech 4:6). Therefore, assuming that 4Q76 does indeed represent a similar text

80. Regarding the textual difficulties of the MT here, see Andrew E. Hill, *Malachi: A New Translation with Introduction and Commentary*, AB 25D (New Haven: Yale University Press, 2008), 249–54.

81. Follingstad describes this type of כי as a marker of "(assertive) polar focus" (see Follingstad, *Deictic Viewpoint*, 157).

82. See the discussions on כי־אם on pp. 113 and 129.

to the *Vorlage* of the Twelve, it is reasonable, based on the translations of כי אם elsewhere in the Twelve that attest to an understanding of its various functions, to posit that the translator made a context-based decision to translate the collocation here with ἀλλὰ ἐάν.

In sum, though the occurrences of ἀλλά are few in the Twelve, they do help to provide a clearer picture of how the translator approached their *Vorlage*. In order to use a DM that is not clearly lexically motivated by the underlying Hebrew or, at the least, is one possible but certainly not the stereotypical option, it is necessary for the translator to have some awareness of the flow of the discourse and to be able to assess the relations between pieces of information. The occurrences of ἀλλά further build upon, even if only a little, the emerging picture of the translator. They are aware of more than just the most immediate context and are willing to forego stereotyped equivalents in favor of representing their understanding of how the discourse fits together. This is not to say that "their understanding" is necessarily different than the meaning conveyed by the Hebrew. On the contrary, their renderings are often fitting translations of their source. However, as discussed in §1.3, Hebrew is much less explicit with regard to relations between propositions, having fewer DMs that do more jobs or having different constructions altogether to accomplish what some Greek DMs accomplish. Thus, when translating the Hebrew, the translator was often faced with more than one possible and viable option for rendering their source text, not just because some of the Hebrew DMs are polysemous but also because the context would allow for more than one interpretation, for example, Mal 2:16—the corrective reading works, but understanding כי as marking a causal clause also fits very well in the context. Without an awareness of context, the translator could not have found reason to use ἀλλά where they do.

## 4.4. Conclusion

Throughout this section, I have argued that ἀλλά has one core pragmatic function: it instructs the recipient to process its host utterance as a corrective to information within his or her mental representation of the discourse. In §§4.1 and 4.2, I examined a representative sample of ἀλλά from third to first century BCE papyri and from the LXX Pentateuch, respectively. These investigations led to the conclusion, discussed in full in §4.2.2, that the DM's core pragmatic function is signaling a corrective relation. Despite a couple minor differences, it was also shown that this claim finds support in other recent Greek linguistic studies, both in Classical Greek and later Koine. In §4.2.3, I discussed the significance of ἀλλά with regard to the study of LXX translation technique. Only on rare occasion can one suggest that ἀλλά may have been used for no other reason than pure lexemic representation. In most occurrences, the DM is not lexically motivated by the underlying Hebrew. Granted, it often accomplishes a similar pragmatic effect as what it is rendering, but even then, a translator chose ἀλλά rather than a lexical or stereotyped equivalent. Moreover, the element(s) rendered by ἀλλά are typically functionally polysemous, exhibiting related but different functions in various contexts and constructions. Assuming they were aware of these various functions, then, a translator had to decide how the Hebrew was functioning, which would be based on their understanding of the discourse and how the pieces of information fit together. Thus, the use of ἀλλά, in most instances, evinces translators who were aware of more than the immediate context and translated accordingly. Lastly, in §4.3, I investigated the few occurrences of ἀλλά in the Twelve. These also revealed a translator who was not concerned with precise lexical or stereotypical representation, but sought to convey the relations they saw in their source text idiomatically in the Greek. This further builds on the developing picture of the translation technique of the Twelve from previous chapters as striving for a faithful rendering of the *Vorlage*, which included maintaining an awareness of the flow of the discourse and an assessment of the context.

# 5
# ἀλλ᾽ ἤ

In the Twelve, of the ten occurrences of ἀλλά, seven are collocated with the disjunctive ἤ.[1] In the rest of the LXX, while ἀλλά does occur more frequently than ἀλλ᾽ ἤ, there is a relatively high percentage of the collocation. Of the 557 instances of ἀλλά in the Greek Old Testament, 138 of them are collocated with ἤ.[2] That is roughly 25 percent of the occurrences of ἀλλά. When compared to the New Testament, this percentage is put in stark relief. Of the 603 instances of ἀλλά in the New Testament, only two are collocated with the disjunctive particle (Luke 12:51 and 2 Cor 1:13). That is a percentage of 0.33. This is a notable difference of use that may suggest ἀλλ᾽ ἤ was a feature of early Koine Greek that was disappearing from the language. According to the data provided below in §5.2, such a decline may also be represented in the papyri of the third to first centuries BCE.[3] Despite the frequency of this collocation in the early koine period and especially in the LXX, it receives practically no attention in Greek lexica and grammars nor in scholarship on LXX translation technique. At worst, the collocation is ignored altogether; at best, it is assumed to be functionally equivalent to ἀλλά without any reason given. The intent of this chapter is to investigate a representative sample of occurrences of ἀλλ᾽ ἤ in the papyri and LXX in order to determine, first, its pragmatic function and, second, what such an understanding of the collocation contributes to the study of LXX translation technique.

1. I am assuming that it is ἀλλά and not ἄλλο in ἀλλ᾽ ἤ. See n. 4 below.
2. This is based on a search of R-H.
3. However, see my comments at the beginning of §5.2.

## 5.1. ἀλλ᾽ ἤ in Greek Scholarship

The treatment of ἀλλ᾽ ἤ in Greek scholarship typically comes in one of three categories: it is regarded as an exceptive, as functionally equivalent to ἀλλά, or as a corrective like ἀλλά but with an added emphatic nuance.[4] Each one of these will be discussed in turn.[5]

The idea that ἀλλ᾽ ἤ is an exceptive, and thus comparable to εἰ μή and ἐὰν μή, is found in Denniston's *Greek Particles*. When ἀλλ᾽ ἤ precedes only one word or a single phrase, he renders it as "except"; when the collocation introduces the second of two coordinated phrases, he renders it as "except that" or "but merely."[6] It is interesting that he suggests the gloss "but merely." While it may be used in exceptive contexts, the focus of such a construction is not on the exception being made but rather on the corrective and exclusive nature of what follows. This may seem slightly pedantic, but it is important to note the difference between exceptive and corrective relations. I regard exception as a subset of correction, being a narrower type of it. This is because exceptives, as demonstrated in chapter 3, portray an event or excluded set member as a corrective that counters previously processed truth-propositional content. Correctives, on the other hand, as exemplified by ἀλλά in chapter 4, correct and realign a presumed piece of information in the reader's mental representation but do not interact with truth-propositional content. In this way, exceptives have a more specific contextual requirement for use. The collocation "but merely" belongs to the corrective superset, as it does not have the contextual requirement that it counter truth-propositional content. However, because it has the added constraint of exclusivity, that is, focusing on the singularity or exclusive nature of what follows, it may be used in what would otherwise be an exceptive context, since exclusion is typically

4. In Greek scholarship, there is no consensus as to whether the ἀλλ᾽ of ἀλλ᾽ ἤ represents the particle ἀλλά or the adjective ἄλλο, though the typical accentuation used reveals a preference for ἀλλά (see Philomen Probert, *A New Short Guide to the Accentuation of Ancient Greek*, Advanced Language Series [London: Bristol Classical Press, 2003], §§78, 275, 277). As will be seen in the examples below, the data indicate that ἀλλά is the more reasonable assumption given the closer functional conformity between ἀλλά and ἀλλ᾽ ἤ.

5. Le Moigne has investigated instances of ἀλλ᾽ ἤ in LXX Isaiah, but this will be discussed in §5.3 below.

6. Denniston, *Particles*, 24.

inherent to exceptions.[7] Because of this, an implicitly exceptive relation between two propositions would provide an excellent context for highlighting the inherent exclusion to the excepted content. The decision to use an exclusive corrective construction rather than an exceptive would then depend on the communicative intent of the speaker. Do they want to focus on the material's status as an exception, countering truth-propositional content, or on it being the exclusive corrective to what preceded? Thus, an exclusive corrective construction such as "but merely" can occur in an exceptive context, owing to its exclusivity constraint, but it can also be used in contexts inappropriate to an exceptive marker such as "except that," owing to its membership in the corrective superset. On this latter type of context, to use one of Denniston's examples, consider Xenophon, *Oec.* 2.13:

> *Οὔτε γὰρ αὐτὸς ὄργανα χρήματα ἐκεκτήμην, ὥστε μανθάνειν, οὔτε ἄλλος πώποτέ μοι παρέσχε τὰ ἑαυτοῦ διοικεῖν* <u>*ἀλλ᾽ ἢ*</u> *σὺ νυνὶ ἐθέλεις παρέχειν.*
> For, I myself had neither procured the necessary instruments, so as to learn, nor did another ever supply me his own instruments to administer a household *all' ē* you now want to supply.

Denniston translates the last clause as "It is only you now that are willing."[8] This is an instance of Denniston's "but merely" use, represented by the cleft construction "It is only." It is unlikely that ἀλλ᾽ ἤ is functioning as an exceptive. An exceptive relation between the two propositions would be forced and would result in semantic incoherence given the lack of a clear exception being made (hence why Denniston does not translate the collocation as "except" or "except that"). Moreover, given the context, Denniston's translation makes sense in its own right, but accepting the translation as a proper and valid rendering requires one to posit a different function for ἀλλ᾽ ἤ. It is not exceptive here but rather an exclusive corrective construction.

Some other grammarians have also posited an exceptive function for ἀλλ᾽ ἤ, such as Friedrich Blass, Albert Debrunner, and Robert Funk, and also Herbert Smyth.[9] James Moulton and Nigel Turner, similarly, regard

---

7. I.e., [not X except $X_1$] assumes an exclusive correction, though its focus is on the exceptive relation between the utterances.

8. Denniston, *Particles*, 24.

9. BDF, §448(8); Smyth, §2777.

the two instances of ἀλλ᾽ ἤ in the New Testament as communicating the same exceptive force as εἰ μή.[10] F. C. Conybeare and St. George Stock, based on their work in the LXX, consider some occurrences of ἀλλ᾽ ἤ to be exceptive, though they do not regard this as the collocation's primary function.[11] Similarly, Edwin Mayser views ἀλλ᾽ ἤ as exceptive but only when following a negation.[12] With regard to lexica, LSJ provides the glosses "except, but" for the collocation, BDAG translates it as "except," and Takamitsu Muraoka posits an exceptive function for some of the collocation's occurrences.[13]

Others have argued that the collocation functions exactly like ἀλλά. Margaret Thrall states that while ἀλλ᾽ ἤ can signal exception in Koine, many occurrences of the collocation in the New Testament, LXX, and papyri are clearly not exceptive and instead witness to a functional equivalence to ἀλλά.[14] In addition, Mayser notes that ἀλλ᾽ ἤ, when not following a negation, is no different from ἀλλά.[15] Muraoka, though positing an exceptive use for some occurrences of ἀλλ᾽ ἤ, also regards the phrase as being able to function just like ἀλλά.[16]

Lastly, there is the claim that the collocation has the same pragmatic function as ἀλλά but expresses a more emphatic nuance. Conybeare and Stock, for example, write, "In most of these passages [i.e., the occurrences of ἀλλ᾽ ἤ in Swete's LXX] ἀλλ᾽ ἤ is simply a strengthened form of ἀλλά. If it differs at all from it, it is in the same way as 'but only' in English differs from the simple 'but.'"[17] It is interesting that Conybeare and Stock provide the gloss "but only," as such is an exclusive corrective construction, similar to glosses used by both Denniston and Smyth. Johannes Louw and Eugene Nida also regard ἀλλ᾽ ἤ as a stronger form of ἀλλά, stating that the collocation is a more emphatic phrase marking contrast.[18] Similarly, MGS glosses the collocation as "but how!" and adds the comment "of indignant surprise."[19]

---

10. Moulton and Turner, *Grammar*, 330.
11. Conybeare and Stock, *Grammar*, §108.
12. Mayser, *Grammatik*, §164.35.
13. LSJ, s.v. "ἀλλ᾽ ἤ"; BDAG, s.v. "ἀλλά"; *GELS*, s.v. "ἀλλά."
14. Thrall, *Greek Particles*, 16–20.
15. Mayser, *Grammatik*, §164.18.
16. *GELS*, s.v. "ἀλλά."
17. Conybeare and Stock, *Grammar*, §108.
18. L-N, §89.125.
19. MGS, s.v. "ἀλλά."

The history reveals that Greek scholarship is divided. While there is more of a consensus that ἀλλ᾽ ἤ is an exceptive marker, there are notable voices who understand the collocation as resembling ἀλλά, whether equivalent to it or also adding an emphatic nuance. Moreover, though the terminology is never used, some in fact seem to view ἀλλ᾽ ἤ as an exclusive corrective construction, based on their renderings of it when translated in context or on glosses provided. In what follows, in order to move beyond this standstill, a representative sample of occurrences of ἀλλ᾽ ἤ in the papyri and LXX will be investigated, and an attempt will be made to discern and describe the collocation's discourse-pragmatic function and how it guides the reader in processing the text and building the mental representation of it.

## 5.2. The Use of ἀλλ᾽ ἤ in the Papyri

In the papyri of the third century, ἀλλ᾽ ἤ occurs twenty-nine times. In the second century, there are twelve instances of ἀλλ᾽ ἤ, most of them being used formulaically in a set of related papyri.[20] In the first century, there are none. As I mentioned in §5.1 above, the decline of the use of ἀλλ᾽ ἤ, as witnessed to between the LXX and New Testament, may also be represented in the papyri. However, there is a significant decline in extant papyri between the third and first centuries BCE, which may skew our results.[21]

### 5.2.1. P.Lond. 7.2006 (248 BCE)

In this letter to Zenon, a certain Jason (presumably an employee of Zenon's) has run into financial issues. He needs to pay six months' worth of wages to some shepherds but, as he writes in his letter, is unsure from where to take the money. He explains to Zenon that the typical sources of funding are either not available or sufficient. Moreover, funds are short for other transactions, such as for some cheese Zenon instructed Jason to purchase. Here we find an instance of ἀλλ᾽ ἤ.

> (15) κ̣α̣ὶ τὸν τυρὸν ὃν γράφεις ἡμῖν πα[ρ]αλαμβάνειν ἐκ ι (δραχμῶν) τὸ τάλαντον οὐχ̣ εὑρίσκει \τὸ τά(λαντον)/ <u>ἀλλ᾽ ἢ</u> (δραχμὰς) ς.

20. UPZ 1.52, 1.53, 1.54, 1.55.

21. See T. V. Evans, "The Potential of Linguistic Criteria for Dating Septuagint Books," *BIOSCS* 43 (2010): 10–11.

> (15) And the cheese about which you wrote to us to receive for a sum of ten drachmae, he cannot find the sum *all' ē* six drachmae.

It may be the case that the relation between the statement "he cannot find the sum" and the following "six drachmae" is exceptive, as the context does allow for it ("he cannot find the sum *except* six drachmae"). However, the more conventional εἰ/ἐὰν μή would be the natural choice if such were the case. Moreover, exception, though arguably possible, does not quite fit the context. A sum of ten drachmae is not a set, or at least not a typical set, from which members may be excepted. A *sum*, by definition, is a totality and therefore cannot be modified by an exception. It is like using the qualifier "all." If I were to say, "I cannot find all of my students except these two," though my interlocutor may understand me, the sentence is not well formed because an exception is not made. It remains true that I cannot find all of my students and thus the truth-propositional content of the utterance is not countered, which it should be if an exception were being made.[22] Instead, I would need to either say, "I cannot find all of my students *but only* these two" or "I cannot find *any* of my students *except* these two." The former retains "all" but corrects the potential assumption that no students were found. The latter is exceptive but required "all" to be changed to "any." In the same way, the truth-propositional content of "he cannot find the sum" is not countered by "six drachmae." It remains true that the sum cannot be found.

If ἀλλά underlies ἀλλ' ἤ and one were to regard the particle as exhibiting its normal pragmatic function, informing the reader of an upcoming correction to preceding material or to an assumption arising from what preceded, then they could understand it to be signaling a corrective to the preceding proposition: "He cannot find the sum *but rather* six drachmae." This may be possible, but if this were the intended relation between propositions, ἀλλά would be the obvious and more simple choice, not ἀλλ' ἤ.

One would do well to ask what is relevant about the "six drachmae." The purpose for adding "six drachmae" after "he cannot find the sum" is to communicate that this is all the person has; he can find only six drachmae and it is not enough. A restrictive or exclusive relation between propositions would not be obtained through asyndeton, so it would need a dedicated DM in order to be communicated. Thus, it would seem that ἀλλ'

22. See the discussion on exceptives in ch. 3.

ἤ is signaling an exclusive correction ("He cannot find the sum *but only* six drachmae"), correcting the potential assumption that the person has no money at all and at the same time focusing on the fact that this is the only portion of the sum that he has.[23] This would make sense given the context and also has the advantage of regarding both particles as contributing to the function of the collocation (if the first member of the collocation is ἀλλά). The particle ἀλλά retains its corrective function ("but") and the disjunctive ἤ takes on a more idiomatic role ("only"). However, it is possible that ἤ taking on the role of an exclusive marker could be construed as an extension of its use as a marker of an alternative, in that, in a context in which the first option is eliminated and corrected, the disjunctive is no longer concerned with presenting an alternative (in fact, it is no longer possible!) and must present the only remaining option. In other words, the interaction with the context and with the procedural constraint that ἀλλά signals leaves ἤ without a first option and so it then must narrow its focus to the only "option" left.

5.2.2. P.Cair.Zen. 2.59270 (251 BCE)

In this letter, Spondates corresponds with Zenon concerning deliveries of wood in response to a prior request from Zenon. An instance of ἀλλ᾽ ἤ can be found when Spondates clarifies whether acacia wood is needed.

> (5) γέγραφα σοι ἵνα εἰδῇις διότι ξύλων ἀκανθίνων οὐχ ὑστεροῦσι, <u>ἀλλ᾽ ἤ</u> ἔχουσι ἱκανά, συκαμινίνων δὲ χρεία ἔσται
> (5) I have written to you in order that you know they are not lacking acacia wood, *all' ē* they have enough. Now, there is a need for sycamore wood.

The collocation cannot be exceptive, as the context would not allow it. However, the relation between the propositions could very well be one of correction: "They are not lacking acacia wood, *but/rather* they have enough." The relevance of the proposition "they have enough" is that it provides the corrective for the preceding proposition. Thus, ἀλλά would be the most natural DM to use between these two propositions. This would

23. Claude Orrieux takes the ἀλλ᾽ ἤ here in the same way, translating it with the French restrictive construction *ne … que* (*Les Papyrus de Zenon: L'horizon d'un grec en Egypte au IIIe siècle avant J.C.*, Deucalion [Paris: Macula, 1983], 143).

be similar to the instances of ἀλλά in Gen 40:23 and Exod 16:19–20a, observed in chapter 4, where the DM introduces material that is essentially tautologous.[24] The preceding negated information is, for all intents and purposes, restated as a positive corrective. Instead, though, the author uses ἀλλ᾽ ἤ. It may be the case that the collocation is functionally equivalent to ἀλλά. As with example 1, though, an exclusive corrective reading is possible here. In this way, ἀλλ᾽ ἤ would accomplish an exclusive-marking function in addition to what ἀλλά alone accomplishes, thereby allowing the two DMs to be regarded as related functionally but not as completely equivalent. Thus, the Greek would be rendered: "They are not lacking acacia wood, *but* they *only* have what is sufficient." The choice to use ἀλλ᾽ ἤ instead of ἀλλά, then, is motivated by the desire to express the restricted nature of what is being communicated. While there is no lack of acacia wood, neither, it would seem, is there an abundance. "ἀλλά they have what is sufficient" does not inform Zenon whether it is enough wood for just the time being or enough for the next year; "ἀλλ᾽ ἤ they have what is sufficient" assures him that there is not a pressing need for acacia wood but also informs him that there could be one soon.

### 5.2.3. P.Cair.Zen. 3.59492 (third century BCE)

Zenon had previously instructed Paosis to tell him if anyone treats him unjustly. Paosis now writes to Zenon because of the unjust predicament in which he finds himself.

> (5) γίνωσκε οὖν Ἡρακλίδην τὸν ἐπὶ τῶν μυρίων ἀπαγαγών με εἰς τὸ δεσμωτήριον τετιμώρηταί με εἰσπράσσων (δραχμὰς) ρ. ἐμοὶ δὲ ὑπάρχει οὐθὲν ἀλλ᾽ ἢ ὅσα μοι Ὧρος κατέλιπεν
> (5) So, know that Herakleides, the leader of the ten thousand, after taking me to prison, has avenged himself upon me by exacting one hundred drachmae. Now there is nothing to me *all' ē* as much as Horos left to me.

This instance of ἀλλ᾽ ἤ occurs in what could be taken as an exceptive context.[25] However, the salience and relevance of the information follow-

24. See pp. 170–71.

25. Note Orrieux's translation: "Or je ne possède rien sinon ce que m'a laissé Horos" ("But I do not possess anything *except* what Horos left me"). Orrieux, *Les Papyrus de Zenon*, 129.

ing ἀλλ᾽ ἤ is in its exclusive nature more-so than it being an exception. Thus, ἀλλ᾽ ἤ is both fitting and natural in the context. It alerts the reader to process what follows as a corrective to the preceding "nothing to me" and to focus on the limitation: "There is nothing to me *but only* as much as Horos left to me."

### 5.2.4. P.Hamb. 1.27 (250 BCE)

The author writes to Zenon with regard to a number of business matters in Philadelphia.[26] One such matter concerns a lack of fodder, owing to a certain Onnophris's inability or lack of desire to provide what was previously arranged.

> (15) εἰ δέ σοι φαίνεται, καλῶς ποιήσεις ἀποστείλας (δραχμὰς) η, ὅπως δώ[σω ὑπ(ὲρ) γεωρ]γῶν· εἰσὶν γὰρ εἰς ιβ ἀρ(ο)ύ(ρας) τῶν δ (δραχμῶν) \ τῶι μι[σ]θίωι/. χόρτον <γὰρ> ⟦ἡμῖν⟧ οὐκ ἔδωκεν ἡμῖν Ὀννῶφρις ἀλλ᾽ ἢ [τ]εσ[σεράκοντα ἀρ(τάβας)] τῶν υ ὧν ἔγραψας αὐτῶι, ὥστε λυσιτελεῖ μισθώσασθαι ἢ χορτάσματα ζητεῖν.
> (15) Now, if it seems fitting to you, please send eight drachmae, so that I may give it on behalf of the farmers. For they are in twelve fields for four drachmae for the tenant.[27] For Onnophris did not give pasturage to us *all' e* forty artaba of the four hundred about which you wrote to him, with the result that it is better to hire or to request fodder.

The author could have used ἀλλά to express the corrective relation between the propositions, but instead chooses ἀλλ᾽ ἤ. Like ἀλλά, it signals a corrective replacement to the preceding, but its exclusive constraint explicitly communicates the degree to which Onnophris did not meet Zenon's wishes. He did not give them pasturage *but only* forty of the four hundred artaba (presumably of fodder)![28] The use of ἀλλά would have

---

26. The author's name is unknown.

27. Earlier in the letter, the author notes that there are only three farmers!

28. Presumably, the pasturage is needed for animals to feed but Zenon also specifically requested four hundred artaba of fodder in addition. Another way to read this would be to understand the χόρτον that Onnophris did not provide as fodder, which leads to a different meaning, namely, "Onnophris did not give fodder to us *but only* forty artaba of the four hundred." In this case, εἰ/ἐὰν μή could have been used, given the counter to the truth-propositional content of the preceding. The fact that ἀλλ᾽ ἤ is used instead would seem to be due to its limiting constraint being more relevant given the situation than an explicit exceptive constraint. The difficulty with this latter

been sufficient to relate the two propositions and highlight the corrective, owing to the increased processing effort required by the construction. However, by using ἀλλ᾽ ἤ, the author provides a limitative frame of reference through which the reader will process the corrective. In addition, in this context, the exclusive serves to communicate a more explicitly emphatic utterance than would have been achieved by ἀλλά.

### 5.2.5. The Function of ἀλλά as Evinced in the Papyri

Given the small amount of data in the papyri, a tentative suggestion is provided here. It appears that ἀλλ᾽ ἤ has a very specific pragmatic function: marking an exclusive corrective relation. The DM informs the reader that what follows is relevant in that it is a correction to the preceding information and also narrows the reader's focus to the salient exclusive or limited element of the correction.

## 5.3. The Use of ἀλλ᾽ ἤ in the LXX

Of the thirty-five occurrences of ἀλλ᾽ ἤ in the Pentateuch and the Twelve, it is used to render כי אם the most with thirteen occurrences, followed by nine instances in which the Hebrew text simply reads כי. On the whole, then, while the translators understandably use ἀλλ᾽ ἤ in contexts in which כי אם occurs in the Hebrew *Vorlagen*, there is a wider spectrum of use that goes beyond quantitative representation of the Hebrew and, perhaps in a few instances at least, beyond qualitative representation as well. A full count of the occurrences of the phrase in the Twelve and Pentateuch is provided below in the table below.

| Underlying Hebrew: | Number of Instances |
|---|---|
| כי אם | 13 |
| כי | 9 |
| Ø | 2 |
| אפס | 2 |
| אך | 2 |

option, though, is discerning why the author used χόρτον for "fodder" when he uses a more specific term (χορτάσματα) at the end. Hence why I have taken χόρτον as pasturage above.

| | |
|---|---|
| בלתי | 1 |
| אם־לא | 1 |
| בלתי־אם | 1 |
| הלוא | 1 |
| ואם | 1 |
| זולתי | 1 |
| רק | 1 |

### 5.3.1. Examples from the LXX

In Gen 24:38, Abraham's servant recounts how he was instructed not to take a wife for Isaac from the Canaanites but rather from Abraham's extended family.

> (24:37) καὶ ὥρκισέν με ὁ κύριός μου λέγων Οὐ λήμψῃ γυναῖκα τῷ υἱῷ μου ἀπὸ τῶν θυγατέρων τῶν Χαναναίων, ἐν οἷς ἐγὼ οἰκῶ ἐν τῇ γῇ αὐτῶν, (38) ἀλλ' ἤ εἰς τὸν οἶκον τοῦ πατρός μου πορεύσῃ καὶ εἰς τὴν φυλήν μου καὶ λήμψῃ γυναῖκα τῷ υἱῷ μου ἐκεῖθεν.
> (24:37) And my lord made me swear saying, "You will not take a wife for my son from the daughters of the Canaanites, among whom I am living in their land. (38) *All' ē* you will go to the house of my father and to my tribe and you will take a wife for my son from there."

> אם־לא אל־בית־אבי תלך ואל־משפחתי ולקחת אשה לבני
> "But you will go to the house of my father, to my family. And you will take a wife for my son."

As Abraham's family are not Canaanites themselves, ἀλλ' ἤ cannot be signaling an exception. What is relevant about the information following ἀλλ' ἤ is that it serves as a correction to an element of the preceding. *Instead* of a Canaanite wife, Abraham's servant is to find a wife from within the non-Canaanite family. Thus, it would seem that ἀλλ' ἤ is functioning at least in a very similar manner to the particle ἀλλά. In fact, in Gen 24:4, when Abraham gives this command to his servant, the translator renders the underlying כי with ἀλλά:

> μὴ λάβῃς γυναῖκα τῷ υἱῷ μου Ἰσαὰκ ἀπὸ τῶν θυγατέρων τῶν Χαναναίων, μεθ' ὧν ἐν ἐγὼ οἰκῶ αὐτοῖς ἀλλ' εἰς τὴν γῆν μου, οὗ ἐγενόμην, πορεύσῃ καὶ εἰς τὴν φυλήν μου καὶ λήμψῃ γυναῖκα τῷ υἱῷ μου Ἰσαὰκ ἐκεῖθεν.

> You will not take a wife for my son Isaac from the daughters of the Canaanites, among whom I am living. Rather, you will go to my land, where I was born, and to my tribe, and you will take a wife for my son Isaac from there.

Thus, it would appear that one could posit some extent of functional equivalence between ἀλλά and ἀλλ᾽ ἤ.[29]

One may also be able to make a case for ἀλλ᾽ ἤ expressing a more emphatic nuance. Given the כי in 24:4 that is represented by ἀλλά and the אם־לא in 24:38 that is represented by ἀλλ᾽ ἤ, it is plausible that the LXX translator decided to use a more emphatic form of ἀλλά to match the emphatic affirmative that אם־לא expresses, particularly after an oath.[30] It could be argued that the decision to use ἀλλ᾽ ἤ was based solely on a need to quantifiably represent both lexemes in the underlying Hebrew. However, while I do not deny that quantitative representation was likely a consideration, the translator of LXX Genesis does feel free elsewhere to render single lexemes with ἀλλ᾽ ἤ (Gen 21:26; 45:8) and two lexemes with ἀλλά (Gen 15:4; 32:28 [29 MT]; 35:10; 40:14). Thus, this occurrence of ἀλλ᾽ ἤ may evince a pragmatic function like ἀλλά but with an added emphatic force.

Another option is to regard ἀλλ᾽ ἤ as an exclusive corrective marker, which suits the context well and still has the potential rhetorical effect of expressing emphasis. By signaling a correction and focusing on the exclusivity of something, emphasis may naturally arise. The difference between "You will not take a daughter from the Canaanites, *but* you will go to my land" and "You will not take a daughter from the Canaanites, *but* you will *only* go to my land" is first the exclusivity signaled by "only" and second the emphasis that arises owing to the use of "only."

By rendering אם־לא with ἀλλ᾽ ἤ, the translator goes beyond lexical representation (e.g., εἰ μή, which would have resulted in incoherence). Instead, it would seem that owing to his understanding of the text and the flow of the discourse, the translator decided to convey the relation with a pragmatically similar device in koine idiom.

---

29. It should be noted that there are manuscripts that add ἤ in Gen 24:4 as well as manuscripts that omit the ἤ in Gen 24:38.

30. BDB, s.v. "אִם"; *DCH*, s.v. "אִם"; Gesenius, *Hebräisches und Aramäisches Handwörterbuch*, s.v. "אִם."

Another example may be found in Deut 4:12. Here, Moses is speaking to Israel and reminding them of the theophany at Mt. Horeb and the declaration of the covenant.

> καὶ ἐλάλησεν κύριος πρὸς ὑμᾶς ἐκ μέσου τοῦ πυρός· φωνὴν ῥημάτων ὑμεῖς ἠκούσατε, καὶ ὁμοίωμα οὐκ εἴδετε, ἀλλ' ἢ φωνήν·
> And the Lord spoke to you from the midst of the fire; you hear the sound of words, but you did not see a form, *all' ē* a voice.
>
> וידבר יהוה אליכם מתוך האש קול דברים אתם שמעים ותמונה אינכם ראים זולתי קול
> And YHWH spoke to you from the midst of the fire. You heard the sound of words, but you did not see an image—only a voice.

The relevant relation between propositions here is one of correction. As no truth-propositional content is being countered, an exceptive relation would be incoherent. Rather, optimal relevance is achieved in the communicative act by the hearer understanding that φωνήν was the thing experienced *instead of* or *in place of* seeing a ὁμοίωμα. Thus, again, ἀλλ' ἤ appears to guide the reader in the building of his mental representation of the text by signaling that what follows should be processed as a corrective to what preceded. However, if this was the intended mental route, why not use ἀλλά? It was more prevalent in the language, at least by what one can observe in the papyri, LXX, and New Testament. Moreover, ἀλλ' ἤ is only representing one lexeme in the Hebrew, זולתי. If the collocation has the same function as ἀλλά and the underlying Hebrew being rendered is one word and not two, ἀλλά would seem to be the much more reasonable choice. Thus, it is likely that ἀλλ' ἤ is accomplishing something more than ἀλλά. Similar to the above examples from Gen 24 and the papyri, ἀλλ' ἤ may be functioning as an exclusive corrective—"you did not see a form *but* (you heard) *only* a voice." In context, an exclusive constraint is understandable and adds to the communication. It serves to drive home the point that they saw no form and heard only a voice out of the midst of the fire. In addition, if ἀλλ' ἤ does have an exclusive-signaling function, it is a fitting rendering of זולתי here, which can signal exclusivity and is regularly translated as such in this instance.[31] Granted, ἀλλ' ἤ adds the corrective

---

31. So also John William Wevers, *Notes on the Greek Text of Deuteronomy*, SCS 39 (Atlanta: Scholars Press, 1995), 73. Consider some modern translations of the

element of ἀλλά to the utterance, but given the tendency toward explicit interclausal relations in Greek, this should not be too surprising. Moreover, it is a fitting rendering given the context and given that a corrective relation can be implicitly perceived in the Hebrew. Lastly, it is interesting to note that both NETS and the LES translate ἀλλ' ἤ as "only" here. Similarly, LXX.D translates it with "nur," and *Bd'A* renders it as "seulement."

In Exod 16, the people of Israel start complaining to Moses and Aaron. They are tired of walking in the wilderness and they are famished. They find this new way of life so terrible that they go so far as to wish they had died in Egypt. Moses and Aaron address the congregation to inform them that God will provide meat and bread for them. In addition, they remind Israel against whom the people are truly complaining.

> (16:8) *καὶ εἶπεν Μωυσῆς Ἐν τῷ διδόναι κύριον ὑμῖν ἑσπέρας κρέα φαγεῖν καὶ ἄρτους τὸ πρωὶ εἰς πλησμονήν, διὰ τὸ εἰσακοῦσαι κύριον τὸν γογγυσμὸν ὑμῶν, ὃν ὑμεῖς διαγογγύζετε καθ' ἡμῶν· ἡμεῖς δὲ τί ἐσμεν; οὐ γὰρ καθ' ἡμῶν ὁ γογγυσμὸς ὑμῶν ἐστιν, ἀλλ' ἢ κατὰ τοῦ θεοῦ.*
> (16:8) And Moses said, "When the Lord gives you meat to eat at evening and bread at morning to sate you, because the Lord heard your grumbling that you are grumbling against us, and what are we? For your grumbling is not against us, *all' ē* against God."
>
> ויאמר משה בתת יהוה לכם בערב בשר לאכל ולחם בבקר לשבע בשמע יהוה את־תלנתיכם אשר־אתם מלינם עליו ונחנו מה לא־עלינו תלנתיכם כי על־יהוה
> And Moses said, "When YHWH gives you meat to eat in the evening and bread in the morning to fill you, because YHWH heard your murmurings that you are murmuring against us, and what are we? Your murmurings are not against us, but against YHWH."

Similar to what has been observed thus far, this occurrence of ἀλλ' ἤ cannot be construed as an exceptive marker, as no exception is being made. Rather, as is typical for the particle ἀλλά, the proposition preceding ἀλλ' ἤ negates a set ("us") and the proposition following ἀλλ' ἤ affirms an element of an entirely different set ("God"). Given this, the collocation appears to function in a similar capacity to ἀλλά. It is alerting the reader that what follows is a corrective (in this case, a replacement) to what pre-

Hebrew: "only," NET, NRSV, NIV, KJV, ESV; "ne … que," Nouvelle Edition de Genève, BDS, LSG; "non … che," NR; "soltanto," CEI; "nur," Schlachter; "sólo," LBLA, NBD, NBLH, NTV, NVI.

ceded. In this sense, ἀλλά could have been used rather than ἀλλ' ἤ. In fact, it would have been the simpler choice—one particle to signal correction instead of two particles to signal the same. Thus, in addition to the corrective constraint, the collocation may be construed as also communicating an exclusive relation. Pragmatically, this signals to the reader to restrict his focus from Moses and Aaron not just to God but to God *alone*, which then entails a rhetorical effect of more emphatically and more forcefully singling out the recipient of the people's complaining.

It is significant that the underlying Hebrew is כי, since it would be better represented quantitatively by ἀλλά as well as qualitatively (the Exodus translator even renders כי with ἀλλά once elsewhere; Exod 23:24). The fact that they do not demonstrates an engagement with and interpretation of the text. Their translation instructs the reader to process the text so that what was implicit in the Hebrew is now explicit in the Greek. It seems likely that this was done in order to bring about the rhetorical emphatic effect.

Leviticus 21 details rules for living for the priests of Israel. In verse 14, the Lord provides instructions regarding whom the high priest may marry.

> χήραν δὲ καὶ ἐκβεβλημένην καὶ βεβηλωμένην καὶ πόρνην, ταύτας οὐ λήμψεται, <u>ἀλλ' ἤ</u> παρθένον ἐκ τοῦ γένους αὐτοῦ λήμψεται γυναῖκα·
> Now, a widow, a woman who has been cast out, a woman who has been defiled, or a prostitute, these he will not take, *all' ē* he will take a virgin from his kin as a wife.

> אלמנה וגרושה וחללה זנה את־אלה לא יקח כי אם־בתולה מעמיו יקח אשה
> A widow, a woman who has been cast out, or a defiled harlot, these he will not take. Instead, he will take a virgin from his people as a wife.

The high priest is limited to only one kind of woman for marriage, a virgin from his own kin. The virgin is not a member of the previously negated set (widow, divorcee, defiled woman, prostitute). This is made all the more clear by what immediately follows in verse 15: "And he will not profane his children among his people." It is because the virgin is construed as a member of an entirely different set that she is acceptable as a wife, in that, unlike the other women, she will bear nondefiled children. Thus, ἀλλ' ἤ cannot be an exceptive marker here, as it would not signal a counter to truth-propositional content. Thus, instead of ἀλλ' ἤ marking an exceptive relation, the collocation signals, similar to what has been observed in the above examples, a correction to preceding content and restricts the reader's focus to the sole acceptable alternative, thus: "*rather*, he will *only* take a virgin from his kin as a wife."

The translator could have translated the underlying כי אם with the often pragmatically equivalent *εἰ μή* or *ἐὰν μή*. The fact that he did not evinces his knowledge that כי אם can function either as an exceptive or as a broader corrective, since he does suitably translate the Hebrew collocation with *ἐὰν μή* elsewhere (Lev 22:6).[32] Moreover, this demonstrates the translator's awareness of what is being communicated in context, since he allows the surrounding context to influence his choice of DM.

Another example of *ἀλλ' ἤ* may be found in Num 13:29. Here, the spies that were sent into Canaan have returned to the people of Israel and are detailing what they saw.

> (13:28) *καὶ διηγήσαντο αὐτῷ καὶ εἶπαν Ἤλθαμεν εἰς τὴν γῆν, εἰς ἣν ἀπέστειλας ἡμᾶς, γῆν ῥέουσαν γάλα καὶ μέλι, καὶ οὗτος ὁ καρπὸς αὐτῆς· (29) ἀλλ' ἢ ὅτι θρασὺ τὸ ἔθνος τὸ κατοικοῦν ἐπ' αὐτῆς, καὶ αἱ πόλεις ὀχυραὶ τετειχισμέναι καὶ μεγάλαι σφόδρα, καὶ τὴν γενεὰν Εναχ ἑωράκαμεν ἐκεῖ,*
> (13:28) And they explained to him and said, "We came into the land, into which you sent us, a land flowing with milk and honey, and this is its fruit. (29) *All' ē* that the people living in it are bold, and the cities are fortified, having been walled and very large, and we have seen the race of Anak there."

> ויספרו־לו ויאמרו באנו אל־הארץ אשר שלחתנו וגם זבת חלב ודבש הוא וזה־פריה: אפס כי־עז העם הישב בארץ והערים בצרות גדלת מאד וגם־ילדי הענק ראינו שם
> (13:27) And they told him and said, "We went into the land to which you sent us. And, indeed, it is flowing with milk and honey, and this is

32. In fact, Follingstad regards כי אם as marking "contrastive exhaustive-listing focus" (Follingstad, *Deictic Viewpoint*, 156). He writes, "It not only excludes, but replaces and corrects a presupposition that goes against the exclusion. It does this 'exhaustively' —i.e., not X **only** Y" (156–57, emphasis original). Follingstad regards "exceptive כי אם" as a type of use that falls within (or is a subset of) the broader contrastive exhaustive-listing focus category (see his discussion in §F.3.2.1.2). Locatell also notes the exceptive and restrictive uses of כי אם and comments on the conceptually fluidity between the two (Locatell, "Grammatical Polysemy in the Hebrew Bible," 260–61). Thus, it makes sense why one may observe *εἰ/ἐὰν μή*, *ἀλλά*, and *ἀλλ' ἤ* are all used to translate כי אם in the LXX. None of them cover the exact same territory of כי אם (*ἀλλ' ἤ* comes very close, but is not as productive and contextually neutral as כי אם), but they all functionally overlap with the Hebrew collocation.

its fruit. (28) Nevertheless ("only that"), the people living in the land are strong, and the cities are unassailable and very large. And we also saw the descendants of Anak there."

The translator could have used the restrictive πλήν to render אפס, which can function as a restrictive.[33] The Greek particle would work in the context and suitably represent the Hebrew. The use of ἀλλ᾽ ἤ instead demonstrates the translator's desire to explicitly signal a correction to the assumption that arises from 13:28, that because the land is so good, the people should settle there. By using ἀλλ᾽ ἤ, the translator makes explicit the correction in the spies' words, that one should not assume based on what has been said that the people should settle in the land, rather they have reasons for staying out of the land! The additional exclusivity function of ἀλλ᾽ ἤ makes it more suitable than ἀλλά, first because it matches the function of the underlying אפס and second because its pragmatic function naturally entails, given the context, an emphatic rhetorical nuance. Thus, this may be an example of an extension of the DM's use, in that it may have been chosen for the occasionally associated rhetorical effect of marking emphasis rather than for the pragmatic function of marking exclusivity itself.[34]

In Lev 21:2, there is an occurrence of ἀλλ᾽ ἤ that one could argue marks an exceptive relation.

(21:1) Καὶ εἶπεν κύριος πρὸς Μωυσῆν λέγων Εἰπὸν τοῖς ἱερεῦσιν τοῖς υἱοῖς Ἀαρὼν καὶ ἐρεῖς πρὸς αὐτούς Ἐν ταῖς ψυχαῖς οὐ μιανθήσονται ἐν τῷ ἔθνει αὐτῶν, (2) ἀλλ᾽ ἢ ἐν τῷ οἰκείῳ τῷ ἔγγιστα αὐτῶν, ἐπὶ πατρὶ καὶ μητρί, καὶ υἱοῖς καὶ θυγατράσιν, ἐπ᾽ ἀδελφῷ (3) καὶ ἀδελφῇ παρθένῳ τῇ ἐγγιζούσῃ αὐτῷ τῇ μὴ ἐκδεδομένῃ ἀνδρί, ἐπὶ τούτοις μιανθήσεται.
(21:1) And the Lord said to Moses, "Speak to the priests, the sons of Aaron and you will say to them: They will not be defiled by the dead among their people, (2) *all' ē* by their nearest kin, for father and mother and sons and daughters, for a brother (3) and a virgin sister who was close to him and did not have a husband. For these he may be defiled."

---

33. See *HALOT*, s.v. "אֶפֶס"; BDB, s.v. "אֶפֶס"; Wilhem Gesenius, *Hebräisches und Aramäisches Handwörterbuch*, s.v. "אֶפֶס."

34. This less prototypical use would still bear sufficient resemblance to the prototypical ἀλλ᾽ ἤ, given both the corrective element and the frequent potential for an emphatic nuance in many of the DM's contexts of use. As is frequently the case with fuzzy boundary uses of language elements, the interaction between the DM and the surrounding context would clarify for the recipient the communicative intent behind the DM.

> ויאמר יהוה אל־משה אמר אל־הכהנים בני אהרן ואמרת אלהם לנפש לא־יטמא בעמיו: כי אם־לשארו הקרב אליו לאמו ולאביו ולבנו ולבתו ולאחיו: כולאחתו הבתולה הקרובה אליו אשר לא־היתה לאיש לה יטמא
>
> (21:1) And YHWH said to Moses, "Speak to the priests, the sons of Aaron, and you will say to them: He will not defile himself for a dead person among his people. (2) Except for his close relative, for his mother and for his father and for his son and for his daughter and for his brother (3) and for his virgin sister who is close to him who did not have a husband; for her, he may defile himself."

The exceptive relation between propositions is evident. A set is negated—"they will not be defiled by the dead among their people"—and then members from that set are reintroduced as exceptions—"their nearest kin." There is a clear exception being communicated. The question, then, is whether ἀλλ' ἤ may be used to signal exception or if the translator is using it as an exclusive corrective as in the above examples. First, as previously discussed, the Leviticus translator is aware that כי אם can function as either a corrective or an exceptive. In Lev 22:6, a clearly exceptive context, the translator renders כי אם with ἐὰν μή, and in Lev 21:14, a clearly corrective context in which an exceptive reading would be incoherent, he renders it with ἀλλ' ἤ. If he had wanted to focus on the exceptive relation, there is no reason why the translator could not have used εἰ μή or ἐὰν μή. Thus, already, there is reason to think that the translator may be using ἀλλ' ἤ to focus on a different relation. Moreover, everything that has been observed up to this point suggests that ἀλλ' ἤ is a marker of an exclusive corrective relation. Second, recalling the discussion in §5.1, exceptives and exclusive-markers share some overlap when it comes to suitable contexts of use. All exceptions inherently assume some element of exclusion; not all exclusive-markers, however, assume exception, as the above examples all illustrate. Because of this, two deductions may be made: First, it is possible for an exclusive to replace an exceptive when the communicator wants to focus on the exclusion more-so than the exception. Second, the converse of this, that an exceptive can replace an exclusive, is of course not necessarily true; an exceptive marker will often not be able to be substituted for the exclusive marker.

Based on this, the most reasonable approach to this occurrence of ἀλλ' ἤ, and others like it, is to regard it as maintaining its exclusive corrective function. This does not eliminate the inherent exception in the context, instead it simply guides the reader to focus on the exclusivity or restriction of the excepted element, rather than on the exception itself.

Thus: "They will not be defiled by the dead among their people, *but only* by their nearest kin."

### 5.3.2. A Cognitive-Functional Description of ἀλλ᾽ ἤ

Based on what has been observed in the LXX, the description of ἀλλ᾽ ἤ provided in §5.2.5 may be confirmed. It seems evident that the DM has a very specific pragmatic function: marking an exclusive corrective relation.[35] Thus, in an example such as Exod 16:8, *οὐ γὰρ καθ᾽ ἡμῶν ὁ γογγυσμὸς ὑμῶν ἐστιν, ἀλλ᾽ ἢ κατὰ τοῦ θεοῦ*, the reader's mental route is to first process the negated proposition that the people's grumbling is not against Moses and Aaron. Second, ἀλλ᾽ ἤ informs the reader that they should continue building the mental representation of the text by regarding what follows as offering new information that is a correction to what preceded. Not only that, but the correction has an exclusive force. It is *only* this thing, nothing else. Third, the reader processes "against God" as the exclusive correction, understanding the proposition's relevance as informing them of where the grumblings of the previous proposition are actually directed if not to Moses and Aaron. In addition, there is rhetorical purpose in using ἀλλ᾽ ἤ, in that it seems that the exclusive-signaling force of ἀλλ᾽ ἤ may entail, at least in some contexts, a certain level of emphasis.

With regard to how ἀλλ᾽ ἤ has been described in Greek scholarship, the description offered here finds many suggestions with which to agree, some with which to disagree, and offers a slightly different way of conceiving of the collocation. I find the suggestion that the collocation is a marker of exception to be unconvincing. In many contexts, such simply does not work as an analysis of the DM. Granted, ἀλλ᾽ ἤ can and does occur in exceptive contexts, but that does not necessarily indicate an exceptive-marking function, especially when εἰ/ἐὰν μή are available and typical. Rather, the exclusive-signaling element of ἀλλ᾽ ἤ naturally lends the collocation to exceptive contexts. This is to be expected, as

35. This understanding of the collocation has also been indirectly suggested by Drummen, based on her research on ἀλλά. While she notes the common acceptance of the collocation as an exceptive, she translates an occurrence of it from Aristophanes's *Frogs* with "but only," noting the incompatibility of exception to the context, and then remarks, "Even if we *are* dealing with the idiomatic expression ["except that"] here, I believe the correcting function of the particle can certainly be felt" (Drummen, "Discourse Cohesion in Dialogue," 147).

there is a relationship between restriction and exception evinced cross-linguistically.[36] They are distinct functions, but they share functional overlap. Nevertheless, the function of ἀλλ᾽ ἤ as I have described it can be maintained even in contexts in which an exceptive marker would be acceptable. Some in Greek scholarship even saw this themselves, it would seem, by glosses given for ἀλλ᾽ ἤ like "but merely." The use of ἀλλ᾽ ἤ in an exceptive context, then, is a meaningful choice to focus on the inherent exclusivity more-so than the exception.[37] I am in agreement with those scholars who suggest that ἀλλ᾽ ἤ has the same function as ἀλλά. I would only add that it has an additional exclusive-signaling function as well, which makes the choice to use ἀλλ᾽ ἤ in a context wherein ἀλλά would suffice a meaningful one. Lastly, the suggestion that ἀλλ᾽ ἤ is an emphatic form of ἀλλά is both correct and incorrect. Its exclusive-signaling function does give the collocation a stronger force than ἀλλά, but to call that "emphatic" runs the risk of missing the restriction that is being communicated. However, as was observed in some of the examples above, the exclusive relation, in certain contexts, can entail an emphatic nuance being added to the correction.

Thus, the following summary description may be offered. The DM ἀλλ᾽ ἤ functions within the cognitive domain and signals an exclusive corrective relation. Like ἀλλά, it signals that what follows is a corrective to some element within the recipient's mental representation of the discourse. Unlike ἀλλά, it has the added constraint of narrowing the recipient's focus to the salient exclusive or limited element of the corrective. This exclusive-marking constraint naturally lends ἀλλ᾽ ἤ to be used in exceptive contexts, though the use of ἀλλ᾽ ἤ rather than a clear exceptive marker likely points to the desire to narrow focus on the exclusive correction being made. In some contexts, there appears to be an added emphatic nuance that arises from using ἀλλ᾽ ἤ. This may be an additional motivation in using the collocation at times.

---

36. Bernd Kortmann, *Adverbial Subordination: A Typology and History of Adverbial Subordinators Based on European Languages*, EALT 18 (Berlin: de Gruyter, 1997), 87, 199.

37. At the same time, we must be open to the possibility of a polysemic analysis in which the function of ἀλλ᾽ ἤ allowed for the development of a strictly exceptive sense. However, given the sparsity of data, the fact that the DM was falling out of use, and the fittingness of exclusive correction in the exceptive contexts in which it appears, I am hesitant to posit this.

### 5.3.3. ἀλλ᾽ ἤ and LXX Translation Technique

This understanding of ἀλλ᾽ ἤ has certain implications for the study of LXX translation technique and for how one understands the translator's motivations. First, it can be said that the translators examined here did not necessarily feel constrained to render any one lexeme or any collocation in the Hebrew Bible with ἀλλ᾽ ἤ. Thus, text-critically, one must be careful of postulating a certain Hebrew lexeme or collocation in a translator's *Vorlage* solely on the basis of ἀλλ᾽ ἤ. Second, the fact that the collocation can be used when the underlying Hebrew reads כי אם or כי or asyndeton or אפס or אך or any of the other lexemes listed at the beginning of §5.3 demonstrates that the translators, at least those examined above, felt free to translate according to their own understanding of how the propositions were related to one another, which also required a certain level of contextual awareness on their part. Lastly, related to the previous point, the choices made by the translators provide insight into their interpretation of the source texts. For example, when ἀλλ᾽ ἤ is used and the underlying Hebrew appears to have had כי, an interpretative move has been made on the part of the translator. Even if some of those occurrences of כי could be regarded as signaling a corrective, many of them cannot be, or at the least, they could equally be regarded as explanatory/causal markers, which would have been more suitably translated by γάρ, διότι, or ὅτι. When the relation between clauses in Hebrew is asyndetic, one should immediately question why the translator used ἀλλ᾽ ἤ rather than mirroring the asyndeton in Greek. The translator's decision to use ἀλλ᾽ ἤ, in most instances, witnesses to their interpretation of the context as well as a desire to explicitly mark the relations between propositions as they conceived of them. Even rendering כי אם with ἀλλ᾽ ἤ witnesses to more than a simply quantitative and more-or-less qualitative representation. The collocation כי אם can be corrective or exceptive. To translate this into Greek, the translator was required to look to the surrounding context to understand what was being communicated.

This can also be seen in Le Moigne's work on particle use in LXX Isaiah.[38] In his brief discussion of ἀλλ᾽ ἤ, which occurs four times in the book, he demonstrates that the translator did not use the DM as a stereotypical rendering of any one lexeme or collocation in his *Vorlage*. Assuming a

38. Le Moigne, "Le livre d'Ésaïe dans la Septante," ch. 7 §A.4.

similar *Vorlage* to the MT, in the DM's four occurrences in LXX Isaiah, it renders something different each time. In Isa 42:19, it stands in once for כי אם and once for the preposition כ. In Isa 62:9, the MT attests to כי. In Isa 66:2, ἀλλ᾽ ἤ is a plus. With respect to this last use, Le Moigne writes, "Without a doubt, the translator wanted to make the function of the last noun phrases more explicit."[39] But this can be extended to the other instances as well. In each case, the translator did not have to use ἀλλ᾽ ἤ. The fact that he did attests to his understanding of the context and a desire to convey that understanding.[40]

---

39. Le Moigne, "Le livre d'Ésaïe dans la Septante," ch. 7 §A.4.a: "Le traducteur a sans doute voulu rendre plus explicite la fonction des derniers syntagmes nominaux."

40. It is worth discussing the data in LXX Isaiah and Le Moigne's analysis. In three of its four occurrences in the book, Le Moigne regards the DM as exceptive, translating it as "sinon" in Isa 42:19 (twice) and "si ce n'est" in Isa 66:2. He regards its use in Isa 62:9 as equivalent to ἀλλά, though he entertains the idea that it may be exceptive there as well (Le Moigne, "Le livre d'Ésaïe dans la Septante," ch. 7 §A.4.b). In the three examples that Le Moigne regards as exceptive, ἀλλ᾽ ἤ is preceded by a rhetorical question: (Isa 42:19a–b) καὶ τίς τυφλὸς ἀλλ᾽ ἢ οἱ παῖδές μου καὶ κωφοὶ ἀλλ᾽ ἢ οἱ κυριεύοντες αὐτῶν; "And who is blind *all' ē* my servants and deaf *all' ē* the ones who lord it over them?"; (Isa 66:2b) καὶ ἐπὶ τίνα ἐπιβλέψω ἀλλ ἢ ἐπὶ τὸν ταπεινὸν καὶ ἡσύχιον καὶ τρέμοντα τοὺς λόγους μου; "On whom will I look *all' ē* on the humble and quiet and the one who trembles at my words?" These examples illustrate the discussion above with respect to the pragmatics of ἀλλ᾽ ἤ, its suitable contexts of use, and the shared functional space between restrictives and exceptives. In these three examples, εἰ/ἐὰν μή could have easily been used. Whether ἀλλ᾽ ἤ itself focuses on the exception is dependent entirely on what happens in the mind of the recipient when the rhetorical question, ἀλλ᾽ ἤ, and its host utterance are processed together. With εἰ/ἐὰν μή after an interrogative, such as Esth 6:6 examined in ch. 3, it seems clear that the reader would assume a negated set out of which to extract an excepted member. Perhaps that is also the case with ἀλλ᾽ ἤ. Though, even then, it would seem likely that ἀλλ᾽ ἤ would be used specifically to focus the reader's attention on the limitative relation. At the same time, given what has been observed in this chapter, it may be the case that ἀλλ᾽ ἤ stays closer to ἀλλά. In this case, it counters the assumption that there are many who are blind and deaf and points the reader to the exclusive corrective. This could be rendered in English by something along the lines of: "Who is blind? *Just* my servants. Who is deaf? *Just* the ones who lord it over them" and "On whom will I look? *Only* on the humble and quiet and who trembles at my words." The fourth instance of the DM is in Isa 62:8b–9: Εἰ ἔτι δώσω τὸν σῖτόν σου καὶ τὰ βρώματά σου τοῖς ἐχθροῖς σου, καὶ εἰ ἔτι πίονται υἱοὶ ἀλλότριοι τὸν οἶνόν σου, ἐφ᾽ ᾧ ἐμόχθησας· ἀλλ ἢ οἱ συνάγοντες φάγονται αὐτὰ καὶ αἰνέσουσιν κύριον, καὶ οἱ συνάγοντες πίονται αὐτὰ ἐν ταῖς ἐπαύλεσιν ταῖς ἁγίαις μου. "I will not again give your grain and your food to your enemies, and foreign sons will not again drink your wine, for which you labored. *all' ē* the ones who gather will

## 5.4. ἀλλ' ἤ in the Twelve

In the Twelve, there are seven occurrences of ἀλλ' ἤ. Aside from one textually difficult occurrence (Mal 2:15), they all render either כי (Hos 1:6, 7:14; Amos 7:14; Zech 8:12) or כי אם (Mic 6:8; Zech 4:6). In each case, the DM can be observed as functioning as a marker of an exclusive corrective relation. A few will be surveyed here.

In Hos 1:6, the Lord declares that he will no longer show mercy to Israel. He will now align himself against them. To connect these two utterances, the translator has the Lord using the collocation ἀλλ' ἤ.

> *καὶ συνέλαβεν ἔτι καὶ ἔτεκε θυγατέρα. καὶ εἶπεν αὐτῷ Κάλεσον τὸ ὄνομα αὐτῆς Οὐκ ἠλεημένη, διότι οὐ μὴ προσθήσω ἔτι ἐλεῆσαι τὸν οἶκον Ισραηλ, ἀλλ' ἢ ἀντιτασσόμενος ἀντιτάξομαι αὐτοῖς.*
> And Gomer became pregnant again and bore a daughter. And the Lord said to him, "Name her 'Not Pitied,' for I will no longer show mercy to the house of Israel, *all' ē* opposing, I will align myself against them."

> ותהר עוד ותלד בת ויאמר לו קרא שמה לא רחמה כי לא אוסיף עוד ארחם את־בית ישראל כי־נשא אשא להם
> And Gomer conceived again and gave birth to a daughter. And the Lord said to me, "Name her 'Not Pitied,' for I will not again have compassion on the house of Israel that I would in any way forgive them."

The proposition following ἀλλ' ἤ, "opposing, I will align myself against them," is cast as an exclusive corrective to the preceding: "I will not show mercy to the house of Israel, *instead*, *only* opposing, I will align myself against them." It is not just that the Lord will not show mercy and will instead oppose Israel. He will *instead only* oppose Israel. The Lord is portrayed by the translator as communicating that this is his only course of

---

eat them and praise the Lord, and the ones who gather will drink them in my holy residences." Given the narrow dataset of LXX Isaiah, Le Moigne tries to force this instance to behave like the others, suggesting, "We could thus paraphrase the whole as 'I will not give your goods to anyone (except you), no one (except you) will eat them" (ch. 7 §A.4.b: "On pourrait ainsi paraphraser l'ensemble 'je ne donnerai tes biens à personne [si ce n'est toi], personne [si ce n'est toi] les mangera'"). If one considers the prototypical usage of the DM attested by a wider dataset, its use in Isa 62:9 looks perfectly normal. The truth-propositional content of the preceding is not countered and the DM introduces the exclusive correction: "*but only* the ones who gather will eat them."

action with reference to Israel. This, then, may also have the added rhetorical effect of emphasizing the Lord's proclamation.

Assuming that the reading attested in the MT mirrors the *Vorlage* of the Twelve, then one can observe the translator taking something that was implicit in their source text and making it explicit in their translation. The exclusive constraint of ἀλλ᾽ ἤ takes the reader down a more specific mental pathway than the underlying Hebrew does. The translator could have mirrored their *Vorlage* with ἀλλά. The fact that they did not demonstrates a translator who was willing to go beyond lexemic and quantitative representation and translate instead according to their interpretation of the text.[41]

In Zech 4, the prophet is speaking with an angel, who is explaining the visions that Zechariah is witnessing. In verse 6, the angel relates a vision to Zerubbabel's task of rebuilding the temple.

> *καὶ ἀπεκρίθη καὶ εἶπε πρός με λέγων Οὗτος ὁ λόγος κυρίου πρὸς Ζοροβαβελ λέγων Οὐκ ἐν δυνάμει μεγάλῃ οὐδὲ ἐν ἰσχύι, ἀλλ᾽ ἤ ἐν πνεύματί μου, λέγει κύριος παντοκράτωρ.*
> And he answered and said to me, "This is the word of the Lord to Zerubbabel: 'Not by great power nor by strength, *all' ē* by my spirit, says the Lord Almighty.'"
>
> ויען ויאמר אלי לאמר זה דבר־יהוה אל־זרבבל לאמר לא בחיל ולא בכח כי אם־ ברוחי אמר יהוה צבאות
> And he answered and said to me, "This is the word of YHWH to Zerubbabel: 'Not by strength and not by power, but instead by my spirit, says YHWH of Hosts.'"

The collocation works very well in this context. It instructs the reader to process the text and build their mental representation of it by regarding the following information as a corrective to what they have already processed and as an exclusion that narrows their focus on the one salient thing being communicated: *only* by the Lord's spirit will Zerubbabel accomplish his task. Understandably, given the context, an emphatic force naturally arises out of the pragmatics of the collocation. By using ἀλλά, the translator could

41. Quantitative representation does not seem to be a primary consideration for the translator of the Twelve, as they use ἀλλά in place of כי אם in Amos 8:11 and ἀλλ᾽ ἤ in place of the single lexeme כי in four of the collocation's seven occurrences (Hos 1:6; 7:14; Amos 7:14; Zech 8:12).

have instructed the reader, more or less, in the same mental processing route, but by using ἀλλ' ἤ, the explicit exclusion heightens the strength of the communication. Moreover, in the Hebrew, this is an instance of כי אם that exemplifies Follingstad's suggestion that it, at its core, focuses on an exclusion that corrects a presupposition.[42] Though the overlap between כי אם and ἀλλ' ἤ is not perfect, they are remarkably similar in their core functions. While the translator of the Twelve could have used ἀλλ' ἤ owing only to their exegesis of the text, it is possible that they chose the DM because of its fittingness to render the Hebrew collocation. Even then as has been discussed, in order to translate כי אם into Greek, because of the overlap it shares with various Greek DMs, the translator had to allow contextual factors play into their translation. In any case, this occurrence of ἀλλ' ἤ again demonstrates a translator who was aware of context and was able to encode their conception of the flow of the discourse into their translation.

In Amos 7:14, the prophet is answering Amaziah, who has told him to prophesy elsewhere. Defending his prophetic ministry in Israel, Amos begins by noting his humble beginnings as a shepherd and gardener and, in the following verses, that the Lord took him from his way of life and set him on his prophetic path.

> *καὶ ἀπεκρίθη Αμως καὶ εἶπε πρὸς Αμασίαν Οὐκ ἤμην προφήτης ἐγὼ οὐδὲ υἱὸς προφήτου, ἀλλ' ἤ αἰπόλος ἤμην καὶ κνίζων συκάμινα·*
> And Amos answered and said to Amaziah, "I was not a prophet nor a son of a prophet, *all' ē* I was a goat herder and a mulberry ripener.
>
> ויען עמוס ויאמר אל־אמציה לא־נביא אנכי ולא בן־נביא אנכי כי־בוקר אנכי ובולס שקמים
> And Amos answered and said to Amaziah, "I was not a prophet, and I was not a son of a prophet. For, I was a herdsmen and a ripener of sycamore figs.

By using ἀλλ' ἤ, the translator signals an exclusive corrective relation between the propositions. The relevance of the statement "I was a goat herder and a mulberry ripener" to the communication is fully realized in light of the constraint that ἀλλ' ἤ bears on the reader's processing and subsequent interpretation. The statement is a corrective to what preceded and restricts and narrows the reader's focus to Amos's humble role as nothing

42. See Follingstad, *Deictic Viewpoint*, 156–57.

more than a laborer. Amos had no claim to the prophetic office. *Instead*, he was *only* a goat herder and mulberry ripener. The underlying כי in the translator's source text could have been suitably rendered with γάρ, διότι, or even ἀλλά. The translator's choice to use ἀλλ' ἤ appears to be a motivated one to make explicit what they considered to be the salient relation between the propositions.

The instances of ἀλλ' ἤ in the Twelve all indicate a translator who was more involved in theirs work than simply finding matching lexemes in their target language. By using the DM, the translator demonstrates their understanding of the discourse and instructs the reader down the same mental pathway. In most cases, the DM appropriately renders a similar pragmatic device in the underlying Hebrew, כי or כי אם, but even then, the translator had many options available to them. They had to decide, based on their reading of the text, what relation was relevant to what was being expressed. When translating כי, in particular, they also made the decision to signal an exclusive relation, even though it was not signaled in their *Vorlage*. In the end, the use of ἀλλ' ἤ in the Twelve contributes to the picture of a translator who engaged with the text and did not always shy away from employing natural Greek idiom when their interpretation called for it, even though it frequently did not precisely mirror the Hebrew.

## 5.5. Conclusion

In sum, ἀλλ' ἤ is a collocation that provides a unique contribution to the discourse but has often been overlooked. Though closely related to ἀλλά, it provides an additional constraint that has communicative value and should therefore be appreciated. In LXX scholarship, its use provides insight into the translators and the choices they made when rendering their *Vorlagen* into Greek. With the occasional exception of כי אם, other DMs would better replicate the structure of the underlying Hebrew. By using ἀλλ' ἤ, the LXX translators reveal their interpretation of the text, demonstrate their willingness to move beyond simple replication of their *Vorlagen*, and evince an ability to indicate textual relations by means of natural koine idiom.

# 6

# μέν

The particle μέν appears twice in the Twelve: Hag 1:4 and Zech 1:15. That μέν appears at all is highly significant, as, unlike the DMs investigated in the preceding chapters, there is nothing remotely close to a lexical equivalent to μέν in Biblical Hebrew. For a translator to choose to employ the particle even though it does not represent a lexeme in their *Vorlage* suggests that they were not only willing to go beyond lexical representation of their source text but also intent on facilitating the reader's construction of a specific mental representation of the text.

The situation is the same with regard to most occurrences of μέν throughout the LXX, in that, one does not have the option of positing qualitative (or, often, even quantitative) representation as the motivation behind its use. Owing to this, one must ask what could have motivated the translators to use μέν *at all*? In order to answer this question, it is crucial to determine what μέν accomplishes in the early koine period.

In traditional grammars and lexica, a few functions are typically attributed to μέν. Most often, it is understood as marking a correlation between its host utterance and a following corresponding utterance introduced by another particle, normally δέ.[1] When not followed by a particle that introduces a corresponding utterance (traditionally labeled "μέν *solitarium*"), μέν is either understood as marking a correlation with material that is implied and must therefore be supplied by the reader or as an affirmative

1. E.g., Denniston, *Particles*, 359, 369–84; BDF, §447; Wallace, *Greek Grammar*, 672; Porter, *Idioms*, 212; Winer, *New Testament Greek*, 551; Robertson, *Grammar*, 1151; Smyth, §§2903–15; Abel, *Grammaire du Grec Biblique*, §78*k*; K-G 2.2:264; Dana and Mantey, *Manual Grammar*, §232; Young, *New Testament Greek*, 200; Green, *Grammar of the Greek Testament*, 344–45; Danker, *Greek-English Lexicon*, s.v. "μέν"; BDAG, s.v. "μέν"; L-N, §§89.104, 89.136, 91.3; *GELS*, s.v. "μέν."

or emphatic particle.[2] The former use, marking a correlation with implied material, is, in fact, how Denniston exclusively describes μέν *solitarium*. He writes:

> The explanation of μέν *solitarium*, in general, is either that the speaker originally intends to supply an answering clause, but subsequently forgets his intention … or, far more frequently, that he uses μέν, like γε, in contrast with something which he does not, even in the first instance, intend to express in words, or even (sometimes) define precisely in thought.[3]

Thus, apart from a few that posit an emphatic or affirmative function, grammars and lexica have primarily understood μέν to signal a correlation between its host utterance and forthcoming content, whether an explicit utterance or implied material. Some of the grammarians (e.g., Smyth and Robertson) frame the correlative relationship in terms of contrast, especially when discussing the μέν … δέ construction.

## 6.1. The Use of μέν in the Papyri

Extant papyri between 300 BCE and 1 CE witness to approximately seven hundred occurrences of μέν.[4] Many of these instances appear formulaic, where μέν is used in very similar legal contexts, sometimes even with the exact same wording, only applied to a different situation. Very frequently, the particle is soon followed by a connective (usually δέ) that occurs in a corresponding sentence or clause. Thus, in many of the examples below, the discussion will focus not only on μέν but also its relation to the following connective.

---

2. As a marker of correlation, see, e.g., Robertson, *Grammar*, 1152; Green, *Grammar of the Greek Testament*, 345; Smyth, §2896; BDAG, s.v. "μέν" 2; LSJ, s.v. "μέν" 2; *DFNTG*, 170; Stephen H. Levinsohn, *Textual Connections in Acts*, SBLMS 31 (Atlanta: Scholars Press, 1987), 143. As an affirmative or emphatic particle, see, e.g., Porter, *Idioms*, 212; Chamberlain, *Grammar of the Greek New Testament*, 161; L-N, §91.6; Danker, *Greek-English Lexicon*, s.v. "μέν."

3. Denniston, *Particles*, 380.

4. A search on papyri.info on 9 July 2014 for the lemma "μεν" resulted in 831 hits. Of those hits, 117 were not the particle μέν but were rather part of another word (e.g., a first-person plural active verb). This brought the count down to 714. However, of those 714, there were 143 instances in which μέν is postulated as having been written where there is a now a lacuna in the papyrus and 41 instances in which two or three of the letters of the particle are illegible.

### 6.1.1. P.Cair.Zen. 1.59019 (260–258 BCE)

The author of this letter is an associate of Zenon's and is writing to update him on business matters.[5] In line 5, the author informs Zenon of the price he will try to negotiate for (as indicated elsewhere in the letter) the curing of dice from gazelle bones. In line 11, the author promises to write more to Zenon soon.

> (5) [περὶ δ]ὲ τῆς θεραπείας πειρασόμεθα μὲν χαλκιαίους, εἰ δὲ μή γε, διχαλκιαίους· … (11) τὰ δὲ λοιπά σοι γράψω ἀκριβέστερον, νῦν μὲν γάρ μοι οὐκ ἐξεποίησεν. πειρῶ δέ μοι ὅτι τάχο̣ς̣ γρ̣ά̣φειν [περὶ] [πάντω]ν.
> (5) With regard to the services rendered, we will try *men* to make it cost one chalkous, but (*de*) if we really cannot, a double chalkous. … (11) I will write the rest to you much more precisely, for *men*, it is not possible for me now, but (*de*) I am attempting to write very soon concerning everything.

Immediately observable are the δέ that quickly follow each instance of μέν, each one having the same moderate scope as the preceding μέν. In both cases, the corresponding sentences are concerned with presenting two different options with regard to one overarching topic that was introduced prior to μέν. The first μέν follows a statement of the overarching topic—services rendered—and introduces the author's statement that he will try to negotiate the cost to be one chalkous. This is quickly followed by the corresponding δέ and its host utterance. The author states that, if one chalkous cannot be negotiated, the cost will be a double chalkous. The two sentences are intrinsically linked. Together, they provide the relevant information with respect to the topic at hand. The negotiations for the cost to cure dice will result in an agreement to pay either one chalkous or two chalkoi.

The second μέν is collocated with γάρ and is thus part of offline material that provides explanatory information in relation to the preceding proposition, "I will write the rest."[6] The μέν introduces a statement that explains why further writing will take place in the future: the author does not currently have the time available to him. However, this is not all he has to say on the matter. The corresponding sentence, connected by δέ,

---

5. The author's name is unknown.

6. On the function of γάρ, see *DGGNT*, 51–54. See also Sicking, "Devices for Text Articulation," 20–25.

serves to reassure Zenon that, despite the lack of time, the author is trying to write as soon as possible concerning every matter. Thus, here as well, the *μέν* … *δέ* construction provides the reader with two pieces of related information that together form an utterance that is highly relevant with regard to the overarching topic expressed in the preceding statement ("I will write the rest").

### 6.1.2. P.Cair.Zen. 1.59107 (257 BCE)

In this letter, Apollonios writes to Panakestor about a boat that the latter requested. Apollonios explains why the boat has not been sent and suggests a path forward.

> (1) Ἀπολλώνιος Πανακέστορι χαίρειν. τ̣ὸ̣ [π]λοῖον ἔτι πρότερον ἀπεστάλκειμεν ἄν σοι, ἀλλ' ὁρῶμεν μ̣έ̣[γα ἀνή]λ̣ω̣μ̣α̣ ἐσόμενον εἰς τοὺς ναύτας. <u>εἰ μὲν οὖν</u> δύνασαι τῶν ἐν Κερκῆι τισὶν δοῦναι, οἵτινες ἐργῶνται καὶ δια[θ]ρ̣έψο̣υ̣σ̣ι̣ τ̣οὺ̣ς ν̣[αύ]τ̣[α]ς, ὅταν δέ σοι (5) χρεία ἦι τοῦ πλοίου ἀποχρήσουσι, γράψον ἡμῖν· ἀποστελοῦμεν γάρ σοι. <u>εἰ δὲ</u> μή, οὐχ ὁρῶ πῶς δυνάμεθα καθημένοις τοῖς ναύταις τὸν πλεῖστον χρόνον τοὺς μισθοὺς διὰ παντὸς διδόναι.
>
> (1) Apollonios to Panakestor. Greetings. We would have already sent the boat to you earlier, but we see a great expense in the future for the sailors. So, if *men* you are able to give (it?) to some (boatmen?) in Kerke,[7] whoever will work and will support the sailors, then whenever you have enough (5) need for the boat, write to us. We will send to you. But (*de*) if not, I cannot see how we are able to continually offer wages to sailors who are sitting around most of the time.

Owing to the cost of maintaining sailors, Apollonios has reservations about sending a boat to Panakestor. Apollonios thus presents two options concerning the situation. First, introduced by *μέν*, he states that should Panakestor be able to make arrangements for the sailors to be supported, then when the boat is needed, he should write to Apollonios again.[8] The

---

7. This line is difficult. Apollonios seems to be suggesting that Panakestor find some associates (boatmen in Kerke?) who would have use of the boat and would thus maintain the sailors. Presumably, in this arrangement, Panakestor would then have the right to use the boat whenever he needed it. See Edgar, *P.Cair.Zen*, 124.

8. It may be tempting to view the apodosis, ὅταν δέ σοι χρεία ἦι τοῦ πλοίου ἀποχρήσουσι, γράψον ἡμῖν· ἀποστελοῦμεν γάρ σοι, as a part of the *μέν* … *δέ* construc-

corresponding option, introduced by δέ, is then presented: If Panakestor cannot pay and maintain sailors, then Apollonios does not see how the costs for sailors who are sitting around most of the time can be covered. The obvious implication here is: "If you cannot figure out how to maintain the sailors, you are not getting the boat." Thus, the μέν ... δέ construction is used with two related sentences that together convey a whole utterance that is crucially relevant to the discourse topic stated at the beginning of the letter (intention to send the boat but reluctance to do so owing to the cost of the sailors). Note, too, that the particles also correspond in their moderate scope over the conditional clauses.

Also significant here is the εἰ μέν ... εἰ δέ construction. In the papyri, this construction is not infrequently used when there are two contrasting options for a given situation.[9] It seems to have been a set phrase. This is not to say its use was purely formulaic, but that there was a fittingness to its use in certain contexts in conjunction with the discourse-pragmatic functions of the DMs involved.

### 6.1.3. P.Mich. 3.190 (172 BCE)

This is a portion of a contract between Theokles and Aristokles. Theokles agrees to lend Aristokles money, and the contract stipulates the time period, interest rate, and matters concerning repayment. These lines in particular detail when repayment should happen and what will happen should Aristokles fail to do so.

> ἀποδότω δὲ Ἀριστοκλῆς Θεοκλεῖ τὸ προγεγρα(μμένον) δά(νειον) τὰ γ (τάλαντα) καὶ τὰς ψπ τοῦ χα(λκοῦ) καὶ τὸν γενόμενον αὐτῶν τόκον ἐν μηνὶ Ἀπελλαίωι, Αἰγυ(πτίων) δὲ Παῦνι, τοῦ ι (ἔτους). ἐὰν δὲ μὴ ἀποδῶι, ἀποτεισάτω τὸ μὲν δά(νειον) ἡμιόλι[ο]ν τὸν δὲ τόκον ἁπλοῦν καὶ ἡ πρᾶξις ἔστω Θεοκλεῖ πράσσ[ο]ν[τι] Ἀριστοκλῆν ἢ τὴν ἔγγυον αὐτ[ο]ῦ καὶ παρ᾽ ἑνὸς α[ὐ]τῶν οὗ ἂν αἱρῆται καὶ παρ᾽ ἀμφοτέρων καθάπερ ἐκ δίκης.
> Now, let Aristokles repay to Theokles the aforementioned loan: 3 talents, 780 in bronze money, and the interest, in the month of Apellaios (or Pauni in the Egyptian calendar) in the tenth year. But, if he does not repay, let him pay as penalty the *men* loan plus 50 percent and (*de*)

---

tion. However, as one can observe in this example and in others below, εἰ μέν corresponds to a forthcoming εἰ δέ. The two work together to provide two contrasting options to one situation.

9. This construction will be observed again in the LXX data below.

simple interest. (25) Theokles will have the right to exact payment from Aristokles or his surety, whichever of them he may choose, or upon both, exactly as is right.

Rather than offering two corresponding, contrasting options for one situation as in the above examples, this μέν … δέ construction presents two corresponding, *non*contrasting pieces of one situation, in which the latter piece builds on the former. After providing the terms for the repayment of Theokles's loan to Aristokles, the author lays out the penalty if Aristokles does not pay Theokles back. The penalty is divided into two parts. The first, occurring with μέν, is that Aristokles will have to pay the loan plus another 50 percent. The second, signaled by δέ, is that Aristokles will still have to pay the interest on top of the 150 percent remittance. Thus, the two distinct pieces of information relevant to the topic of penalties are introduced by μέν … δέ, and together, they form the whole picture. Though the μέν … δέ construction presents two pieces of one situation rather than two options with regard to one situation, as the instances above do, one may observe in this example two similar contextual features: (1) One utterance is followed by another that adds distinct but corresponding information to the former, and (2) both together provide the relevant details to a preceding established topic. It should be noted that the scope of the particles is different here than in the other letters examined so far. In examples 1 and 2, μέν and δέ occurred with a moderate scope. Here, however, they both have a narrow scope, introducing noun phrases that serve as the direct objects of ἀποτεισάτω.[10]

### 6.1.4. P.Oxy.12.1465 (100–1 BCE)

This letter concerns the theft of wheat from two threshing floors near the village Isieion Pekysios. After describing the situation, the author ends the letter with a request that the thieves be sought out and the goods retrieved.[11]

10. This narrow scope may be determinative in the position of μέν after τό rather than after ἀποτεισάτω. For what appears to be a clearer example of this, see example 5 below.

11. The names of the author and recipient are lost as is any explicit indication of their relationship or their vocations.

> (10) ἀξιῶ συντ[ά]ξα̣ι̣ ἐ̣[κ]ζ̣η̣τ̣ήσαντα̣ς̣ τ̣ο̣ὺ̣ς̣ α̣[ἰτίο]υ̣ς̣ καταστῆσαι ἐπὶ σέ, ὅπως ἐγὼ μὲν τὰ εἰλημμένα κομίσωμαι, οἱ δὲ φανησόμενοι αἴτιοι τύχω[σ]ι ὧν προσήκει πρὸς (15) ἐπίστασιν ἄλλων, ἵν' ὦ ἀντειλημμένος.
> (10) I think we ought to arrange a group to seek out the guilty to bring them to you, so that I *men* may recover the things that have been taken, and (*de*) the guilty who will be revealed may get that which is fitting, as a (15) deterrent to others—so that I may provide help.

The author wants the thieves to be sought out and then follows with the reason why he desires this. The reason consists of two separate outcomes. First, opening with μέν and the fronted topic ἐγώ, it is so that he can reclaim what has been stolen. Second, continuing with δέ and the preposed topic switch to οἱ φανησόμενοι αἴτιοι, it is so that the guilty may be punished and be a deterrent to others. The two statements, if isolated, would have nothing to do with the other. However, the μέν ... δέ construction ties them together, informing the reader that the connection between the two is relevant to the request that precedes them. They form an argument as to why the suggestion ought to be followed.

Note that, as with the previous example from the papyri, the two utterances introduced by μέν and δέ do not contrast with one another. They provide two distinct but complementary parts of a whole. It is also worth highlighting the fronting of topics in both sentences. Though such fronting explicitly indicates a topic switch, these sentences are nevertheless tied together and meant to be read as integrally linked.

### 6.1.5. UPZ 1.125 (89 BCE)

This papyrus is similar to example 3 above, being a contract for a loan between two parties, Peteimouthes and Konouphis, and detailing the penalties should Peteimouthes not pay it back.

> (20) ἐὰν δὲ μὴ ἀποδῶι καθό(τι) γέγραπται, ἀποτεισάτω Πετειμούθης Κονούφει τὸ μὲν δάνειον ἡμιόλιον παραχρῆμα καὶ τοῦ ὑπερπεσόντος χρόνου τοὺς τόκους ὡς τοῦ στατῆρ[ο]ς χαλκοῦ δραχμῶν ἑξήκοντα κατὰ μ[ῆ]να καὶ τὸ βλάβος καὶ τοῦ (25) παρασυγγραφεῖν εἰς τὸ βασιλικὸν ἐπίτιμον ἀργυρίου δραχμὰς τέσσαρας καὶ ἡ πρᾶξις ἔστω Κονούφει καὶ τοῖς παρ' αὐτοῦ ἔκ τε αὐτοῦ Πετειμούθου καὶ ἐκ τῶν ὑπαρχ[όντ]ων αὐτῶι πάντω[ν π]ρ[ά]σσοντι [κ]αθάπερ ἐκ δίκης. ἡ δὲ συγγραφὴ ἥδε κυρία ἔστω πανταχοῦ.
> Now, if he does not pay as it is written, Peteimouthes must pay as penalty (20) to Konouphis the *men* loan plus 50 percent immediately and

> (*kai*) the overtime interest (about sixty bronze drachmae monthly to the stater), (25) and (*kai*) the damage, and (*kai*), for breaking contract, a penalty of four silver drachmae for the treasury. And Konouphis and those from him shall have the right of exaction both from him, Peteimouthes, and from all those present with him when he did it. Now, let this contract be authoritative everywhere.

While in content this occurrence of μέν is similar to example 3 above, it differs significantly from the previous examples, in that, instead of a μέν … δέ construction, one can observe here μέν followed by the connective καί. Moreover, rather than there being one particle that corresponds with the μέν, there are three—each particle introduces a different direct object for ἀποτεισάτω. Apart from that, it is as one would expect. The phrase hosting μέν is the beginning of a series of utterances that detail the main idea. Each phrase that follows provides further information that is distinct and yet linked thematically to the rest. The phrase hosting μέν indicates the loan plus 50 percent extra as the first penalty to be paid, and the following three phrases introduced by καί indicate that overtime interest, the damage, and the fee for breaking contract, respectively, must also be paid.[12] The utterances are relevant to the same overarching topic, the penalty to Peteimouthes, but each one covers a distinct piece of that topic. Together, they provide the whole picture.

This example may raise several questions. One may ask whether μέν … καί is a legitimate construction, why the author used καί rather than δέ, and why I do not consider the sentence containing δέ at the end of the quotation to correspond to the material in which μέν is found. To the first question, μέν … καί can be observed in many papyri as well as in the

12. It is possible that the next καί clause is also linked to the μέν, but given other examples, such as example 3 above, in which one will normally observe a μέν … δέ construction introducing the objects of ἀποτεισάτω, I am inclined to think that the thematic relation between μέν and the first three καί encourages the link whereas the switch of topic, verb mood, and change of scope in the following καί clause allows the reader to move away from the μέν … καί construction. The same can be said of example 3 above (though the καί follows μέν … δέ there, rather than μέν … καί). Further, as has been observed up to this point, μέν and the corresponding utterance(s) that follow it provide pieces of information that together form a relevant utterance to the preceding topic, which in this case is monetary repayment.

LXX.[13] Although it is typical to find δέ following μέν, such is not necessary in order for μέν to function.[14] To the second question, this is best answered by appealing to the author's conception of the discourse. Where one author wants to mark a new segment, another may feel that simple connection suffices. As was observed in chapter 2, while there are certain contexts in which segmenting the discourse would be more natural and certain contexts in which it would be less natural, marking a distinct information unit is rarely ever a black-and-white decision. It depends on how the author conceives of the movement of the discourse and their assumptions about the reader. In this case, the author did not consider the successive utterances to be distinct segments within the discourse that built on each other, but rather simply as connected utterances of equal status. Regarding the third question, as has been observed thus far, μέν is typically followed by material that corresponds with it in two ways: First, the utterances share thematic coherence. The DM will present one piece or side of a situation, the related material will present the next corresponding or contrasting piece(s), and together they provide a connected, relevant communication to an overarching topic. Second, when μέν is coordinated with a following DM(s), the scope of μέν will determine the scope of that particle. For instance, in examples 1, 2, and 4, μέν occurs with a moderate scope, and the following δέ do as well. When μέν occurs with a narrow scope, as it does here in example 5 and also in example 3, the following καί and δέ, respectively, also occur with a narrow scope. In these two papyri, μέν occurs within the noun phrase, between the definite article and the

---

13. See the example below in Isa 6:2. See also Denniston, *Particles*, 374–77; F. A. Paley, *A Short Treatise on The Greek Particles and Their Combinations according to Attic Usage* (Cambridge: Deighton, Bell, 1881), 35; *GELS*, s.v. "μέν."

14. It makes sense that δέ frequently follows μέν, given the functions of the two particles (the function of μέν will be discussed in §6.1.7 below), but frequency and suitability do not therefore disallow μέν from being coordinated with another particle or no particle at all. While μέν … δέ is the prototypical construction, δέ is not a necessary piece of it—μέν is sufficient itself. (I am thankful to Kris Lyle for a conversation in which he talked about μέν and its combinations with other particles in terms of sufficient conditions rather than necessary. It was very helpful to my thinking on the matter. See also the discussion on prototypical categorization in §1.2.2.3) Moreover, as Aitken has shown, it was easy for a scribe to use μέν and to not include a corresponding particle (Aitken, "Characterization of Speech," 28). See also the discussion regarding variables to the use of μέν on p. 235 as well as the remarks on *men solitarium* in §6.2.1.

noun, and introduces the object of the verb *ἀποτεισάτω*; the subsequent *καί* (example 5) and *δέ* (example 3) build on that, adding related material that details what else must be paid and maintaining a narrow scope within the same verb phrase. To sum up, then: (1) the *δέ* at the end of this example occurs in material that is not closely related to the material of the *μέν* clause, (2) example 3 contains a *μέν* … *δέ* construction that is parallel to the *μέν* … *καί* observed here, and (3) the *δέ* at the end of this example has a broader scope than *μέν*. Owing to these considerations, I am convinced that the *μέν* in example 5 is indeed correlated with the following *καί*.

### 6.1.6. PSI 4.322 (266/5 BCE)

In this brief letter, Apollonios writes to Zenon and instructs him to wait for a boat that is on its way.

> Ἀπολλώνιος Ζήνωνι χαίρειν. ὅτ' ἔγραψ[άς μοι,] ἐπιστολὴν ἀπεστάλκεμεν ἐξ Ἀλεξα[νδρείας] καὶ Ἀνδρονίκωι τῶι ἐν Πηλουσίωι οἰκονόμω[ι τὸ] πλοῖόν σοι (5) μισθώσασθαι. ὑπόμεινον οὖν ἕω̣[ς ἂν] παραγένηται. ἔδει <u>μὲν</u> γάρ σε δ̣ιόρθω̣[σιν] ἐκ Γάζης ἡμῖν προεπιστε̣ῖ̣λ̣α̣ι. ἔρρωσο.
> Apollonios to Zenon. Greetings. Because you wrote to me, we had sent a letter from Alexandria and to Andronicus the house-steward in Pelousion to (5) hire the boat for you. So, remain there until it arrives. For, *men* it was necessary that you send the payment to us in advance from Gaza. Farewell.

Based on this correspondence, we know that Zenon wrote to Apollonios earlier, requesting that he hire the boat and, it would seem, informing him that the money would be sent or had already been sent. Apollonios responds, stating that a letter has been sent to hire the boat and, in his last sentence, informing Zenon that it was necessary the payment be sent in advance. Curiously, *μέν* is used in this final sentence. It cannot be signaling a link to forthcoming material as there is none. Thus, it may be the case that this *μέν* instead signals a corresponding implication that the reader is expected to supply, namely that the money took some time to arrive, which presumably caused Apollonios to delay in sending the letter to hire the boat.[15]

15. See pp. 209–10 for traditional grammars and lexica that posit that the reader must supply the implication. I think something similar is happening in

### 6.1.7. The Function of μέν as Evinced in the Papyri

Based on what has been observed in the papyri, the following may be posited. In every case:

1. Μέν introduces an utterance that corresponds with one or more following thematically linked utterances.
2. These utterances are usually introduced with a corresponding particle, typically δέ, and the scope of the particle mirrors the scope of the preceding μέν.
3. When the corresponding utterances are processed together, they may be viewed as a whole, that is, a coherent discourse unit providing information relevant to a particular accessible (typically previously activated) overarching topic.
4. The utterances that follow and correspond with μέν are necessary, in that, the discourse would be incomplete without them as they provide necessary corresponding information. In relation to the μέν utterance, the following utterance(s) will often provide distinct but linked information or "the other side of the coin."

Thus, it would seem that μέν functions within both the cognitive and metatextual domains. Cognitively, μέν is anticipatory, in that it alerts the reader to forthcoming material that needs to be processed together with the host utterance in which μέν occurs. Metatextually, the DM signals the beginning

papyri such as UPZ 2.181; *BGU* 3.993dupl; PSI 9.1018; and PSI 9.1022. In these, what appears to be a formulaic shorthand is being used: ἐφ' ἱερέων Πτολεμαίου μὲν Σωτῆρος τῶν ὄντων καὶ οὐσων, "In the presence of the current priests and priestesses of Ptolemy *men* Savior." Cf. this with other papyri that are more elaborative, such as P.Lond. 3.879: ἐφ' ἱερειῶν Πτολεμαίου μὲν Σωτῆρος καὶ βασιλέως Πτολεμαίου θεοῦ Εὐεργέτου καὶ Σωτῆρος ἑαυτῶν Εὐχαρίστου, "In the presence of the priests of Ptolemy *men* Savior and King, Ptolemy God, be praised, and Savior himself, be thanked." See also P.Adl. G1; P.Dryton. 1.2; and P.Dryton. 1.11. In these papyri, the other titles of the Ptolemaic king follow directly after Σωτῆρος. It would seem that the papyri that contain μὲν Σωτῆρος and then move on (typically to the location of the priests or to a statement informing the reader of who the public notary was) are implying the corresponding materials, suggesting that the reader should supply the rest of the king's titles.

of a distinct kind of discourse unit that comprises two or more thematically linked utterances that provide relevant information to a preceding topic.[16]

It is readily apparent that the μέν in examples 3 and 5 are narrow in scope. The following related utterances, which μέν anticipates, are corresponding noun phrases, and the feeling with which one is left after reading them is that a small list has progressively been built. Contrast this with the μέν with a moderate scope in the other examples from the papyri. In those, the DM is functioning at the sentence level, and so the reader is often given the next related piece of information or, sometimes, "the other side of the coin" in the corresponding sentences. In all of these cases, the function of μέν is the same, but the scope is a factor that affects the resultant meaning and how the discourse comes together.[17]

As a final remark, it should be noted that there is a continued awareness of μέν in this period and some of its set phrases, such as εἰ/ἐὰν μέν and μὲν γάρ, even in documents such as these. That is to say, since μέν is, as Lee states, associated with "good" style, its use in the papyri, particularly private letters, is not necessarily expected.[18] Granted, one can observe a certain penchant for literary style in the work of many of the scribes whose letters and legal documents are available to us, but much of it is simply everyday Greek. It is important, then, to note that μέν was being used even in these documents during this time. Its proper use provides a picture of both the scribes' ability with the language as well as their rhetorical prowess, and the use of set phrases reveals that these idioms were still in use in the early koine period.

---

16. In cases in which there is no prior material, and thus no established topic, such as in Acts 1:1, I would still argue that, prototypically, μέν will introduce and anticipate material relevant to a preceding topic. In the few cases where that pattern is not followed, the reader is expected to be able to pragmatically presuppose the overarching topic. In the case of Acts 1:1, the topic would seem to be the author's writings to Theophilus. The μέν clause details the first, the Gospel of Luke, and the current document is his second, continuing where the first left off.

17. μέν with a broad scope will be discussed below in §6.2.

18. Lee, *Greek of the Pentateuch*, 98. Willy Clarysse notes that the μέν … δέ construction is not uncommon in legal documents but that its use in private letters "show a conscious effort to enhance the style" ("Linguistic Diversity in the Archive of the Engineers Kleon and Theodoros," in *The Language of the Papyri*, ed. T. V. Evans and Dirk D. Obbink [Oxford: Oxford University Press, 2010], 38).

## 6.2. The Use of μέν in the LXX

In the LXX, there are, at most, fifty-six occurrences of μέν.[19] Approximately 75 percent of these are paired with a following δέ. Other than five instances, μέν always appears, in the case of narrative, inside of speech, or in the case of nonnarrative, in contexts in which the author/speaker is addressing the reader (e.g., Proverbs). The DM never qualitatively represents a Hebrew lexeme and it is doubtful that it ever quantitatively represents a Hebrew lexeme.[20]

Since there are only two occurrences of μέν in the Twelve, a representative sample from the rest of the LXX will first be examined. After determining how the particle is used in relation to its function in contemporaneous papyri and with regard to the translational nature of the LXX, then the two instances in Haggai and Zechariah can be investigated.

### 6.2.1. Examples from the LXX

The first instance of μέν in the LXX can be found in Gen 18:12. This well-known passage tells the story of how a son was prophesied to be born to Abraham and Sarah, despite their old age.

> (18:10–12) And he said, "When I return, I will come to you during this season at this time, and Sarah your wife will have a son." And Sarah listened at the door of the tent behind them. (Now, Abraham and Sarah were old, having advanced in days, and Sarah's periods stopped happening.)

> (18:12) ἐγέλασεν δὲ Σαρρα ἐν ἑαυτῇ λέγουσα Οὔπω μέν μοι γέγονεν ἕως τοῦ νῦν, ὁ δὲ κύριός μου πρεσβύτερος.
> Now, Sarah laughed to herself saying, "Not yet *men* has it happened to me up to this point, and (*de*) my lord is old!"

> ותצחק שרה בקרבה לאמר אחרי בלתי היתה־לי עדנה ואדני זקן
> And Sarah laughed to herself saying, "After I am worn out, I will have pleasure? And when my lord is old?!"

19. The exact number is likely somewhere between fifty-four to fifty-six occurrences. A couple instances of μέν are textually suspect.

20. Even if some instances of μέν do quantitatively represent an underlying Hebrew lexeme, they would account only for a very small percentage of its occurrences in the LXX.

This is an example of the type of context in which μέν (and particularly μέν … δέ constructions) is typically used in the LXX, in that, (1) it usually occurs at the sentence level with the correlated utterance immediately following and (2) there is an explicit shift of referent from the DM's host utterance to the related utterance. Often, the shift of referent will be an explicit topic switch and will also cooccur with a new frame of reference for the following sentence. This is the case here. The primary referent and topic of the μέν clause is μοι, whereas the utterance introduced by δέ switches to ὁ κύριός μου. In addition, the frame of reference shifts from οὔπω to no explicit frame (logically, the temporal setting of the δέ clause switches to the present).[21] The frequent referent, topic, and/or framing shift is not all that surprising as a typical feature of contexts in which μέν is found. Since the particle anticipates related material that completes the information given in the μέν utterance, it is reasonable to expect that the following material will thus add another dimension to the information under discussion, whether by focusing on an alternate participant or by providing a different frame of reference. From a cognitive perspective, it may also be the case that μέν makes the processing task easier for the reader. Instead of having to infer the connection between utterances, the presence of μέν signals to the reader that, despite the fact that there may be a participant shift or a new frame of reference (or a new, distinct information unit when δέ is involved), these utterances are closely related and need to be read together. Thus, in contexts with elements of discontinuity between utterances, μέν can be a simple and elegant solution that ensures how the reader processes and understands.

Returning to the example from Genesis, Sarah has two connected points to make in response to the proclamation in verse 10: (1) that she has not had a child up to this point and (2) that Abraham is old (the implication being *too* old to father children). By using μέν at the beginning of her speech, the translator alerts the reader that the present statement (Οὔπω μέν μοι γέγονεν ἕως τοῦ νῦν) and a corresponding, upcoming utterance (ὁ δὲ κύριός μου πρεσβύτερος) are to be taken together as a unit that provides further relevant information to a preceding topic (in this case, the proclamation in 18:10). Further, not only are there elements of discontinuity between the two sentences, but semantically, both utterances are

21. The explicit shift of referent, topic, and/or framing was a typical feature in the papyri as well.

necessary to the argument that Sarah is making. Either utterance alone would leave open the possibility for the implicature "but maybe it could happen;" together, though, they effectively communicate the intended meaning of Sarah's words: There is no way she will bear a son for Abraham.

It would seem, then, that even though δέ alone would have been sufficient, the translator felt the correspondence between the sentences and their relation to the overarching topic to be strong enough to merit the use of μέν. This required an awareness of the forthcoming content on the part of the translator as well as a conscious decision to use a lexeme that does not have an equivalent in their *Vorlage*.[22]

In Gen 43:14, Jacob finally agrees to let his sons take Benjamin to Egypt. His final sentence to them contains a μέν *solitarium*:

> ὁ δὲ θεός μου δῴη ὑμῖν χάριν ἐναντίον τοῦ ἀνθρώπου, καὶ ἀποστείλαι τὸν ἀδελφὸν ὑμῶν τὸν ἕνα καὶ τὸν Βενιαμίν· ἐγὼ μὲν γάρ, καθὰ ἠτέκνωμαι, ἠτέκνωμαι.
> Now, may my God give you grace before the man, and may he send your brother, the one (Simeon) and Benjamin. For I *men*, just as I am childless, I am childless.

> ואל שדי יתן לכם רחמים לפני האיש ושלח לכם את־אחיכם אחר ואת־בנימין ואני כאשר שכלתי שכלתי
> And may God Almighty give you mercy before the man, and may he let your other brother and Benjamin go free with you. And I, just as I am childless, I am childless.

While this may appear problematic, it may be the case that the translator understood Jacob to be intentionally leaving the corresponding clause implied. This, then, would be an instance of μέν anticipating implied material that the reader is expected to supply, as was observed in example 6. By using μέν here in Gen 43:14, then, a certain weight is added to Jacob's words. He is pictured as cutting himself off, too distressed, dejected, and

---

22. While one may attempt to argue that μέν quantitatively represents אחרי, it matters little. First, nowhere else in Genesis, or the rest of the LXX insofar as I am aware, does μέν stand in place of אחרי, so it certainly was not a conventional quantitative representation. Further, even if the presence of אחרי did motivate the translator to place something in their translation, why μέν? It is not coincidence that the context is a perfect fit for the DM.

angry to continue talking. This is all the more possible since Jacob has made it clear that he blames his sons for this situation. In Gen 42:36, Jacob says to them: Ἐμὲ ἠτεκνώσατε· Ἰωσὴφ οὐκ ἔστιν, Συμεὼν οὐκ ἔστιν, καὶ τὸν Βενιαμὶν λήμψεσθε, "You made me childless! Joseph is not, Simeon is not, and you will take Benjamin!" While it is difficult to know for certain, the fact that μέν functions prospectively throughout the LXX and papyri and that other grammarians have observed μέν implying a corresponding clause influences me to regard this instance in a similar way.[23] Given that μέν occurs inside of a γάρ clause that is supporting what Jacob wants God to do, the implied material could offer the contrasting circumstance should God give them success (all the more reason not to say it, as it would foster a hope that may well be dashed) or could simply be an affirmation that Jacob does not wish to lose any more children, which can be left unsaid as it is easily assumed.[24]

Another example of an implied corresponding clause can be found in Exod 4:23. In the verses prior, the Lord is speaking with Moses, instructing him as to what will happen when he returns to Egypt. He then begins to tell Moses what he should say to the pharaoh:

> *εἶπα δέ σοι Ἐξαπόστειλον τὸν λαόν μου, ἵνα μοι λατρεύσῃ· εἰ μὲν οὖν μὴ βούλει ἐξαποστεῖλαι αὐτούς, ὅρα οὖν ἐγὼ ἀποκτενῶ τὸν υἱόν σου τὸν πρωτότοκον.*
> And I said to you, "Send my people out, in order that they might serve me. If *men* then, you do not want to send them out, see, then, I will kill your firstborn son!"

> ואמר אליך שלח את־בני ויעבדני ותמאן לשלחו הנה אנכי הרג את־בנך בכרך
> And I said to you, "Let my son go so that he may serve me." But you refused to let him go. Behold! I am going to kill your son, your firstborn!

The first difference one will notice after reading the Greek and the Hebrew is that the Greek version of Exod 4:23 is mitigated in comparison. As Le

23. For the prospective use of μέν, see pp. 209–10. Contra Lee (*Greek of the Pentateuch*, 99), I do not regard this (or any) μέν as emphatic. Lee does acknowledge the use of μέν to imply corresponding material but nevertheless regards this instance as emphatic. Regarding so-called emphatic μέν, see n. 59 below.

24. Thus, the entire unit would either be something to the effect of "For, I *men* just as I have been made childless, I have been made childless. But (δέ) if God gives you grace and sends your brother, then" or "For, I *men* just as I have been made childless, I have been made childless. But (δέ) I do not wish to lose any more children."

Boulluec and Sandevoir state, "By introducing a conditional, the translator makes explicit the possibility that remains open: A change of pharaoh's attitude."[25] The μέν appears to have been motivated in like manner. By its presence, it signals a cohesive unit relevant to the preceding topic, thus implying the corresponding εἰ δέ clause: "But if you do want to send them out, I will not kill your firstborn son." The Exodus translator, then, who demonstrates a high competence in translation and ability with the Greek language, is able to both use idiomatic, literary Greek and mitigate the Lord's speech by using the set phrase εἰ μέν.[26]

The DM is also found in Exod 32:32. Here Moses is pleading with the Lord to forgive Israel for their sin of idolatry. After acknowledging the people's sin (32:31), he offers the Lord two contrasting options hoping that he will choose one.

> (32:31) And Moses turned to the Lord and said, "I am asking, Lord, these people have sinned a great sin, and they made for themselves golden gods.

> (32:32) καὶ νῦν εἰ μὲν ἀφεῖς αὐτοῖς τὴν ἁμαρτίαν, ἄφες· εἰ δὲ μή, ἐξάλειψόν με ἐκ τῆς βίβλου σου, ἧς ἔγραψας.
> But now, if *men* you will forgive them the sin, forgive. But (*de*) if not, wipe me out from your book that you wrote."

> ועתה אם־תשא חטאתם ואם־אין מחני נא מספרך אשר כתבת
> "But now, if you will carry away their sin, but if not, please wipe me out from your book that you wrote."

Similar to example 2, this passage contains two conditional clauses, each hosting one member of a μέν … δέ construction. The effect of the construction is to tie the two clauses together and relate them to the topic of Israel's sin, giving the feeling, in this context, of an argument being built. After Moses presents his first plea—if you will forgive, then do it—the

25. Le Boulluec and Sandevoir, *L'Exode*, 102: "En introduisant une conditionnelle, le traducteur explicite la possibilité qui demeure ouverte : un changement d'attitude chez Pharaon" (See also LXX.D 1:284).

26. For the competence of the LXX translator, see Aejmelaeus, *Parataxis in the Septuagint*, 180. Note also the repetition of οὖν, an odd feature that may indicate the translator's desire for literary embellishment (see Aitken, "Characterization of Speech," 31).

corresponding option is given: if you will not, then punish me for their sin. The relation between these two conditionals is an important one; they necessarily travel together. As there is no lexical element in the Hebrew text that would have motivated the use of μέν here, not even quantitatively; it appears that the inherent semantic connection between the two conditionals, as two contrasting options that complete each other and are together relevant to Moses's plea to the Lord, was the motivating factor for the translator. The effect of placing μέν ... δέ in Moses's plea to the Lord is that it presents Moses as making a two-part statement to the Lord that he wants to be processed together. This is not to say that μέν is *required* for the Lord to understand the relation between Moses's sentences and their relevance to a preceding topic, it is not; however, by creating the expectation for a related utterance, the particle strengthens the relation, thereby highlighting the whole plea that Moses is making to the Lord and ensures that it is not missed.[27] Consider the traditional gloss for the μέν ... δέ construction: "On the one hand ... on the other." In English, this construction is never semantically necessary, but native speakers still use it often in everyday speech. It instructs the recipient that, with regard to the topic under discussion, there are two utterances—one given now and one anticipated—that together will provide a relevant communication. The recipient thus expects another necessary, related utterance, and the connection between the two and their relation to the preceding is ensured to not be missed, just like μέν. In this case, Moses is described as effectively saying to the Lord, "On the one hand (this is not everything I have to say on the matter of Israel's sin—there is more!), if you will forgive their sin, then do it, but on the other hand, if you will not forgive, then wipe me from your book (just whatever you do, please don't punish them!)!" As Aitken has argued, "In the few instances of the μέν/δέ contrast the translators would have had to have made a conscious effort to include the relevant particles."[28] Owing to this, that the translator uses μέν here *at all* demonstrates the desire to encode the text based on their conception of it, to help guide the reader in their interpretation of it, and to do so in idiomatic Greek. This

27. As Runge writes, "The presence of μέν only serves to highlight and strengthen what was already present, ensuring that the reader or hearer does not miss the speaker's intended connection" (*DGGNT*, 77). I would only add: and understands that the forthcoming connected material needs to be read together with the present material to achieve optimal relevance with regard to an overarching topic.

28. Aitken, "Characterization of Speech," 28–29.

last point should not be missed. By using the set phrase εἰ μέν … εἰ δέ, one is perhaps left with an impression of the translator's sense for a slightly higher register of Greek. This both attests to the translator's proficiency and is a further consideration for why μέν occurs here. As with example 2 above, there is a fittingness of the set phrase to the context. The translator may have been motivated to use μέν not only because of the suitability of its discourse-pragmatic function to the context but also because of a sense for the idiom and a reflex to place μέν … δέ after the two εἰ that open up contrasting conditionals.

The DM may also occur with a broad scope. In Lev 4:3, μέν is used to explicitly relate verses 3–12 to subsequent developments, all of which further detail what the Lord says in verse 2.[29]

> (4:2) "Speak to the sons of Israel saying, 'If a person unintentionally sins against the Lord from the commands of the Lord, which one should not do but does any one of them:
>
> (4:3) ἐὰν <u>μὲν</u> ὁ ἀρχιερεὺς ὁ κεχρισμένος ἁμάρτῃ τοῦ τὸν λαὸν ἁμαρτεῖν, καὶ προσάξει περὶ τῆς ἁμαρτίας αὐτοῦ, ἧς ἥμαρτεν, μόσχον ἐκ βοῶν ἄμωμον τῷ κυρίῳ περὶ τῆς ἁμαρτίας αὐτοῦ· (4) καὶ προσάξει τὸν μόσχον παρὰ τὴν θύραν τῆς σκηνῆς τοῦ μαρτυρίου ἔναντι κυρίου, καὶ ἐπιθήσει τὴν χεῖρα αὐτοῦ ἐπὶ τὴν κεφαλὴν τοῦ μόσχου ἔναντι κυρίου καὶ σφάξει τὸν μόσχον ἐνώπιον κυρίου.… (13) Ἐὰν <u>δὲ</u> πᾶσα συναγωγὴ Ἰσραὴλ ἀγνοήσῃ, καὶ λάθῃ ῥῆμα ἐξ ὀφθαλμῶν τῆς συναγωγῆς, καὶ ποιήσωσιν μίαν ἀπὸ πασῶν τῶν ἐντολῶν κυρίου, ἣ οὐ ποιηθήσεται, καὶ πλημμελήσωσιν, (14) καὶ γνωσθῇ αὐτοῖς ἡ ἁμαρτία, ἣν ἥμαρτον ἐν αὐτῇ, καὶ προσάξει ἡ συναγωγὴ μόσχον ἐκ βοῶν ἄμωμον περὶ τῆς ἁμαρτίας, καὶ προσάξει αὐτὸν παρὰ τὰς θύρας τῆς σκηνῆς τοῦ μαρτυρίου.
> (4:3) If *men* the anointed high priest sins so that the people sin, and he will bring for his sin that he committed a calf without blemish from the herd to the Lord for his sin. (4) And he will bring the calf near the door of the tent of witness before the Lord, and he will place his hand on the head of the calf before the Lord, and he will slay the calf in front of the Lord.… (13) But (*de*) if all the congregation of Israel is ignorant, and the matter escapes the notice of the eyes of the congregation, and they do one thing from all the commandments of the Lord that is not to be done, and they err, (14) and the sin in which they sinned becomes known to them, and the congregation will bring a calf without blemish from the herd for the sin, and they will bring it near the door of the tent of witness.

29. So also Lee, *Greek of the Pentateuch*, 98–99.

> אם הכהן המשיח יחטא לאשמת העם והקריב על חטאתו אשר חטא פר בן־בקר תמים ליהוה לחטאת ... (13) ואם כל־עדת ישראל ישגו ונעלם דבר מעיני הקהל ועשו אחת מכל־מצות יהוה אשר לא־תעשינה ואשמו
>
> (4:3) If the anointed priest sins so that the people are guilty, then he will offer for the sin that he committed a bull of the herd without blemish to YHWH as a sin offering.... (13) And if the whole congregation of Israel errs and the matter is hidden from the eyes of the assembly, and they do one thing from all the commandments of YHWH that are not to be done and are guilty.

This continues even beyond the issue of the congregation's sin. In 4:22, 27, and 5:1, the sacrifice instructions for the ruler who sins, the person who sins, and the person who does not act as a witness though he is able, respectively, are given—each one with a corresponding ἐὰν δέ and preposed topic switch. Thus, this occurrence of μέν is particularly significant as the scope of the particle is rather broad and it is connected not to one corresponding utterance but four. More than previous examples, this instance of the particle raises the question: What could have motivated the translator to insert μέν though it represents nothing in his *Vorlage* and given that its host utterance is not *immediately* followed by a corresponding one? By using μέν, the translator explicitly connects the portions of the speech together and effectively subsumes the entire rest of the speech under the topic given in verse 2, unintentional sins.[30] The presence of the particle creates an expectation in the reader of corresponding material, and because of this, the reader must cognitively "hold on to" what they have read. Thus, when the reader reaches the corresponding materials, they know to process them together with the utterance in which μέν appeared. The reader is then acutely aware of the connections between the sections, and it is ensured that, in the building of their mental representation of the text, they will relate them all together and understand the cohesive unit to be relevant to the preceding topic. What is especially important is that this kind of macrolevel use of μέν requires a translator who *knows* the content of his *Vorlage*. A translator who is only aware of the most immediate context would be

---

30. Contra John William Wevers, who misses the connection to later content, instead claiming that the μέν here expresses "certainty" (*Notes on the Greek Text of Leviticus*, SCS 44 [Atlanta: Scholars Press, 1997], 35). On whether such a function is appropriate, see n. 49 below.

unable to utilize μέν in this way.[31] Also of note, similar to example 2 and Exod 32:32 above, is the use of the set phrase ἐὰν μέν … ἐὰν δέ (… ἐὰν δέ…, etc.) here. As with the Exodus translator, the Leviticus translator evinces the ability and desire to render the Hebrew with idiomatic Greek and indicates what may have been another contributing factor to the decision to use μέν here: the sense for the idiom and its fittingness as a set phrase to the context. Note too that the use of μέν results in structuring a mental representation in a way that is not explicitly achieved by the underlying Hebrew.[32]

There are also a few examples in the LXX of μέν … καί (… καί), similar to what was observed in example 5.[33] One of these appears is Isaiah's vision of the Lord in Isa 6:2. In verse 1, Isaiah sees the Lord sitting on his throne. His eyes then examine the space around the throne, wherein he sees two seraphim standing at either side of the Lord.

> καὶ σεραφιν εἱστήκεισαν κύκλῳ αὐτοῦ, ἓξ πτέρυγες τῷ ἑνὶ καὶ ἓξ πτέρυγες τῷ ἑνί, καὶ ταῖς <u>μὲν</u> δυσὶ κατεκάλυπτον τὸ πρόσωπον <u>καὶ</u> ταῖς δυσὶ κατεκάλυπτον τοὺς πόδας <u>καὶ</u> ταῖς δυσὶν ἐπέταντο.
> And seraphim were standing around him, one had six wings and the other had six wings. And with *men* two wings, they were covering their

31. The Leviticus translator, in particular, enjoyed using μέν at this level of discourse. Compare this example with Lev 3:1 and 7:2. In all of these examples, sacrifice instructions are being given for various scenarios with ἐὰν μέν opening and preparing the reader for forthcoming content—contexts that certainly lend themselves to ἐὰν μέν. Another μέν with a broad scope, though not as large as the Leviticus examples, may be observed in Job 12:3, with the corresponding material in Job 12:7.

32. Also interesting is the way in which the translator approaches conjunctive *vav*. As can be observed in this passage and also throughout Leviticus, this translator prefers to use καί for *vav* even when leaving it untranslated would be preferred (such as in the apodosis of a conditional). Despite this proclivity for quantitative representation of the connections between propositions in their *Vorlage*, the translator still uses δέ here. This is significant for the study of translation technique. Just because a translator may tend to translate one way or another, one can only make general comments about that tendency. The OG translators were not bound by any one methodology. This is why the Helsinki School is right to insist that the study of translation technique describe the end product of a translator's work rather than ascribe to them a particular methodology.

33. Similar in that μέν … καί … καί may be observed. The scope of μέν, however, is narrower in example 5 than it is here.

faces; and (*kai*) with two wings, they were covering their feet; and (*kai*) with two wings, they were flying.

שרפים עמדים ממעל לו שש כנפים שש כנפים לאחד בשתים יכסה פניו ובשתים יכסה רגליו ובשתים יעופף

Seraphim are standing above him. Each one has six wings. With two wings, they are covering their faces; and with two wings, they are covering their feet; and with two wings, they are flying.

As with example 5, instead of viewing each successive corresponding sentence as a development on the theme-line, the translator simply connects them with καί.[34] Similar to Lev 4:3, μέν is used in a context wherein all of the corresponding utterances are detailing a preceding statement of a larger category. In Lev 4:3, it was the overarching category of unintentional sins; here, it is "six wings." In order to highlight this connection between sentences and explicitly convey that they are a tightly bound unit relevant to the preceding, the translator employs μέν. As with the previous examples, there is no lexical motivation from the Hebrew source to use μέν nor is the particle semantically necessary to the discourse. The use of μέν, then, must have been a contextually motivated pragmatic decision on the part of the translator. The three sentences all work together to paint one picture of the seraphim beside the Lord, and μέν ensures that the picture is processed as one cohesive unit.[35]

### 6.2.2. A Cognitive-Functional Description of μέν

The examples that have been examined thus far are representative of what one can observe throughout the LXX. There is nothing in the LXX that is categorically different from what was observed in the papyri. Thus, the following description may be offered for μέν.

The DM μέν functions within the cognitive and metatextual domains. Its discourse-pragmatic function is (1) to alert readers to forthcoming necessary, corresponding, and semantically related material that needs to be processed

---

34. Of course, as with any occurrence of καί in the LXX when there is a *vav* in the underlying Hebrew, interference from the source language should certainly be kept in mind as a potential factor for the choice of καί.

35. Though he does not discuss μέν in pragmatic terms, the connection to the two following καί is noted in Le Moigne, "Le livre d'Ésaïe dans la Septante," ch. 4 §A.1 μέν en 6.2.

together with the host utterance in which μέν occurs and (2) to instruct readers to build their mental representation of the discourse by regarding the resultant grouping as a coherent unit that provides relevant information about a preceding or presupposed topic. In addition, the material μέν anticipates will occur at the same level of discourse as the DM's host utterance. By nature of the expectation μέν effects, the information associated with the DM should remain activated in a reader's mental representation, at least up to the point when the reader arrives at the related material.

This description of μέν is similar to that of de Kreij's, based on his investigation of the particle's use in early Classical Greek (Homer and Pindar). He describes μέν as having "specialized in cueing projection," demonstrating how it can function with a large scope, "projecting the progression of a discourse," and how it can be used with a smaller scope to prepare the reader for an upcoming correlated statement (such as in a μέν … δέ construction).[36] He concludes:

> Projection can account for a range of pragmatic functions that μέν has in Homer, Pindar, and beyond. First, the particle serves as metalanguage to guide the hearer through the discourse, often foreshadowing transitions to new moves within the discourse. In this function, its scope extends over its entire host act, and there is no particular relation between μέν and the word that precedes it. Second, μέν can have scope over the preceding word, with a range of possible effects. In Homer and Pindar not every μέν entails a δέ: when μέν has large scope, the projection can be fulfilled with any particle that can continue the discourse, or no particle at all. If μέν has small scope, it most typically forms part of a μέν–δέ construction, which in later literature covers the majority of μέν instances.[37]

Likewise, Drummen, commenting on the particle's use in Aeschylus, Sophocles, Euripides, and Aristophanes, writes:

> μέν is generally described as setting up an expectation for some part to follow. That is, in pragmatic terms, it projects another discourse act….

36. Bonifazi, Drummen, and de Kreij, *Particles in Ancient Greek Discourse*, 477, 484.

37. Bonifazi, Drummen, and de Kreij, *Particles in Ancient Greek Discourse*, 489. However, I would categorize many of de Kriej's examples of μέν with a small scope as having a medium scope. This is because he is focusing on the word that precedes μέν, whereas I consider μέν to be introducing its entire host utterance, which can be a phrase, clause, or larger unit.

> Besides indicating that more narrative steps will follow in story-telling monologues, speakers can also use μέν, for example, to mark a juxtaposition of (parts of) conditions, arguments, or points of view.[38]

The suggestion that projection is the core pragmatic feature of μέν matches what was observed and described above in the papyri and LXX. However, projection alone seems insufficient and too broad. At least in what can be observed in early koine material, it is the projection of (1) *semantically related material* that is (2) *relevant to a preceding or implied topic* that is core to the particle's usage. The suggestion that μέν projects semantically related material aligns with Bakker's description of it based on his work in Attic Greek. With regard to the μέν … δέ construction, he argues that it "effects a coherence in the discourse that is semantic (content-oriented), in that the information is felt to be incomplete when either member is lacking," and regarding μέν, "The presence of *mén* … does no more than signal that the clause will acquire its intended meaning only in combination with the following one, to which it anticipates."[39] Similarly, *CGCG* writes that μέν "indicates **incompleteness** or **open-endedness**—μέν signals that its host segment in itself does not provide all the necessary information; it raises the expectation that another text segment will follow to provide an addition or contrast."[40] Based on their work in the New Testament,

---

38. Bonifazi, Drummen, and de Kreij, *Particles in Ancient Greek Discourse*, 896.

39. Bakker, "Boundaries, Topics, and the Structure of Discourse," 300, 301. Bakker posits an additional category for the μέν … δέ construction. He argues it can be used as a discourse structuring device by which μέν signals that the current discourse segment is complete and coming to a close and δέ begins a new discourse topic (302–5). (Sicking provides a similar argument with regard to some occurrences of μὲν οὖν … δέ; "Devices for Text Articulation," 27.) I have not seen any μέν in the papyri, the LXX, or the New Testament that functions in this way. If it is a legitimate category, it would seem to have phased out by the koine period. Unfortunately, what Bakker does not provide is an explanation as to how the two functions of the μέν … δέ construction that he sees are related, how one could have developed from the other, or how they are distinguished from one another. As it stands, since I am focusing on the use of DMs in Koine, an in-depth evaluation of Bakker's second category would be outside of the purview of this investigation. However, do note Levinsohn's discussion of Acts 8:25, which contains a μέν (οὖν) … δέ (8:26) similar to the examples Bakker gives. Levinsohn argues that the μέν (οὖν) is transitional and its host-utterance backgrounded and that the μέν is prospective, anticipating the δέ, which picks up the mainline of the narrative (Levinsohn, *Textual Connections*, 146–47).

40. *CGCG*, §59.24, emphasis original.

Levinsohn and Runge both argue along similar lines as Bakker. Levinsohn uses the term "prospective" to describe μέν, noting that the traditional Greek grammarians considered it as always prospective, and Runge states that "Μέν signals the presence of one common constraint: anticipation of a related sentence that follows."[41]

The descriptions above are not an entirely new or different way of describing μέν. As noted earlier, the traditional grammars and lexica make similar claims; they only lack the pragmatic perspective that is a more recent development in linguistic scholarship.[42] Denniston, for example, recognizes that μέν often corresponds with following related material and thus devotes much of his chapter on the particle to a function he calls "preparatory."[43] Likewise, Smyth spends about half of his section on μέν discussing its correlation with following clauses.[44] Robertson also sees a correlative function in μέν, and Jannaris states that such was the function of μέν, as opposed to its emphatic sister μήν.[45] However, some of these view the correlation primarily as one of contrast, especially in μέν … δέ constructions. As observed in the examples earlier and corroborated by the

41. Levinsohn quotation from *DFNTG*, 170; Runge quotation from *DGGNT*, 75. In a personal communication with me on 31 October 2013, Levinsohn noted that the credit for the term "prospective" when describing μέν should go to T. E. Page, *The Acts of the Apostles* (London: Macmillan, 1886), 94. It should be noted that Levinsohn also argues the information introduced by μέν, at least in narrative, will often be of "secondary importance in comparison with that introduced with δέ" (*DFNTG*, 170). Based on the occurrences of μέν I have examined in the papyri and LXX, I am convinced that Runge is correct in his observation that "The downgrading effect that Levinsohn asserts is better explained by the nature of the offline information that it often introduces than by the particle itself" (*DGGNT*, 76 n. 7). Granted, Levinsohn's claim is made with regard to the particle's use in narrative and most of what I have examined is nonnarrative (whether legal documents or direct speech within a narrative), but its use in nonnarrative as well as in examples from narrative like Exod 13:21 (ὁ δὲ θεὸς ἡγεῖτο αὐτῶν, ἡμέρας μὲν ἐν στύλῳ νεφέλης δεῖξαι αὐτοῖς τὴν ὁδόν, τὴν δὲ νύκτα ἐν στύλῳ πυρός·, "Now, God was leading them, by day *men*, in a pillar of cloud to show them the way, and (*de*) by night, in a pillar of fire") have led me not to regard prominence of the anticipated information as a function of μέν itself. It should be noted that Levinsohn does use the qualifiers "frequently" and "often," thus indicating that the downgrading is not viewed as central to the particle's function.

42. See pp. 209–10.

43. Denniston, *Particles*, 369–84.

44. Smyth, §§2901c, 2903–2913.

45. Robertson, *Grammar*, 1151–53; Jannaris, *Greek Grammar*, §1744.

more recent investigations into μέν in Classical Greek and the New Testament, μέν simply anticipates related material, which may or may not be contrastive. Though the particle may be particularly well suited to drawing attention to a contrast, such is simply a natural result of its pragmatic function. There are plenty of instances in which μέν or μέν … δέ cannot be construed as contrastive (such as every papyri example given above besides the two from the Zenon corpus). As discussed in chapters 2 and 4 with regard to δέ and ἀλλά, contrast is a semantic element of the linguistic context; signaling it is not a distinct function of μέν, δέ, or μέν … δέ.[46]

However, in all of these descriptions, the relation between μέν and its corresponding utterances, on the one hand, and that which precedes them is hardly discussed. Traditional scholarship says nothing about the motivation to use μέν within its wider context. Similarly, even though de Kreij, Drummen, Bakker, Runge, and Levinsohn provide excellent descriptions of what μέν accomplishes from a discourse-pragmatic perspective, they do not fully answer the question of why an author or translator would use it.[47] As was argued above based on the examples from the papyri and LXX, an author or translator uses μέν because the resulting unit that it signals—that is, both the host utterance of μέν and the anticipated material following—provides further relevant information to a particular preceding topic. This is the strength of describing μέν not just from a discourse-pragmatic perspective but also by drawing some insights from relevance theory.[48] Normally, readers expect optimal relevance at each step as they progress through a text, but μέν signals to them that, with regard to a particular preceding topic, optimal relevance is not achieved by simply reading on to the present material but by reading and processing it together with the anticipated material. By describing μέν from these two angles, we obtain a

46. See also Runge's discussion of contrast and μέν … δέ in Matt. 3:11 in *DGGNT*, 77.

47. This is not to say that de Kreij, Drummen, Bakker, Runge, and Levinsohn do not discuss the preceding context at all, but rather that the discussions are very minimal. Levinsohn, in fact, writes, "It is most common in the narrative sections of Acts for *men* to occur in connection with an initial response to the last event recorded. The presence of *men* anticipates a second response by the same subject … or by the addressee of the initial response.… Furthermore, if the event which led to the initial response had a stated or implied goal, *men* anticipates the realization of that goal in the later response" (Levinsohn, *Textual Connections*, 144).

48. See, e.g., the studies in Blass, *Relevance Relations in Discourse*; and Blakemore, *Relevance and Linguistic Meaning*.

fuller understanding of how it guides the reader in the construction of his mental representation of the text.

Based on what has been observed in third to first century BCE Greek and the descriptions of μέν given by de Kreij, Drummen, and Bakker for Attic Greek and Runge and Levinsohn for Biblical Greek, it would seem that μέν did not undergo any significant diachronic change.[49] Its use as an anticipatory marker, able to function at any level of the discourse, persists through time and across genres. Regarding variables to its use, while I would argue that μέν is sufficient in itself, prototypical μέν is exemplified in the μέν … δέ construction.[50] Slightly less typical, though still quite frequent, is μέν with a corresponding connective that is not δέ. Following that is μέν with no corresponding connective.[51]

### 6.2.3. μέν and LXX Translation Technique

The fact that μέν appears *at all* in the LXX is significant. The particle has no lexical equivalent in Hebrew and rarely, if ever, quantitatively represents an underlying Hebrew constituent; moreover, the translators were obviously still hesitant to employ the particle.[52] Thus, by its very use, it offers salient insights into the translator who did employ it. First, it evinces a translator who was aware of the wider linguistic context. In almost every case, the

49. There is evidence that μέν at one point had an emphatic function, which some posit as a use in the koine period (see nn. 2 and 23 above). However, as I have demonstrated elsewhere, prospective μέν developed from an old emphatic function, and that function had *already* phased out in Classical Greek (being left to μήν). It is an interesting historical footnote about the development of the DM but nothing more. See the discussion in Christopher J. Fresch, "Is There an Emphatic μέν? A Consideration of the Particle's Development and Its Function in Koine," *NTS* 63 (2017): 261–78.

50. One does wonder why the two particles are so well-suited to one another. Perhaps it is because they both operate within the metatextual domain. It may also be the case that it is the forthcoming segmentation signaled by δέ that motivates the use of μέν, to ensure in those particular contexts that the reader read the two or more discourse chunks together.

51. See also the discussion in n. 14 above. The edge of the fuzzy boundary would be μέν that implies corresponding material.

52. This can be most readily seen when one considers the use of the particle in the nontranslated material of the LXX, which is a smaller corpus than the translated books of the Hebrew Bible. Compared to the ~55 occurrences of μέν in the translated material, there are 120 other instances of μέν in the LXX. See also Le Moigne, "Le livre d'Ésaïe dans la Septante," ch. 4, A. Étude de μέν; Conybeare and Stock, *Grammar*, §39.

use of the particle could not be motivated if the translator was aware of only the most immediate context. Second, it indicates how the translator read and interpreted the material in their *Vorlage*. They regarded these words, clauses, sentences, or paragraphs introduced by μέν to be connected to semantically corresponding, forthcoming, relevant material in relation to an overarching topic. Third, the fact that the translator would use the particle when faced with such material *despite the lack of a corresponding lexical equivalent* evinces that they were willing to call attention to the connection between those utterances and found the connection to be important enough to merit employing a lexeme that did not correspond to a lexeme in their *Vorlage*. Fourth, the use of μέν by a translator demonstrates the desire to render their source text into idiomatic Greek.[53] Finally, in addition to encoding their understanding of the *Vorlage's* discourse into their translation by using μέν, the translator may also seek to elevate the rhetoric by the particle's use. The particle is not a necessary piece of the translation; it is helpful in that it makes the communication clearer and delimits possible interpretations, but it is not necessary, semantically or syntactically. Neither does it lexically relate to anything in the underlying Hebrew. Both of these are reason enough for a LXX translator to forego its use, which they appear to have done most of the time. Understanding the function of the particle provides much insight, but a rhetorical motivation in combination with it may provide an even clearer picture. Willy Clarysse, commenting on the use of μέν in papyri notes, "Μέν … δέ is common in rhetorical showcases, e.g. in legal texts, but rare in private letters. The examples [in private letters] show a conscious effort to enhance the style of these private letters."[54] Lee also notes the association of μέν with "good" style.[55] It may be that this provided a level of extra motivation for at least some of the handful of instances where it appears in the translated books of the LXX. Consider also that of those approximately fifty-five instances of μέν, almost 30 percent and just over 12 percent occur in the set phrases εἰ/ἐὰν μέν and μὲν γάρ, respectively. This may indicate a reflex to use the idiom where it is felt especially appropriate rhetorically.

53. So also Lee, "Features of the Speech of Jesus," 3, who remarks generally on the LXX translators, following a discussion on μέν, "The translators were not necessarily constrained by the original in their use of particles, just as in general they show readiness … to employ idiomatic Greek where appropriate."

54. Clarysse, "Linguistic Diversity," 38.

55. Lee, *Greek of the Pentateuch*, 98.

It is also important to note that the use of *μέν* affects the building of the reader's mental representation of the text in a way that is not achieved in the underlying Hebrew texts. This is not to say that a significantly different interpretation or meaning will be obtained in every or even most instances, but *μέν* does instruct the reader in a way that the Hebrew does not, in that it explicitly signals to the reader to anticipate related material and that relevance to a preceding topic will be fully realized by relating it to the connected utterances. In this way, too, *μέν* eases the processing effort on the part of the reader.

Therefore, a description of a translator's translation technique must account for the use of *μέν*; it cannot simply be ignored. For each translator, deeper investigation may be done than is possible in this chapter as to what further possible factors may have influenced them to use the particle.[56] Nevertheless, the facts remain that its uses in the LXX are in line with its discourse-pragmatic function observed elsewhere, that it shows some ability on the part of the translator to translate idiomatically, that it is never qualitatively motivated and hardly, if ever, quantitatively motivated, and that in order to use it, the translator had to have some conception of the wider context as they translated as well as the freedom to encode that conception into the text.

## 6.3. μέν in the Twelve

Now that the papyri and the LXX have been thoroughly investigated in their use of *μέν*, we can return to the two instances of the particle in the Twelve.

**Haggai 1:4**
(1:2–3) Thus says the Lord Almighty saying, "These people are saying, 'The time has not come to build the house of the Lord.'" And a word of the Lord came by the hand of Haggai the prophet saying,

(1:4) Εἰ καιρὸς ὑμῖν <u>μέν</u> ἐστι τοῦ οἰκεῖν ἐν οἴκοις ὑμῶν κοιλοστάθμοις, ὁ δὲ οἶκος οὗτος ἐξηρήμωται;
"Is it time for you *men* to live in your paneled houses, but (*de*) this house to be left devastated?"

56. For an example of this, see my discussion regarding the two *μέν* in the Twelve in §6.3 below as well as Le Moigne's investigation of *μέν* in Isaiah ("Le livre d'Ésaïe dans la Septante," ch. 4 §A. Étude de *μέν*).

העת לכם אתם לשבת בבתיכם ספונים והבית הזה חרב
"Is it time for you to dwell in your covered houses, while this house is desolate?"

**Zechariah 1:15**
*καὶ ὀργὴν μεγάλην ἐγὼ ὀργίζομαι ἐπὶ τὰ ἔθνη τὰ συνεπιτιθέμενα ἀνθ' ὧν ἐγὼ μὲν ὠργίσθην ὀλίγα, αὐτοὶ δὲ συνεπέθεντο εἰς κακά.*
And I am extremely angry at the nations who joined together in an attack—because I *men* was angry a little, but (*de*) they joined together in an attack for evil.

וקצף גדול אני קצף על־הגוים השאננים אשר אני קצפתי מעט והמה עזרו לרעה
And I am extremely angry at the nations at ease, with whom I was angry a little, but they have helped in wickedness.

The translator of the Twelve had no lexical motivation to use *μέν* in either of these verses. Neither instance of the particle represents any lexeme of the Hebrew, qualitatively or quantitatively. This raises the question as to why the translator would use the particle at all. One can observe in both verses that *μέν* occurs inside of material that, while important, is not the end of the conversation. Rather, in both cases, there is a final point yet to be made that correlates with the former material in which *μέν* appears but that serves as the last word on the topic under discussion (Haggai: the unwillingness to rebuild the temple; Zechariah: the Lord's anger with the nations). In Hag 1:4, the Lord questions his people's comfortable living and then effectively condemns them for it as he reminds them that his temple remains devastated. In Zech 1:15, the Lord states that he was already angry against the attacking nations, but his great anger is the combination of that prior anger with his response to their joining in an attack for evil, this latter point seemingly being the proverbial "last straw."

In light of what has been observed throughout the papyri and the rest of the LXX, the uses of *μέν* in Hag 1:4 and Zech 1:15 are very fitting. In both verses, the particle anticipates related, forthcoming material, highlights the connection between its host utterance and that material, and makes explicit that the cohesive unit, as a whole, not just *μέν*'s host utterance, is relevant to a preceding topic. Thus, in both cases, the resultant effect is that an argument is being built against Israel and the nations, respectively. It would seem to be these connections and their relevance to the overarching topic that motivated the translator to insert *μέν*. The particle thus instructs the reader to build their mental representation with anticipation of related material in mind, that there is more yet to be said that completes the meaning of the utterance as a whole and is thus relevant to the preceding, and thereby ensures the reader does not miss the connection.

In comparing the Greek with the underlying Hebrew, it is important to point out, as was observed with the other LXX examples, that by inserting μέν into these verses, the translator creates an explicit connection and expectation for the reader, influencing their mental representation of the text in a way that is not achieved in the Hebrew. Moreover, the translator who uses μέν to alert the reader that the present material is incomplete and the full meaning and its relevance is realized in connection with forthcoming content is certainly communicating their own understanding of the content. Also, with regard to the translator's translation technique, as with the other instances of the DM in the LXX, the presence of lexically unmotivated μέν evinces the ability and desire of the translator to go at least occasionally beyond lexical constraints to render their source text into idiomatic (and perhaps stylized) Greek.

It may be asked why the translator only uses μέν in these two verses but nowhere else in the Twelve. A satisfactory answer will likely never be provided, but there are some considerations worth noting. First, it is worth keeping in mind that μέν was largely avoided by the LXX translators, as it did not represent an underlying Hebrew lexeme. This is all the more evident when one encounters the many more occurrences of μέν in the handful of nontranslated books.[57] Second, if the Twelve was translated by a group of translators, then it is possible that Hag 1 and Zech 1 in the LXX are the work of one translator from that group.[58] This is at least conceivable, since the two chapters are close together in proximity and Haggai and Zech 1–8 are thematically related and may have even constituted a collected corpus prior to the formation of the Book of the Twelve.[59] Third, there are key contextual and theological factors that bear mentioning.

57. See n. 52 above.

58. See §1.4.

59. See Nogalski, *Micah–Malachi*, 493–94, 765, 806–7; Carol L. Meyers and Eric M. Meyers, *Haggai, Zechariah 1–8: A New Translation with Introduction and Commentary*, AB 25B (Garden City, NY: Doubleday, 1987), xliv–xlviii; Martin Leuenberger, "Time and Situational Reference in the Book of Haggai: On Religious- and Theological-Historical Contextualizations of Redactional Processes," in *Perspectives on the Formation of the Book of the Twelve: Methodological Foundations—Redactional Processes—Historical Insights*, ed. Rainer Albertz, James D. Nogalski, and Jakob Wöhrle, BZAW 433 (Berlin: de Gruyter, 2012), 157–58; Martin Hallaschka, "From Cores to

With regard to Hag 1:4, it is on the correlated points, with an understanding that the current status of the Lord's temple is the primary issue, that the following verses build. Haggai 1:5–11 begin a connected but new discourse unit, as signaled by the heavy pragmatic encoding in verse 5 with a temporal shift (καὶ νῦν) and forward-pointing τάδε along with the formulaic speech frame τάδε λέγει κύριος παντοκράτωρ. The content of these verses reminds the people again of their laziness and sin (1:6) and then commands them to go up to the mountain, cut trees, and build the Lord's house so that he can take pleasure in it and be honored (1:8), all the while experiencing the Lord's judgment (1:9–11). Similarly, the verses following Zech 1:15 build off of its correlated points. A connected but distinct shift occurs in verse 16, as signaled by the DM διὰ τοῦτο, the forward-pointing τάδε, and the redundant quotative speech frame λέγει κύριος.[60] The Lord then declares that he will return to Jerusalem with compassion (1:16, picking up on 1:14), he will rebuild his temple, that good things will happen in the cities (1:17), Jerusalem will be abundantly settled (2:4), the Lord will be a wall of fire around and become glory in Jerusalem, and that those who plundered the Lord's people, those against whom 1:15 is directed, will become spoil for their own slaves (2:8–9). Thus, in both cases, the discourses that follow Hag 1:4 and Zech 1:15 owe their contents (or at least much of them) to the correlated utterances in question. It is also interesting to note that the rebuilding of the Lord's temple is a primary, if not the primary, point in both discourses. It is not difficult to imagine that, given the manner in which the discourses build off of the respective correlated utterances and, perhaps, the importance of the assurance that the temple will be rebuilt, the translator saw a need to make sure the starting points of those discourses were not overlooked by the reader and was thus motivated to use μέν to highlight and strengthen the connection between utterances. This would ensure the connection would not be missed and would also draw more attention to the motivations behind the respective following discourses.[61]

---

Corpus: Considering the Formation of Haggai and Zechariah 1–8," in Albertz, Nogalski, and Wöhrle, *Perspectives on the Formation of the Book of the Twelve*, 171–89.

60. On διὰ τοῦτο and redundant quotative speech frames in Koine, see *DGGNT* §§2.6, 7.2.2, 7.3.2.

61. Michel Casevitz, Cécile Dogniez, and Marguerite Harl, *Les Douze Prophètes: Aggée, Zacharie*, Bd'A 23.10–11 (Paris: Cerf, 2007), 74–75, 226–27, do not comment on either of these instances of μέν. This is an unfortunate oversight but is typical of

More interesting, though, than why the particle only occurs twice in the Twelve is that it occurs at all. The translator of the Twelve generally tried to stick rather close to their *Vorlage*, and yet μέν is still used twice and used well. That μέν appears at all in the Greek translation of the Twelve indicates that it is alive and well in the language and being used.

As a final thought, related to this last point, it is interesting to note that the μέν … δέ construction is generally regarded as having declined in use in Postclassical Greek and is a feature of a more formal style of communication.[62] If this is the case, then its occurrences in the Twelve (and the rest of the LXX) are all the more extraordinary. This is not to say that the particles are merely inserted to mimic classical style; their placement in Hag 1:4 and Zech 1:15 are perfectly fitted to the context, both from a discourse-pragmatic perspective, as just argued, and from a rhetorical one, given the argumentative context of both passages. However, their presence does evince the translator's familiarity with a slightly higher register of Greek.

## 6.4. Conclusion

A few issues were not touched on that bear mentioning here. First, as I have mentioned elsewhere with regard to οὖν based on Aitken's work, direct speech seems to have invited more freedom from the translators to engage in good, literary Greek.[63] The fact that most of the occurrences of μέν occur inside of direct speech in the LXX may be further evidence of this. Second, Aitken has helpfully demonstrated the rhetorical effect μέν may have in the LXX to convey a literary style, showing even that in Gen 18:12 (examined above), "it elevates Sarah's speech to a more formal and literary level."[64] Such effects are outside of the purview of this chapter, but I include it here as a helpful reminder that literary style and rhetoric are

current work on the Greek text of the Septuagint, which tends to examine the text solely from syntactic/semantic and qualitative/quantitative viewpoints, ignoring the pragmatic features of the language.

62. See Lee, "Features of the Speech of Jesus," 1–7; Clarysse, "Linguistic Diversity," 38; Aitken, "Characterization of Speech,", 28; Moulton and Turner, *Grammar*, 331. However, see also Thrall, *Greek Particles*, 2–3, who offers a necessary warning in relying too much on the papyri to provide evidence for the decline of particle use in Koine Greek.

63. Fresch, "Peculiar Occurrences of οὖν"; Aitken, "Characterization of Speech," 30–31.

64. Aitken, "Characterization of Speech," 28–29.

further considerations when evaluating any text and should be featured more in discussions regarding the LXX translators. This is not to say that style and rhetoric override the function of a DM; they do not, but there is no reason that the use of a DM in a certain context could not have more than one motivation.[65] Related to these points is the potential explanatory power of sociolinguistics. Lee explains, "The way something is said varies with the *situation* in which it is said. The main ingredients of situation are who is speaking, to whom they are speaking, what kind of utterance it is, and in what real-life context it is said. Vocabulary and other features of language are adjusted, that is, choices are made from a range of variables, to fit the situation."[66] As Lee goes on to demonstrate, social situation is an important factor to consider when examining the language of the Greek Old Testament that provides illuminating insights.[67] While sociolinguistic explanations of μέν are not sufficient in themselves to explain its use, they may provide further insight into the motivations of a translator.

---

65. Such is the feeling one gets when Clarysse, concerning the papyri, notes, "*Μέν* … *δέ* is common in rhetorical showcases, e.g. in legal texts, but rare in private letters. The examples above show a conscious effort to enhance the style of these private letters" (Clarysse, "Linguistic Diversity," 38). Or Lee, who writes, based on the tendency for μέν (… δέ) to occur in educated, official letters rather than private letters, which are more likely to mirror everyday speech, "It seems clear, then, that quite early in the Koine μέν (… δέ) was no longer the living idiom that it undoubtedly had been in Classical Greek but had become, on the whole, a sign of an attempt at more educated Greek, a prestige feature consciously used" (Lee, "Features of the Speech of Jesus," 2). But of course μέν (… δέ) is used *correctly* and *with good reason* in the koine material, whether private letters, the LXX, or the New Testament. When it is used, it is fitting to the contexts in which it appears. Lee's statement, in particular, would be tantamount to someone two thousand years from now arguing: "Since 'consequently,' 'to be certain,' 'whereas,' and 'tantamount' were declining in use in twentieth to twenty-first century English and, when they did occur, tended to be found in dissertations and legal documents but not in private correspondences, it is clear that the words had become a sign of an attempt at more educated English." The conclusion, obviously, does not necessarily follow from the premise. Though a lexeme is rare in everyday speech and private correspondences and may, in fact, reflect a higher register or a more stylized idiom, it does not therefore indicate that every occurrence of that linguistic unit must have been nothing more than a rhetorically motivated attempt at a more educated-sounding correspondence. Issues of register, style, and social context ought to be considered, but they alone cannot account for a DM's use.

66. Lee, *The Greek of the Pentateuch*, 46.

67. Lee, *The Greek of the Pentateuch*, 47–72.

In the end, we are again provided with a picture of the LXX translators, and the translator of the Twelve in particular, that evinces an awareness of the wider linguistic context and a freedom to translate accordingly into idiomatic Greek. More than most of the DMs examined throughout this investigation, the fact that μέν is used at all in the LXX is surprising, given both its decline in Greek and its lack of a Hebrew equivalent. Paying attention to the use of μέν is important in the study of LXX translation technique. It would appear that the LXX translators who utilized the particle were not always content to mirror their *Vorlagen* exactly but were willing to insert the particle owing to their interpretation of the text before them and with a view to communicate clearly to the reader.

# 7
# Conclusion

Discourse markers are valuable components of language that serve to instruct the recipient of a communication how to integrate new material into one's own mental representation of the discourse. The object of this study has been to investigate a selection of DMs in early Koine Greek—namely, δέ, εἰ/ἐὰν μή, ἀλλά, ἀλλ' ἤ, and μέν—in order to discern their unique functions and to demonstrate their significance to the study of LXX translation technique.

Throughout this study, it has been observed how traditional descriptions of DMs typically do not accurately portray what DMs accomplish. This is due to the descriptions not being functional in nature and the unique features of DMs (interaction with the mental representation, scope assignments, function within macrofunctional domains) not being recognized. However, this is not to say that the traditional grammars and lexica never provide any insight into the DMs. On the contrary, they frequently demonstrate a deep understanding of the Greek language and an intuitive sense for what the DMs accomplish. On the other hand, though, they lack the linguistic framework, especially one well suited to DMs in particular, and the wealth of typological data available today. In addition, even though there has been linguistically informed scholarship on DMs in Classical and Postclassical Greek, grammars and lexica, on the whole, either have not caught up with or have simply not paid attention to such studies. Thus I have attempted in my interaction with traditional Greek scholarship to confirm their descriptions where possible, at other times to break new ground, and, only when necessary, to provide a corrective.

## 7.1. The Value of Functional Descriptions

In my investigations, following current trends in linguistic scholarship on DMs, I sought to provide functional descriptions of the DMs based on their uses in the documentary papyri and LXX. Thus, rather than attributing the semantics of surrounding contexts to the DMs, I posited prototypical functions and extensions from the prototype that could be observed across the data sets. These descriptions focus on how each DM instructs the reader to build their mental representation of the discourse and process the text. In each chapter, I demonstrated that the posited functions had more explanatory power and described what each DM accomplishes more accurately. In all of this, the value of modern linguistic theory was evident. The work that has been done, and that informed my theoretical framework, on discourse comprehension, mental representations, functional grammar, cognitive linguistics, discourse grammar, discourse analysis, pragmatics, and linguistic typology was demonstrated to be valuable and crucial to the study of Koine Greek linguistics.

It was also observed that my findings found support as well as further confirmed the work of other scholars who have engaged in similar discourse-pragmatic investigations in Classical and later Koine Greek. Additionally, in each case, I was able to offer further refined descriptions of the DMs.

## 7.2. Insight into the Language of the LXX

In each investigation, the documentary papyri of the third to first centuries BCE were analyzed first, owing to their witness to natural koine idiom. In this way, the papyri served as a control group against which the data in the LXX could then be compared. The LXX, as a translation, may not always witness to genuine koine idiom, owing to interference from the source language, so a control group is both valuable and necessary. One insight that arose from this, though, was the comparable use of the DMs in both corpora. In other words, in the LXX, there was essentially no difference in function for any of the DMs investigated. This is particularly significant as discussions continue concerning the linguistic nature of the Greek translations of the Old Testament. Though linguistic interference certainly does occur and each translator must be analyzed individually, one may observe in the use of these DMs consistent usage that reflects the Greek idiom of the day. Thus, it is my hope that this study will encourage more scholarship that investigates the Greek of the LXX on its own terms and in its own right.

## 7.3. Discourse Markers and LXX Translation Technique

One intention of this study was to demonstrate the value and significance of DMs to the study of translation technique. As was repeatedly observed, DMs, though quantitatively representing an element of the underlying Hebrew in many instances, are often not lexically motivated by their *Vorlagen*. Because of this and because of the pragmatic contributions DMs make to the discourse, attention to DMs can provide unique insight into how a translator conceived of the structure and flow of the discourse and intended for the reader to process the text. For example, it was demonstrated that δέ signals an explicit discourse structure by indicating distinct information units. This is not always explicitly (or even implicitly) mirrored in the Hebrew. Instead, it witnesses to the translator's conception of the discourse.

Significantly, it was demonstrated that DMs frequently evince an awareness of a wide context on the part of the translator. By their very nature as grammatical phenomena with discourse implications, DMs are contextually motivated, discourse-driven devices. In addition, since they connect to the mental representation under construction, they interact with information beyond the linguistic context that is presumed to be in the mind of the reader or that the author/translator wants to activate in the mind of the reader, whether potential assumptions, inferences, or evaluations. Therefore, a translator, in order to justify the choice to use a DM, must have had reason to do so based on their own conception of the discourse and how to facilitate its successful communication. This was clear in every investigation. For instance, εἰ/ἐὰν μή, ἀλλά, and ἀλλ᾽ ἤ, in order to be used, had to be motivated by a contextual awareness and a consideration of the construction of the reader's mental representation. A contextual awareness was especially critical for the use of these DMs owing to the fact that all three of them would often render the same Hebrew DMs (given the polysemy of the Hebrew DMs). Of course, the requirement of contextual motivation and a consideration of the reader's mental representation is nowhere more clearly seen than in μέν. The Greek DM does not even have a partial equivalent in Hebrew, and its use continually evinces a contextual awareness on the part of the LXX translators and a desire to encode the discourse idiomatically, according to their conception of it, and in such a way as to guide the reader in their processing of it.

Moreover, as I argued in chapter 1, it is reasonable to assume that the nonlexically motivated renderings of DMs are not the only instances during the translation work in which a translator was aware of the wider context and the flow of the discourse.[1] Rather, unless it is postulated that the contextually fitting nonlexically motivated renderings are *accidents*, they evince a contextual awareness that was likely maintained, more or less and to greater or lesser extent, *throughout* the translation process. How a translator uses DMs provides insight not only into how they conceived of the discourse but also into their level of contextual awareness. Thus, DMs have much to offer the study of translation technique. They uniquely contribute to the discourse, do not always match the underlying Hebrew, and explicitly demonstrate how a translator comprehended the text and pieced it together. Attention to DMs also has the advantage of moving us beyond the, in Joshua Harper's words, "overly simplistic dichotomy between 'literal' and 'free.'"[2] This dichotomy is problematic in most of its applications, but it is especially unhelpful with regard to DMs. Even a translator who may be consistently characterized as producing a literal translation will occasionally use a nonlexically motivated DM that pragmatically produces the same effect as the underlying Hebrew by different means. A proper understanding of and attention to DMs enables the Septuagintalist to study how a translator engaged with their *Vorlage* at those critical hinges between discourse contents and attempted to produce a text that conveyed the *Vorlage*'s meaning, or their conception of it, in idiomatic Greek.

Lastly, this study reveals the need for deep engagement with the translators themselves. Often, the study of translation technique provides statistical data with little linguistic and contextual analysis. While it is interesting to compile data on how a translator renders a Hebrew lexeme or how a Greek lexeme is used throughout a corpus vis-á-vis the underlying Hebrew, these data require rigorous interpretation. We must ask *why* the translator makes the *choices* they do, considering the context, the structure of the discourse, the facilitation of successful communication, and numerous other factors as well. Statistical data can be helpful, but they are only a starting point. Without interpretation of them and an examination of the

1. See pp. 36–37.
2. Harper, *Responding to a Puzzled Scribe*, 22.

translator who produced them, they do not sufficiently describe the translation or the translator. There is much that we stand to gain by broadening our framework to enable us to ask more questions of the translator so as to gain a more robust and nuanced perspective of them and their work.

## 7.4. Insight into the Twelve

Throughout this study, the translator of the Twelve was specifically examined in order to provide a more in-depth look at how a translator engaged with their *Vorlage* and used the DMs under investigation. In every chapter, it was observed that the translator did not feel especially constrained to lexically represent the underlying Hebrew in every instance. Instead, the translator regularly evinces a contextual awareness, a consideration of the flow of the discourse, and a concern for successful communication that influences their use of DMs. The DMs never feel out of place nor rhetorically motivated, but are rather used for the pragmatic and communicative purpose of aiding readers in their comprehension of the text and in the building of their mental representation of the discourse. Moreover, the translator's use of the DMs frequently demonstrates a desire to render the meaning of their source text. Though they often do not "literally" represent the Hebrew, they nonetheless, in most cases, convey the meaning of it (or a viable meaning if the Hebrew could be read in more than one way). In addition, there are instances in which the pragmatics of the Hebrew are exactly matched by the pragmatics of the Greek, though by different means, possibly witnessing to an impressive linguistic intuition on the part of the translator. By paying careful attention to the use of DMs in the Twelve, then, one is presented with a picture of a translator who was concerned both to create an idiomatic Greek text and to faithfully convey the meaning of the original.

## 7.5. Suggestions for Further Research

### 7.5.1. Greek Linguistics

Greek linguistics stands to benefit greatly from modern linguistic theory and from moving out of the typical corpora into less explored areas. First, there are many DMs in Greek, particularly in Postclassical Greek, yet to be investigated from a cognitive-functional perspective. It is my hope that others will see the value in this study and go on to contribute to our understanding of the functions of these DMs. Second, I hope to have demonstrated the value of both the documentary papyri and the LXX to linguistic inquiry. Both of these corpora, particularly the papyri, have much yet to offer to our knowledge of Greek, not only with regard to DMs.

### 7.5.2. LXX Studies

In connection with the above, there are other Greek DMs that occur in the LXX that offer insight into how the translators conceived of the discourse and understood their source texts. Having proper understandings of these DMs will directly benefit the study of translation technique, will affect our reading and interpretation of the texts, and will have implications for textual criticism. Moving beyond the realm of DMs, modern linguistic theory in general has not been widely adopted and applied in LXX scholarship. As I hope to have demonstrated here, there is much to be gained from interdisciplinary studies that are informed by linguistic scholarship and investigate how it may benefit the field of LXX studies.[3]

One topic not addressed in previous chapters is whether this study speaks into the issue of how we conceptualize the nature of the Septuagint as a translation. This is outside the purview of the present study, but a note must be made given the insistence of LXX scholars to continue this conversation. In brief, within LXX scholarship, there is disagreement as to whether we should conceive of the LXX as the text-as-produced (the text *qua* translation) or the text-as-received (the translation *qua* text).[4] In other words, are the translations subservient to the Hebrew source and intended to guide the reader back to it (text-as-produced) or are they to be read as Greek texts in their own right (text-as-received)? Of course, such a framing is inherently flawed. It assumes a polar opposition, begging the question. As a part of this debate, different translation theories have been argued for and applied, such as the interlinear paradigm, descriptive translation studies, polysystem theory, and skopos theory.[5] No solution

3. On this, see also Fresch, "Septuagint and Discourse Grammar."

4. Cameron Boyd-Taylor, "What Is the Septuagint?," in Salvesen and Law, *Oxford Handbook of the Septuagint*, 28.

5. For the interlinear paradigm, see, e.g., Albert Pietersma and Benjamin G. Wright III, "To the Reader of NETS," *NETS*, xii–xx; Pietersma, "Beyond Literalism: Interlinearity Revisited," in *"Translation Is Required": The Septuagint in Retrospect and Prospect*, ed. Robert J. V. Hiebert, SCS 56 (Atlanta: Society of Biblical Literature,

to these discussions will be provided here, but suffice it to say that DM usage does not neatly fit with a dichotomous framing of text-as-produced versus text-as-received, and thus it should nuance how we conceptualize the nature of the translation. On the one hand, statistically, the use and nonuse of DMs in the LXX is generally not what we would expect in koine texts based on extant data. For example, *καί* occurs with more frequency and δέ with less. This may be due to interference from the source text and ought to be considered. However, more significantly, a proper understanding of DMs poses problems for any conceptualization that simply assumes the translations are subservient to their Hebrew sources and intended to guide the reader back to them. As has been demonstrated throughout this study, DMs are significant devices that can have a critical effect on how one conceives of the structure and meaning of a text. As was seen in the Twelve throughout this study (and also in the Pentateuch and other translated books), DMs often do not guide the reader back to the Hebrew source. Their uses are varied, they frequently do not represent the underlying Hebrew quantitatively and/or qualitatively, they rarely are stereotyped equivalents for any Hebrew lexeme, and they sometimes guide the reader down distinctly different mental pathways vis-á-vis the Hebrew source. Moreover, it was observed that the translators were motivated to use DMs by their own conception of the flow and structure of the discourse. The very fact that DMs are used in the LXX *at all* and used according to koine idiom evinces a translation that is, at least in this respect, idiomatic in the target language, produced in and for the receptor culture, and not concerned with isomorphic or lexical transfer. Given this, as far as it concerns DMs, one is hard-pressed to fit them within a paradigm that is committed to conceptualizing the translation as subservient to the Hebrew source. In

2010); Cameron Boyd-Taylor, *Reading between the Lines: The Interlinear Paradigm for Septuagint Studies*, BTS 8 (Leuven: Peeters, 2011); Boyd-Taylor, "In a Mirror, Dimly—Reading the Septuagint as a Document of Its Times," in *Septuagint Research: Issues and Challenges in the Study of the Greek Jewish Scriptures*, ed. Wolfgang Kraus and R. Glenn Wooden, SCS 53 (Atlanta: Society of Biblical Literature, 2006). For descriptive translation studies, see, e.g., Boyd-Taylor, *Reading between the Lines*; J. Ross Wagner, *Reading the Sealed Book: Old Greek Isaiah and the Problem of Septuagint Hermeneutics* (Waco, TX: Baylor University Press, 2013). For polysystem theory, see, e.g., Dries De Crom, "A Polysystemic Perspective on Ancient Hebrew-Greek Translation," *JAJ* 11 (2020): 163–99; Dhont, *Style and Context of Old Greek Job*. For skopos theory, see, e.g., Carsten Ziegert, "Kultur und Identität: Wörtliches Übersetzen in der Septuaginta," *VT* 67 (2017): 648–65.

any case, the extent to which this study or others like it may impact these discussions within LXX scholarship is something that deserves to be considered in further research.

## 7.6. Abbreviated Descriptions of the Discourse Markers

In closing, I provide here distilled descriptions of the DMs investigated in this study. These descriptions are meant to be quick reference tools for the benefit of the reader and are not meant to supplant their full descriptions within their chapters.

### Δέ

Δέ organizes and structures discourse. At its core, it signals a break between segments, introducing a new, distinct information unit. Depending on its scope assignment and the thematic discontinuities cooccurring with it, δέ may correspond with a new development within the discourse such as a new scene or a new topic to be discussed, a new subtopic within a larger unit or the next part of an argument being built, parenthetical information, or small steps that merit being separated out as distinct units.

### Εἰ/ἐὰν μή

Εἰ/ἐὰν μή signals an exception, informing the reader that the DM's host utterance is relevant in that it counters the truth-propositional content of recently acquired information. When the DM occurs with a moderate scope, the previously processed information is typically modalized, resulting in its truth-propositional content being viewed as contingent on whether the material introduced by εἰ/ἐὰν μή is realized. When the DM occurs with a narrow scope, it typically introduces an excepted member of a previously asserted set, thus countering the truth-propositional content of previously processed information.

### Ἀλλά

Ἀλλά instructs the recipient to regard the information introduced by the particle as a corrective to some element within their mental representation of the discourse for the purpose of realigning it according to the communicator's concerns. The information being corrected may be textually based, an assumption, an implication, or a discourse topic—whatever is most manifest and relevant to the recipient upon processing the correction and integrating it into the mental representation (i.e., takes the least amount of processing effort).

Ἀλλ᾽ ἤ

Ἀλλ᾽ ἤ signals an exclusive corrective relation. Like *ἀλλά*, it signals that what follows is a corrective to some element within the recipient's mental representation of the discourse. Unlike *ἀλλά*, it has the added constraint of narrowing the recipient's focus to the salient exclusive or limited element of the corrective.

Μέν

Μέν (1) alerts readers to forthcoming necessary, corresponding, and semantically related material that needs to be processed together with the host utterance in which *μέν* occurs and (2) instructs readers to build their mental representation of the discourse by regarding the resultant grouping as a coherent discourse unit that provides relevant information about a preceding or presupposed topic.

# Bibliography

Abdelwahed, Youssri. "The Illumination of Lamps (Lychnokaia) for Neith in Sais/Esna in Greco-Roman Egypt." *Abgadiyat* 10 (2015): 31–45.

Abel, Félix Marie. *Grammaire du Grec Biblique suivie d'un choix de papyrus*. 2nd ed. Paris: Gabalda et Fils, 1927.

Addinall, Peter. "Exodus III 19B and the Interpretation of Biblical Narrative." *VT* 49 (1999): 289–300.

Aejmelaeus, Anneli. "Characterizing Criteria for the Characterization of the Septuagint Translators: Experimenting on the Greek Psalter." Pages 54–73 in *The Old Greek Psalter: Studies in Honour of Albert Pietersma*. Edited by Robert J. V. Hiebert, Claude E. Cox, and Peter J. Gentry, JSOTSup 332. Sheffield: Sheffield Academic, 2001.

———. "The Function and Interpretation of כי in Biblical Hebrew." *JBL* 105 (1986): 193–209.

———. *Parataxis in the Septuagint: A Study of the Renderings of the Hebrew Coordinate Clauses in the Greek Pentateuch*. Dissertationes Humanarum Litterarum 31. Helsinki: Suomalainen Tiedeakatemia, 1982.

———. "The Septuagint of 1 Samuel." Pages 123–41 in *On the Trail of the Septuagint Translators: Collected Essays*. Rev. ed. Leuven: Peeters, 2007.

———. "The Significance of Clause Connectors in the Syntactical and Translation-Technical Study of the Septuagint." Pages 43–57 in *On the Trail of the Septuagint Translators: Collected Essays*. Rev. ed. Leuven: Peeters, 2007.

———. "Translation Technique and the Intention of the Translator." Pages 59–69 in *On the Trail of the Septuagint Translators: Collected Essays*. Rev. ed. Leuven: Peeters, 2007.

———. "What Can We Know about the Hebrew *Vorlage* of the Septuagint?" Pages 71–106 in *On the Trail of the Septuagint Translators: Collected Essays*. Rev. ed. Leuven: Peeters, 2007.

———. "What We Talk about When We Talk about Translation Technique." Pages 205–22 in *On the Trail of the Septuagint Translators: Collected Essays*. Rev. ed. Leuven: Peeters, 2007.

Aijmer, Karin. *Understanding Pragmatic Markers: A Variational Pragmatic Approach*. Edinburgh: Edinburgh University Press, 2013.

Aijmer, Karin, Ad Foolen, and Anne-Marie Simon-Vandenbergen. "Pragmatic Markers in Translation: A Methodological Proposal." Pages 101–14 in *Approaches to Discourse Particles*. Edited by Kerstin Fischer. SiP 1. Amsterdam: Elsevier, 2006.

Aitken, James K. "Characterisation of Speech in the Septuagint Pentateuch." Pages 9–31 in *The Reception of the Hebrew Bible in the Septuagint and the New Testament: Essays in Memory of Aileen Guilding*. Edited by David J. A. Clines and J. Cheryl Exum. Sheffield: Sheffield Phoenix, 2013.

———. "Introduction." Pages 1–12 in *The T&T Clark Companion to the Septuagint*. Edited by James K. Aitken. London: Bloomsbury T&T Clark, 2015.

Allan, Rutger J. "Sense and Sentence Complexity: Sentence Structure, Sentence Connection, and Tense-aspect as Indicators of Narrative Mode in Thucydides' *Histories*." Pages 93–121 in *The Language of Literature: Linguistic Approaches to Classical Texts*. Edited by Rutger J. Allan and Michel Buijs. ASCP 13. Leiden: Brill, 2007.

Ariel, Mira. "Discourse, Grammar, Discourse." *Discourse Studies* 11 (2009): 5–36.

Arnold, Bill T., and John H. Choi. *A Guide to Biblical Hebrew Syntax*. Cambridge: Cambridge University Press, 2003.

Ausloos, Hans. "Translation Technique." Pages 165–82 in *The Oxford Handbook of the Septuagint*. Edited by Alison G. Salvesen and Timothy Michael Law. Oxford: Oxford University Press, 2021.

Bagnall, Roger S., and Raffaella Cribiore. *Women's Letters from Ancient Egypt, 300 BC–AD 800*. Ann Arbor: University of Michigan Press, 2006.

Bagnall, Roger S., and Peter Derow. *The Hellenistic Period: Historical Sources in Translation*. Malden, MA: Blackwell, 2004.

Bakker, Egbert J. "Boundaries, Topics, and the Structure of Discourse: An Investigation of the Ancient Greek Particle δέ." *Studies in Language* 17 (1993): 275–311.

Bandstra, Barry Louis. "The Syntax of Particle 'KY' in Biblical Hebrew and Ugaritic." PhD diss., Yale University, 1982.

Barr, James. *The Typology of Literalism in Ancient Biblical Translations*. MSU 15. Göttingen: Vandenhoeck & Ruprecht, 1979.

Basset, Louis. "Ἀλλ' ἐξόλοισθ' αὐτῳ κοαξ: Réexamen des emplois de ἀλλά à la lumière de l'énonciation dans *Les Grenouilles* d'Aristophane." Pages 75–99 in *New Approaches to Greek Particles: Proceedings of the Colloquium Held in Amsterdam, January 4–6, 1996, to Honour C. J. Ruijgh on the Occasion of His Retirement*. Edited by Albert Rijksbaron. ASCP 7. Amsterdam: Gieben, 1997.

Bazzanella, Carla. "Discourse Markers in Italian: Towards a 'Compositional' Meaning." Pages 449–64 in *Approaches to Discourse Particles*. Edited by Kerstin Fischer. SiP 1. Amsterdam: Elsevier, 2006.

Black, Stephanie L. *Sentence Conjunctions in the Gospel of Matthew: καί, δέ, τότε, γάρ, οὖν and Asyndeton in Narrative*. JSNTSup 216. London: Sheffield Academic, 2002.

Blakemore, Diane. *Relevance and Linguistic Meaning: The Semantics and Pragmatics of Discourse Markers*. CSL 99. Cambridge: Cambridge University Press, 2002.

Blass, Regina. *Relevance Relations in Discourse: A Study with Special Reference to Sissala*. CSL 55. Cambridge: Cambridge University Press, 2006.

Bonifazi, Anna, Annemieke Drummen, and Mark de Kreij. *Particles in Ancient Greek Discourse: Exploring Particle Use across Genres*. Hellenic Studies 79. Washington, DC: Center for Hellenic Studies, 2016.

Boring, M. Eugene. *Mark: A Commentary*. NTL. Louisville: Westminster John Knox, 2006.

Boyd-Taylor, Cameron. "In a Mirror, Dimly—Reading the Septuagint as a Document of Its Times." Pages 15–31 in *Septuagint Research: Issues and Challenges in the Study of the Greek Jewish Scriptures*. Edited by Wolfgang Kraus and R. Glenn Wooden. SCS 53. Atlanta: Society of Biblical Literature, 2006.

———. *Reading between the Lines: The Interlinear Paradigm for Septuagint Studies*. BTS 8. Leuven: Peeters, 2011.

———. "What Is the Septuagint?" Pages 13–32 in *The Oxford Handbook of the Septuagint*. Edited by Alison G. Salvesen and Timothy Michael Law. Oxford: Oxford University Press, 2021.

Brannan, Rick. "The Discourse Function of ἀλλά in Non-Negative Contexts." Pages 263–88 in *Discourse Studies and Biblical Interpretation: A Festschrift in Honor of Stephen H. Levinsohn*. Edited by Steven E. Runge. Bellingham, WA: Logos Bible Software, 2011.

Brinton, Laurel J. "Discourse Markers." Pages 285–314 in *Historical Pragmatics*. Edited by Andreas Jucker, and Irma Taavitsainen. Handbooks of Pragmatics 8. Berlin: de Gruyter, 2010.

Brown, Gillian, and George Yule. *Discourse Analysis*. CSL. Cambridge: Cambridge University Press, 1983.

Butler, Christopher S. *Approaches to the Simplex Clause*. Volume 1 of *Structure and Function: A Guide to Three Major Structural-Functional Theories*. SLCS 63. Amsterdam: Benjamins, 2003.

Callow, Kathleen. "The Disappearing Δέ in 1 Corinthians." Pages 183–93 in *Linguistics and New Testament Interpretation: Essays on Discourse Analysis*. Edited by David Alan Black, Katharine G. L. Barnwell, and Stephen H. Levinsohn. Nashville: Broadman, 1992.

Carlson, Robert. "Narrative Connectives in Sùpyìree." Pages 1–19 in *Coherence and Grounding in Discourse: Outcome of a Symposium, Eugene, Oregon, June 1984*. Edited by Russell S. Tomlin. TSL 11. Amsterdam: Benjamins, 1987.

Casevitz, Michel, Cécile Dogniez, and Marguerite Harl. *Les Douze Prophètes: Aggée, Zacharie*. Bd'A 23.10–11. Paris: Cerf, 2007.

Chafe, Wallace. "Cognitive Constraints on Information Flow." Pages 21–51 in *Coherence and Grounding in Discourse: Outcome of a Symposium, Eugene, Oregon, June 1984*. Edited by Russell S. Tomlin. TSL 11. Amsterdam: Benjamins, 1987.

———. "The Deployment of Consciousness in the Production of Narrative." Pages 9–50 in *The Pear Stories: Cognitive, Cultural, and Linguistic Aspects of Narrative Production*. Edited by Wallace L. Chafe. Advances in Discourse Processes 3. Norwood, NJ: Ablex, 1980.

Chamberlain, William Douglas. *An Exegetical Grammar of the Greek New Testament*. New York: Macmillan, 1941.

Clarysse, Willy. "Linguistic Diversity in the Archive of the Engineers Kleon and Theodoros." Pages 35–50 in *The Language of the Papyri*. Edited by T. V. Evans, and Dirk D. Obbink. Oxford: Oxford University Press, 2010.

Conybeare, F. C., and St. George Stock. *A Grammar of Septuagint Greek*. New York: Ginn & Co., 1905. Repr., Grand Rapids: Zondervan, 1980.

Cowles, Heidi Wind. "The Psychology of Information Structure." Pages 287–318 in *The Expression of Information Structure*. Edited by Manfred Krifka and Renate Musan. Expression of Cognitive Categories 5. Berlin: de Gruyter, 2012.

Cox, Claude. “Tying It All Together: The Use of Particles in Old Greek Job.” *BIOSCS* 38 (2005): 41–54.

Croft, William, and D. Alan Cruse. *Cognitive Linguistics*. CTL. Cambridge: Cambridge University Press, 2004.

Cross, Frank Moore. “4QExodb.” Pages 79–95 in *Qumran Cave 4: VII, Genesis to Numbers*. Edited by Eugene Ulrich and Frank Moore Cross. DJD XII. Oxford: Clarendon, 1994.

Cumming, Susanna, and Ono Tsuyoshi. “Discourse and Grammar.” Pages 112–37 in *Discourse as Structure and Process*. Edited by Teun A. van Dijk. Discourse Studies 1. London: Sage, 1997.

Dana, H. E., and Julius R. Mantey. *A Manual Grammar of the Greek New Testament*. Upper Saddle River, NJ: Prentice Hall, 1957.

Dancygier, Barbara, and Eve Sweetser. *Mental Spaces in Grammar: Conditional Constructions*. CSL 108. Cambridge: Cambridge University Press, 2005.

Danker, Frederick William. *The Concise Greek-English Lexicon of the New Testament*. Chicago: University of Chicago Press, 2009.

De Crom, Dries. “A Polysystemic Perspective on Ancient Hebrew-Greek Translation.” *JAJ* 11 (2020): 163–99.

Denniston, J. D. *The Greek Particles*. 2nd ed. Oxford: Clarendon, 1959.

Dhont, Marieke. “Septuagint Translation Technique and Jewish Hellenistic Exegesis.” Pages 21–33 in *T&T Clark Handbook of Septuagint Research*. Edited by William A. Ross and W. Edward Glenny. London: T&T Clark, 2021.

———. *Style and Context of Old Greek Job*. JSJSup 183. Leiden: Brill, 2018.

Dijk, Teun A. van. “The Study of Discourse.” Pages 1–34 in *Discourse as Structure and Process*. Edited by Teun A. van Dijk. Discourse Studies 1. London: Sage, 1997.

Dines, Jennifer M. “The Minor Prophets.” Pages 438–55 in *The T&T Clark Companion to the Septuagint*. Edited by James K. Aitken. London: Bloomsbury T&T Clark, 2015.

———. *The Septuagint*. Understanding the Bible and Its World. London: T&T Clark, 2004.

———. “The Septuagint of Amos: A Study in Interpretation.” PhD diss., University of London, 1992.

———. “Stylistic Invention and Rhetorical Purpose in the Book of the Twelve.” Pages 23–48 in *Et sapienter et eloquenter: Studies on Rhetorical and Stylistic Features of the Septuagint*. Edited by Eberhard Bons and Thomas J. Kraus. FRLANT 241. Göttingen: Vandenhoeck & Ruprecht, 2011.

Dogniez, Cécile. "The Twelve Minor Prophets." Pages 307–20 in *The Oxford Handbook of the Septuagint*. Edited by Alison G. Salvesen and Timothy Michael Law. Oxford: Oxford University Press, 2021.

Dooley, Robert A., and Stephen Levinsohn. *Analyzing Discourse: A Manual of Basic Concepts*. Dallas: SIL International, 2001.

Drummen, Annemieke. "A Construction-Grammar Analysis of Ancient Greek Particles." Pages 42–68 in *Toward a Cognitive Classical Linguistics: The Embodied Basis of Constructions in Greek and Latin*. Edited by Egle Mocciaro and William Michael Short. Berlin: de Gruyter, 2019.

———. "Discourse Cohesion in Dialogue: Turn-Initial ΑΛΛΑ in Greek Drama." Pages 135–54 in *Discourse Cohesion in Ancient Greek*. Edited by Stéphanie Bakker and Gerry Wakker. ASCP 16. Leiden: Brill, 2009.

Durham, John I. *Exodus*. WBC 3. Waco, TX: Word, 1987.

Eddinger, Terry W. *Malachi: A Handbook on the Hebrew Text*. BHHB. Waco, TX: Baylor University Press, 2012.

Emmott, Catherine. *Narrative Comprehension: A Discourse Perspective*. Oxford: Oxford University Press, 1999.

Evans, T. V. "The Potential of Linguistic Criteria for Dating Septuagint Books." *BIOSCS* 43 (2010): 5–22.

———. "Standard Koine Greek in Third Century BC Papyri." Pages 197–206 in *Proceedings of the Twenty-Fifth International Congress of Papyrology Ann Arbor, July 29–August 4, 2007*. Edited by Traianos Gagos. Ann Arbor: Scholarly Publishing Office, 2010.

Evans, T. V., and Dirk D. Obbink. "Introduction." Pages 1–12 in *The Language of the Papyri*. Edited by T. V. Evans, and Dirk D. Obbink. Oxford: Oxford University Press, 2010.

Fauconnier, Gilles. *Mental Spaces: Aspects of Meaning Construction in Natural Language*. Cambridge: MIT, 1985. Repr., Cambridge: Cambridge University Press, 1994.

Fischer, Kerstin. "Frames, Constructions, and Invariant Meanings: The Functional Polysemy of Discourse Particles." Pages 427–47 in *Approaches to Discourse Particles*. Edited by Kerstin Fischer. SiP 1. Amsterdam: Elsevier, 2006.

———. "Towards an Understanding of the Spectrum of Approaches to Discourse Particles: Introduction to the Volume." Pages 1–20 in *Approaches to Discourse Particles*. Edited by Kerstin Fischer. SiP 1. Amsterdam: Elsevier, 2006.

Follingstad, Carl Martin. *Deictic Viewpoint in Biblical Hebrew Text: A Syntagmatic and Paradigmatic Analysis of the Particle* כי. Dallas: SIL International, 2001.

Foolen, Ad. "Polysemy Patterns in Contrast: The Case of Dutch *Toch* and German *Doch*." Pages 59–72 in *Pragmatic Markers in Contrast*. Edited by Karin Aijmer and Anne-Marie Simon-Vandenbergen, SiP 2. Amsterdam: Elsevier, 2006.

Fresch, Christopher J. "Discourse Markers in Lexica and the Benefit of Functional Descriptions: A Case Study of δέ." In *Koine Greek and the Evidence of Documentary Sources*. Edited by Trevor Evans and Genevieve Young-Evans. Forthcoming.

———. "Illuminating the Path Ahead for Septuagint Studies: A Consideration of John A. L. Lee's *The Greek of the Pentateuch*." *JSCS* 54 (2021): 25–42.

———. "Is There an Emphatic μέν? A Consideration of the Particle's Development and Its Function in Koine." *NTS* 63 (2017): 261–78.

———. "The Peculiar Occurrences of οὖν in the Septuagint of Genesis and Exodus." Pages 455–72 in *XV Congress of the International Organization for Septuagint and Cognate Studies, Munich, 2013*. Edited by Wolfgang Kraus, Michaël van der Meer, and Martin Meiser. SCS 64. Atlanta: SBL Press, 2016.

———. "The Septuagint and Discourse Grammar." Pages 79–92 in *T&T Clark Handbook of Septuagint Research*. Edited by William A. Ross and W. Edward Glenny. London: T&T Clark, 2021.

Funk, Robert W. *A Beginning-Intermediate Grammar of Hellenistic Greek*. 3rd ed. Salem, OR: Polebridge, 2013.

Geeraerts, Dirk. "Introduction: A Rough Guide to Cognitive Linguistics." Pages 1–28 in *Cognitive Linguistics: Basic Readings*. Edited by Dirk Geeraerts. CLR 34. Berlin: de Gruyter, 2006.

Georgakopoulou, Alexandra, and Dionysis Goutsos. *Discourse Analysis: An Introduction*. Edinburgh: Edinburgh University Press, 1997.

Gesenius, Wilhelm. *Hebräisches und Aramäisches Handwörterbuch über das Alte Testament*. Edited by Rudolf Meyer et al. 18th ed. Berlin: Springer, 2013.

Gignac, Francis Thomas. *A Grammar of the Greek Papyri of the Roman and Byzantine Periods, Vol. 1: Phonology*. Milan: Istituto Editoriale Cisalpino—La Goliardica, 1976.

Givón, Talmy. "The Grammar of Referential Coherence as Mental Processing Instructions." *Linguistics* 30 (1992): 5–56.

———. *On Understanding Grammar*. Perspectives in Neurolinguistics and Psycholinguistics. New York: Academic Press, 1979.

———. *Syntax: An Introduction*. Vol. 2. Rev. ed. Amsterdam: Benjamins, 2001.

Glenny, W. Edward. *Finding Meaning in the Text: Translation Technique and Theology in the Septuagint of Amos*. VTSup 126. Leiden: Brill, 2009.

———. *Micah: A Commentary Based on Micah in Codex Vaticanus*. Septuagint Commentary Series. Leiden: Brill, 2015.

Graesser, Arthur C., Morton A. Gernsbacher, and Susan R. Goldman. "Cognition." Pages 292–319 in *Discourse as Structure and Process*. Edited by Teun A. van Dijk. Discourse Studies 1. London: Sage, 1997.

Green, Samuel G. *Handbook to the Grammar of the Greek Testament*. Rev. and improved ed. London: Religious Tract Society, 1886.

Hallaschka, Martin. "From Cores to Corpus: Considering the Formation of Haggai and Zechariah 1–8." Pages 171–89 in *Perspectives on the Formation of the Book of the Twelve: Methodological Foundations—Redactional Processes—Historical Insights*. Edited by Rainer Albertz, James D. Nogalski, and Jakob Wöhrle. BZAW 433. Berlin: de Gruyter, 2012.

Halliday, M. A. K., and Christian Matthiessen. *An Introduction to Functional Grammar*. 2nd ed. London: Arnold, 1994.

Halliday, M. A. K., and Ruqaiya Hasan. *Cohesion in English*. English Language Series 9. Harlow: Longman, 1976.

Hansen, Maj-Britt Mosegaard. "A Dynamic Polysemy Approach to the Lexical Semantics of Discourse Markers (with an Exemplary Analysis of French *toujours*)." Pages 21–41 in *Approaches to Discourse Particles*. Edited by Kerstin Fischer. SiP 1. Amsterdam: Elsevier, 2006.

———. *The Function of Discourse Particles: A Study with Special Reference to Spoken Standard French*. Pragmatics and Beyond NS 53. Amsterdam: Benjamins, 1998.

Harper, Joshua L. *Responding to a Puzzled Scribe: The Barberini Version of Habakkuk 3 Analysed in the Light of the Other Greek Versions*. LHBOTS 608. London: Bloomsbury T&T Clark, 2015.

Hasselgård, Hilde. "'Not *Now*': On Non-correspondence between the Cognate Adverbs *now* and *nå*." Pages 93–113 in *Pragmatic Markers in Contrast*. Edited by Karin Aijmer and Anne-Marie Simon-Vandenbergen. SiP 2. Amsterdam: Elsevier, 2006.

Heckert, Jakob K. *Discourse Function of Conjoiners in the Pastoral Epistles*. Dallas: Summer Institute of Linguistics, 1996.

Hill, Andrew E. *Malachi: A New Translation with Introduction and Commentary*. AB 25D. New Haven: Yale University Press, 2008.

Hoey, Michael. *Textual Interaction: An Introduction to Written Discourse Analysis*. London: Routledge, 2001.

Horrocks, Geoffrey. *Greek: A History of the Language and Its Speakers*. 2nd ed. Chichester: Wiley-Blackwell, 2010.

Hughes, Rebecca, and Michael McCarthy. "From Sentence to Discourse: Discourse Grammar and English Language Teaching." *TESOL Quarterly* 32 (1998): 263–87.

Hunt, A. S., and C. C. Edgar. *Select Papyri, Vol. 2: Non-Literary Papryi; Public Documents*. LCL. Cambridge: Harvard University Press, 1934.

James, Patrick. "Papyri, Language of." Pages 11–14 in vol. 3 of *Encyclopedia of Ancient Greek Language and Linguistics*. Edited by Georgios K. Giannakis. 3 vols. Leiden: Brill, 2014.

Jannaris, Antonius N. *An Historical Greek Grammar: Chiefly of the Attic Dialect*. New York: Macmillan, 1897. Repr., Hildesheim: Olms, 1968.

Johnson-Laird, P. N. "Mental Models in Cognitive Science." *Cognitive Science* 4 (1980): 71–115.

Johnstone, Barbara. *Discourse Analysis*. 2nd ed. Introducing Linguistics 3. Malden, MA: Blackwell, 2008.

Khan, Geoffrey. *Studies in Semitic Syntax*. London Oriental Series 38. Oxford: Oxford University Press, 1988.

Kintsch, Walter. *Comprehension: A Paradigm for Cognition*. Cambridge: Cambridge University Press, 1998.

Kortmann, Bernd. *Adverbial Subordination: A Typology and History of Adverbial Subordinators Based on European Languages*. EALT 18. Berlin: de Gruyter, 1997.

Lambrecht, Knud. *Information Structure and Sentence Form: Topic, Focus, and the Mental Representations of Discourse Referents*. CSL 71. Cambridge: Cambridge University Press, 1998.

Langacker, Ronald W. *Cognitive Grammar: A Basic Introduction*. Oxford: Oxford University Press, 2008.

———. "Cognitive Grammar." Pages 87–109 in *The Oxford Handbook of Linguistic Analysis*. Edited by Bernd Heine and Heiko Narrog. Oxford: Oxford University Press, 2010.

Langendonck, Willy van. "Iconicity." Pages 394–418 in *The Oxford Handbook of Cognitive Linguistics*. Edited by Dirk Geeraerts and Hubert Cuyckens. Oxford Handbooks. Oxford: Oxford University Press, 2007.

Le Boulluec, Alain, and Pierre Sandevoir. *L'Exode*. Bd'A 2. Paris: Cerf, 1989.

Le Moigne, Philippe. "Le livre d'Ésaïe dans la Septante: Ecdotique, stylistique, linguistique." PhD diss., L'École pratique des hautes études, 2001.

Lee, John A. L. *The Greek of the Pentateuch: Grinfield Lectures on the Septuagint 2011–2012*. Oxford: Oxford University Press, 2018.

———. "Some Features of the Speech of Jesus in Mark's Gospel." *NovT* 27 (1985): 1–26.

Leuenberger, Martin. "Time and Situational Reference in the Book of Haggai: On Religious- and Theological-Historical Contextualizations of Redactional Processes." Pages 157–70 in *Perspectives on the Formation of the Book of the Twelve: Methodological Foundations—Redactional Processes—Historical Insights*. Edited by Rainer Albertz, James D. Nogalski, and Jakob Wöhrle. BZAW 433. Berlin: de Gruyter, 2012.

Levinsohn, Stephen H. "Self-Instruction Materials on Non-narrative Discourse Analysis."

———. *Textual Connections in Acts*. SBLMS 31. Atlanta: Scholars Press, 1987.

Lewandowska-Tomaszczyk, Barbara. "Polysemy, Prototypes, and Radial Categories." Pages 139–69 in *The Oxford Handbook of Cognitive Linguistics*. Edited by Dirk Geeraerts and Hubert Cuyckens. Oxford: Oxford University Press, 2007.

Lewis, Diana M. "Discourse Markers in English: A Discourse-Pragmatic View." Pages 43–59 in *Approaches to Discourse Particles*. Edited by Kerstin Fischer. SiP 1. Amsterdam: Elsevier, 2006.

Locatell, Christian S. "Grammatical Polysemy in the Hebrew Bible: A Cognitive Linguistic Approach to כִּי." PhD diss., University of Stellenbosch, 2017.

Longacre, Robert E., and Shin Ja J. Hwang. *Holistic Discourse Analysis*. 2nd ed. Dallas: SIL International, 2012.

Louw, Johannes P., and Eugene A. Nida. *Greek-English Lexicon of the New Testament Based on Semantic Domains*. 2 vols. New York: United Bible Societies, 1989.

Maschler, Yael, and Deborah Schiffrin. "Discourse Markers: Language, Meaning, and Context." Pages 189–221 in *The Handbook of Discourse Analysis*. Edited by Deborah Tannen, Heidi E. Hamilton, and Deborah Schiffrin. 2nd ed. BHL. Chichester: Wiley Blackwell, 2015.

Mayser, Edwin. *Grammatik der Griechischen Papyri aus der Ptolemäerzeit, 2.3: Synthetischer Teil*. Leipzig: Teubner, 1934.

McLay, R. Timothy. *The Use of the Septuagint in New Testament Research*. Grand Rapids: Eerdmans, 2003. .

Meinhold, Arndt. *Maleachi*. BKAT 14.8. Neukirchen-Vluyn: Neukirchener Verlag, 2006.

Merwe, Christo H. J. van der. "Discourse Linguistics and Biblical Hebrew Grammar." Pages 13–49 in *Biblical Hebrew and Discourse Linguistics*. Edited by Robert D. Bergen. Dallas: Summer Institute of Linguistics, 1994.

Meyers, Carol L., and Eric M. Meyers. *Haggai, Zechariah 1–8: A New Translation with Introduction and Commentary*. AB 25B. Garden City, NY: Doubleday, 1987.

Moltmann, Friederike. "Exception Sentences and Polyadic Quantification." *Linguistics and Philosophy* 18 (1995): 223–80.

Moulton, James H., and Nigel Turner. *A Grammar of New Testament Greek, Vol. 3: Syntax*. London: T&T Clark, 1963.

Muraoka, Takamitsu. "In Defence of the Unity of the Septuagint Minor Prophets." *Annual of the Japanese Biblical Institute* 15 (1989): 25–36.

Nemo, François. "Discourse Particles as Morphemes and as Constructions." Pages 375–402 in *Approaches to Discourse Particles*. Edited by Kerstin Fischer. SiP 1. Amsterdam: Elsevier, 2006.

Nogalski, James D. *The Book of the Twelve: Micah–Malachi*. SHBC 18b. Macon, GA: Smyth & Helwys, 2011.

Nyan, Thanh. "From Procedural Meaning to Processing Requirement." Pages 167–88 in *Approaches to Discourse Particles*. Edited by Kerstin Fischer. SiP 1. Amsterdam: Elsevier, 2006.

Olofsson, Staffan. *The LXX Version: A Guide to the Translation Technique of the Septuagint*. ConBOT 30. Stockholm: Almqvist & Wiksell, 1990.

Orrieux, Claude. *Les Papyrus de Zenon: L'horizon d'un grec en Egypte au IIIe siècle avant J.C.* Deucalion. Paris: Macula, 1983.

Page, T. E. *The Acts of the Apostles*. London: Macmillan, 1886.

Paley, F. A. *A Short Treatise on The Greek Particles and Their Combinations according to Attic Usage*. Cambridge: Deighton, Bell, 1881.

Palme, Bernhard. "The Range of Documentary Texts: Types and Categories." Pages 358–94 in *The Oxford Handbook of Papyrology*. Edited by Roger S. Bagnall. Oxford: Oxford University Press, 2009.

Pérez-Jiménez, Isabel, and Norberto Moreno-Quibén. "On the Syntax of *Exceptions*: Evidence from Spanish." *Lingua* 122 (2012): 582–607.

Perkins, Larry J. "Exodus: To the Reader." *NETS*, 43–51.

Pietersma, Albert. "Beyond Literalism: Interlinearity Revisited." Pages 3–21 in *"Translation Is Required": The Septuagint in Retrospect and Prospect*. Edited by Robert J. V. Hiebert. SCS 56. Atlanta: Society of Biblical Literature, 2010.

Pietersma, Albert, and Benjamin G. Wright III. "To the Reader of NETS." *NETS*, xiii–xx.

Polak, Frank H. "Context Sensitive Translation and Parataxis in Biblical Narrative." Pages 525–39 in *Emanuel: Studies in Hebrew Bible, Septuagint and Dead Sea Scrolls in Honor of Emanuel Tov*. Edited by Shalom M. Paul. VTSup 94. Leiden: Brill, 2003.

Pons Bordería, Salvador. "A Functional Approach to the Study of Discourse Markers." Pages 77–99 in *Approaches to Discourse Particles*. Edited by Kerstin Fischer. SiP 1. Amsterdam: Elsevier, 2006.

Porter, Stanley E. *Idioms of the Greek New Testament*. 2nd ed. Biblical Languages: Greek 2. London: Continuum, 2005.

Probert, Philomen. *A New Short Guide to the Accentuation of Ancient Greek*. Advanced Language Series. London: Bristol Classical Press, 2003.

Redeker, Gisela. "Discourse Markers as Attentional Cues at Discourse Transitions." Pages 339–58 in *Approaches to Discourse Particles*. Edited by Kerstin Fischer. SiP 1. Amsterdam: Elsevier, 2006.

Renaud, B. *La Formation du Livre de Michée: Tradition et Actualisation*. Études bibliques. Pendé: Gabalda et Cie, 1977.

Robertson, A. T. *A Grammar of the Greek New Testament in the Light of Historical Research*. Nashville: Broadman, 1934.

Roulet, Eddy. "The Description of Text Relation Markers in the Geneva Model of Discourse Organization." Pages 115–31 in *Approaches to Discourse Particles*. Edited by Kerstin Fischer. SiP 1. Amsterdam: Elsevier, 2006.

Runge, Steven E. "Teaching Them What Not to Do: The Nuances of Negation in the Greek New Testament." Paper presented at the Annual Meeting of the Evangelical Theological Society. San Diego, November 2007. https://tinyurl.com/SBL0414a.

Sanderson, Brandon. *Dawnshard*. New York: Tor, 2021.

Sasson, Jack M. *Jonah: A New Translation with Introduction and Commentary*. AB 24B. New York: Doubleday, 1990.

Satterthwaite, Philip E. "Judges." Pages 102–17 in *The T&T Clark Companion to the Septuagint*. Edited by James K. Aitken. London: Bloomsbury T&T Clark, 2015.

Scarlata, Mark W. "Genesis." Pages 13–28 in *The T&T Clark Companion to the Septuagint*. Edited by James K. Aitken. London: Bloomsbury T&T Clark, 2015.

Scheppers, Frank. *The Colon Hypothesis: Word Order, Discourse Segmentation and Discourse Coherence in Ancient Greek*. Brussels: VUBPress, 2011.

Sicking, C. M. J. "Devices for Text Articulation in Lysias I and XII." Pages 1–66 in *Two Studies in Attic Particle Usage: Lysias & Plato*. Mnemosyne Supplements 129. Leiden: Brill, 1993.

Simon, Uriel. *Jonah: The Traditional Hebrew Text with the New JPS Translation*. Translated by Lenn J. Schramm. JPS Bible Commentary. Philadelphia: Jewish Publication Society, 1999.

Ska, Jean Louis. "Note sur la traduction de *welō'* en Exode III 19b." *VT* 44 (1994): 60–65.

Slings, S. R. "Adversative Relators between PUSH and POP." Pages 101–29 in *New Approaches to Greek Particles: Proceedings of the Colloquium Held in Amsterdam, January 4–6, 1996, to Honour C. J. Ruijgh on the Occasion of His Retirement*. Edited by Albert Rijksbaron. ASCP 7. Amsterdam: Gieben, 1997.

Smith, Ralph L. *Micah–Malachi*. WBC 32. Waco, TX: Word, 1984.

Soisalon-Soininen, Ilmari. "Beobachtungen zur Arbeitsweisez: Der Septuaginta–Übersetzer." Pages 319–29 in *Isac Leo Seeligmann Volume: Essays on the Bible and the Ancient World*. Edited by Alexander Rofé, and Yair Zakovitch. Jerusalem: Rubinstein, 1983.

Stenström, Anna-Brita. "The Spanish Discourse Markers *O Sea* and *Pues* and Their English Correspondences." Pages 155–72 in *Pragmatic Markers in Contrast*. Edited by Karin Aijmer, and Anne-Marie Simon-Vandenbergen. SiP 2. Amsterdam: Elsevier, 2006.

Stuart, Douglas. *Hosea–Jonah*. WBC 31. Waco, TX: Word, 1987.

Sweeney, Marvin A. *The Twelve Prophets, Volume 2: Micah, Nahum, Habakkuk, Zephaniah, Haggai, Zechariah, Malachi*. Berit Olam. Collegeville, MN: Liturgical Press, 2000.

———. *Zephaniah: A Commentary*. Hermeneia. Minneapolis: Fortress, 2003.

Taylor, John R. *Linguistic Categorization*. 3rd ed. Oxford Textbooks in Linguistics. Oxford: Oxford University Press, 2003.

———. *The Mental Corpus: How Language Is Represented in the Mind*. Oxford: Oxford University Press, 2012.

———. "Prototype Effects in Grammar." Pages 562–79 in *Handbook of Cognitive Linguistics*. Edited by Ewa Dąbrowska, and Dagmar Divjak. Handbooks of Linguistics and Communication Science 39. Berlin: de Gruyter, 2015.

Theocharous, Myrto. *Lexical Dependence and Intertextual Allusion in the Septuagint of the Twelve Prophets: Studies in Hosea, Amos and Micah*. LHBOTS 570. New York: Bloomsbury, 2012.

Thrall, Margaret E. *Greek Particles in the New Testament: Linguistic and Exegetical Studies*. NTTS 3. Leiden: Brill, 1962.

Tjen, Anwar. *On Conditionals in the Greek Pentateuch: A Study of Translation Syntax*. LHBOTS 515. New York: T&T Clark, 2010.

Travis, Catherine E. "The Natural Semantic Metalanguage Approach to Discourse Markers." Pages 219–41 in *Approaches to Discourse Particles*. Edited by Kerstin Fischer. SiP 1. Amsterdam: Elsevier, 2006.

Tucker, W. Dennis, Jr. *Jonah: A Handbook on the Hebrew Text*. BHHB. Waco, TX: Baylor University Press, 2006.

Verhoeven, Ludo, and Charles Perfetti. "Advances in Text Comprehension: Model, Process and Development." *Applied Cognitive Psychology* 22 (2008): 293–301.

Verschueren, Jef. *Understanding Pragmatics*. Understanding Language. London: Arnold, 1999.

Vianès, Laurence. *Les Douze Prophètes: Malachie*. Bd'A 23.12. Paris: Cerf, 2011.

Vivien, Ler Soon Lay. "A Relevance-Theoretic Approach to Discourse Particles in Singapore English." Pages 149–66 in *Approaches to Discourse Particles*. Edited by Kerstin Fischer. SiP 1. Amsterdam: Elsevier, 2006.

Wagner, J. Ross. *Reading the Sealed Book: Old Greek Isaiah and the Problem of Septuagint Hermeneutics*. Waco, TX: Baylor University Press, 2013.

Wakker, Gerry C. *Conditions and Conditionals: An Investigation of Ancient Greek*. ASCP 3. Amsterdam: Gieben, 1994.

———. "'Well I Will Now Present My Arguments': Discourse Cohesion Marked by οὖν and τοίνυν in Lysias." Pages 63–81 in *Discourse Cohesion in Ancient Greek*. Edited by Stéphanie Bakker and Gerry Wakker. ASCP 16. Leiden: Brill, 2009.

Wallace, Daniel B. *Greek Grammar beyond the Basics*. Grand Rapids: Zondervan, 1996.

Waltereit, Richard. "The Rise of Discourse Markers in Italian: A Specific Type of Language Change." Pages 61–76 in *Approaches to Discourse Particles*. Edited by Kerstin Fischer. SiP 1. Amsterdam: Elsevier, 2006.

Watson, Wilfred G. E. *Classical Hebrew Poetry: A Guide to Its Techniques*. JSOTSup 26. Sheffield: JSOT Press, 1986.

Wevers, John William. *Notes on the Greek Text of Exodus*. SCS 30. Atlanta: Scholars Press, 1990.

———. *Notes on the Greek Text of Genesis*. SCS 35. Atlanta: Scholars Press, 1993.

———. *Notes on the Greek Text of Deuteronomy*. SCS 39. Atlanta: Scholars Press, 1995.

———. *Notes on the Greek Text of Leviticus*. SCS 44. Atlanta: Scholars Press, 1997.

———. *Notes on the Greek Text of Numbers*. SCS 46. Atlanta: Scholars Press, 1998.

White, John L. *Light from Ancient Letters*. Philadelphia: Fortress, 1986.

Williams, Ronald J. *Williams' Hebrew Syntax*. Rev. and expanded by John C. Beckman. 3rd ed. Toronto: University of Toronto Press, 2007.

Winer, G. B. *A Treatise on the Grammar of New Testament Greek*. Translated by W. F. Moulton. 9th ed. Edinburgh: T&T Clark, 1882.

Wolff, Hans Walter. *Obadiah and Jonah: A Commentary*. Translated by Margaret Kohl. CC. Minneapolis: Augsburg, 1986.

Yiftach-Firanko, Uri. "Law in Graeco-Roman Egypt: Hellenization, Fusion, Romanization." Pages 541–60 in *The Oxford Handbook of Papyrology*. Edited by Roger S. Bagnall. Oxford: Oxford University Press, 2009.

Young, Richard A. *Intermediate New Testament Greek: A Linguistic and Exegetical Approach*. Nashville: Broadman & Holman, 1994.

Yule, George. *Pragmatics*. Oxford Introductions to Language Study. Oxford: Oxford University Press, 1996.

Zeevat, Henk. "A Dynamic Approach to Discourse Particles." Pages 133–48 in *Approaches to Discourse Particles*. Edited by Kerstin Fischer. SiP 1. Amsterdam: Elsevier, 2006.

Zerwick, Maximilian. *Biblical Greek: Illustrated by Examples*. Translated by Joseph Smith. Rome: Pontifical Institute Press, 1963.

Ziegert, Carsten. "Kultur und Identität: Wörtliches Übersetzen in der Septuaginta." *VT* 67 (2017): 648–65.

# Index of Ancient Sources

Documentary Papyri

Pseudepigrapha



Dead Sea Scrolls



Greco-Roman Literature

# Index of Modern Authors

CPSIA information can be obtained
at www.ICGtesting.com
Printed in the USA
LVHW070045250623
750567LV00007B/61